DISCOVERING BERLIOZ

ESSAYS, REVIEWS, TALKS

DISCOVERING BERLIOZ

ESSAYS, REVIEWS, TALKS

DAVID CAIRNS

Foreword by
SIR JOHN ELIOT GARDINER

David Cairns on Music
Volume One

Musicians on Music
No. 12

To Rosemary, and in honour of Colin Davis
and his forebears and successors

This collection first published by Toccata Press, 2019.

British Library Cataloguing in Publication Data
A catalogue record for this book is available from the British Library.

ISBN 978-0-907689-58-4
ISSN 0264-6889

Set in 11 on 12 point Minion Pro
by Kerrypress Ltd, St Albans

Contents

List of Illustrations

Foreword
SIR JOHN ELIOT GARDINER

In his own words, David Cairns' longstanding commitment and devotion to Hector Berlioz has been 'body and soul'. He belongs to a handful of English musical enthusiasts for whom discovering Berlioz, in the 1950s, was a defining moment in their lives. If the late Colin Davis was the composer's most persuasive advocate in the concert hall and opera house, David Cairns provided the crucial intellectual and literary underpinning. Together they swung the tide in favour of one of the most misrepresented and controversial of Romantic composers. I count myself fortunate to have been inspired by the advocacy of both men. They first drew my attention to the fervent workings of Berlioz's supercharged imagination and to the glorious music it engendered. Anyone familiar with Cairns' translation of Berlioz's *Memoirs* or, still more, his magisterial two-volume biography of the composer will welcome this volume of essays spanning fifty years. The writing bears the hallmarks of Cairns' style – the way he combines passion with scholarship, zeal in defence of his hero with a measured assessment of his foibles and wounds (some of which were self-inflicted). There are insights aplenty and clues to unravelling the troubled skein of his life and creativity.

Prelude
LIFE WITH BERLIOZ

'They are finally going to play my music': Berlioz's deathbed prophecy, a century and a half after his death, is being richly fulfilled. How different sixty years ago, when the announcement that the Royal Opera House was staging his little-known epic opera *The Trojans* aroused no more than mild curiosity, and the composer, though he had his fervent admirers, was generally still a disputed figure in the history of music. In the event the production of *The Trojans* at Covent Garden in 1957, revived in 1958 and 1960, made a huge stir and began the change in Berlioz's fortunes, revealing to a host of listeners a composer quite different from the view of those who professed to know about such things.

To put matters right and make amends became the cause, the mission, of a group of young British musicians and music-lovers, of whom I was one. The stars were working for us. Colin Davis – who had discovered Berlioz when playing clarinet in 'The Flight into Egypt' from *The Childhood of Christ* under Roger Désormière at William Glock's Bryanston Summer School, and had then had the chance to explore his music further during his years in Glasgow as assistant conductor of the BBC Scottish Orchestra – was back in London, at Sadler's Wells, and with the Chelsea Opera Group (COG), of which I was co-founder, he conducted a series of Berlioz concerts (sung in English) every summer for the next five years (1961–65). It was a time of huge excitement: we had Colin with us again, and we, and he, were renewing the adventures of the first, Mozart-dominated period of COG (1950–57), with the added spice of getting to know music both strange and of extraordinary beauty and intensity. In particular, *Romeo and Juliet* and *Benvenuto Cellini* were unknown territory. Above all, there was *The Trojans*, which, though some of us had heard it, we didn't know from the inside. It transfixed us. Our passion was typified by the response of John Anderson, one of the violinists, who at the end of a rehearsal of Act 1 exclaimed, his face shining with a holy radiance: 'It's beyond anything!'

The two-part performances, in 1963 and 1964, brought together a number of people who would become prominently associated with the study of Berlioz's life and the advancement of his music: Hugh Macdonald (second violin, who had edited the full score for his Ph.D.), Julian Rushton (percussion and conductor of the offstage bands in Act 1), Nicholas Snowman (chorus tenor), Richard Macnutt (chorus bass) and myself (percussion). The experience fuelled our determination to have the full score published and the whole work recorded; and in pursuit of these goals (finally attained in 1969, the centenary of the composer's death), some of us would meet, usually in one of those conspiratorial alcoves at Durrant's Hotel (off Baker Street), after concert performances conducted by Colin Davis with the London Symphony Orchestra and the Philharmonia at the Festival Hall – with Colin there, too, as were Ernest Fleischmann and, often, John Warrack – and plan how to achieve them. By then the Berlioz Centenary Committee, created by Russell Brown and chaired by Lord Drogheda, was in existence and had set up the sub-committee which became, under Hugh Macdonald's direction, the Bärenreiter New Berlioz Edition.

By that time, I was body and soul for Berlioz. My commitment was sealed one night at Covent Garden, at that climactic moment in the first act of *Les Troyens* when, Cassandra's horrified vision of the sack of Troy and of Corebus's death having caused her to faint in his arms, the cellos and double basses softly echo the rhythmic motif of her prophecy, under still, diminished-seventh harmonies. As I listened, I felt the composer's compassionate love for his doomed heroine rise up and take possession of me, my whole being reached out in answer, and I thought: I will do everything I can for you.

It had by no means always been so. Ten years earlier the very notion would have struck me as laughable. I had been brought up to believe good things of France (where my mother had worked during the First World War, in an army canteen in Le Havre), and with a love of the French language. And before the Second World War a Frenchwoman from Annecy, Marthe Perret, who taught in an English grammar school, used to stay with us in the holidays; we read the Babar books in the original and spoke French at mealtimes. Then, after the War, came the intoxicating invasion of French films, *Les Enfants du Paradis*, *La Kermesse héroïque*, *Carnet de bal*, *Le Jour se lève*, *Quai des brûmes*, *Drôle de drame* and the rest. But my musical upbringing remained almost exclusively German. I had heard the 'Royal Hunt and Storm' (from Act 4 of *Les Troyens*), performed by Beecham and the London Philharmonic in Boston Stump, as long ago as 1945, but it can't have made much impression on me, for I have no recollection of it. I remember, a few years later, during a passionate argument in which I defended Brahms against a Francophile, anti-Brahmsian friend, quoting Emma Woodhouse's description of Mrs Elton, in Jane Austen's novel, to

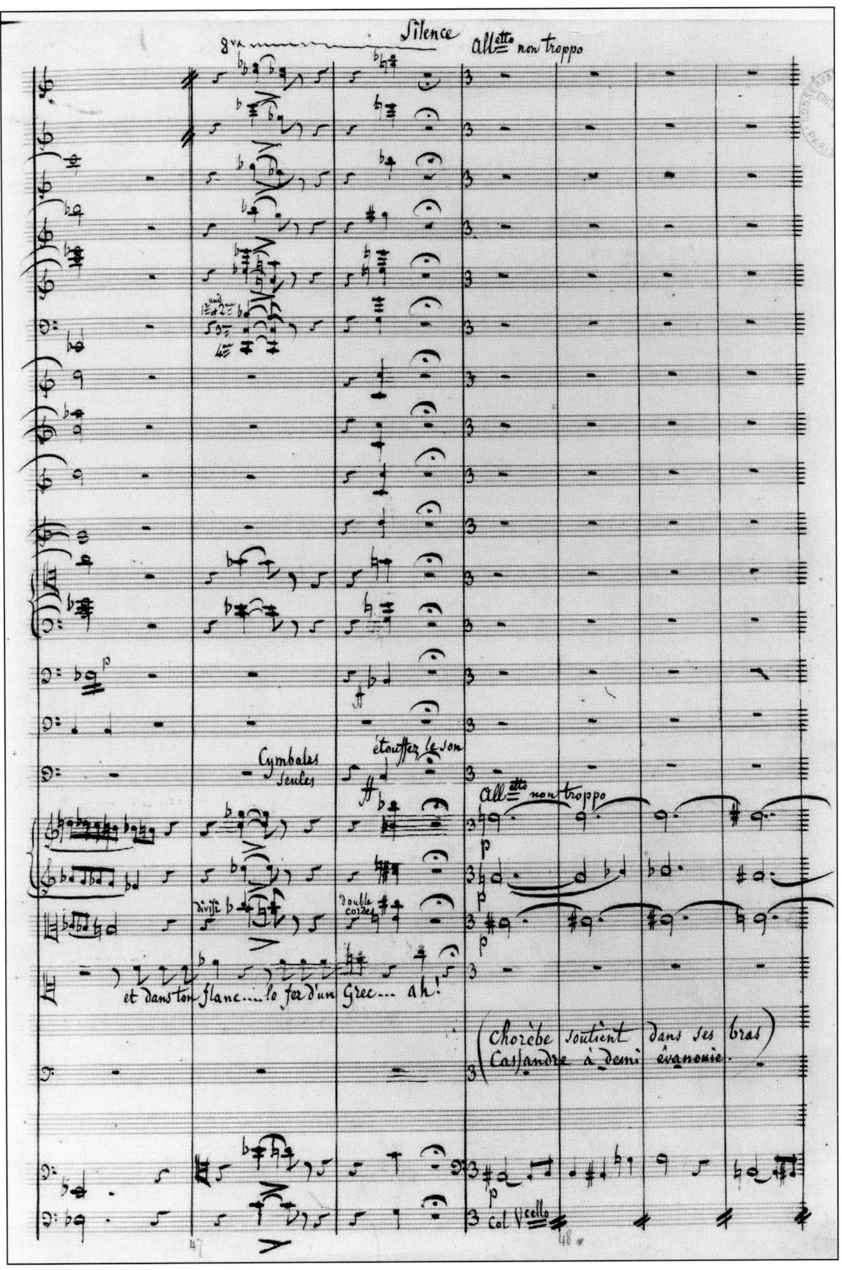

Les Troyens, *Act 1, autograph full score, with Cassandre 'à demi évanouie'*

dismiss Berlioz as a 'coarse vulgarian'. As I recall elsewhere,[1] I sat stony-faced through a recording of the *Symphonie fantastique* which my sister Margaret urged me to listen to. For her, she said, the first time she heard Berlioz's music was like being in a foreign country and suddenly hearing your own language spoken. For me, it was double Dutch.

I was over 30, with more than twenty years of devotion to classical music, of living it in my inmost being, before anything changed. Yet perhaps, in the end, it had to happen and it was written on my cards – as I came to realise many years later when, in 2003 (the bicentenary of Berlioz's birth), a television company from Grenoble came over to explore the sites associated with his visits to London. I took them to the house in Queen Anne Street where he stayed in 1851, when he was a member of the international jury on musical instruments at the Great Exhibition (and where a blue plaque commemorating the fact had been fixed to the façade in 1969). Inside the house we were handed a sheet of paper which listed the people who had lived there during its long history. I discovered that in the year of my birth the house was occupied by the man who, though not a family friend or a relation, had been chosen as my godfather (for, so it seems, diplomatic reasons – my father was working for him at the time). The discovery cast a new light on the name of my first girlfriend, famous in family lore. I encountered her at the age of three, on Bamburgh beach in Northumberland, and – so I was told – the moment I set on eyes on her, I clasped her in my arms and covered her with kisses. She was called Stella. She was the star of the shore, Stella littorae, not Stella montis as Berlioz called the goddess of his childhood, but it was near enough: Bamburgh was as much my sacred ancestral territory as Mont-Saint-Eynard and the Isère were his. What till then had seemed no more than an amusing coincidence now took on an air of destiny. I saw that, after all, I had had no choice.

The translation of Berlioz's *Memoirs* which I began in 1963 took much longer than I had imagined it would. It is a long book; and, in addition, as I worked on it, I came to see that to do the job thoroughly I must make various editorial additions: a selection of contemporary descriptions of Berlioz, a glossary of the characters and institutions figuring in the book, an investigation chapter by chapter into the veracity or otherwise of Berlioz's account of his life, and a list of sources, in Berlioz's other books and in his newspaper writings, that contributed to the *Memoirs*. I had been up all night compiling this final appendix when I received a letter from the publisher, Cassell, informing me that they were not going to 'proceed with

[1] *Cf.* pp. 29–30, below.

My three-year-old self with Stella, Bamburgh, 1929

publication of the above-mentioned title' – this despite the fact that all that was then missing were a couple of sheets of A4: they had everything else. Luckily my agent, Bertie van Thal of London Management, acted swiftly, telephoned Livia Gollancz, proprietor of Victor Gollancz Ltd., and a taxi transported the manuscript from Red Lion Square to Henrietta Street the same morning. Gollancz (and Knopf in the USA) published it in March 1969, in time for the centenary of Berlioz's death.

A month later, in April, I read a paper on '*Les Troyens* and *The Aeneid*' at the spring conference of the Royal Musical Association and, that evening, took the night train to Scotland to give talks on *The Trojans* in Edinburgh, Glasgow and Aberdeen (ahead of the Scottish Opera production). By then I was working at Philips Records, where we were planning the complete recording of the opera, based on the Covent Garden production that was due in September, and using the full score and parts recently published by Bärenreiter for the New Berlioz Edition. At the same time I was busy with the Arts Council exhibition 'Berlioz and the Romantic Century', designed by Alan Tagg, that was to open at the Victoria and Albert Museum in October – for which the head of exhibitions at the Council, Elizabeth Davison, and I made visits to Paris and La Côte-Saint-André to choose objects for display. For it I devised a scheme of nine chronological sections, and for its catalogue, masterminded and edited by Elizabeth, I wrote an introduction and also a biographical summary for each section. The official opening of the exhibition took place an hour-and-a-half after the seventeenth of the eighteen recording sessions for *Les Troyens*, involving a rapid dash from Walthamstow Town Hall to South Kensington after three

58 Queen Anne St, London, W1, with the plaque commemorating Berlioz's residence

hectic hours in which we recorded the big finale of Act 3 – a session that had been thrown into doubt at the last minute by a dramatic telephone call from Roger Soyer, who was singing the role of Narbal. 'Monsieur Cairns, une véritable catastrophe': he was buying a new car and had had to surrender his passport to the police, and so would not be able to arrive in time. I told him that he must, as this was the only opportunity to record the scenes he was singing in, and somehow he did. In November we recorded the *Grande Messe des morts* (Requiem) in Westminster Cathedral, and in December heard the playback of the recording of *Les Troyens* and passed it for production. On the last evening of 1969 I listened on the gramophone to the 'Convoi funèbre' from *Roméo et Juliette* and the Prelude to *Les Troyens à Carthage* and then, on the stroke of midnight, sent a large rocket blazing into the night sky from the back garden of our house in Putney.

Meanwhile, on the strength of my edition of the *Memoirs*, I had been asked by Tom Rosenthal, managing director of Thames and Hudson, to write a biography of Berlioz. It seemed the logical thing to do and I accepted. The commission was for a single-volume life, to be delivered in four years' time. I little suspected how much of my existence it would consume, or that one volume would metamorphose inexorably into two.

The pieces in this book, spanning more than fifty years and linked by a record of the circumstances that gave rise to them, together form a narrative of my relationship with Berlioz and his music – the earliest, the introduction I wrote in 1962 for the Peregrine edition of *Evenings in the Orchestra* (*Les Soirées de l'Orchestre*), the most recent the texts of talks on the *Grand Traité d'Instrumentation et d'Orchestration Modernes*, given to a Members' Weekend of the Berlioz Society in November 2014, and on 'Berlioz and Song', given at the Oxford Lieder Festival in October 2015, and some thoughts on Berlioz's interest in early music, published in the *Berlioz Society Bulletin* No. 207, in March 2019. The contents of the book are arranged in roughly chronological sequence: boyhood, La Côte-Saint-André, the fascination of Chateaubriand's *Génie du Christianisme*, their crucial influence on his art; the role of the traditional French romance in his output; Berlioz's relations with his sisters; the early *Messe solennelle*; the successive revelations of Shakespeare and Beethoven which turned the provincial youth brought up in a musical wilderness into the composer of the *Symphonie fantastique*; then a discussion of the *Fantastique* and its relation to so-called programme music; Italy and its influence (second only to that of his childhood); a discussion of Berlioz the writer; two major scores of the mid- and late 1830s, *Benvenuto Cellini* and *Roméo et Juliette*, and the *Grand Traité*; then Germany; *La Damnation de Faust*, and the criticisms it provoked, leading to a consideration of attitudes to Berlioz's music over the years; *Les Nuits d'été;* his dealings with the powers that be and his fluctuating social and political ideas; finally, *Les Troyens*, and then a glance at the future. Part I begins with a survey of religion in the life and works of the composer. He chose to open his *Memoirs* with remembrance of his first communion. Ironic in tone though it is, the choice is not accidental: it seems to me to offer an essential clue to his personality.

Inevitably, in a collection such as this, made up of pieces written at different times and for different occasions, there is some overlap between one piece and another. In editing them I have tried to keep repetition to a minimum. Even so, some quotations, facts and observations appear more than once, wherever I feel they are necessary to the narrative or argument in question: to cite a few examples, Berlioz's 1862 article on *Fidelio*; the recurrence, in his music, of the sound of girls' voices that left so deep a mark on him at his first communion; the magical moment when he comes upon a piece of blank manuscript paper, waiting for orchestral music to be inscribed on it; the persistent and pervasive influence of ancient liturgical chants heard in boyhood; Le Sueur's reminiscences of public music-making under the Revolution; the dream of performing the *Eroica* on the plains of Troy; the vital stimulus of the Bonn Beethoven Festival to the composition of *La Damnation de Faust*; Shakespeare's role in *Les Troyens;* the 1957 Covent Garden production of the opera, its transforming effect on the composer's reputation, and Robert Collet's review in *The Score*; the swipes I take at Hippeau, Boschot and Newman for their carping strictures on the *Memoirs;* my debt to Katharine Boult's translation of that work.[2] I hope that nonetheless such repetitions will not be thought to outstay their welcome. I must also apologise for inconsistencies in the naming of some of Berlioz's works, which – depending on the context – are given either in French or in English.

Berlioz, in his last days, was haunted by the fear that his music would not survive when he was no longer there to perform it. He was only too aware how difficult his works were to play and to conduct. It was, he said, 'precisely their expression, their inner fire and rhythmic originality' that made them hard to get right:

> To perform them well, everyone concerned, the conductor most of all, must feel as I feel. I thought I would have apoplexy when I heard the *King Lear* overture in Prague, directed by a kapellmeister of incontestable merit. It was approximately right; but in such cases approximately right is totally wrong.[3]

His exceptional power and magnetism as a conductor, of other music as well as his own (Beethoven, Gluck, Mendelssohn), are well attested: among others, by Charles Hallé ('he was the most perfect conductor that I ever set eyes on, one who held absolute sway over his troops, and played upon them as a pianist upon the keyboard'[4]), by Hans von Bülow, by Pauline Viardot, by César Cui ('of all the conductors we have heard in Petersburg, Berlioz is unquestionably the greatest'[5]). But what would be the fate of his music when he wasn't there to show how it should go?

As it happened, he need not have worried. The line held. Today, a century and a half after Berlioz's death, 'the great Hector's sword' (to borrow the words of Ulysses in *Troilus and Cressida*) has not 'lacked a master': it is in the hands of enough conductors who know how to wield it. So perhaps, instead – quoting his beloved Shakespeare again – we may say: 'Rest, rest, perturbéd spirit'.

[2] *The Life of Hector Berlioz, as written by himself in his letters and memoirs*, J. M. Dent, London/E. P. Dutton, New York, 1903.

[3] *The Memoirs of Hector Berlioz*, transl. and ed. David Cairns, Everyman, London, 2002 (hereafter *Memoirs*), p. 526.

[4] *Life and Letters of Sir Charles Hallé*, Smith, Elder and Co., London, 1896, p. 64.

[5] Quoted in Vladimir Vasilievich Stasov, *Selected Essays on Music*, transl. Florence Jonas, Cresset Press, London, 1968, p. 166.

Acknowledgements

The book is dedicated first to my wife Rosemary, who supported and encouraged me lovingly and unstintingly and was actively involved with me throughout the half-century and more of my Berliozian (and Mozartian) projects, and, second, to the conductors who have wielded 'the great Hector's sword' in our own day: Colin Davis, Roger Norrington, John Eliot Gardiner, Mark Elder, Adrian Brown, Robin Ticciati, Antonio Pappano, Andrew Davis, Edward Gardner, Pat Miller, James Levine, John Nelson, Serge Baudo, François-Xavier Roth, Sylvain Cambreling, Valery Gergiev (to name only those known to me) – for there has never been a time when so many conductors were eager to perform his music; then, going back to the past, Arturo Toscanini, Dmitri Mitropoulos, Hamilton Harty, Thomas Beecham, Charles Munch, and, further still, the doughty phalanx of German musicians who believed in him and championed his music in the last decades of the nineteenth century and the beginning of the twentieth: Charles Hallé, Hans von Bülow, Hans Richter, Felix Mottl (who would not tolerate criticism of Berlioz – 'there is no *but*'[1]), Gustav Mahler, Felix Weingartner, Artur Nikisch and, in his native France, Edouard Colonne, who began the renascence soon after Berlioz's death, and then passed the baton to his pupil and first violist Pierre Monteux.

As President of the Berlioz Society, I suppose I don't need permission to reproduce items that were printed in its *Bulletin* (of which I am also editor). But I should like to thank the publishers of the books and journals in which other articles first appeared, for kindly allowing me to reprint them here. They are Penguin Allen Lane and the University of California Press, Cambridge University Press, University of Rochester Press, Everyman, Verlag Dohr, Köln, *The Sunday Times*, *Gramophone*, Testament and *Symphony*.

For the illustrations, my thanks go to the Bibliothèque nationale de France, Département de la Musique, for a page of the autograph full score of *Les Troyens*, Act 1 (p. 15), the first page of the autograph full score of the *Grande Messe des morts* (p. 64), a page of the autograph full score of *Les Troyens*, Act 5 (p. 81), the first page of the autograph full score of the 'Offertoire' (*Grande Messe des morts*) (p. 119), the autograph letter to Humbert Ferrand of 6 February 1830 (p. 158), page two of the autograph full score of the

[1] *Cf.* Georges de Massougnes, *Hector Berlioz: son œuvre*, Calmann-Lévy, Paris, 1919, p. 138.

Edouard Colonne

Hans von Bülow

Felix Mottl

Charles Hallé

Hans Richter

Felix von Weingartner

Arthur Nikisch

Gustav Mahler

Charles Munch

Sir Hamilton Harty

Sir Thomas Beecham

Pierre Monteux

Symphonie fantastique (p. 168), a page of Gluck's *Iphigénie en Tauride* in Berlioz's hand (p. 179), a page of the autograph full score of the Sextet from Act 2 of *Benvenuto Cellini* (p. 214), a page of the autograph full score from the finale of *Roméo et Juliette* (p. 228) and the autograph sketch of 'Absence' from *Les Nuits d'été* (p. 290); to Michael Mullen of the Royal College of Music for the opening pages of the autograph manuscript of the *Messe solennelle* (pp. 113 and 118), courtesy of the St Carolus Borromeuskerk, Antwerp; to the Musée Berlioz, La Côte-Saint-André, for an autograph page of the *Memoirs*, chapter 4 (p. 75), an anonymous caricature of Berlioz from 1845 (p. 83), the portrait of Adèle Suat (p. 93), the portrait of Nancy Berlioz (p. 98) and three autograph pages of the *Memoirs* (pp. 75, 234 and 311); to the Morgan Library and Museum, New York (Fenderson Collection) for an autograph page of the *Memoirs*, chapter 22 (p. 49), the autograph letter to Nancy Berlioz of 28 July 1827 (p. 96), three autograph pages of the *Memoirs* (pp. 49, 123 and 130), the autograph letter to the Princess Sayn-Wittgenstein from 24 June 1856 (p. 136); to the Kunsthalle, Hamburg, for Claude Lorrain's *View of Carthage with Dido and Aeneas* (p. 55); to Madame Marie Coumes and Madame Bernard, Librairie Pinault, Paris, for the autograph letter to Albert Du Boys from 20 July 1825 (p. 109); to the National Gallery, London, and Neil Evans for Corot's *Roman Campagna with Claudian aqueduct* (p. 182); to the Stiftung Weimarer Klassik und Kunstsammlungen, Weimar, for Lauchert's portrait of Berlioz (p. 258); to June Mendoza for the portrait of Colin Davis (p. 366); to the Athenaeum and its archivist, Jennie de Protani, for the page of the Club minutes from 1848 (p. 366); and to Chris Christodoulou for his photographs of Sir John Eliot Gardiner and Sir Roger Norrington (p. 371).

I should like also to thank the many friends whose interest and enthusiasm and knowledge lie behind, and have contributed to, my writings on Berlioz over the years: Adrian Brown, Siân Edwards, John Eliot Gardiner, Roger Norrington, Robin Ticciati; Peter Bloom, David Charlton, Jonathan Elkus, Kern Holoman, the late Katherine Kolb, Ralph Locke, Hugh Macdonald, Richard Macnutt, Michael Rose; my colleagues on the committee of the Berlioz Society – Alastair Aberdare, Linda Edmondson, Christopher Follett, Brian Godfrey, Simon Jones, Shelagh Marston, Peter Payne, Helen Petchey, Martin Price, Adam Ridley, Julian Rushton; John M. Anderson, Michel Austin, Gunther Braam, the late Harold Hughes, Monir Tayeb; Jean-Pierre Bartoli, Catherine Massip, Cécile Reynaud, Rémy Stricker; and in La Côte-Saint-André – at the Musée Berlioz, the Festival, and the Association nationale Hector Berlioz – Lucien Chamard-Bois, Gérard Condé, Christiane Dauwe, Arlette Ginier-Gillet, Annie Jeannenez, Frédérique Laudinet,

Bruno Messina, Corinne Morel, Delphine Sabouraud, Chantal Spillemaecker, the late François Thévenet and Antoine Troncy.

Special tributes to Julian Rushton and Chris Follett for nobly reading the entire text, and for their comments and corrections, to Adam Ridley for his wise advice, to Peter Bloom for countless kindnesses and, for their generous help with the illustrations, to Monir Tayeb, Gunther Braam, Paul Ryan, Peter Bloom and Bryan Sherwood. Tanya Tintner did sterling service in bringing order to the first draft of my text; and Máire Taylor's alertness as proof-reader likewise requires a note of gratitude.

Finally, grateful thanks to Martin Anderson for giving me a hospitable home at Toccata Press, and for his vigilant eye and command of the whole project.

PREAMBLE

A Tragic Life

The deadline for delivery of the manuscript of my biography of Berlioz to Thames and Hudson (1973) had long passed before I began to write. The early 1970s were spent researching among the family papers preserved in the Paris apartment of Yvonne Reboul-Berlioz – where, as I wrote in the preface to the first volume, 'I began to get a picture of the environment from which the composer sprang, and the idea of the book I should write about him first took shape' – and also among the archives of the École de Médecine and the Opéra. It was not till the late 1970s that I started writing, in a room in Wolvesey Palace lent me by the Bishop of Winchester, John Taylor, and his wife, Peggy. I was living in Winchester, where my wife, Rosemary, was deputy head of Danemark School. Jacques Barzun chided me humorously for choosing to work under the wing of the Anglican church on Berlioz, who had scathing things to say about such 'schisms'. But our house in Wharf Hill was very small, and the space and quiet I enjoyed in the bishop's palace were exactly what I needed. I wrote this prologue there, and I reproduce it here, to launch this book and as my credo.

For a long time the music of Berlioz remained a sealed book to me. Each person comes to a particular composer in his or her own way and time; no rules govern the processes of musical discovery. But circumstances of cultural climate and environment may delay it. The more conditioned we are to the music we know, the more, unconsciously, we expect the unfamiliar to approximate to it. Bruckner's formal designs are usually incomprehensible, to begin with, to someone accustomed to Brahms'; and most people know Brahms' symphonies before they encounter Bruckner's. There are musicians and music-lovers who are drawn to Berlioz's music irresistibly and for whom its idiosyncrasies of style are no barrier; in their deepest being it sounds a note of instant recognition. To many others it seems alien when they first hear it and perhaps for long afterwards, as it did to me. I was brought up from the age of eight or nine in the German tradition: first Bach, then a few years later Beethoven, finally Brahms. Composers not squarely in that tradition were assimilated with difficulty if at all. (Even Mozart seemed trivial.) I remember one day, when I was in my early twenties, my sister Margaret coming home in some excitement with a recording of the

Fantastic Symphony that she had just heard. She insisted on my listening to it then and there. It made absolutely no sense to me.

Nearly ten years passed before anything occurred to change this attitude. My musical tastes grew outwards from their Germanic centre, but on the rare occasions when I heard any Berlioz, I could make little of it. Then in 1957 Covent Garden produced *The Trojans*. I went to the dress rehearsal and the premiere. Unlike many, *bouleversés* by the experience (the origin of the modern Berlioz revival), I was only partly persuaded. But had I not had to go abroad immediately after the first night, I should certainly have returned to Covent Garden for a later performance, for by then my interest had been aroused. Not long before, my cousin Teddy Hodgkin had played me the old 78 recording by Jean Planel of 'Le Repos de la sainte famille' from *The Childhood of Christ* and had lent me the *Memoirs* (in the Everyman edition, with its racy, sympathetic translation by Katharine Boult). I was charmed by the strange sweetness and purity of the piece, and I was riveted by the book: the personality of the author intrigued and attracted me. I felt I must reconsider my rejection of his music and have another shot of it.

The opportunity came a few months later. The Chelsea Opera Group performed *The Damnation of Faust* under Meredith Davies. I played in the orchestra, in the percussion section. We had half a dozen rehearsals. Gradually, in the course of them, the barriers fell away and enlightenment dawned – until I realised with delight that the language which ten years before had been so much gibberish to my musical understanding had become familiar and made sense, thrilling, unimagined sense after all.

I give these personal details not simply to show how I became interested in Berlioz but as a means of illustrating the general problem his music can pose. In a musical culture still predominantly Teutonic, Berlioz's language even now can take a lot of learning. For long there were powerful extraneous factors obstructing the process of learning it. The 'Berlioz Problem' was a nineteenth-century creation, but it lasted well into the twentieth. Musical opinion labelled him a freak; and in no area of human activity are received ideas more tenacious and myths harder to dispel. It became customary to think of him as a phenomenon uniquely eccentric and *sui generis* and of his admirers as a race apart.

To some extent the problem was that of all new music, dependent for its acceptance on conductors and musicians capable of mastering its technical and stylistic demands, so that the performances it receives communicate it faithfully and do not distort it beyond comprehension. But in the case of Berlioz the music tended to remain new, not receiving enough performances to become familiar, and making technical and stylistic demands of a formidable kind. It was not so much that it exploited the most advanced instrumental techniques, and invented a few new ones, as that it did so in the service of a style that musicians necessarily found hard to understand because its most prominent features were precisely those that the nineteenth century was busy forgetting: extended melody and complex, irregular rhythm. In an age dominated by Wagnerian harmonic polyphony, music based on opposite methods was wide open to misunderstanding. Its composer could only appear an outsider subject to no laws, and one whose methods seemed at odds with his aims. The two 'sides' of his art, the Romantic and the Classical, were seen as the reflection of deep unresolved tensions in his nature, poles between which his magnetic but unstable genius flickered ungovernably.

Attempts made to place him during his lifetime had led only to confusion. In the conservative mind he became associated with the deeply feared new movements in Germany (which were believed to imperil the very survival of music). This strange error helps to account for the extraordinary ferocity with which his French critics attacked him. Such an idea – Berlioz as disciple of Wagnerism – could have been thought up only in France. But there was a kind of excuse for it in the success he always seemed to be having with the Germans. In fact, if his works excited more response beyond the Rhine than in his native country, that was because there was a serious concert-going public in Germany, ready and curious to listen to new things, new styles and forms, and not because of any strong German affinities in his music. His roots were in France, in the music of French composers or composers assimilated to the French tradition. But this cardinal truth was hidden, both by the novel aspects of his music and because the tradition was in decline by the time he emerged as a composer to be reckoned with. Gluck, Spontini, Le Sueur, Méhul, Cherubini – they were his chief influences in the years when he was learning to speak with his own voice. A decade later they were *passés*.

Here is one source of the Berlioz legend. He had roots but they were concealed because the music from which they stemmed had ceased to be familiar. People were conscious only of the strangeness of his style, combined with something disconcertingly old-fashioned. In a musical society divided by rival factions, his music satisfied no single orthodoxy. To the academic establishment, always peculiarly narrow and rule-obsessed in France, it was unacceptable by reason of its disregard of the 'principles of correct composition' – principles that Beethoven himself deserved the severest censure for flouting – and by reason of its restless modernity. But the modernists, though excited by it and in particular by its enrichment of the expressive possibilities of the orchestra, could not wholly accept it either: its antecedents, its whole bent, were too directly opposed to theirs.

Berlioz and Wagner both set out from Beethoven (the discovery of whose music marked the final and decisive stage in Berlioz's artistic formation); but they took quite different directions, and it was the Wagnerian that appeared to lead to the future. At the very moment when Wagner was writing his most advanced score, *Tristan und Isolde*, the score that was to have such a marked influence on the music of the next 50 years, Berlioz was summing up his life's work in a classical epic of the ancient world, steeped in the spirit of Gluck and Spontini, Claude Lorrain, Virgil, Shakespeare – *The Trojans*. When Berlioz went through the score of *Tristan* that Wagner presented to him, he found the harmonic idiom incomprehensible. Yet this same conservative, whose *Treatise on Modern Instrumentation and Orchestration* takes a good third of its examples from the operas of Gluck composed 70 or 80 years earlier, can introduce the *Treatise* with the late-twentieth-century watchword: 'Any sound-producing body utilised by the composer is a musical instrument'.

Berlioz's isolation should not be exaggerated. He had his admirers and champions, German, Russian and English, but French as well, to whom his music, 'paradoxes' and all, spoke directly, without impediment. And so far from leading nowhere, it was to influence composers as diverse as Bizet, the Russian Five, Mahler, Busoni and Stravinsky. But, as he himself recognised, his time had yet to come. If much in his works sprang from a past already fading from memory when he first presented them, much was ahead of its time and awaited an age capable of responding to it. Extended melody, harmony treated expressively rather than functionally (as in the Austro-German tradition), rhythmic innovation, form created afresh for the particular context, timbre and space as compositional elements, open orchestral textures, and a lean and lucid sound with no trace of the all-pervasive instrument of nineteenth-century composition, the piano – such things had so to speak to be rediscovered before a style based of them could be at all widely understood.

Above all, it needed the advent of a retrospective age in which all epochs are potentially equal, all styles admissible, where one thing is no longer judged by another, and the only laws a piece of music must be true to are its own. Modern culture's comprehensive awareness of the past, its revival of more and more forgotten works, and at the same time the profound upheavals in musical composition, have between them virtually abolished the concept of a norm against which music such as Berlioz's could be measured and found wanting. The historical factors that made him seem a freak have run their course. Thanks to much more frequent performance and to recording, his works are no longer more talked of than listened to. They have become familiar.

The classic case of the Berlioz score that everyone knew about and hardly anyone knew was *The Trojans*. Its discovery, at Covent Garden in 1957, was correspondingly revelatory in its effect. At a stroke the picture changed. The significance of those performances was summed up at the time by Robert Collet in *The Score*:

> What seems immediately to have struck many people [...] was that this music was utterly different from the idea of Berlioz handed out to us by writers on music, and not only the stupid ones. Until very recently it was customary to hear quite knowledgeable musicians and amateurs talk of Berlioz as a wayward Byronic eccentric, with an interest in the orchestra that was unusual for his day, and an undoubted gift for musical *grotesquerie*, but otherwise a striking figure in musical history rather than a truly great composer. No one who has listened to *The Trojans* with even partial understanding can accept such a superficial and one-sided view any longer.[1]

He was speaking of musical opinion in Britain, a country with a tradition of interest in Berlioz going back to the composer's visits to London a century earlier. But the consequences – of which the publication of the full score, more than a century after its composition, and the issue of a complete recording were only the most obvious – were to be felt far beyond Covent Garden.

The last few years have seen Berlioz, the quondam bugbear of the professors, become a respectable subject of academic research. Scholars have begun to examine his scores without prejudice and to find out what they contain and how they are written. The study of his compositional procedures now going on in European and American university music departments is bringing to recognition a composer radically different from the wild man of myth who composed by flashes of lightning and was great, if at all, by accident. It has become normal to treat him like other composers. Even a French critic might hesitate before expressing himself in the language and tone of Émile Vuillermoz in his *Histoire de la Musique*, published in 1949: 'Musicians suffer [...] from the slapdash nature of his writing, the clumsiness of his style and his incoherent and chaotic methods of composition'.[2]

The distinguished French musician Henry Barraud has declared that Vuillermoz's pronouncements on music in general reveal an incompetence so profound as to render everything he wrote null and void.[3] Yet it is not enough simply to dismiss such a passage as too extreme to bother about. Its

1 *The Score*, Vol. 20, June 1957, p. 68.
2 Arthème Fayard, Paris, 1949, p. 238.
3 During an address to the Colloque Berlioz, Bibliothèque nationale de France, October 1975.

hysteria may have something to say not merely about the writer but about the music that had so disagreeable an effect on him. The old received idea of Berlioz as subverter of artistic law and order continues to arouse feelings of insecurity. And not only the idea but the music itself, and notably its sense of violence: violence barely contained and sometimes bursting out with frightening force – what Berlioz's contemporary the critic Blaze de Bury called 'the smell of carnage that rises from some of his scores'[4] (a quality critics also found in the paintings of Delacroix), and that Colin Davis has described as his ability to 'generate terror'. There is in his music, especially the music of his youth, an electrical atmosphere by which some people are unsettled as by certain kinds of weather. It is, maybe, as natural for one person to make him a scapegoat as for another to identify with his heroic struggles and love him for his very humiliations.

Even when one takes him for himself and not as a symbol, there may remain barriers. His is not consoling music. Its nerves are exposed. With all its ardours and exaltations, it is disturbingly alive to the torments of human existence, outside and within. Its passionate sense of beauty carries an acute awareness of how frail and ephemeral beauty is. It understands the tragic limitations of life, the discrepancy between imagination and fact, the chaos that waits beyond the edge of civilisation, the terror of isolation in an empty universe. There is a core of reserve at the heart of its most fiery intensities. You cannot wallow in it. It can be intoxicating, but to the spirit more than to the senses.

In this he differs from the Romantic composers who were his contemporaries. Their aims may have been similar to his; their methods are not. His art objectifies the emotions that inspire it. He stands apart, too, from most of his fellow artists in France, the writers and painters. For all the similarities, he seems beside them a figure from an older time. He may share their postures and preoccupations, their literary enthusiasms, their beliefs, their subjects, their self-consciousness as artists, their attachment to the contrast of extremes, and their sense of the past. But his nostalgia is more deeply ingrained, more ancient. Again and again one hears in his music this note of antiquity: sometimes as a sadness 'old as man's weariness', sometimes as a freshness from the youth of the world. It is this indefinable but unmistakable tone that made Heine compare him to a 'colossal nightingale, a lark the size of an eagle, such as we are told existed in primordial times',[5] and that a modern writer, Victor Gollancz, has defined

[4] *Musiciens du passé et du présent et de l'avenir*, Calmann-Lévy, Paris, 1880, p. 357. De Bury also complains of 'cette horrible grimace qui balafre comme un signe de malédiction l'altière beauté de son œuvre' ('the shocking grimace that disfigures, like a kind of curse, the proud beauty of his work').

[5] In *Lutetzia. Vermischte Schriften,* Hoffmann und Campe, Hamburg, 1854, Vol. III, p. 272.

as an 'ache for an earlier, a kind of pre-moral beauty'.[6] The yearning for a golden age is no mere conventional pose with Berlioz; it is a condition of his existence. When, after writing his Virgilian epic *The Trojans*, he said that he had spent his life 'with that race of demigods',[7] he was stating the truth.

Such an artist, compounded of such seeming opposites, could not have been other than problematical, just as his career as a composer in mid-nineteenth-century Paris could only be a record of frustrations and unfulfilled hopes and the isolated triumphs that win a battle but not the war. Some have sought to explain the ill luck that seems to cling to him throughout his life, and to pursue him in death, by reference to malevolent destiny: he was 'born under an evil star'. Others have interpreted it as self-induced, the projection of inner contradictions: Berlioz was the author of his own misfortunes. But the explanation is simpler. Certainly his music would have created difficulties – of comprehension, interpretation, performance – whatever age he had lived in. Like biblical man, he was 'born to trouble as the sparks fly upward'. But the problem was exacerbated by history. And, French to the marrow though he was, he chose the worst possible age and environment to live in. 'What the devil was the Good Lord thinking of when he had me born in "this pleasant land of France"?'[8] His *cri du cœur* says it all. The contradictions were between an artist of his ideals and the values and organisation of musical culture in contemporary Paris; and the outcome was inevitable. It was no accident that the two chief roads to success, the Opéra and the Conservatoire, were both barred to him; no accident that the spiritual heir of eighteenth-century *tragédie-lyrique*, who had been brought up to believe that the theatre was the natural goal of a composer, composed fewer than half a dozen operas, only one of which was commissioned by a Paris opera house; no accident that the greatest French composer between Rameau and Debussy remained outside the establishment; that the finest conductor of his time was passed over in favour of lesser talents whenever there was a post to be filled; that the Société des Concerts performed his music on only two occasions in the first 35 years of its prestigious existence; that he obtained no settled position in French musical life; that in consequence he had to fight every inch of the way, hardly ever enjoying the freedom he needed, forced to dissipate his energies on peripheral activities; and that in the end the struggle wore out his resilient spirit, and the repression of his creative fires burned him up, silencing his eager genius at its height.

[6] *Journey towards Music*, Gollancz, London, 1964, pp. 38–39.

[7] *Correspondance générale*, Vol. V, 1855–59, ed. Hugh J. Macdonald and François Lesure, Flammarion, Paris, p. 694.

[8] *Memoirs*, p. 95.

Ernest Newman, surveying the obstacles that Berlioz had to battle against throughout his career, concluded that 'the work he actually did […] seems only the more wonderful'.[9] True: *The Trojans*, the Requiem, *Les Nuits d'été*, *The Damnation of Faust*, *The Childhood of Christ*, the *Fantastic Symphony* exist, and they have never been more widely performed or more clearly understood. But when one considers what he might have done in other circumstances, and the works that were fated to remain locked in his imagination, never to receive form, how can one think of his life as other than tragic?

[9] Peter Heyworth (ed.), *Berlioz, Romantic and Classic. Writings by Ernest Newman*, Gollancz, London, 1972, p. 65.

Autobiography/Biography

This essay – written for Peter Bloom's compendium Berlioz: Scenes from the Life and Work *(University of Rochester Press, Rochester, NY, 2008) – discusses the relationship between autobiography and biography in which any biographer of Berlioz is inevitably involved, and shows the spirit in which I set out to write mine.*

Berlioz's autobiography, like his music, had commonly been regarded with scepticism. The more I worked on it the more I realised that here, too, was an attitude that cried out for correction. After it had first appeared, in 1870, the book, christened by Charles Villiers Stanford 'Berlioz's masterly work (? of fiction)',[1] was ready prey for commentators bent on proving its author at best a fantasist and at worst a liar. But it became increasingly clear to me that here was a far more accurate account than I had been led to believe.

Cross-questioning an autobiography demands a care and judiciousness that Berlioz's inquisitors, prominent among them Edmond Hippeau, Adolphe Boschot and Ernest Newman, were often guilty of forgetting. They forgot, too, in their zeal for refutation, that it is unwise to make assumptions based merely on the absence of corroborating documents. From his premise of Berlioz the fantasist with a fatal weakness for tall stories, Hippeau suspected that the episode of the enthusiast at the performance of Sacchini's *Œdipe à Colone* in chapter 15 ('Deep Feelings of a Mathematician')[2] was an invention. Berlioz's veracity would be vindicated when a letter from him to the man in question, Le Texier or Le Tessier, came to light, in which he speaks of the ecstasy to which Sacchini and Dérivis (the Oedipus) had reduced them both.[3]

Certainly, Berlioz loves a good story, and he knows how to tell it. The dramatised dialogues that enliven the *Memoirs* – the conversations with Pingard the Institute usher, the argument with Cherubini over the proposed use of the Salle du Conservatoire for his concert in May 1828, the exchange

[1] *Pages from an Unwritten Diary*, Edward Arnold, London, 1914, p. 68.

[2] *Memoirs*, p. 60.

[3] *Correspondance générale*, Vol. I, 1803–32, ed. Pierre Citron, Flammarion, Paris, 1972, pp. 80–81; Edmond Hippeau, *Berlioz intime*, E. Dentu, Paris, 1883, pp. 32–33. Hippeau also imagined he had caught Berlioz out changing the name of his fellow protester at the Opéra from Saint-Ange (in his earlier book *Voyage musical en Allemagne et en Italie*) to de Pons. But they were the same person: Saint-Ange was de Pons' professional name.

between Le Texier and the orange-eating billiards aficionado Léon de Boissieux during the trio 'O doux moments' in *Œdipe,* the humorous account of Karl Guhr, the Frankfurt kapellmeister, with his 'Sacré nom te Tieu (S.N.T.T.)' – may well have been touched up a little;[4] but no one now feels impelled to insist that they never took place. Berlioz was one of those people – we all know them – who attract bizarre events. Unusual things happened to him.

Some of the dialogues may even be more or less verbatim. There is no reason to doubt that Horváth, the Budapest newspaper editor, on examining the score of the 'Hungarian March', expressed anxiety about Berlioz's stating the Rákóczy theme *piano* at the opening of the piece and that Berlioz replied: 'Don't worry, you shall have such a forte as you never heard in your life', or that, conducting the first performance, he 'shot [Horváth] a glance as if to say, "Well, are you still nervous, or are you satisfied with your forte?"'[5] In Berlioz's newspaper account of the sequel to the concert, when an excited Hungarian bursts into the artists' room and, embracing him convulsively, blurts out his admiration in a Mr Jingle-like staccato, the words 'Allemands chiens' ('German dogs') found in the later *Memoirs* are missing. One can dismiss the phrase as an example of subsequent embroidery for effect, as has been done. Or – I think, more reasonably and plausibly – one can interpret its omission from the original account as having been due to diplomacy and tact, given that that account described a tour of German lands and was aimed at a largely German readership. These are random examples. The general process of exoneration was long and arduous; but it resulted in an autobiography that is worthy, as a whole, of respect and that can be used with confidence as a prime source for the composer's life.

The *Memoirs* are a constant challenge and stimulus to the biographer, both in what they reveal and even more in what they don't. Every biographer of Berlioz is by definition locked into a close but critical relationship with them. Writing his biography is both helped by his own account of it and, in a sense, required by it. Once I had translated and annotated it and, in the process, had acquired some familiarity with the composer's life, I was more or less obliged to take the next step. The book does not set out to give the full story. It is no day-to-day record or anything like it (it is far less explicit than Chateaubriand's *Mémoires d'outre-tombe,* the detailed, intimate account of an artist's existence, whose impending publication may have spurred Berlioz to begin his own in 1848). He has, he says in his Preface, no desire to write

[4] *Memoirs,* pp. 91–97, 74–76, 59–60 and 265–66.

[5] *Memoirs,* p. 416 (*Journal des débats,* 19 October 1847; republished in Hector Berlioz, *Critique musicale,* Vol. 6 (1845–48), ed. Anne Bongrain and Marie-Hélène Coudroy-Saghaï, Buchet-Chastel, Paris, 2008, p. 339). Lázár Petrichevich Horváth was editor of the newspaper *Honderü.*

confessions: he will tell only what he wants to tell about his personal life. He wishes simply to correct certain misstatements about his career, describe the influences that have shaped his art, and give an idea of the difficulties an aspiring composer faces in France, while at the same time offering 'a few useful hints'. It is, expressly, a tale with many gaps in it.

To fill them, while also testing and confirming, or not, its statements of fact, was made far easier by a mass of documents and published studies that were not available to (or not consulted by) earlier biographers – publications prompted by, and in turn furthering, the modern revival and reappraisal of Berlioz's music. This new knowledge has been particularly useful in the mapping of the least well-known period of his life, his childhood and his early years in Paris. There is now a whole intricate network of interrelated material for the biographer to work on. The letter to Le Texier cited above is one of hundreds that have appeared – letters revealing all kinds of insights and information that make possible a fuller picture of his life and personality. Taken in conjunction with his journalistic writings – now much more accessible than before and often containing autobiographical material – and with the large number of often revealing papers in public archives or in private collections, they enable us to form a more rounded portrait of the man and of his struggles: what he called his 'Thirty Years War against the routineers, the professors and the deaf'.[6]

To take one example, the lists of orchestral musicians, with their addresses and fees, which have survived in the composer's hand for the year 1835 and which are preserved in 'Berlioz papiers divers' in the Département de la Musique of the Bibliothèque nationale de France, illustrate in the most vivid way possible what it took to organise his Paris concerts in the 1830s, when he had to assemble his orchestra each time from scratch, player by player. In another library, the Bibliothèque municipale de Grenoble, an autograph document – a two-page sketch for one of the monologues in *Le Retour à la vie* – makes it clear that the work was conceived and begun before Berlioz left Paris for Italy and was originally associated with his love for Camille Moke: the 'return to life' it celebrated was his Camille-inspired recovery from the Harriet Smithson obsession.[7]

Sometimes, of course, new knowledge creates new uncertainties. The *baccalauréat* records in Grenoble provide the pleasant information that one of the Latin passages Berlioz was asked to translate in March 1821 was the

[6] From the autograph *Manuscript List of 1855* (*cf.* D. Kern Holoman, *Catalogue of the Works of Hector Berlioz*, New Berlioz Edition, Vol. 25, Bärenreiter, Kassel, 1987, p. 510).

[7] *Cf.* David Cairns, *Berlioz,* Vol. 1: *The Making of an Artist 1803–1832*, Allen Lane, London, 1999 (hereafter Cairns, *Berlioz,* Vol. 1), p. 471 and the note on p. 622; *Lélio ou Le Retour à la vie*, ed. Peter Bloom, New Berlioz Edition, Vol. 7, Bärenreiter, Kassel, 1992, pp. VIII–IX.

description, in Book 2 of the *Aeneid*, of Cassandra dragged captive from Minerva's sanctuary. But the records also suggest that he flunked his *bac* the first time he presented himself, in December 1820. An intriguing thought: but what exactly lay behind this surprising failure – what personal dramas, what domestic tensions – posterity, unfortunately, has no idea.

The family papers preserved by the descendants of Berlioz's sister Nancy have proved particularly rich, and it was for me a stroke of fortune to be able to spend weeks searching through them in the apartment of Yvonne Reboul-Berlioz in the rue de Ranelagh, Paris XVI.[8] Its prize possession was the *Livre de Raison* of Dr Louis Berlioz, the composer's father, who, for over twenty years, from 1815 to the late 1830s, entered in it a detailed record of his family and household and the running of his estate. The book gives the inventory of his extensive library (where his son first acquired his lifelong passion for reading) and of his surgical instruments, and, in addition, an account of the two occupations of La Côte-Saint-André by allied troops, in 1814 and 1815, which would be of interest to historians of the Napoleonic Wars.

The *Livre de Raison* was known to earlier Berlioz specialists, but none of them before Pierre Citron, general editor of the *Correspondance générale d'Hector Berlioz,* seems to have grasped its importance for their work and realised what a mine of information it is. Boschot refers to it only in passing. If he had studied it in earnest and read Dr Berlioz's homilies on politics and society, he could never have portrayed him as a reactionary or made such an insistent point of Berlioz's being brought up the 'fils d'un ultra'. Julien Tiersot quotes at length from it in the first volume of his edition of Berlioz's letters,[9] but it is by no means certain that he ever consulted it in person. The extracts he prints are jumbled about in the wrong order. In particular, Dr Berlioz's father's anti-republican sentiments are systematically erased. Missing, too, are the statements that the family's seventeenth-century ancestor Claude Berlioz was illiterate and that Hector Berlioz married Harriet Smithson 'malgré les parens'. Expunging the anti-republican sentiments could be Tiersot's work, but the removal of the other two items suggests the bourgeois prejudices of the then owner,

[8] *Cf.* David Cairns, 'The Reboul–Berlioz Collection' in Peter Bloom (ed.), *Berlioz Studies*, Cambridge University Press, Cambridge, 1992, pp. 1–7. Madame Reboul was the widow of Nancy Pal's great-grandson Admiral Georges Reboul, who took the name Reboul-Berlioz. Yvonne Reboul herself was directly descended from Henry Pal, brother of Nancy's husband Camille Pal. Part of the collection was bequeathed to the Musée Berlioz at La Côte-Saint-André by Yvonne's daughter Catherine Vercier. The rest is in the possession of the families of her two other children, Guy Reboul-Berlioz and Martine Perrin. *Cf.* also pp. 377–78, below.

[9] Julien Tiersot (ed.), *Hector Berlioz, Les Années romantiques, 1819–1842*, Calmann-Lévy, Paris, 1904, pp. xxxi–xl.

Livre de Raison
De
Louis Joseph Berlioz
Docteur Médecin résidant
à la Côte St André

Commencé le 1er Janvier 1815.

Dr Louis Berlioz and his Livre de Raison

Marie Masclet-Reboul (Nancy's granddaughter), who – if my conjecture is right – transcribed selected paragraphs for Tiersot rather than letting him see the book for himself.

If Tiersot did see it, he failed to read far enough to understand that Dr Berlioz recorded more than (in Tiersot's words) the list of 'dépenses, recettes etc. de sa maison, pêle-mêle avec d'autres indications': in particular, precious information about the chronology of Berlioz's student years, including the dates of his departure for Paris after summer or autumn vacations at La Côte – entries that reveal, among other things, that chapter 10 of the *Memoirs,* which ostensibly describes a single return visit, is in fact a conflation of several visits, and that Berlioz went back in 1822, 1823, 1824 and 1825 (though not in 1826, the year to which biographers used to ascribe it). These simple dates show how protracted was the family dispute over the eldest son's career. Not till 1826, five years after he first went to Paris, did Berlioz feel sufficiently independent and sure of himself to resist the order to return home.

The *Livre de Raison* also reveals where and when the new flute that Berlioz says he set his heart on[10] was purchased and how it was made and constituted ('red ebony, with eight keys and a slide, both silver, and a foot joint in C'); when, too, Dr Berlioz bought him his guitar. Over and above its value as a source of these and similar biographically fruitful details, the book is important in its totality, as illuminating the environment of Berlioz's

[10] *Memoirs*, p. 18.

boyhood and the values and beliefs that led Dr Berlioz to oppose his son's vocation so bitterly, though in the end to no avail.

Important as it is, however, it is far from being the only treasure of the Reboul Collection. For the first volume of the *Correspondance générale* alone – the period least rich in Berlioz letters – the collection produced nearly 30 that had been unknown till a few years before. Hidden away in drawers, too, were dozens of letters written by Berlioz's son Louis, from his childhood to within a few months of his death, which cast new light on their troubled but in the end close and loving relationship. There were others no less useful for the biographer, especially for the years when no or very few Berlioz letters existed: from Berlioz's uncle, the music-loving cavalry captain Félix Marmion; from Marmion's former lover, Madame Husson, which show that his seventeen-year-old nephew confided his secret ambitions to his uncle ('you must be finding it hard not to sympathise with your nephew in his enthusiasm for music'); from Dr Berlioz himself, which reveal him to have been a more volatile and irrational creature than either his view of himself or his portrait in the *Memoirs* would have us believe, and which also correct the traditional view of his marriage; from Joséphine Berlioz, Hector's mother; from her old school friend, Nancy's godmother Nancy Clappier, gossipy missives full of shrewd observations bearing on Berlioz's life and character; and many letters from Adèle Berlioz to her sister Nancy, with little titbits like the remark, near the end of their brother's year in Italy: 'Talking of noses, no news of Hector', or the information that in 1846 Berlioz seems to have been seriously thinking of splitting up with Marie Recio.

Not least, there are the diaries (*tableaux journaliers*) that Nancy kept off and on from 1822 to 1825 and the more sporadic *cahiers de souvenirs* from the late 1820s and early 1830s, the years first of Berlioz's most fraught relations with the family over his career, and then of his return as second prizewinner of the Prix de Rome (when his friend Humbert Ferrand visits La Côte and comes under Nancy's sharp-eyed scrutiny), and of his love-affair with Camille Moke. In addition to the valuable information they provide, the diaries make much clearer her ambiguous, fluctuating relationship with her brother – at one period in their lives very close. They also illuminate the character of Nancy herself, 'so like her brother in many respects, stirred by similar longings and idealisms, prey to similar despairs but, unlike him, without the means of escape'.[11]

Apart from a brief and garbled reference by Boschot, I found no sign that any Berlioz scholar before Citron realised what a vital source these diaries

[11] Cairns, 'The Reboul-Berlioz Collection', in *Berlioz Studies*, *op. cit.*, p. 14.

are or even knew of their existence. In them one reads of the excitement at La Côte at the news of Hector's engagement to Camille (it is from Nancy that we learn that Camille called him 'le fiancé de mon cœur'). Thanks to the eighteen-year-old Nancy's daily entries we experience at first hand the tumult of the household during the last days of Berlioz's five-week visit in June–July 1824 – a visit that had seemed to begin so well but that ended in anguish – and glimpse the intense emotional strain that he was subjected to, only twenty years old and in many ways young for his age.

> We were hardly back before Mama realised that Hector had sent his trunk off and would soon be following. On discovering it she broke down and wept a lot and berated him quite harshly, but justifiably. He took it with a most distressing air of unconcern. He can't wait to go.
>
> We talked of my brother this afternoon. My father is dreadfully affected by it all. 'I have always been unfortunate,' he said. 'My childhood was not happy, my youth was very stormy, and now the son who was to have been my consolation is destroying the happiness I might have had.'
>
> This evening Papa has just exhausted his remaining eloquence in an attempt to move my brother and bring him back to a more sensible line of conduct. He replies with the absurd argument that he was 'born like this'. He curses his existence.

Sadly, Nancy the reporter is not on hand either in August–November 1825, when Dr Berlioz, angered by the success of the *Messe solennelle*, makes his last sustained attempt to dissuade his son – the diary had stopped in March 'until such time as I can paint a less gloomy picture' (though we do have a letter in which Nancy speaks of the 'wall of separation' between father and son) – or in autumn 1822, or in spring 1823 when, as I have argued, the confrontation with his mother described in chapter 10 of the *Memoirs* very probably took place.[12] For that crucial period of the conflict we can, however, to some extent fill the void by reading – again in the Reboul Collection – the letters of Félix Marmion, that shrewd observer and ambivalent go-between who always took a keen interest in his nephew's affairs.

Nancy's diary can also be frustrating by falling silent just when it has whetted your appetite. In April 1822, when Berlioz's cousin and fellow medical student Alphonse Robert pays a surprise visit to La Côte, one reads that he 'told us a lot about their way of life [in Paris], Hector's in particular' and, a few days later, that 'Monsieur Alphonse spoke to us a great deal about the theatre'. That is all. What wouldn't one give for a full account of those conversations!

[12] Cairns, *Berlioz*, Vol. 1, pp. 120–22 and 159–60.

Such frustrations are the common lot of biographers, especially if their subject lived a long time ago, when contemporary testimony is likely to be sparse. Even when there is testimony, too often there can be no certainty. But biographers are 'hot for certainty': we fasten on passing witness and are prone to set it in stone.[13] Here is a tiny example. Replying to his mother's offer of some new clothes, Berlioz says, in a letter of 1836, that a few shirts would be welcome but he doesn't need an overcoat: 'Pour le manteau, je n'en porte jamais' – 'I never wear one'.[14] Evidently that was so in 1836; but does that mean one can state, as a fact, that Berlioz never wore an overcoat, *tout court*? One might conclude otherwise from the famous photograph taken by Nadar[15] in 1857, where he is shown draped in an ample coat, were it not that the coat belonged not to him but to the studio, and figures in other Nadar portraits.[16] Yet would Berlioz have agreed to be portrayed in it if he 'never wore one'?

Reminiscences of Berlioz by friends and acquaintances, of which there are many, are subject like any others to the natural uncertainties and distortions of the human memory, as well as being influenced by the nature and degree of closeness of the relationship in question. Ernest Legouvé writes fascinatingly and at length about Berlioz in his *Soixante ans de souvenirs*[17] and one would not be without it. But many of the events he describes took place half a century earlier. How trustworthy is he? Certainly not when he says that Berlioz was not widely read and had only a very limited knowledge of literature. Berlioz's letters and published writings are peppered with allusions to Racine, Molière, Corneille, Boileau, La Fontaine – they are so much part of the furniture of his mind that they almost cease to be quotations – as well as to Shakespeare (he cites more than 30 of the plays), and he was a voracious reader of contemporary publications. The inescapable conclusion is that for whatever reason (diffidence in the presence of an eminent literary figure?) he did not choose to discuss the topic with Legouvé.[18]

[13] The tenor Michael Kelly, who took the roles of Don Basilio and Don Curzio in the premiere of *Le nozze di Figaro*, claims that Mozart's favourite number in the opera was the sextet. He does so in a volume of memoirs written many years later. Mozart may well have made such a remark in passing, at a particular moment. But can one therefore say: 'We know which Mozart's favourite number was'?

[14] *Correspondance générale*, Vol. II, 1832–42, ed. Frédéric Robert, Flammarion, Paris, 1975, p. 274.

[15] Nadar was the pseudonym of Gaspard-Félix Tournachon (1820–1910), who was also a caricaturist, journalist and novelist – and also a balloonist and proponent of manned flight. Debussy, Gounod and Liszt were among the other composers he photographed.

[16] *Cf.* Gunther Braam (ed.), *The Portraits of Hector Berlioz*, New Berlioz Edition, Vol. 26, Bärenreiter, Kassel, 2003, pp. 174–75.

[17] Ernest Legouvé, *Soixante ans de souvenirs*, Imprimerie A. Lahure, 2 vols., Paris, 1886.

[18] Neville Cardus (in *Sir Thomas Beecham: A Memoir*, Collins, London, 1961), says that Beecham was not interested in either politics or religion. But he was. As Edmund Tracey observed in a review of the

Berlioz in Nadar's famous 1857 portrait – wearing the studio greatcoat

For that matter, can one trust Legouvé's story of Marie Recio knocking on Harriet Smithson's door and saying triumphantly: 'You're not Madame Berlioz, you're the old, rejected one, I am the real Madame Berlioz, the young and pretty one'?[19] Could Marie have been so cruel, so odious? Yet could even a romancer as inveterate as Legouvé have invented it? One simply doesn't know. On the other hand, his story of the six-year-old Louis woken in the night by the noise of his mother upbraiding his father, and running to her and crying 'Mama! Don't be like Madame Lafarge' – the murderess whose trial in 1840 was the talk of France – has, it seems to me, the ring of truth.[20] In the end, however, one can only go with what judgement and instinct suggest.

Equally, when one has a sudden hunch, one should be prepared to back it – as I did when it occurred to me that the famous incident of Habeneck's 'pinch of snuff', commonly pooh-poohed but attested by independent witnesses, may have taken place not at the premiere of the Requiem but at the public dress rehearsal. Hunches, needless to say, are not necessarily right. In trying to conceive Berlioz's increasingly anxious state of mind as he made his way to the rue de la Tour des Dames to call on the great Talma and ask him to include *Beverley* in his benefit performance at the Théâtre-Français in April 1824 (in the end he felt too shy to accost him), I assumed that he went there from his lodgings in the rue Saint-Jacques, and I walked the distance myself to see how long it would have taken him (about 45 minutes), his nervousness growing all the while. But supposing he went not from his lodgings but from the Bibliothèque du Conservatoire – a haunt of his – or from Le Sueur's house in the rue Sainte-Anne?

Sometimes the evidence is conflicting. On the question of Berlioz's piano-playing, or lack of it, is one to believe the witness who says that all he could do was pick out a tune with one finger or the one who says that, although no pianist in any conventional sense, he could give a remarkable impression of a piece of music?[21]

Another biographical hazard is that the surviving testimony, in the form of letters, may well contain allusions that will escape an outsider. This is particularly so of family letters. Families have their private codes, their familiar jokes which do not have to be spelled out and which are necessarily lost on others. When Mozart tells his father that he has written

---

book, 'It takes two to make a conversation. Perhaps Sir Thomas decided that religion and politics were not Mr Cardus's strongest suits'.

[19] Legouvé, *op. cit.*

[20] *Ibid.*

[21] Respectively Legouvé, *ibid.*, and Auguste Barbier, *Souvenirs personnels et silhouettes contemporaines*, E. Dentu, Paris, 1883; *cf.* Michael Rose, *Berlioz Remembered*, Faber and Faber, London, 2001, respectively pp. 61 and 49.

The opening of Berlioz's 1822 manuscript containing arias from Gluck's two Iphigénie *operas*

the symphony he is sending him (for a celebration by the Haffner family) in D 'because you prefer that key',[22] there is surely more in the remark than meets the eye. Behind the correspondence of the Berlioz family, like any other's, must lie a whole world of shared experience, and of shared humour, that is largely denied to everyone else. Communications between friends, too, may contain references that the correspondents take for granted and that are therefore hidden from others. When Berlioz told Ferdinand Hiller that he was writing *La Belle voyageuse* very slowly, 'a few bars at a time, like a counterpoint lesson', one should surely not take it literally; he was, very probably, teasing Hiller – there was a lot of that in their relationship. Hiller may well have said Berlioz composed too quickly, and this was his (jesting) response.[23]

One asset a biographer needs but cannot rely on is luck – the serendipity, for instance, that led Richard Macnutt unsuspectingly to a particular shelf in the back room of a shop off the quai des Grands-Augustins in Paris, where he found a 120-page manuscript containing arias from Gluck's two *Iphigénie* operas in a familiar hand, written out by Berlioz from the full scores in the Conservatoire Library in 1822, a discovery that made thrillingly alive and real the passage in chapter 5 of the *Memoirs*, where Berlioz speaks of reading and re-reading Gluck's scores, copying them and learning them by heart, going without sleep because of them and forgetting to eat. 'When I was at last able to hear *Iphigénie en Tauride* I vowed as I left the Opéra that in spite of father, mother, uncles, aunts, grandparents, and friends, I would be a musician.'[24]

Again and again, when working on the *Memoirs*, I found that the records of the time confirm this or that detail in the book, even when it seems exaggerated or purely fanciful. To take one example among many, Berlioz makes comic play with the fact that the text of the Prix de Rome cantatas usually began with a sunrise,[25] and that it is typical of him ('eternally at odds with life and with the Academy') that when he eventually won the prize, in 1830, it was with a sunset. Sure enough, the archives of the Institut de France record sunrises in 1822, 1823 and 1825: 'Le jour a pénétré sous cet épais ombrage', 'L'aube a doré les monts d'une clarté nouvelle', 'La fraîcheur du matin ranime la nature'.[26]

Not that such accuracy is always the case. The emphasis of the *Memoirs* on the crucial role of Gluck in Berlioz's apprenticeship is indeed borne

[22] Emily Anderson (transl.), *The Letters of Mozart and his Family*, 3rd edn., Macmillan, London, 1985, p. 810.

[23] Ferdinand Hiller, *Künstlerleben*, DuMont-Schauberg, Cologne, 1880, p. 105.

[24] *Memoirs*, p. 23.

[25] *Memoirs*, pp. 87 and 117.

[26] In the cantatas *Geneviève de Brabant*, *Thisbé* and *Ariane à Naxos*, by J.-A. Vinaty.

désigner parmi les aspirants les cinq ou six élèves les plus avancés.
Le sujet du grand concours devait être une scène lyrique sérieuse pour une ou deux voix *et orchestre*; et les candidats, afin de prouver qu'ils possédaient le sentiment de la mélodie et de l'expression dramatique, l'art de l'instrumentation et les autres connaissances indispensables pour écrire passablement un tel ouvrage, étaient tenus de composer *une fugue vocale*. On leur accordait une journée pour ce travail. *Chaque fugue devait être signée*.

Le lendemain, les membres de la section de musique de l'Institut se rassemblaient, lisaient les fugues, et faisaient un choix trop souvent entaché de partialité, car un certain nombre des manuscrits *signés* appartenait toujours à des élèves de MM. les académiciens.

Les votes recueillis et les concurrents désignés, ceux-ci devaient se représenter bientôt après pour recevoir les paroles de la scène ou cantate qu'ils allaient avoir à mettre en musique, et *entrer en loge*. M. le Secrétaire perpétuel de l'académie des beaux arts leur dictait collectivement le classique poème, qui commençait presque toujours ainsi:

« Déjà l'aurore aux doigts de rose.

ou:

« Déjà le jour naissant ranime la nature.

ou:

« Déjà d'un doux éclat l'horizon se colore.

ou:

« Déjà du blond Phœbus le char brillant s'avance.

ou:

« Déjà de pourpre et d'or les monts lointains se parent. –

etc, etc.

Berlioz makes fun of the inevitable sunrise in Prix de Rome cantatas in his Memoirs.

out by the evidence; but it led him, when recalling those heady events 25 years later, to shorten the period of his medical studies and represent his abandoning of them as more clear-cut than it was. Here other evidence can be drawn on – medical registers, Opéra archives, documents unearthed by the researches of Donnet and Moureaux – to correct the account in the *Memoirs*.[27] The revival of *Iphigénie en Tauride* at the Opéra on 21 August 1822 recorded in the Opéra archives and in the *Almanach des Spectacles* was unquestionably decisive, but the medical and musical careers overlapped for several months – indeed until the providential closure of the École de Médecine in late November 1822 – as can be seen from the school registers, where Berlioz's signature at the beginning of each of the four terms shows that he completed the first-year course, undoubtedly passing the end of term exams and obtaining the *certificat d'assiduité* that every student had to present when signing on for the new term.

Although luck cannot be summoned, it can be encouraged. Opportunism seems to me an essential tool of a biographer. If your subject is ever-present in your mind, if you are constantly, even if half the time unconsciously, on the *qui vive*, unlooked-for pieces of information will seek you out. You never know when one is going to fall into your lap. Though F. R. Leavis used to scorn the Sunday book-reviews as worthless, I am grateful for them. It was happening to read a review of a biography of the famous German scientist and explorer Alexander von Humboldt (whom Berlioz would meet on his visits to Germany) that put me in the way of solving a minor puzzle of the *Memoirs*: the identity of the 'oiseau colossal' soaring above the snows of Chimborazo[28] to which Berlioz compares the lonely, exalted spirit of Beethoven, after hearing Anton Bohrer and friends play the *Adagio* of one of the late quartets.[29] Newman liked to make fun of Berlioz and his 'colossal bird'. But the review, in describing Humboldt at 23,000 feet in the Andes watching a solitary condor circling far above him, led me to the answer. I already knew, from the inventory in the *Livre de Raison*, that Humboldt's *Tableaux de la Nature* was one of the books in Dr Berlioz's library. The young Berlioz, with his interest in exploration and in science (which will persist all his life and be reflected in his writings), certainly read it and found there the solitary condor, as I did when I borrowed it from the London Library. After that, it was no surprise to find, in the same book,

[27] V. Donnet and C. Moureaux, 'Le Baccalauréat-ès-sciences d'Hector Berlioz', in *Marseille médical*, 106e année, No. 3, 1969, p. 160.

[28] The significance of Chimborazo, a currently inactive stratovolcano in Ecuador, is that in the early nineteenth century it was considered to be the highest mountain on Earth – and the equatorial bulge does indeed mean that its summit is the furthest from the centre of the planet. Measured from sea level, however, there are over 100 peaks in the Himalayas which are higher than Chimborazo.

[29] *Memoirs*, p. 362; *cf.* also pp. 138–39, below.

Alexander von Humboldt, painted by Julius Schrader in 1859, with Chimborazo in the background

the South American boa constrictor that covers its victim with a mucous slaver before swallowing it, and which Berlioz remembered as he stood on the tilting deck of the Sardinian brig, during the perilous crossing to Leghorn in 1831, and watched the waves foaming over it, 'comme les boas d'Amérique, qui couvrent leur victime de leur bave avant de la dévorer'.[30]

[30] *Correspondance générale*, Vol. I, p. 417.

To another Sunday review I owe the less important but piquant discovery that William Hazlitt was in Paris in 1824, reporting on it for *The Morning Chronicle,* and went to the Opéra and heard Piccinni's *Didon,* very probably on a night when Berlioz (who never missed a performance if he could help it) was in the audience – though Berlioz would not have shared his opinion of Dérivis, the Iarbas, whom Berlioz and his friends much admired but whom Hazlitt, like Berlioz's hated *dilettanti,* thought a crude and over-vehement singer: 'Ten bulls could not bellow louder, nor a whole street-full of frozen-out gardeners at Christmas'.[31]

It goes without saying that it is an advantage for biographers to like their subjects – to feel drawn to the person in the first place and to continue to, even after years spent in their intimate company. Berlioz has been, for me, never a mere 'subject' – to borrow the word used, in both French and English, to designate the corpse that he dissected at the Hospice de la Pitié while humming Salieri and Spontini – but a living person, whom, whatever his faults, I have never felt the desire to debunk or cut down to size. Besides, he could do it so well himself. One of the attractions of the *Memoirs* is his self-deflating irony, the way he will bring his most inspired flights of fancy down to earth.

This is a characteristic of his writing in general, as when, in a *feuilleton,* after imagining that if he 'were rich, really rich, like those poor deluded souls who give a singer five hundred francs for a cavatina worth five sous', he would buy the plains of Troy from the Sultan and set sail with a choice orchestra to the Troiad, there to perform the *Eroica* in a specially constructed temple of music, he modulates abruptly to a performance of the same work at the Salle du Conservatoire (off the rue Bergère, now in the Ninth Arrondissement):

> a damp and grimy little hall where a few oily chandeliers define the murk, and you see pale women raising their eyes heavenward in studied poses and rubicund men struggling not to fall asleep or nodding their heads out of time with the music and smiling as the anguished orchestra utters its cries of pain.[32]

Berlioz, as Edward Cone remarked, may be his own best critic.[33] But one does not have to agree when he describes himself, in a letter of 1864, as a writer who 'searches for the word that will convey what he feels, without ever finding it – I write with too much violence; I would like to calm down but can't. This lends the movement of my prose an uneven, lurching

[31] William Hazlitt, *Notes of a Journey through France and Italy*, Hunt and Clark, London, 1826, p. 160.

[32] *Revue et gazette musicale*, 28 January 1841; republished in *Critique musicale*, Vol. 4 (1839–41), ed. Anne Bongrain et Marie-Hélène Coudroy-Saghaï, Buchet-Chastel, Paris, 2003, pp. 437–39..

[33] Edward Cone, *Music: A View from Delft. Selected Essays*, ed. Robert P. Morgan, University of Chicago Press, Chicago, 1989, p. 217.

gait, like the steps of a drunken man'.[34] One may note that the passage is an example of a characteristic found here and there in the *Memoirs:* the tendency, not unknown in autobiographers, to make himself out a more extreme, eccentric fellow than he really is ('I know nothing about painting and have little feeling for conventional beauty'[35]), and to heighten his quirks and prejudices – what he himself calls in chapter 38 of the *Memoirs* 'the proneness of artists to write for effect'. But I have to warm to someone so free from self-love or complacency, so alert to puncture any conceit in himself, so honest. He takes himself seriously – why not? – but he never takes himself too seriously. He is well aware of his cussedness, his black moods. The crotchety description of the Salle du Conservatoire and its audience quoted above is humorous in both senses of the word (as well as being necessary for the balance and irony of the piece). He knows perfectly well that the reader will accept it in that light, as the momentary spasm of irritation in one who has written so many rhapsodies about the hall and its memorable concerts that he will be forgiven this brief *jeu d'esprit* in another key.

His playfulness rarely deserts him. In his writings, as in his music, there is scant danger of dullness. I remember Daniel Barenboim saying of the music, at a time when he was conducting a good deal of it with the Orchestre de Paris: 'It grows'. That is true of Berlioz's achievement and personality as a whole. He does not let you down. During all the years I have spent immersing myself in them I have not once tired of him. Amid the traumas and vicissitudes of a tragic life, the acute sufferings physical and emotional – which, being the person he was, he lived to the top of his bent – he hardly ever loses his resilience, his humour, his quickness and energy of mind, his mordant sense of irony, his fertile imagination, his curiosity.

His last but one *feuilleton* in the *Journal des débats,* written in the midst of frequent bouts of severe pain and anxious preoccupation with the coming production of *Les Troyens,* is a flight of fancy that uses the revival of Albert Grisar's *opéra-comique Les Amours du diable* as the launch-pad for a futuristic vision of the Earth made one world by air travel, and himself issuing orders to his orchestral attendant as the next musical festivity draws near: 'Where's Vieuxtemps? And Becker?' 'They're in Sydney, sir.' 'Go and fetch them. And Sivori, and Bottesini, and Piatti?' 'Sir, they're in Canton, Timor, and Mindanao.' 'All right, pick them up as you pass, they're on your route. [...] I want these virtuosos five days from now'.[36]

[34] *Correspondance générale*, Vol. VII, 1864–69, ed. Hugh J. Macdonald, Flammarion, Paris, 2001, p. 102.

[35] *Memoirs*, p. 250. Yet he refers appreciatively to Claude, Michelangelo and Canova, among others.

[36] *Journal des débats*, 3 September 1863.

To read Berlioz is a constant pleasure. He is irrepressible. 'Où diable le bon Dieu avait-il la tête?', he demands of the Good Lord's decision to make him a Frenchman.[37] His enthusiasm refuses to be quenched. To the end he will proselytise his gods, never quite giving up hope. In the late, long essay on *Fidelio* (which Wagner admired), after analysing the work number by number in a style that, as is his wont, mingles the poetic and the technical, he concludes:

> [*Fidelio*] belongs to that powerful race of maligned works [...,] the vitality of which is so intense that nothing can prevail against them – like those sturdy beeches born among rocks and ruins, which end by splitting the stone and breaking through the walls, and rise up proud and verdant, the more solidly rooted for the obstacles they have had to overcome in order to force their way out; whereas the willows that grow without effort on the banks of a river fall into the mud and rot, forgotten. [...] Who knows that light will not dawn sooner than one thinks, even for those whose spirits are closed at the moment to this beautiful work, as they are to the marvels of the Ninth Symphony and the last quartets and the great piano sonatas of that inspired, incomparable being. Sometimes, when one looks at a particular part of the heaven of art, a veil seems to cover 'the mind's eye' and prevent it from seeing the stars that shine there. Then all of a sudden, for no apparent reason, the veil is rent and one sees, and blushes to have been blind so long.[38]

Beethoven is his god, and Gluck and Virgil, and Shakespeare, not *le bon Dieu*, who has a rather rough ride in Berlioz's writings and letters:

> Yet another of my friends is dead. [...] The Good Lord is gunning us down ['le bon Dieu nous mitraille']. I hope he's missing you all at Weimar.[39]

> Five days ago [...] I was in a state of ecstasy – I had played my first act [of *Les Troyens]* through mentally from beginning to end. There's nothing so absurd as an author who, imitating the Good Lord, considers his work on the seventh day and 'finds it good'. But imagine: apart from two or three pieces I had forgotten the whole thing – hence my delight. [...] The only part I hadn't written was the mime scene for Andromache. Its importance daunted me. Now it too is done, and of the whole act I think it's the piece that comes off best. [...] I wept buckets over it. Imitating the Good Lord again, you see – though a lively sensibility was not his strong point, if one is to believe that appalling old rogue Moses.[40]

[37] *Memoirs*, p. 95.

[38] *Journal des débats*, 19 and 22 May 1860, reproduced in *À travers chants* (1862), ed. Léon Guichard, Gründ, Paris, 1971, pp. 88 and 102.

[39] *Correspondance générale*, Vol. V, p. 301.

[40] *Ibid.*, p. 424.

The letters written during the months of the composition of *Les Troyens* – April 1856 to March 1858 – show Berlioz at the top of his form. The creative exuberance released by the achieving of a lifetime's ambition overflows into his correspondence. It documents the making of the opera in exceptionally full and vivid detail; with no other work of his can one follow the progress so closely. For that reason, when I came to these years in my biography of Berlioz, I decided that the whole section should consist simply of extracts from the letters: I would leave him to speak for himself and tell the story of his 'ardent existence' in those two years in his own words.

I did so, as well, in pursuance of a governing idea. In the same spirit, I persuaded the publisher to reproduce Claude's late Virgilian painting *Vue de Carthage avec Didon et Enée* on the back of the dust jacket of the second volume. *Les Troyens,* I argued, is the work that lends unity to Berlioz's life, that makes sense of it. In the light of its greatness – so long denied – one can see that he did fulfil himself. I chose the opera, perhaps at first only half-consciously, as the central motif of the book, beginning with the Latin lessons in his father's study, the tears shed for Dido, and the Virgilian epiphany at Vespers in the church at La Côte, continuing with the discovery of Gluck's 'reconstructions of the ancient world' and the revelatory performances by Madame Branchu ('*tragédie-lyrique* incarnate') in *Iphigénie en Aulide*, *Alceste*, Piccinni's *Didon* and Spontini's *Olympie*, then flowering under the sun of Italy with the guitar improvisations in the Campagna and the mirage of his Virgilian heroes as he looks down on the coast of Naples from the heights of Posilippo. After that, there is never a time when Virgil is not his companion and the work not present by implication, like an underground river running beneath the external reality of his life. In the early 1850s it rises to the surface. With the encouragement of Princess Carolyne Sayn-Wittgenstein, he finally commits himself to it and writes the work that he knows will be the culmination of his existence.

The fate of the opera – sliced in two, the Carthage acts alone given, themselves mutilated – is all too well known. It was the crowning blow. The pages in the *Memoirs* recounting the opera's 'damn'd defeat' are the bitterest in the book. In Gounod's phrase, 'like his heroic namesake Hector, he died beneath the walls of Troy'.[41]

Berlioz would not have agreed with Tolstoy, who entitled his tale of an innocent man sent to Siberia for a murder he did not commit and exonerated years later, at the point of death, 'God sees the truth but waits'. But he would surely have relished the poetic justice whereby it was his long-suffering opera that, nearly a century later, began the upturn in his

[41] *Cf.* Gounod's preface to *Berlioz, Lettres intimes*, Calmann-Lévy, Paris, 2nd edn., 1882, p. vii.

Claude Lorrain, View of Carthage with Dido and Aeneas, *1675 or 1676*

fortunes that has gone from strength to strength in the succeeding 50 years. His dying words, 'They are finally going to play my music'[42] – a prophecy that certainly meant France (it was already being played in Germany and Russia) – were vindicated in 2003, 200 years after his birth, when at the Théâtre du Châtelet, directly opposite the Théâtre-Lyrique where Berlioz had watched his visionary masterpiece brought low, Paris cheered *Les Troyens* to the echo.

[42] Ernest Reyer, 'Hector Berlioz: biographical notes and personal reminiscences,' in *Century*, XVII, December 1893, p. 305.

I

EARLY LIFE

The Distant God

'The Distant God' originated as a talk given at the Berlioz Society Members' Weekend at the Art Workers' Guild in Bloomsbury in November 2011 and published in the Berlioz Society Bulletin *No. 188 (August 2012).*

Berlioz makes no bones about his attitude to established religion. He may not dislike the Catholic Church as intensely as Verdi (who showed his deep revulsion in the brutal, implacable music he wrote for the Grand Inquisitor in *Don Carlos*) – indeed, he may even have a soft spot for certain aspects of it. Nonetheless he is pretty cynical on the subject, pretty dismissive.

Monks, in particular, are a frequent butt of his sardonic humour: the monks of Subiaco, with their brisk trade in rose petals which are marketed as a cure for convulsions, and the show they make of the miraculous muskets whose owners overloaded them but were saved from death by 'calling on the saint in the act of firing';[1] other monks of the Abruzzi, who consort with brigands;[2] his sceptical reaction to the claim of his friend Crispino that he spent his two years in the galleys at Civitavecchia 'not for stealing but for good honest shots and mighty knife-thrusts at strangers in the mountains', on which Berlioz comments: 'he had probably not killed so much as a monk';[3] his description of the palatial monastery of Monte Cassino: 'the mind boggles at the sums that must have been spent on the treasures in the church alone';[4] and, finally, his word-play on the singer Adelina Patti and the proverbial *opportet pati* ('suffering is our lot'), which 'monks translate as "bring the pâté"' ('for lovers of music', of course, he concludes, it has to be translated as 'we must have Patti').[5]

If he is no friend to the Church, he is the sworn enemy of God. His frequent expressions of dissent, whether stoic, ironic, or bitter, all point in the same direction. Berlioz is at pains to present himself as an atheist; he luxuriates in his disbelief. God, if he does exist, is bad news. The Good Lord gets a consistently poor press in Berlioz's writings and correspondence.

[1] *Memoirs*, p. 159.

[2] *Ibid.*, p. 155.

[3] *Ibid.*, p. 164.

[4] *Ibid.*, p. 184.

[5] Entry in Patti's autograph album, 1863–1908 (Christie's catalogue, week of 4 December 1978). *Cf.* also *Journal des débats*, 13 January 1863.

A 'lively sensibility', we learn, is not his 'strong point'.[6] 'What an appalling world you cooked up for us, God', he exclaims in a letter to his friend the violinist Ernst. 'Resting on the seventh day was a rotten idea, you would have done far better to go on working – there was still so much to do.'[7] Sending a brand-new triangle to Germany for a performance of *Harold en Italie*, he adds: 'It's made in the image of God, like all triangles, but unlike other triangles, and certainly unlike God, it's in tune'.[8] In chapter 59 of the *Memoirs* (the final chapter as it was originally intended to be), where he makes the famous invocation to Shakespeare ('our father which art in heaven – if there is a heaven'), he rails against the Almighty: 'God standing aloof in his infinite unconcern is revolting and absurd'. Berlioz's personal deity is Shakespeare: 'Thou alone for the souls of artists art the living and loving God'.[9]

The sole essence that he worships is art – 'just about the one thing in this world', he writes, 'that lasts and that one will be sorry to lose. To feel its power and worship its beauty', he goes on, 'it's worth submitting to the confidence trick called life'.[10] Later, in the final section of the *Memoirs*, he describes walking by the Seine at Asnières one summer evening with his son Louis and Stephen Heller, talking of Shakespeare and Beethoven and all three of them working themselves 'into a state of intense exaltation. [...] We agreed that it is good to be alive to adore the beautiful'.[11] Art, yes, God, no – 'absolument pas', as Lacenaire says in *Les Enfants du paradis*. And of all the arts, music is the greatest. *Music* is religion. One is reminded of Beethoven's declaration: 'Music is the wine of a new creation. And I am Bacchus, who presses out the wine for human beings'.

True, Berlioz devotes the opening chapter of his *Memoirs* to his first communion, but – on the surface, at least – chiefly to mock his naïve, childish faith:

> I was brought up, needless to say, in the Catholic and Apostolic Church of Rome. This religion – charming now that it no longer burns people – was for seven whole years the joy of my life and, although we have long since parted company ['bien que nous soyons brouillés ensemble depuis longtemps'], I have always retained most tender memories of it. [...] I heard Mass every day and took communion every Sunday, and went regularly to confession in order to say to my director, 'Father, I have done nothing'. To which the good

6 *Correspondance générale*, Vol. V, p. 424.

7 *Ibid.*, Vol. III, 1842–50, ed. Pierre Citron, Flammarion, Paris, 1978, p. 632.

8 *Ibid.*, Vol. VI, 1859–60, ed. Hugh J. Macdonald and François Lesure, Flammarion, Paris, 1995, p. 245.

9 *Memoirs*, p. 505.

10 *Correspondance générale*, Vol. III, p. 655.

11 *Memoirs*, p. 549.

man would reply, 'Very well, my child, continue'. I followed this counsel all too faithfully for a number of years.[12]

It could be objected that, whatever he may have said on the subject, the fact remains that three of his major compositions – nearly a quarter of his output – are sacred works, and none of them, the Requiem (1837), the Te Deum (1849) or *L'Enfance du Christ* (1854), the result of a commission, not even the Requiem (the ambition to write it was fully formed well before the occasion that brought it into being); furthermore, to have lavished so much time and energy on religious music when it was in decline in France surely means something.

That is undeniably so; but the motive force behind even these works – the first two, at any rate – could be seen as more secular than strictly religious. From his boyhood Berlioz's imagination, fed by his reading, was fascinated by the idea of music on the grandest scale – music as the soul of a community, a people, as exemplified by the Panathenaia of the ancient Greeks or the celebrations in the Temple of Solomon.

What he learned later from his teacher Jean-François Le Sueur about the huge musical ceremonies in the days of the Revolution and its wars, the symbolic role these great events played in the life of the embattled French people – all this only deepened that fascination and sharpened the desire to revive the tradition, to write not only a *Grande Messe des morts* but also a seven-movement symphony 'in memory of the great men of France' and, when that project remained unrealised for lack of opportunity, a *Funeral and Triumphal Symphony* (1840) in honour of the heroes of the July 1830 Revolution. It is, you could argue, the human connotations of these celebrations – the communal, the social – that stir him, not the divine.

When considering Berlioz's *Grande Messe* (Requiem) and Te Deum, one could also cite the scandalous manner – from the orthodox point of view – in which he handles the sacred texts of the liturgy. He treats them like the dramatist he is, not like the true believer he should be, altering the order of the verses or truncating them as he sees fit.

Thus the depiction of Hell in the 'Rex tremendae' of the Requiem is intensified by bringing forward from later in the *Prose des morts* the words 'confutatis maledictis/flammis acribus addictis' – the accursed delivered to the flames – and also by adding words that don't belong to the *Prose* at all but are taken from a different part of the Mass, the Offertory: 'from the bottomless lake, save them from the lion's mouth, let not Tartarus engulf them, let them not fall into darkness'. These phrases are then largely omitted from the 'Offertoire', which in Berlioz's remodelled tripartite scheme is

[12] *Ibid.*, pp. 5–6.

concerned only with Purgatory, and the truncated text of his 'Offertoire' is further dismembered, the chorus being given only fragments of the liturgy to sing. In obedience to this scheme, the vision of Paradise is made more emphatic by the repetition of the radiant, shimmering 'Sanctus' in place of the 'Benedictus' (which is simply left out), while the separation of Paradise from Purgatory is underlined by removing the words 'to cross over from death to life'. Finally, 'Te decet hymnus' from the opening 'Requiem et Kyrie' is repeated in the concluding movement, to effect the return to the commemorative service of the dead within whose frame the Dante-like vision has been experienced.

The Te Deum shows Berlioz going further still in the liberties he takes with the liturgy. The first two movements may observe the sequence of verses, but after that anything goes: three verses are brought forward from later sections so that a contrasting movement, the gentle, pleading 'Dignare, Domine', can separate the brilliant 'Christe, rex gloriae' from the splendours of the 'Tibi omnes'. Similarly, the 'Te ergo quaesumus' is made to interpose its quiet prayer between the 'Christe' and the monumental 'Judex crederis esse venturus' ('We believe that Thou shalt come to be our Judge'). 'Judex crederis' is in fact only the nineteenth of the canticle's 28 verses; but Berlioz holds it back so that the work may culminate in a suitably apocalyptic movement depicting humanity's fear of judgement. The text of his 'Judex' is itself a mosaic of phrases taken from different parts of the Te Deum.

In all this, you could argue, Berlioz's attitude to the sacred texts is exactly like that of an opera composer who feels free to modify the most venerated stage play or poem if the demands of the music-drama require it. Drama is the be-all and the end-all.

And yet… If we think that that is all it is, we are accepting his words, his special pleading, at their face value. Whatever he may have said, his is a profoundly religious art. It tells us something quite different from the composer's own assertions; it contradicts them. They may 'remain below' – to borrow and invert the words of Claudius, King of Denmark – but the music 'flies up'.

Even in his secular works religious images proliferate. Nor is this just a matter of fashion, the Romantic cult of religion for its picturesque effects: the impulse comes from within himself. Nor, even, is it just one more example of his Protean genius, the ability to create and inhabit diverse worlds, to immerse his whole being in them and become Romeo or Benvenuto or Faust, to feel Dido's agony of spirit in his own spirit – a faculty such as would have enabled him to enter imaginatively into religious emotion and reproduce it. It goes deeper than that: it is a preoccupation, an obsession.

To be sure, Berlioz lost his faith. He and the Church had long since been 'brouillés'. But he never lost the need to believe. The phrase in the *Memoirs* – that the Christian religion was 'for seven whole years' his 'bonheur', 'the joy of my life' – has a significance beyond the irony of its context. The loss of that happiness left a permanent scar.

That, more than any other motives, is why he had to write his Requiem. Its music is full of a poignant regret for the loss of faith, an urgent sense of the need, the desperate need, to believe and to worship. It uses his own doubts to feed into the fears and frail hopes of humanity across the aeons of time, the *saecula saeculorum*. The Revolutionary community celebrated by Le Sueur and Gossec is universalised into the community of the human race through the ages, voicing its eternal longings and confronting its mortality. Through his experience and his understanding of the religious impulse he is able to hear the eternal note and sound it in his music.

This is what gives the *Grande Messe des morts* its force and its power to move and to strike awe and fear. The visions of judgement – the 'Lacrymosa' especially – are formidable. But it is on the human level – humanity's terrible vulnerability – that it appeals: humanity on the edge of eternity ('Hostias', where trombone pedal notes, answered by flutes high above, suggest infinite pulsating space); humanity amid the desolation of an empty universe ('Quid sum miser'); humanity in the Dance of Death, the endless procession of the dead scourged onward towards judgement ('Lacrymosa'); humanity pleading for salvation before the awful majesty of God ('Rex tremendae'); praying from one generation to another ('Offertoire'), hoping against hope ('Requiem et Kyrie'), persuading itself that judgement is still far off ('Dies irae'); humanity striving, out of its terror of extinction, to create a merciful God and a meaningful universe.

From time to time there is a glimpse of hope, as when, in the opening movement, the forlorn descending chromatic phrase in the violins and flutes against the chorus' desolate 'et lux perpetua… luceat eis… et lux…' suddenly yields to a radiant major chord, or when light falls like a benediction on the closing page of the 'Offertoire' (where Berlioz alters the order of the Latin text, making 'promisisti' – 'Thou promised' – the last word sung), as the chant turns from its sad persistent D minor and the whole movement, fugato and chant, resolves in a softly glowing D major. But the prevailing tone is tragic. Through all the contrasts of form and colour and mood, one idea dominates: the bafflement before the enigma of death, in a universe where there may not be a God.

The absence of God is the driving force behind Berlioz's Requiem, the doubt that haunts it. It should not surprise us – everything in him is linked – that while composing the work he should twice have had a dream about the

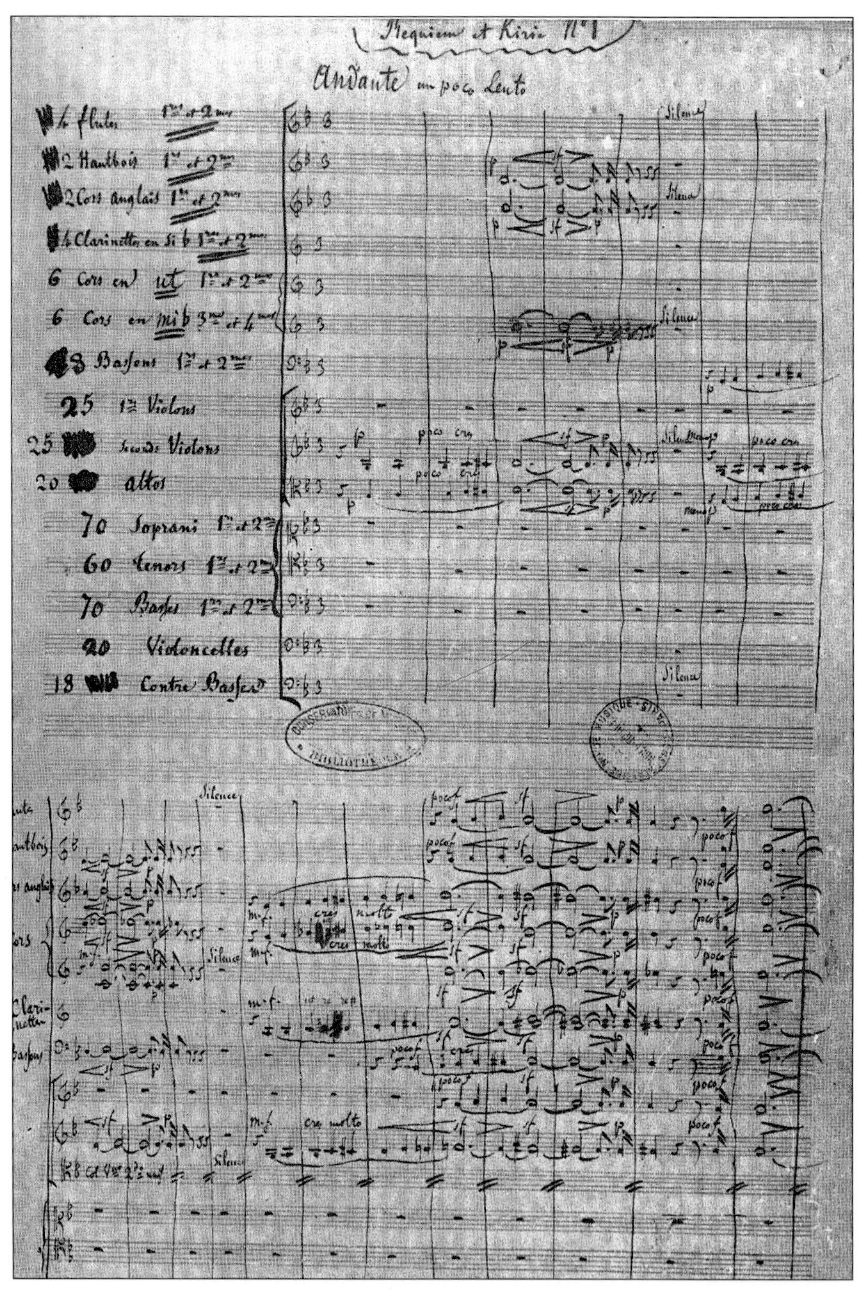

The first page of the manuscript of the Grande Messe des morts

absence of Estelle Dubœuf, the goddess of his boyhood (and of his old age). In the dream he is sitting in her grandmother's garden, at the foot of a tree, alone. Estelle is not there, and he keeps repeating, 'Where is she? Where is she?'[13]

Once he had the commission, and the text of the Mass for the Dead was reshaped to his purpose, he (in his own words) fell upon it

> with a kind of fury. My brain felt as if it would explode, from the pressure of ideas at boiling point. The outline of one piece was barely sketched before the next formed itself in my mind. It was impossible to write fast enough, and I devised a sort of musical shorthand which was of great help to me, especially in the Lacrymosa. All composers know the agony of forgetting ideas and finding that they have vanished forever, for want of time to note them down.[14]

Near the end of his life, having revised the work for publication by Ricordi, Berlioz wrote to his friend Humbert Ferrand: 'If I were threatened with the destruction of all my works save one, it would be for the Messe des Morts that I would beg grace'.[15] We may feel that he should have chosen *Les Troyens*, that summing-up of his existence, and that he would have done had its performance not been dogged by disappointment and defeat and the approximation, the *à-peu-près* that he abhorred and fought against throughout his career. But the choice he does make is significant. The *Grande Messe des morts* enshrines part of his inmost soul. In it he is at one with the visionary events it describes. His imagination is in direct contact with the unending generations of human history, and the music lives their immemorial fears and longings. Dramatic idea and musical process move hand in hand.

He is himself there at the stunned aftermath of the Day of Judgement, in the 'Quid sum miser' and what Wilfrid Mellers calls its 'piteous, fragmentary desolation',[16] the chilling emptiness of the scoring for cors anglais, bassoons and cellos and basses. He is there in the 'Rex tremendae', where the chorus, terrified by the imminent prospect of divine wrath, fails to complete the phrase 'voca me cum benedictis' (like 'confutatis maledictis', a transposition from later in the Mass); unable to utter the words 'among the blessed', their voices break off, the struggling, shouting mob falls silent, as though staring into the bottomless lake, which they evoke in a stammering *sotto voce* over a long, still double-bass note: 'et… de profundo lacu…', the last word emphasised by cavernous clarinet, horn and bassoon octaves. He is there in the pleading 'qui salvandos salvas gratis' ('Thou who freely savest

[13] *Ibid.*, p. 220.

[14] *Ibid.*, pp. 219–20.

[15] *Correspondance générale*, Vol. VII, p. 518.

[16] Alec Harman and Wilfrid Mellers, *Man and his Music*, Barrie and Jenkins, London, 1988, p. 770.

the redeemed'), as the movement resumes after 'let not Tartarus engulf me' (with its expressive flattened sixth in the choral basses and lower strings), and the sopranos, accompanied by the first violins and their tender melodic line, rise from the depths; there, too, when the majesty of the reprised 'Rex, rex tremendae majestatis' is suddenly subdued in a dramatic *pianissimo* as, in answer to massive brass and timpani chords, 'salva me' emerges, each time differently harmonised, more abject. Similarly, he is at one with the multitudes prostrating themselves in awe, in the hushed *pianissimo* at 'Te omnis terra veneratur' in the opening movement of the Te Deum.

Throughout Berlioz's Requiem the contrast between God's awesome power and humanity's utter feebleness, a contrast fundamental to the liturgy, is deliberately emphasised by the textual changes and then carried to extremes by the musical setting, within each movement and between one movement and another. Each of the movements in which the four brass groups are heard is followed by one that is intimate and devotional in character.

Perhaps it is no longer necessary to remind ourselves that the quiet, reflective pieces outnumber the noisy by more than three to one. The multiple brass and percussion are what the *Grande Messe des morts* is still widely known for and still sometimes criticised for, as a 'characteristic' extravagance – as though it were peculiar to Berlioz, whereas in writing for such forces he was simply following in the footsteps of the French composers of the turn of the century; one of them, his teacher Le Sueur, had celebrated the eighth anniversary of the Revolution with a *Chant du 1er Vendémiaire* scored for four separate orchestras, placed each at a corner of the Invalides chapel, where the *Grande Messe des morts* would have its first performance 36 years later.

What is, paradoxically, most striking about Berlioz's treatment of his outsize forces is its restraint. Their full power is unleashed in only three of the ten movements, all three in the section of the work concerned with judgement. There, too, their function is as much architectural as spectacular, clarifying the musical structure, opening new perspectives and at the same time underlining a grandeur that is inherent in the whole style of the music, in its long arcs of melody and its 'still, small voice' of humility as much as in its cataclysms.

The sensational effect of the brass comes also from the contrast it makes with the predominantly austere texture of the music. For much of the time, the twelve horns of the main orchestra are the only brass instruments to offset the large woodwind choir; it is the bleak, mourning sound of the woodwind that leaves the deepest impression on the attentive listener.

It speaks unmistakably of Berlioz the reluctant atheist, of the faith that he had lost but not forgotten.

To be sure, Berlioz the mocker doesn't spare his sentimental twin, and duly appears in order to taunt him. In *La Damnation de Faust* the hero, moved by the Easter Hymn, may think he has recovered his 'wavering beliefs' (the words added for Faust in the second half of the hymn are clearly autobiographical), may indulge in recalling his boyhood and the happiness of 'those days of piety' ('ces jours pieux') and 'the tenderness of prayer': the next instant Mephistopheles the Spirit of Eternal denial is at his side, jeering at this 'child of the holy precincts' whose troubled ears have succumbed to the mere peeling of bells.

Yet those *jours pieux* never cease to summon him back. They are at the centre of his nostalgia. The call of the past increasingly dominates the final decades of his life, perhaps from the moment when, in exile in London, he begins his *Memoirs* by reliving, with an apparent irony that should not deceive us, his first communion, and remembering how, at the sound of the girls' voices of his sister Nancy's convent striking up the Eucharistic hymn, he gave himself to God ('j'étais tout à Dieu') and thought he 'saw heaven open, a heaven of love and pure delight, a thousand times more beautiful than the one I had so often been told about'.[17]

Not that God had become any closer or more benign, or heaven a more probable place. The Te Deum, begun the following year, is more remote, more impersonally ritualistic than the harsh but cathartic Requiem of a decade earlier. Despite richer textures and fuller sonorities, with trumpets, trombones and ophicleides/tubas part of the main orchestral sound, not separate from it, the work is more forbidding, more ancient. The God to whom the words pray, whose infinite majesty they hymn, is yet more distant, and the judgement more relentless still: the repeated 'non confundar in aeternum' of the *Judex crederis* is the ultimate expression of our fears.

Yet, for all that, the child's vision of the blessed country still beckons; the virginal voices of that first epiphany have not faded – they ring out clearly. The sweet insistent sound, which had been a feature of his choral writing since the *Messe solennelle* of 1824–25, and which came back to him as he wrote the first chapter of his *Memoirs*, is more pervasive here than at any time since the Mass. Taking his cue from the words 'To Thee all angels cry aloud', he gives sopranos and altos the modally inflected melody of the 'Tibi omnes' for fully 40 bars of moderate tempo before we hear men's voices; the 'Dignare', 'Domine' and the 'Te ergo quaesumus' are suffused by them; and the central, contrasting 'Salvum fac populum' section of the

[17] *Memoirs*, p. 6.

'Judex crederis', as the pounding rhythms grow less, begins with twenty heart-searching bars for women's voices alone. Only then do the tenors and basses intone their ageless 'per singulos dies' – music that breathes that air of palpable, measureless antiquity that is so familiar and thrilling to those who love Berlioz.

A year after the Te Deum, in 1850, the seed is sown that will grow into his third sacred work, *L'Enfance du Christ.* That it doesn't fall by the wayside or on barren ground is not as accidental as might at first appear. Superficially considered, the coming to fruition could hardly be more haphazard – furtive almost, without the composer's knowledge, he having been so traumatised and nearly bankrupted by the failure of *La Damnation de Faust* that he had resolved never again to put on a major work at his own risk, which meant, in effect, not to compose one. In reality, *L'Enfance du Christ* answered an inner necessity.

The sequence of events and non-events is well known: the organ piece, jotted down in his friend the architect Joseph-Louis Duc's album, metamorphosing into the shepherds bidding farewell to the Holy Family on the eve of the journey to Egypt; the performance of the chorus, filling a gap in the programme of one of the Société Philharmonique concerts, in the guise of a recently discovered fragment by an imaginary seventeenth-century *maître de chapelle*, Pierre Ducré (gratifyingly eliciting the comment, relayed to him by Duc, that 'Berlioz would never be able to write a tune as simple and charming as that little piece by old Ducré'[18]); an overture and a tenor solo composed to go with it, intended for the Philharmonique's next season; the collapse of the Philharmonique; the three movements published as *La Fuite en Égypte* but then set aside (it is performed by François Seghers' Société Sainte Cécile but not by Berlioz); the tenor solo encored a couple of years later at Berlioz's concert in London; further performances of the solo in Germany; the whole *Fuite* given in Leipzig in 1853 to much applause; the composition, at the urging of Berlioz's German admirers, of a sequel, *L'Arrivée à Saïs*, and then of a first part, *Le Songe d'Hérode*, the resulting triptych being intended for Germany; Berlioz deciding to risk losing money after all and perform it in Paris, to please the friends there who still believe in him; three packed performances – four years after the evening at Duc's – and one of the triumphs of his career.

L'Enfance du Christ took many in the audience at the Salle Herz by surprise; this was not at all the Berlioz they were used to. We, with hindsight, can surely say that nothing is more characteristic of him, and also that there was nothing he was more likely to compose (not even *Les Troyens*

[18] *Correspondance générale*, Vol. VII, p. 159.

was more inevitable). 'I begin to live only in the past', he wrote to his sister Adèle in August 1854, shortly after completing the score.[19] The past had been drawing him back ever since he started writing his *Memoirs*, six years earlier; the act of recalling his childhood, followed so soon by the death of his father and his pilgrimage to Meylan and the Saint-Eynard and the scenes of his infatuation with Estelle, marks a change in him, intensifying the nostalgia that lay deep in his nature.

So much of Berlioz's work is prefigured in his early life, so much of the whole character of his art is preconditioned – predestined, we could say – by what he experienced and felt, and read, in those sheltered, momentous years in La Côte-Saint-André and the Dauphiné countryside. In one sense *L'Enfance du Christ* can be seen as a gesture of gratitude to his teacher Le Sueur, whose Old Testament oratorios he listened to on Sundays in the Chapel Royal; there is more than a little of Le Sueur – the composer of *Les Bardes* as well as of *Ruth et Noémi* – in Berlioz's trilogy. But it goes back further than that, to the time when, a boy, he went regularly to the church of La Côte and in doing so absorbed the ancient music of the region. That the solo tenor's first six notes in *La Fuite en Egypte* (to the words 'Les pèlerins étant…') are those of the chant *O filii, o filiae* is only the most striking proof of its influence.

What he heard then chimed with what he found in Chateaubriand's *Génie du Christianisme, ou beautés de la religion chrétienne* (1802), a favourite of his adolescence. The book praised the beauty of Christian ritual, the hymns and prayers of the Catholic Church and the grave, sweet simplicity of the old tunes to which they were sung. Chateaubriand's description of Christianity's central mystery reads, to us, like the scenario of a dramatic work, a challenge to compose it – a challenge made all the more irresistible by its association with another of Berlioz's boyhood idols, the poet of the *Aeneid* and the *Georgics*:

> The Incarnation shows us the Lord of the Heavens in a sheepfold – 'He who commands the thunder wrapped in swaddling clothes, He whom the universe doth not contain confined in the womb of a woman'. Antiquity would have known how to respond to this miracle. What pictures would Homer and Virgil not have left us of the nativity of God in a manger, shepherds hastening to the crib, wise men led by a star, angels coming down into the wilderness, a virgin mother worshipping her newborn son, and all that mingling of grandeur, innocence and enchantment.[20]

[19] *Ibid.*, Vol. IV, 1851–55, ed. Yves Gérard and Hugh J. Macdonald, Flammarion, Paris, 1983, p. 568.

[20] Chateaubriand, *Génie du Christianisme, ou beautés de la religion chrétienne*, Migneret, Paris, 1802 (Garnier-Flammarion, Paris, 1966, Part 1, Book 1, p. 73).

Out of those ancient chants and noëls comes, in part, not only the musical idiom of Berlioz's oratorio but of much in his work in general. How often do we hear in his music the voice of an immemorial past: in the 'Offertoire' cry as of generations without end; in the woodwind's falling phrase, repeated again and again at the words 'miserere nobis', in the 'Dignare, Domine' of the Te Deum. Behind the boyhood song 'Je vais donc quitter pour jamais' lies the *tonus peregrinus* – the plainchant, dating from before Charlemagne, that is said to have originated in the Isère, the region where Berlioz was born, and that reduced him to floods of tears as he listened to the psalm *In exitu Israel* one Sunday at Vespers, his head full of the twelfth book of the *Aeneid*. The chanting of the distant Rogation procession, as the sixteen-year-old boy sits reading in a field, consumed by a devastating sense of isolation, surfaces 25 years later in *La Damnation de Faust*, ironically counterpointing the last stage on the doomed hero's road to ruin.

Thus, when Berlioz composed *L'Enfance du Christ*, whatever people may have thought – critics and sympathisers alike – he did not have to search for a new style. All that changed was the subject. The archaic flavour and purity of expression of the music came naturally to him; they were in his blood. Le Sueur had taught him an interest in modal music that was unusual for the period, and he had employed modal inflexions for special effect. Now that a more systematic use of them was called for, he could resort to them without falling into pastiche. He might have to add a footnote to the first page of the score of the overture to *La Fuite en Égypte*, warning the unwary that the E natural in the theme of the fugato, the flattened seventh of the scale, was not a misprint. (He was wise to do so. I remember, one Christmas, playing on the piano the carol *The Angel Gabriel*, with its modal cadence – A–G natural–A – and my Victorian grandmother, Florrie, exclaiming, 'That's wrong!'.) But the theme is pure Berlioz, however untypical of the mid-nineteenth century. It was no effort for him to compose in this way. On the contrary, it was a joy. He was returning to his roots – to music as ritual, giving expression and shape to the central events of human life, and to the days when religion was his 'bonheur'.

This time there is no sentimental recovery of belief, no cue for Mephisto to rise up and mock. Berlioz's mind remains sceptical. It is an act of piety only in the ancient Roman sense. But his imagination believes. The intensity of remembered emotion is such that he can re-enter the world of the Christmas story and live it as he had once lived it, long ago. It may no longer be possible to be 'tout à Dieu'; that happiness has vanished, never to be recaptured. But he can still hear the virginal tones; he can still close each part of his 'petite sainteté' with the sound of angels' voices – far off but clear – and, for the moment, mean it.

Berlioz and Song

A talk given at the Oxford Lieder Festival Berlioz study day on 24 October 2015.

Berlioz and song? Berlioz and music just for solo voice and piano? A whole study day devoted to it, in the home of the German Lied of all places? Surely a total contradiction in terms! Yet I hope to show that that is not the case – that this is one more of the preconceptions that dogged Berlioz for so long.

Here is another. When his oratorio *L'Enfance du Christ* was first performed, in Paris in 1854, amid all the plaudits for the beauty of the work, there was much astonishment that the master of the grand scale, the grotesque and the macabre should have produced something so gentle and tender, so simple. In his *Memoirs* Berlioz describes receiving a letter, after the premiere, from Heinrich Heine. The poet's wife had come back from the concert enthusing about the new work, which he himself had been too ill to go and hear: 'I fear I shall soon have to leave the Champs-Élysées and go to the other, mythical ones, which won't be nearly so amusing'. In his book *Lutèce* Heine had said that Berlioz had 'little melody [...] and no real simplicity whatever'.[1] He now hastened to recant: 'I hear on all sides that you have plucked a nosegay of the most exquisite blooms of melody and that your oratorio is a masterpiece of simplicity. I can never forgive myself for being so unjust to a friend'.[2] Berlioz, recounting this, goes on:

> I went to see him. As he was starting again on his self-recrimination, I said: 'But in any case, why are you being like a music critic and making categorical statements about an artist when you know only part of his work? You're always thinking of the Witches' Sabbath and the March to the Scaffold, and the Dies irae and the Lacrymosa. Yet I believe I can do, and have done, things that are quite different'.[3]

I dwell on Heine and *L'Enfance du Christ* because some people still think of Berlioz in that way – as (again in Heine's words) 'a colossal nightingale, a lark the size of an eagle, such as existed, we are told, in primordial times'. Berlioz's music, Heine goes on, 'makes me see visions of mammoths and

[1] 'Supplément – Saison musicale, I: Paris, 25 avril 1844', *Lutèce: lettres sur la vie politique, artistique et sociale de la France*, Michel Lévy Frères, Paris, 1855, p. 388.

[2] *Memoirs*, Postscript, pp. 524–55.

[3] *Correspondence Générale*, Vol. IV, pp. 650–51.

other beasts long extinct, fabulous empires of preternatural depravity, and many a cloud-capped impossible wonder'.[4] There is undoubtedly something ancient, a sense of the remote past, of the dawn of history, in Berlioz's music, with all its modernity – and it is still modern: the conductor Antonio Pappano claims it's a serious mistake when planning a concert to put a contemporary work in the same programme as the *Symphonie fantastique*; 'the contemporary work can never compete with the modernity of the Berlioz'.[5] But, to go back to that sense of the colossal: at the same time as being a lark the size of an eagle, he is also just a lark. As I shall try to show, song was at the centre of his musical life. Song goes back to his earliest, formative years.

So much in his art springs from those first years spent in an obscure corner of south-east France, where there was no orchestra, only the very approximate and uncertain wind band of the local National Guard, and no piano, the quintessential nineteenth-century instrument. Berlioz becomes an accomplished flute-player and a competent guitarist, but the nearest he gets to an orchestra – the instrument of which he will be a master – is a blank sheet of music paper with 24 staves on it. What he does have is a boundless and fertile imagination.

And he has song. Song gives him what he calls, in the opening chapter of his *Memoirs*, his first musical experience, when, at his first communion, girls' voices strike up the Eucharistic hymn – a sound that imprints itself so deeply on his consciousness that it will become almost a leitmotiv of his sacred music. The hymn sung at that first communion by the girls of his sister's convent school was a tune from an *opéra-comique* by the eighteenth-century composer Nicolas Dalayrac. Another thing that used not to figure in the popular misconception of Berlioz was his love of the old French operas. What he couldn't stand, and what blighted his life as a critic, was having to review the endless new comic operas that were everlastingly being performed in Paris. But he loved the old ones. Forty years after the Dalayrac epiphany, when he is composing his epic Virgilian opera *Les Troyens*, we find him enthusing about Grétry's *Richard Cœur de Lion*, revived at the Opéra-Comique:

> It's delicious. The Romance galvanises the entire house. The whole thing has a finesse, a truthfulness, an inventiveness and good sense that are captivating. And none of your coarse orchestration. I so much prefer those simple, unassuming orchestral scores with holes in the elbows of their coats, and even in the seat of their pants, to those great loud-mouthed mountebanks

[4] *Op. cit.*, pp. 387–88.

[5] Interview with Alastair Aberdare, *Berlioz Society Bulletin*, No. 197 (September 2015), p. 8.

covered in cheap brass finery who bawl from the height of their soap-boxes: 'Roll up, gentlemen, every place is taken', etc.[6]

Here is the composer of the *Grande Messe des morts* being faithful to his roots. *L'Enfance du Christ* is no anomaly in Berlioz's output: it's a repossession of his boyhood. One of the books this dedicated adolescent reader devoured was Chateaubriand's *Génie du Christianisme*. In it he found a poetic evocation of the ancient hymns and popular rituals of the church. *L'Enfance du Christ*, more than half a lifetime later, is a response to it.

The germ of Berlioz's oratorio is a strophic song, *The Shepherds' Farewell to the Holy Family*. Song was what he grew up with. The first piece that we know of in his musical life, apart from the Dalayrac air, is a folksong. At the age of about twelve he found an old flageolet in the back of a drawer and immediately tried to pick out the popular song 'Malbrouck s'en va-t'en guerre'. His father, disturbed in his study by these untoward squeakings, begged him to stop, but then showed him how to play the instrument. 'Malbrouck', you can't help feeling, was a symbolic choice, with its $\frac{6}{8}$ time, a favourite metre of the mature Berlioz, and its sighing fourth, prophetic of the *idée fixe* of the *Symphonie fantastique*.

Apart from the noëls and chants of the church, and perhaps songs sung in the streets or in the encampments of the foreign troops that occupied the town in 1814 and 1815, the musical fare of La Côte-Saint-André was the romance, that standard form of French song. Romances could be independent pieces but were also commonly extracted from the *opéras-comiques* of composers like Grétry, Boieldieu, Dalayrac, Montini and other now largely forgotten names of the period. They were what the inhabitants of the town knew and liked, and were sung at drawing-room gatherings. Berlioz's uncle Félix Marmion, the dashing cavalry captain who fascinated his nephew with tales of the Napoleonic campaigns, was fond of singing them; his attractive tenor voice was much in demand in the salons of Grenoble.

Not surprisingly, the first major surviving musical manuscript in Berlioz's hand is a *Recueil de romances*, a collection of 25 romances with guitar accompaniment – the accompaniments by him, the tunes from opéras-comiques. The manuscript dates from about 1820, when he was sixteen. He had already begun composing, and again it was natural that his chosen medium would be the romance, the strophic song. The pieces he published soon after arriving in Paris (ostensibly to study medicine) were songs. What is striking about them, with all their imperfections, is that they are the work of an instinctive dramatist, one who is already attempting to colour the

[6] *Correspondance générale*, Vol. V, p. 307.

music in response to the words. It is significant, too, that though he stops publishing songs not long after he becomes a pupil of Jean-François Le Sueur, and his interest shifts to opera and choral music, song doesn't cease to be important in his *œuvre*. In his first nine years in Paris, as a student of medicine, then of music, he steeps himself in the operas of Gluck, Spontini, Méhul and the other composers of the French classical school, he discovers Weber and is bowled over by him, he receives the crucial initiation into Beethoven at the Conservatoire concerts, and he composes the *Symphonie fantastique* in response to the realisation that the Beethovenian symphony is the supreme medium of dramatic music. But what is it that we find right at the beginning of the *Fantastique*? It's a song.

In this section I should like to demonstrate the presence of solo song at the heart of the orchestral abundance of Berlioz's major works, beginning with the *Fantastique*. Some time in his teenage years in the family home at La Côte-Saint-André Berlioz fell under the spell of the French eighteenth-century writer of pastoral idylls Jean-François Florian. He realised, later, how feeble they were, with their tales of shepherds and shepherdesses making gentle, sexless love beside purling brooks or expiring of unrequited passion, but at the time he lapped them up. In particular, he read and re-read Florian's novel *Estelle et Némorin* until he knew it by heart and became Némorin (who like him played the flute). Estelle was only too easily identified with the beautiful Estelle Dubœuf (neighbour of Berlioz's grandfather Nicolas Marmion in the village of Meylan in the hills above Grenoble), six years his senior, with whom he fell in love at the age of about twelve – the goddess, he later said, who 'dictated' much of his music to him, above all in the *Symphonie fantastique*. In his teens, under the overpowering influence of his unattainable love for Estelle, he composed a setting of Florian's lines, 'Je vais donc quitter pour jamais/Mon doux pays, ma douce amie'. It may be significant that it was not one of the songs Berlioz published in the early 1820s, perhaps because it was too personal, too secret, and meant too much to him. So the original song hasn't survived. When, in 1829–30, he was composing his autobiographical symphony, the *Largo* introduction of which is a kind of musical evocation of the state described by Chateaubriand in his novel *René* – 'the state of dreamlike melancholy in which the young imagination feeds on its own impossible desires' – the song came back to him as the very music he needed to express (he said) 'the overpowering sadness of a young heart first tortured by a hopeless love'. The tune as it appears in the Symphony has been shown to fit the opening words of the poem. Its first appearance is on muted strings, in C minor (Ex. 1); then, after a flurry on the full orchestra, it reappears harmonised in the relative major, with a woodwind accompaniment suggestive of the words

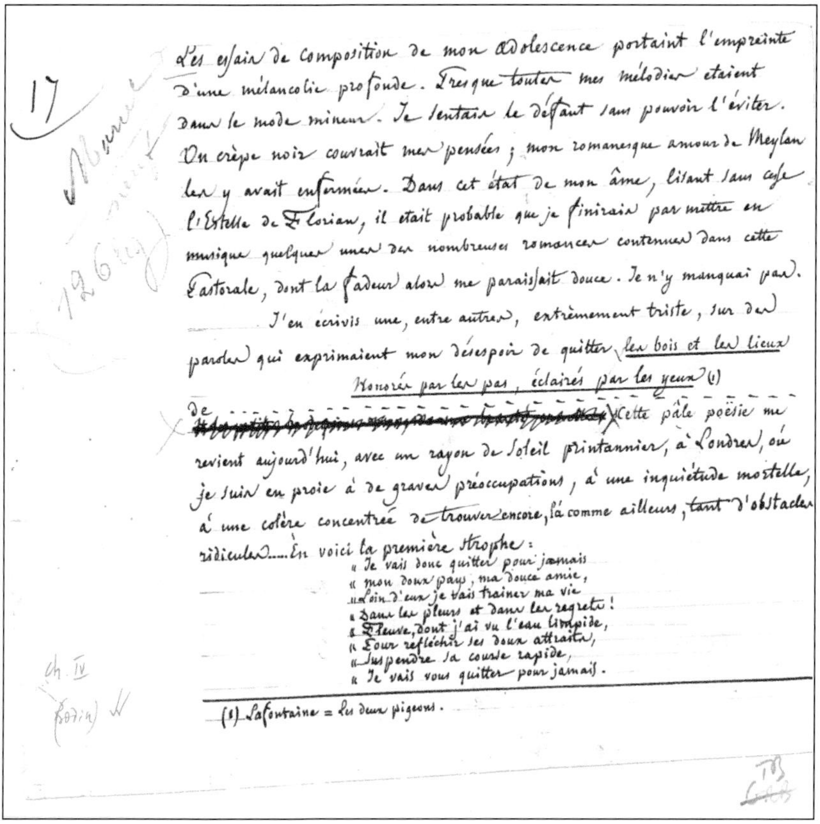

17

Les essais de composition de mon adolescence portaient l'empreinte d'une mélancolie profonde. Presque toutes mes mélodies étaient dans le mode mineur. Je sentais le défaut sans pouvoir l'éviter. Un crêpe noir couvrait mes pensées ; mon romanesque amour de Meylan les y avait enfermées. Dans cet état de mon âme, lisant sans cesse l'Estelle de Florian, il était probable que je finirais par mettre en musique quelques unes des nombreuses romances contenues dans cette Pastorale, dont la fadeur alors me paraissait douce. Je n'y manquai pas.

J'en écrivis une, entre autres, extrêmement triste, sur des paroles qui exprimaient mon désespoir de quitter les bois et les lieux

Honorés par les pas, éclairés par les yeux (1)

de ~~[illegible]~~ Cette pâle poésie me revient aujourd'hui, avec un rayon de soleil printannier, à Londres, où je suis en proie à de graves préoccupations, à une inquiétude mortelle, à une colère concentrée de trouver encore, là comme ailleurs, ~~tant~~ d'obstacles ridicules.... En voici la première strophe :

« Je vais donc quitter pour jamais
« mon doux pays, ma douce amie,
« Loin d'eux je vais traîner ma vie
« Dans les pleurs et dans les regrets !
« Fleuve, dont j'ai vu l'eau limpide,
« Pour refléchir ses doux attraits,
« Suspendre sa course rapide,
« Je vais vous quitter pour jamais.

(1) Lafontaine = les deux pigeons.

ch. IV

Berlioz recalls 'Je vais donc quitter' in the fourth chapter of his Memoirs

about the river, the 'crystal stream' beside which Némorin laments his fate and in which he had once seen his beloved Estelle mirrored.

Ex. 1

'Je vais donc quitter' is apparently the first Berlioz song to be incorporated in a large-scale work. I'd like to single out two more, both of them in his opera *Benvenuto Cellini* and both composed in the mid-1830s, about the time when he was starting to write the opera. The first is a little strophic song to words by Léon de Wailly, one of the opera's librettists: Ex. 2(a) gives a snatch of it. The song re-appears in the music of the Carnival revellers (among them Cellini) who, in the opening scene, sing to the accompaniment of two guitars under the window of the indignant papal treasurer Balducci and his far less unwilling daughter Teresa (Ex. 2(b)).

Ex. 2

(a)

(b)

The other song is 'Je crois en vous' (Ex. 3(a)), which becomes the song of Harlequin, sung by cor anglais and harp, with copious commentary from the women in the crowd, in his contest with the gross Pasquarello during the carnival celebrations in the Piazza Colonna. Berlioz obviously liked the tune, and with reason; it is also made much of in the slow introductory section of the overture (Ex. 3(b)).

Ex. 3

(a)

(b)

My final example of a pre-existing song reappearing in a full-length work is in some ways the most remarkable example of the persistence of Berlioz's attachment to the romances he grew up with. Shortly before he left for Paris at the age of seventeen, he succeeded in having one of his songs, 'Le Dépit de la bergère' (Ex. 4(a) gives the piano introduction), accepted by a Paris publisher. Whether he kept the manuscript or, more probably, remembered the artless tune thought up all those years before, it found a modest place in his last score, as the Sicilienne (Ex. 4(b)) in the comic opera *Béatrice et Bénédict*. Here's another irony: Berlioz, who said he would rather be dead than be caught adding to the pullulating mass of opéras-comiques that polluted the air of Paris, signed off his career with one.

Ex. 4
(a)

One of the many new things Berlioz did in his career was to develop the simple strophic Romance into the through-composed *mélodie* – most obviously in the song-cycle *Les Nuits d'été* but also in pieces like the haunting *Mort d'Ophélie*, the bolero *Zaïde* and *Le Chasseur danois*. At the same time, the strophic song is far from being abandoned. It's so deeply rooted in his being that we find it in two of his grandest works, *La Damnation de Faust* and *Les Troyens*.

To take the *Damnation* first: in the late 1820s, in response to Gérard de Nerval's translation of Part 1 of Goethe's *Faust*, Berlioz composed *Huit Scènes de Faust* ('Eight Scenes from Faust') – actually nine, but formally eight because Marguerite's 'D'amour l'ardente flamme' is combined, audaciously, with the chorus of soldiers shouting in the streets as a background to her tragic reverie. 'D'amour l'ardente flamme' is through-composed, but the *Eight Scenes* also include four strophic songs: 'Le Roi de Thulé', Brander's 'Story of a Rat' ('Histoire d'un rat'), Mephistopheles' 'Flea Song' ('Histoire d'une puce'), and Mephistopheles' Serenade. All four figure in the later *Damnation de Faust*, revised here and there but essentially the same. We hear Berlioz's authentic voice, arguably for the first time in his career, in these short but vivid pieces – his variety, his melodic gift and his ear for colour: the grunting, burbling bassoons and scrabbling strings in the Rat Song (the musical embodiment of the brutal, jeering joviality of the text), the hopping, flea-like violins in the Flea Song, the false geniality of the Serenade, in which the accompaniment of single guitar will become the guitar-like clatter of *pizzicato* strings in the *Damnation*, the solo viola the perfect sound for the remote, imagined sadness of Marguerite's ballad, and the richly expressive cor anglais for the anguish of the *Romance*.

Interestingly, the ballad, 'Le Roi de Thulé', first of the *Eight Scenes*, was written when Berlioz was back in the countryside of his boyhood (Ex. 5 gives the version from *La Damnation de Faust*). The simple strophic form is no barrier to the scope of his imagination.

Ex. 5

I'd like to end with Berlioz's culminating and greatest work, the five-act opera *Les Troyens*. This is an epic on a huge scale. Despite that, at two of the pivotal moments of the drama, the garden scene, where the love of Dido and Aeneas finds its fullest expression, and the beginning of Act 5, where the destiny of the Trojans reasserts its grim inevitability, we have songs. The first is the through-composed 'O blonde Cérès', sung by the court poet Iopas: the restless Dido has asked him to recite his poem about the harvests and the fruits of the earth. The second is the 'Chanson d'Hylas', the song – strophic, but what a song! – of the homesick sailor, sung at the masthead of a Trojan ship at anchor in the port of Carthage (Ex. 6). He dreams of his homeland – which, two passing sentries drily remark, he won't see again. At the end of the third verse he falls asleep, and clarinets complete the melody. Opening the final act, it alters the perspective, casting an unsparing light on what the great issues of war and migration and the displacement of nations mean in the life of an obscure, ordinary individual. For a moment, the heroic preoccupations of the central characters fade into the light of common day. This was a late addition by Berlioz to the opera. It shows his long-lasting devotion to the unassuming musical form that he discovered in his boyhood and never forgot.

Ex. 6

The 'Chanson d'Hylas', from Act 5 of The Trojans

La Côte-Saint-André

The following text is a translation, and revision, of a talk I gave, under the title 'Berlioz et sa cité natale', in the Château at La Côte-Saint-André in the bicentenary year, 2003. At the end I was approached by the mayor and, for a moment, feared that I was about to be given a public rebuke for my disrespectful remarks about the running of the current festival. To my relief, he was all smiles and presented me with a medal.

In July 1831, writing from Italy to his family, Berlioz describes Subiaco – where he is staying, in the foothills of the Abruzzi – as 'a dirty village, dedicated to St André (second point of resemblance to La Côte)'.[1]

I remember, during my visit to La Côte in the summer of 1962, with my wife, our two-year-old son and Richard Macnutt – my first encounter with Berlioz's native country – finding in the Museum an article from a local newspaper, *Le Nouvelliste*, which quoted an ancient inhabitant of the town. Her grandfather, she said, liked to talk of his memories of Berlioz: 'Every so often he'd come back to La Côte. There was a lot of whispering as he passed by – no one dared speak to him any more, he looked so out of sorts with the place'.[2] You get the same impression from the caricature drawn by an anonymous local artist during one of Berlioz's three visits to La Côte in the 1840s.

Not that he preferred Grenoble, a city much admired by his sisters during their girlhood. Grenoble, for him, was merely the gateway to the enchanted kingdoms of Meylan and Murianette and to 'the lovely valley of Grésivaudan where the Isère winds and where I spent the most idyllic hours of my childhood.'[3] For Berlioz, as for Stendhal, Grenoble was the symbol and epitome of bourgeois philistinism and the pursuit of material wealth.

As for La Côte, he would surely have understood the complaints of his mother Joséphine's Grenoblois friends who at the time of her marriage to 'Dr Berlle' regretted that their darling Finette had had to go and live in a distant and dreary little town where nothing of interest or importance ever happened. And he might not have disagreed with his sister Nancy that the town was a centre of gossip 'where the houses are made of glass and

[1] *Correspondance générale*, Vol. I, p. 473.

[2] 2 September 1934.

[3] *Memoirs*, p. 201.

Anonymous caricature of Berlioz, La Côte-Saint-André, c. 1845

domestic affairs are exposed to the four winds'.[4] I am also pretty sure that if he returned to this world he wouldn't think much of the festival that has taken his name in vain – not the festival that Charles Munch dreamed of and his pupil Serge Baudo created (which in the 1980s gave us many fine things, not least two complete productions of *Les Troyens* at a time when Paris was still in outer darkness where that work was concerned, as well as the best staging of *Benvenuto Cellini* yet seen), but the so-called Festival Berlioz that succeeded it, ineptly and unimaginatively run, where I heard – thinking (to adapt Marguerite's words) 'can I believe my ears?' – Berlioz's arrangement of the *Marseillaise* performed *without chorus*, and the Prix de Rome cantata *La Mort d'Orphée* sung by a soprano. I have no wish to bite the hand that fed me – I owe so much to the happy times spent here. Yet one must protest, when there is an occasion for doing so, in the name and for the honour of Berlioz and of his native town. There are people here who are thoroughly versed in his music and his life. It is they who should be in charge of the festival.[5]

For all this ill humour, I don't doubt that Berlioz recognised what he owed, as an artist, to those first seventeen years spent in La Côte – years in which the very remoteness, the absence of events, even the absence of music, were paradoxically so beneficial to him. The landscape too – for it was not just the Isère valley that made a deep impression on him but La Côte and its 'wide, rich plain, green and golden, in its stillness filled with a sense of dreamlike grandeur'.[6] Or again, how fondly he recalled the beauty of the May morning when he took his first communion, walking through the main street of the town towards the convent of the Visitation: 'It was spring, the sun was smiling, a soft breeze played among the whispering poplars, some delicious fragrance filled the air'.[7] The experience stayed with him and was reflected 30 years later in the words added to the 'Easter Hymn', where Faust remembers 'the peace of my days of piety, the sweetness of prayer, the pure delight of wandering, and dreaming, through the green meadows in the infinite light of a springtime sun'.

For us it is obvious that without his Côtois childhood Berlioz would not have been Berlioz. The germ of a large part of his output is there: the Requiem and the Te Deum (in the descriptions he read, and on which his imagination fed, of the grand religious ceremonies of the ancient world, long before his teacher Le Sueur transmitted to him the musical traditions

[4] Letter formerly in the Reboul-Berlioz Collection; quoted in *Correspondance générale*, Vol. II, p. 90.

[5] They are now. Since 2010, under the direction of Bruno Messina and his team, the 'Festival Berlioz' has achieved heights worthy of its name.

[6] *Memoirs*, p. 5.

[7] *Ibid.*

Berlioz's childhood home on the rue de la République in La Côte-Saint-André

of the Revolution and the Consulate, which lie behind both works), the *Symphonie fantastique*, *L'Enfance du Christ*, *La Damnation de Faust*, above all *Les Troyens*, written to 'satisfy a passion that flamed up in my boyhood'.[8]

Certainly, to become the composer we know, he needed the revelations of Shakespeare and Beethoven and the experience of Italy, and he needed dogged determination and concentrated hard work. Yet it is scarcely an exaggeration to say that his *œuvre* already existed in embryo before he left for Paris. Here, if you will allow me, I will quote the passage in my biography of Berlioz that concludes the survey of his boyhood:

> In retrospect, the main themes of Berlioz's existence are laid down in these first seventeen sheltered, momentous years. The very name his parents choose for him is heavy with destiny. Never have boyhood experiences played a more vital part, not only in providing a well of recollected emotion for the artist to draw on but in deciding the character of his art.
>
> Educated at home, he is allowed to preserve unblunted an abnormal capacity for feeling and to develop by wide and voracious reading a superabundant imagination. He shares the dreams of his generation – a fascination with Napoleon and his brilliant, headlong career, a passionate curiosity about far-off lands – and also its nightmares, a chilling sense of isolation, of total estrangement from beauty and love and companionship, attacking without

[8] Letter of 3 March 1858 to Émile Deschamps, *Correspondance générale*, Vol. V, p. 548.

> warning and turning all to dust. His response to nature is awakened in the valleys and mountains and plains of Dauphiné, a landscape whose mixture of grandeur and lucidity, movement and stillness, gleaming peaks, vast blue distances, sinuous contours and swift and violent climatic changes will find a mirror in his music; and from the first this awareness is associated with the onset of romantic passion, expressing itself in hopeless love for a girl six years older than himself, image of the unattainable ideal of which he will be a willing victim all his life. In this hyperactive state his imagination seizes on Virgil, feeding on the tragic passions of the *Aeneid* and creating from its heroic narrative a familiar country to which his soul 'can in a moment travel'. He falls under the spell of religion. Though his beliefs will not survive into adult life, the impression of the Catholic ritual is never effaced; the very loss of faith will leave a powerful imprint on his many sacred works.
>
> Religion, nature, romantic love, adventure, fame, travel, the distant past, a paralysing loneliness – any or all of these are common obsessions of sensitive adolescence. What is uncommon in Berlioz is their tenacity – almost, their purposefulness. It is as though in everything that happens to him he is carrying out a programme. By the time he leaves home and goes to Paris the nature of the artist he is to be is determined in all essentials.[9]

To start with his education. Berlioz thought that being taught at home, not at school, was a handicap, socially speaking – you missed being inured early to the rough and tumble of life. But in every other way, what an advantage! By being educated by a tolerant, open-minded and endlessly curious father, he avoided being subjected to the moulding processes of orthodox education, fatal to the growth of imagination and, in Stendhal's words, to 'the horde of felt emotions that schooling not only doesn't form but prevents from being formed'.[10] On the contrary, he was able to develop, while still young, an intensely active imagination, a wide-ranging mind and independence of thought. It's true that he will call imagination an 'accursed gift that makes our life a perpetual mirage'[11] and believe that anyone dominated by the imagination is by definition 'infinitely unhappy'.[12] Yet for the creative artist this capacity for conceiving extreme states of love, grief, ecstasy, alienation, and experiencing them within himself, was the source of his being. To it he owed not only the intensity of his music but also the vast range it embraces. In creating each work he was absorbed into it, became it, gave it its own unique poetic world. This power of empathy was acquired in boyhood, in the uninhibited cultivation of a vivid imagination and in the books he read and re-read and lived in. The intimate interaction between

[9] Cairns, *Berlioz*, Vol. 1, pp. 93–94.

[10] *Journal*, II, in Henri Martineau (ed.), *Œuvres intimes de Stendhal*, Gallimard, Paris, 1966, p. 584.

[11] *Memoirs*, p. 144.

[12] *Correspondance générale*, Vol. I, p. 367.

books and life characteristic of the adult Berlioz was born in boyhood. It was not simply that he imitated what he read: he was himself Chateaubriand's René, asking nature to give him the beloved his whole being craved; he was Florian's Némorin, prostrate in his grief; he was Rousseau's Saint-Preux (in *Julie*), forgetting his agitation of spirit in the pure air of the mountains; he lived the dying Dido's agony of soul in his soul – a gift that explains the heartrending conviction of the music inspired in him 40 years later by the anguish of the Carthaginian queen.

Chateaubriand's *Génie du Christianisme, ou beautés de la religion chrétienne* is perhaps second only to the *Aeneid* in its impact on the adolescent Berlioz. In it we find many, if not most, of the leading themes of his youthful imaginative life: religion, love, literature, the poetry of Nature, the romance of distant lands, nostalgia for the ancient world, Romantic melancholy. The praise of the hymns and prayers of the Catholic Church, and the ceremonies and processions it evoked – Rogations, Corpus Christi; its evocation of the sacrament of first communion: all this set up resounding echoes in the boy's eager mind.

As I have said, the very poverty of the musical environment of La Côte was in a way a blessing. Berlioz was free to dream of what might be. Those responsible for the exhibition *La Voix du Romantisme* at the Bibliothèque nationale de France in 2003 had the ingenious idea of placing by itself in a glass case a blank piece of manuscript paper, with 24 staves on it but no notes – reference to a symbolic moment in Berlioz's boyhood, when he came upon such a sheet of paper and in an instant glimpsed a whole new, unguessed-at world of music, far off but clear, waiting for him. To hear an orchestra he would have to wait till he arrived in Paris; but from that moment he could imagine one. Similarly, his profound admiration for Gluck, which lasted all his life, first took root in him not by means of direct contact with his music (at that date he knew none of it except one or two pieces arranged with guitar accompaniment) but by reading the long and eulogistic Gluck entry in Michaud's *Biographie universelle*, to which Dr Berlioz subscribed. His full encounter with the music came at the Opéra, soon after he arrived in Paris, and was all the more explosive as a result.

Yes, there was precious little serious music at La Côte-Saint-André, but there were musical impressions, at first sight unpromising but in the event rich in suggestion, and contributing to the formation of Berlioz's musical style. One was his first communion, when the young girls' voices striking up the Eucharistic hymn filled him with 'a mystic yet passionate unrest'[13] and implanted deep in his soul both the idea of music as a dramatic art, giving

[13] *Memoirs*, p. 6.

expression to the central moments of human existence, and the sound of female voices in consort, which will be heard throughout his music from the *Messe solennelle* onwards, but above all in the Te Deum, the work begun not long after he had written the early chapters of his *Memoirs* and relived his boyhood.

From there we come by natural progression to the influence of the music of the church on the young Berlioz: the noëls he hears; the chant *O filii, o filiae*, which will find a clear echo in 'Les pèlerins étant venus' of *La Fuite en Égypte*; the plainchant *Tonus peregrinus*, with its plaintive flattened sixth, which leaves a direct imprint on the childhood song 'Je vais donc quitter pour jamais/Mon doux pays, ma douce amie' that will become the opening melody of the *Symphonie fantastique*. And all this without taking account of the influence of popular song, with its monodies, its irregular phrase-lengths, and its persistent $\frac{6}{8}$, which will leave its trace in Berlioz's style.

More important than anything else, more fertile in its consequences, is the experience of the Rogation procession, whose chanting he listened to one morning in May while sitting in a field (only a step from his home) reading a cloak-and-dagger novel set in Italy.[14] It is important not simply because of its reflection in the slow movement of the *Symphonie fantastique* (the shimmer of the wheatfield, the crying quail, the spacious, shining landscape), nor because of the famous attack of spleen described in chapter 40 of the *Memoirs*: 'le mal de l'isolement' that overcame him that day would inspire the passage where the melody of the *idée fixe*, earthbound, struggles vainly to free itself and take wing and a terrible storm engulfs the orchestra. Nor is it even because the same Rogation chant would be used in *La Damnation de Faust*, in the 'Ride to the Abyss' (last stage in the descent of an ardent, baffled soul towards total isolation). Beyond any particular work, it evokes a major aspect of Berlioz's art – its climate, its atmosphere.

> Absorbed though I was in my reading, my attention was distracted by the faint plaintive sounds of singing coming across the plain at regular intervals. The Rogation procession was passing nearby; the voices I heard were the peasants', chanting the litany of the saints. This time-honoured visitation of the hillsides and the plains in springtime, to ask for heaven's blessing on the fruits of the earth, has something poetic and touching about it that moves me inexpressibly. The procession halted at the foot of a wooden cross decorated with leaves; I saw the people kneel while the priest blessed the land. Then it moved slowly off and the melancholy chanting resumed. From time to time our old curé's quavering voice was clearly audible, with snatches of phrase:
>
> Conservari digneris
>
> (*The peasants*) Te rogamus, audi nos!

[14] F.-L.-C. de Montjoie, *Manuscrit trouvé au Mont Pausylipe*, Le Normant, Paris, 1802.

And the pious throng passed on, further and further into the distance:
(*Decrescendo*)
Sancta Barnaba,
Ora pro nobis!
(*Perdendo*)
Sancta Magdalena,
Ora pro…
Sancta Maria…
Ora…
Sancta…
…nobis
…

Silence… rustle of young wheat swaying in the light morning wind… cry of amorous quail calling to their mates… a bunting, full of joy, singing from the top of a poplar tree… intense peace… a dead leaf falling slowly from one of the oaks… the dull beat of my own heart… Life, surely, was outside me, far away, very far… On the horizon the Alpine glaciers reflected the rays of the mounting sun in great flashes of light… Over there lay Meylan… beyond the Alps Italy, Naples, Posilippo… the characters in my book… burning passions… secret, unfathomable happiness… Away, away! Oh for wings, to devour distance! I must see, admire, I must know love, rapture, the flame of an embrace, I must live life to its limits!… but I am but an earthbound clod. These characters are imaginary, or exist no longer… What love?… What fame?… What heart?… Where is my star, my *Stella montis*? Vanished no doubt for ever… When shall I see Italy? And the fit burst forth in all its fury; I suffered agonies, and lay on the ground groaning, convulsively tearing up handfuls of grass and wide-eyed innocent daisies, struggling against the sensation of *absence*, against an appalling *isolation*.[15]

The description of the procession speaks so clearly of Berlioz's music. It is the ancestor of several movements in which religious processions approach and then move away: the Pilgrims' March in *Harold en Italie*, the prayer in *Benvenuto Cellini*, the entry of the Wooden Horse in *Les Troyens*. It speaks too of his predilection for monotones, movements constructed round a single note or phrase: the 'Convoi funèbre' of *Roméo et Juliette*, the 'Offertoire' with its immemorial cry of souls in purgatory, the unchanging lament of violins and horns in the fourth song of *Les Nuits d'été* ('Sur les lagunes'), the Septet in *Les Troyens*. Or, think of the *perdendo* at the end of pieces like the Pilgrims' March, with its longer and longer silences, the ebbing clarinet melody in *La Mort d'Orphée*, Hylas in *Les Troyens* falling asleep before he can complete his song, the cellos dwindling into silence in 'Sur les lagunes', the reapers passing on their way home from the fields in *Sara la baigneuse*.

[15] *Memoirs*, pp. 174–75.

Think of the long musical vistas that recur throughout Berlioz's music, as a body of sound passes gradually out of earshot – nearly always, however vestigial the sound, charged with a feeling of momentousness: the Pilgrims' March again, the 'Marche nocturne' in *L'Enfance du Christ*, the climax of the third act of *Les Troyens*, the end of *Herminie*, the chorus of soldiers and students winding from sight at the end of Part 2 of *La Damnation de Faust*, leaving behind it, for all its rowdy high spirits, a sense of desolation.

Without doubt, when Berlioz took the road to Paris, at the age of seventeen, he had, as a musician, an enormous amount of catching up to do. He knew practically nothing. He was going to have to work long and tenaciously to master his *métier* – as indeed he did. But the prentice composer who arrived in Paris at the end of October 1821 had received the preparation he needed. Which being so, La Côte-Saint-André has every right to be proud of the title of Berlioz's native town.

Two Sisters

The following account of Berlioz's relations with his sisters Adèle and Nancy draws, here and there, on material quoted in my biography of the composer but also makes use of other documents transcribed during the weeks I spent going through the Reboul Collection of family papers in the 1970s. Nancy's name is given here as she spelled it in adult life, not as her brother's 'Nanci'. She herself used the latter form as a child, then at some point decided to change it, perhaps out of emulation of, and affection for, her godmother Nancy Clappier. Unreferenced quotations are my translations from unpublished letters and from Nancy's diary.

Two sisters might have been three if Louise-Julie-Virginie hadn't died in childhood. All we know of this third offspring of Louis and Joséphine Berlioz is what Dr Berlioz wrote in his *Livre de Raison* – her birth, on 29 September 1807, her death, on 16 April 1815, and the following lines (Napoleon had returned from Elba a few weeks before):

> My daughter Louise had begun complaining of a slight pain in the tonsils (8 April 1815). I did not treat her, as I considered that the illness was not serious enough; several people had been experiencing a similar ailment that month, and those who had received the most thorough treatment for it had not recovered any sooner than those who had been given no medication. For a few weeks there had been no further croup. On the 13th the tonsillitis developed into pharyngeal angina and tubercle. She died at 8 in the morning of the 16th, despite all I could do to save her. Oh my daughter! my country! My heart is broken.

Otherwise the record is silent. What the mysterious Louise was like, how the family reacted to her passing, we have no idea. She is mentioned in none of the correspondence. Nor do we know what Berlioz felt about this sister, four years his junior. For a long time he was close to Nancy, born two years after him, and he doted all his life on Adèle, who was more than ten years younger than he was.

Adèle's death, in 1860, at the age of 45, was a grievous blow to him. 'We loved each other like twins. She was an intimate friend.'[1] Adèle became his chief confidant, after Princess Wittgenstein, during the composition of *Les Troyens*. 'Thinking of you refreshes me', he wrote in October 1856.

[1] *Correspondance générale*, Vol. VI, p. 136.

> You don't know that another link between us has been forged since you seemed to take an interest in this thing that excites and disturbs me, that eats into me, that kills me and makes me live. [Berlioz had shown her the libretto of the opera when she was in Paris not long before.] Unfortunately you don't know music, but at least, now, the literary side of the work (don't laugh at that pretentious word) gives you a means of communication and opens a window through which you can look out on my garden. The idea that you watch me working there is a quite new and delightful sensation. And can you believe it (you must forgive me) – I love you the more for it.[2]

On the face of it, the deep affinity between two such different characters – and between one for whom music is everything and one who 'doesn't know music' – is hard to credit. Adèle's long, rambling letters – a large number survive from the years of her married life – do not suggest a mind of much interest. Their mundane accounts of the daily domestic round are something of a penance to plough through. I well remember what Yvonne Reboul-Berlioz said after she had, at my request, examined the letters in her collection in search of references to Berlioz: 'Que cette femme est assommante!' ('What a bore that woman is!'). There may have been an element of sibling rivalry in the judgement, Madame Reboul being the representative of Nancy's side of the family and therefore predisposed to look down on the other branch. Yet it can't be denied that if Adèle weren't Berlioz's sister, there would not be much to recommend her correspondence.

All the same, it would be a mistake to write her off. She may not have had an intelligence like her brother's, or her sister's, but she had spirit. The Reboul Collection, in the days when I was researching it, contained an extraordinary bundle of letters from the early spring of 1828, documenting an acute family crisis involving Adèle, then thirteen years of age. Her father, thinking it time she was given a better education than she could get at the convent school in La Côte-Saint-André, sent her to Saint Pierre, a girls' boarding school in Grenoble; but she would have none of it. She cried day and night (at times so loudly that her screams could be heard in the street), refused to eat, wouldn't sleep, made violent scenes, vomited and coughed blood. For two months the family was in uproar. Friends and relations were sucked into the drama, and letters, laments, advice, threats poured back and forth: from Adèle herself, to her mother and sister, begging to be brought home; from Louis Berlioz; from Nancy; from Dr Berlioz's brothers, Victor and Auguste, both of whom lived in Grenoble and were recruited to visit the school and reason with her; from Victor's wife the beautiful Laure (the one who, when Berlioz, defending a career in the arts, remarked that to hear her talk one would suppose she would have thought it a scandal if Racine

[2] *Ibid.*, Vol. V, p. 378.

Adèle Suat, née *Berlioz*

had been a member of the family, made the immortal reply: 'Well, my dear, you know, a good name matters more than anything'[3]); from old Grandpère Marmion; from Uncle Félix; from family friends – Nancy Clappier, the Appreins, the Malleins, the Faures, the Rochers; from M. Petit, almoner of the La Côte convent; and from the increasingly despairing headmistress of the school, Louise de Bourcet.

What these documents reveal, among other things, is a quality Adèle's brother would have admired and sympathised with: tenacity. Significantly, it seems not simply to have been extreme homesickness that motivated her but the loss of liberty and – as her uncle Victor said – 'having to attend class regularly, not just when she feels like it'. (She was her brother's twin in that respect.) Evidently she had made up her mind from the first. 'I'm convinced it's calculated', writes Victor. 'Having given up hope of bringing her parents round, she's now set on wearing down the patience of the ladies at the school and forcing them to get rid of her. She's absolutely determined'. And in the end she got her way and was brought home.

The word 'forceful' ('énergique') that Berlioz applies to her is not perhaps so surprising after all. Independence of spirit, determination, seems to have

[3] *Memoirs*, p. 39.

been one of her defining characteristics. In Italy in 1831, climbing in the foothills of the Abruzzi, Berlioz will recall the eleven-year-old Adèle, on one of their annual holidays at Meylan, striding up Mont-Saint-Eynard, 30 paces ahead of the rest of the family.[4] When she comes to marry, she will choose a local notary, Marc Suat, whom her father and sister consider beneath her; Nancy and her husband, Camille Pal, will continue to believe that she could have done better for herself, and Adèle ever after will be prone to see in every gesture of Camille's a veiled insult to her socially inferior husband. (At a family reunion at La Côte in September 1847, Adèle seems to have fired up at something Camille said; Berlioz, in an emollient letter to Nancy, admitted that Adèle had a 'terrible tendency' to imagine wrongs.[5]) But she had the happiest marriage of anyone in the Berlioz family – the only one of them that did.

Perhaps most of all what drew her brother to her was that she accepted him as he was. Unlike Nancy, she had been too young to take part in the first traumatic years of the protracted family quarrel over his career, the effects of which would never quite cease to mark his relations with the others. With them he was constantly having to justify himself, was always expecting to face criticism. With her, he had nothing to prove. She loved him unconditionally. When the rest of the family cut him off for marrying Harriet Smithson, she alone stood by him; she, he told her, would be his family now.[6]

A letter of Adèle's, to Nancy, written soon after Berlioz's return from Rome, gives a picture of the two of them:

> He's really merry, this lovely brother of ours. What a difference from the last time he was here [en route for Rome, and oppressed by anxiety at parting from Camille Moke] – it's not the same man. I was very curious to know what he feels about the treacherous Camille; I was afraid to bring up the subject, but I needn't have worried, he brought it up himself and talked to me at great length about it. […] Since he's been here I've been spending my time very happily. He's working hard [preparing orchestral parts for concerts in Paris], and while he works I keep him company, mending his shirts, which may surprise you; but what is more extraordinary, it doesn't bore me in the least – working for *him* is a delight. I can see you laughing, you beast – but I asked for it by the naïve way I've been carrying on.[7]

The image that sums up their intimacy is a passage in Berlioz's *Memoirs*, written after Adèle's death. It may serve as her epitaph:

4 *Correspondance générale*, Vol. I, p. 474.

5 *Ibid.*, Vol. III, p. 453.

6 *Ibid.*, Vol. II, p. 131.

7 Quoted in Cairns, Vol. 1, pp. 548–49.

> She was a person of such spirit and warmth of heart; she bore so tenderly with the asperities of my nature and was ready to indulge my most childish whims. I remember, one pouring wet morning after my return from Italy, when we were all together at La Côte-Saint-André, suggesting we go for a walk. 'Yes, I'll come', she said. 'Wait a second while I put on my galoshes.' My elder sister said we were a couple of lunatics, no one else could conceivably want to go squelching about the country in weather like this. I fetched a large umbrella and, regardless of the jeers of the rest of the family, Adèle and I descended to the plain and walked for nearly five miles, pressed together under the umbrella, not speaking a word. We loved each other.[8]

In a letter from the same period, to Princess Wittgenstein, describing the same incident, Berlioz adds: 'I loved her much more than I loved the elder sister'.[9] The force of that statement is disconcerting, considering the evidence of how close they had once been. What happened to sour relations with that elder sister, who – the early documents show – was his confidante and intimate friend; who, on her side, writes of 'time hanging heavy till Hector returns', of her 'joy' at his coming, of how he looks when he arrives, in 1828, winner of the Prix de Rome second prize, 'full of fire, of impetuosity, of life, youth, beauty'? Throughout Berlioz's student years, as his letters and her diaries make clear, it is Nancy he confides in, and that not just because Adèle is still too young: they are genuinely close.

In a letter of 2 November 1823 he writes to her – in connection with the family dispute over his choice of career – as to one sympathetic to his troubles, and signs himself 'your brother and your friend for life'.[10] It is to Nancy that he describes in passionate detail his feelings on seeing his first Gluck opera (*Iphigénie en Tauride*).[11] In the years that follow he continues to share with her his deepest thoughts – his experience of Beethoven, of Weber, of Spontini, his response to the July Revolution, his love for Camille Moke, his delight in the novels of Scott and James Fennimore Cooper, his attitude to marriage:

> I can assure you we think the same way about it. Don't worry, never shall I marry for money, even supposing I had the chance. [...] Yes, dear sister, you are absolutely right to look to a husband as a support, a guide, a protector, not a banker.[12]

[8] *Memoirs*, p. 550.

[9] *Correspondance générale,* Vol. VII, pp. 134–35.

[10] *Nouvelles lettres de Berlioz, de sa famille, de ses contemporains, 1803-69*, ed. Peter Bloom, Joël-Marie Fauquet, Hugh J. Macdonald and Cécile Reynaud, Actes Sud and Palazetto Bru Zane, Arles and Venice, 2016, p. 44.

[11] *Correspondance générale,* Vol. I, pp. 36–37.

[12] Letter of 10 January 1829, wrongly assigned to 1828 in *ibid.*, Vol. I, pp. 169–70.

n'aurai pas beaucoup de gloire a avoir
vaincu mes deux adversaires, ils sont loin
de se douter, seulement, de ce que c'est
que la musique dramatique.
Alphonse va passer tout a l'heure
son 3me examen, il renonce cette
année a faire un voyage a la côte
et le remet a la premiere occasion ou nous
pourrons le faire ensemble.

Adieu ma chère Sœur

Jusqu'à ce que je sorte de prison.

Ton frère H. B.

P. S.

Nous aurons tous les soirs sallon de
réception dans la grande cour de l'institut
les amis et connaissances peuvent venir
nous voir de six a 9 heures. Il y a
un surveillant qui prend soin qu'on ne nous
transmette rien du dehors qui puisse avoir
rapport au sujet du concours. —

In a letter to Nancy of 28 July 1827 Berlioz reports on the prison-like conditions in which the Prix de Rome cantatas are composed – in this instance, La Mort d'Orphée, *the first of his four, ultimately successful, attempts to win the prize.*

Two months later, in March 1829, he comes near to telling her of his passion for Harriet Smithson, which he had been keeping rigorously secret from the family; while he writes to her, the current of his thoughts has been leading him dangerously in that direction, ('Pandora's box' is 'beginning to open without my realising it'). The letter – in answer to one from her telling him of the terrible emptiness of her existence and of her distress at her parents keeping all proposals of marriage secret from her – contains the fullest of all Berlioz's avowals of his feeling for Nancy:

> Instead of going to bed I want to reply to you, to speak to you – not of what relates only to me but what touches me because it concerns you. I believe that what is true of real love is also true of friendship – that absence makes it grow. Every time I get a letter from you it seems you have become dearer to me than ever. How I wish I could see you happy! The more I discover sympathetic likenesses between our two characters the more I feel my anxiety about your future redouble. Without doubt, as intelligence and sensibility develop in you, so you become more liable to pain and suffering.[13]

A letter of 17 March 1830, a year later, shows him sympathising passionately with her over their parents' dismissal, without consulting her, of a suitor whom for once she was prepared to accept.[14] Yet, within another two years, relations between brother and sister will have cooled dramatically and the old intimacy will have gone, never to be recovered. Why was that?

There was an affinity between them, but the likenesses he identified were weaker than he believed – or rather, they were real but were qualified by differences in their characters and, still more, by the drastic discrepancy in their respective situations. He confided in her; but his confidences only underlined the chasm between his experience of life and art and hers. In the last resort, Nancy could not be the close friend he sought in her.

We know a good deal about her, thanks to the diaries – the *tableaux journaliers* and the *cahiers de souvenirs* – that she kept off and on between 1822 and 1832 (the year of her marriage). In them we see an adolescent, and then a young woman, who was indeed not happy, one like her brother in many respects, avid for experience, stirred by similar longings and idealisms, prey to similar despairs, but with no means of escape. He got away to Paris, she was trapped.

We see her in intimate teenage conversation with her adored Elise Rocher; agonising over their friendship (does Elise really love her, will Nancy 'lose' her when she leaves to get married and has children?); giggling with her at the oddities and pretensions of the young men of La Côte as they pass them

[13] *Ibid.*, p. 243.
[14] *Ibid.*, Vol. IX, p. 75.

Nancy Berlioz

in the streets; shocked when Elise, member of a larger, more open family, acquaints her graphically with the facts of life. We see her strumming her guitar in the moonlight on the balcony of her room; blocking her ears when the band of the local National Guard, on the Esplanade, plays as only it can; reading incessantly, fiction and non-fiction – Racine, Scott, Madame de Genlis, Madame Campan; self-consciously drafting her letters before sending them, and then still dissatisfied with them; worrying that her nose is too long; fretting at being kept in the dark by her parents about offers of marriage; thrusting her latest *bout-rimé* into the fire rather than show it to Hector's friend Casimir Faure; writing poems in honour of the family parrot Vert-Vert and the English spaniel Fido; penning a tearfully romantic novella whose heroine is beautiful but doomed to die of tuberculosis.

These are not just the usual conventional girlish reflections; they are of interest not simply because of whose sister she was but because Nancy was an independent soul, sharp-tongued, with a will of her own, choosy, someone of keen, sceptical intelligence who in many ways refused to share the narrow provincial outlook of most of her contemporaries. Here she is, writing to her brother from Grenoble:

> Our little cousin [Odile, Victor Berlioz's daughter] is an interesting person, but I can't see her mind developing, given the anti-liberal education she's been receiving. [...] So Mlle de Chichiliane is to marry M. Jacquemet! Rich, but so ugly, so stupid. When I gave vent to what I thought about it, both Uncle Victor and Uncle Félix accused me of being a child, a romantic, and not of this century. What a century! What a view of happiness!

Nancy is known to have turned down several offers of marriage from rich pretenders. In an entry in October 1828 she describes meeting, at Madame Chanron's salon,

> a thin, insignificant, red-faced man with a pointed head. We only just managed by violent efforts to contain our laughter. It turns out he is one of my 'conquests', from Voiron – he asked for my hand two years ago, as I discovered afterwards. One more in my collection of suitors whose names and attractions I know! So it's only those who think of me. To them I must confine my pretensions. I am never to meet anyone to whom I might feel drawn by similarity of taste and situation. Nothing that could appeal to my imagination, capture my esteem, touch my heart and fulfil its secret desires – none of that will ever come my way.

But the diaries show, too, that in other, important ways she is different from her brother. They show that unlike him but like her mother she is devoutly religious (she notes with gratified approval what her brother's friend Humbert Ferrand says about the monastery of the Grande Chartreuse: 'It is not yet heaven but it is no longer earth. Religion, my dear Hector, is not an empty word'). They also show that she is prudish. She may, instinctively, revolt against the restrictive, grossly subordinate position of women in French provincial society, but she absorbs many of the principles, among them that theatre-going (the delight of Nicolas and Félix Marmion) is a grievous sin. When Elise, by now married and living in Valence, confesses to her that she went to see Ducis' *Othello*, and was so moved by it that she went again, to *Hamlet*, Nancy upbraids her severely and tells Elise's aunt, who gives her niece a terrible dressing-down.

Nancy's diary records her confused reaction to Rousseau's novel *Julie, ou la nouvelle Héloïse*, and her embarrassment (and secret excitement?) at its sexual frankness:

> My father read us extracts from the first letters in *La Nouvelle Héloïse*. The language of passion in it is admittedly sublime, and the style thrilling. But anything that goes beyond the bounds of moderation and endangers the soul revolts and disgusts me. I have no hesitation in stating that I would rather die than inspire such feelings and be exposed to the risk of sharing them. Just thinking of them makes my whole being tremble with horror.

Nancy is by no means always the dutiful echo and mouthpiece of her parents. She can be critical of them. But, as the eldest child still living at home, she is in an awkward position, appealed to by both sides. 'As for [Hector]', her mother writes, 'he is as you say madder than ever, thank God his sister is not like him, though he thinks she is.' But it was not as simple as that. In some ways she was like him. Nancy could cope only by agreeing with parents and brother by turns. 'My father has imposed on me an obligation that I find exceedingly painful', she writes in her diary in February 1825, at the height of the crisis precipitated by news of the abortive rehearsal of the *Messe solennelle*, 'that of writing to my brother to charge him with reproaches that are alas only too well deserved.'

As an inveterate moraliser, Nancy may not have been altogether averse to the task; a reply of Berlioz's to one such letter ends: 'When you write, dear sister, try to tone down your reprimands a little'.[15] Yet that wasn't always how she saw it. A few weeks earlier she writes: 'There is something terribly exaggerated in the way [my parents] regard my brother's failings. If he were to cover us with shame and infamy their reaction could not be any stronger.' Here, she is influenced by her godmother Nancy Clappier, Joséphine Berlioz's friend, who points out that Hector's chosen career could be an honourable one – 'they are the *fine arts*, after all' – and who writes to Nancy that she is 'quite of your opinion about Hector. While sympathising with his parents' distress, I cannot help – as I look about me and make comparisons – preferring their son, with his faults, to the vast majority of our young men'.

At another time Nancy fears that her brother 'will poison his parents' existence and shorten the life of my father' – who 'today gave me a look so touching that I could hardly hold back my tears'. At one moment she is feeling deeply for her brother in his plight; at another – daily witness of her parents' anger and bewilderment, caught up in the tension of the household – it is all the fault of his 'folly'. No wonder her attitude fluctuated wildly. She was in an impossible situation.

She was also genuinely ambivalent about him and about what he was doing. 'One can't have a conversation with him about anything but his art', she writes in her diary, during her brother's visit to La Côte in the summer of 1824. 'He goes on and on about his opera [*Les Francs-juges*], but as to anything else….'

How could it have been otherwise? Berlioz himself recognised it. The gulf between them was simply too wide. 'You don't have the powerful distractions that I have', he writes (in the letter of March 1829, quoted above), 'though I

[15] *Ibid.*, Vol. I, p. 150.

believe that coming to Paris, with its atmosphere of new sensations, would make all the difference.' But Nancy would be a married woman in her thirties before she set foot, briefly, in the capital – 'that electrifying city',[16] as her brother called it, 'with all the intelligent people to be found there, the whirl of ideas in which one lived and moved'. The environment she lived in could hardly have been more unlike that. As it was, in contrast to her less complex, less imaginative, less sceptical sister, she never really accepted her brother's vocation. Much as she felt drawn to him and attracted and excited by his ideas, and envious of them, she was prevented both by her nature and by her situation from entering into them.

'Ah, but you speak of the *beautiful*, the great, the sublime', he writes in the letter of March 1829,

> and a host of ideas rise up, all depressing. The sublime is not sublime for everybody. What transports some people is for others unintelligible, sometimes even ridiculous. There are the prejudices that come from education, and then there are the totally different ways people are made.[17]

And he describes how, at a performance of Beethoven's C sharp minor Quartet, only a handful of people, himself among them, were moved by it. The rest found it incomprehensible, even absurd.

Such questions were the very stuff of his mind, his daily preoccupation. The sublime was his natural habitat. She could only dream, and reach vainly for it, like the souls of Virgil's dead stretching their hands in yearning for the retreating shore.

Berlioz, on his side, saw this. 'You don't understand Shakespeare, you aren't carried away by Moore'. How could she be? Above all, music in the sense and to the extent that it was his whole life was closed to her. In 1822, at the Opéra-Comique, 'I thought of you, sister, and how you would have enjoyed it. The Opéra perhaps would give you less pleasure, it's too serious for you'.[18] But the Opéra was where great things happened – from which Nancy was excluded.

Such an assessment may be accurate. It is also condescending – as is what he says about her in the *Memoirs*: that she has 'a good voice but absolutely no natural instinct for music; she is fond of it but has never been able to read it; she can't even decipher a folksong'.[19]

There could have been no bigger barrier between them. And Nancy, self-doubting, impatient of her restricted life, craving in vain the freedom he was

16 *Ibid.*, Vol. III, p. 366.

17 *Ibid.*, Vol. I, p. 244.

18 *Ibid.*, Vol. I, pp. 38–39.

19 *Memoirs*, pp. 14–15.

enjoying, must have sensed it. There is a sadness in the way she sometimes writes of him – 'my brother is more and more distant from us' – but there is envy, too. When her friend Rosanne Goletty (Elise Rocher's cousin) met Berlioz in Paris in 1830, at the time of the preparations for the premiere of the *Symphonie fantastique*, and reported that from what she heard he was 'making his mark' and was likely to 'win a big reputation', Nancy's reply was scornful: 'I should think it *was* time, at 26, to show what one is. But as for his talent and the career he's embraced, a little celebrity is all it is, nothing suggests that he will soon succeed in obtaining something more positive'. His condescension, you feel, was being well repaid.

Already, four years earlier, in an 'Epistle to my brother', in which she tries her hand at a verse-letter in the vein of that interminable troubadour Grandpère Marmion, she is characterising his passion for music as an aberration, an 'error' from which she predicts he will one day be 'cured'. All through those fraught times Nancy is dubious about what her brother holds most dear, about what is his essential being, his *raison d'être*. Such scepticism can only have served to alienate him from her, and her from him. (In the remarks about her in the *Memoirs*, quoted above, there is more than a suggestion that he is getting his own back, even a hint of malice.) That distrust, more than anything, was what blighted their once close and loving friendship. It was part of the whole process, his increasing and inevitable detachment from the family milieu – his world had expanded immeasurably, theirs had stayed the same – but it bore most damagingly and most painfully on his relations with Nancy. (Ten years later, when Nancy visited Paris, she was made keenly aware of their estrangement, to judge by Nancy Clappier's reply to a letter of hers that has not survived: 'the things you say [...] about artists and men of letters. They live in another world [...]. One has to think of them as beings apart; but a brother, [...] that is a blow'.)

Even as late as 1830, not many weeks after her disdainful letter to Rosanne, she could write excitedly in her diary about the news of Hector's new love, Camille Moke, and what she learned of it from Edouard Rocher during a game of *boules* in the Rochers' garden, 'on a subject so dear to my heart'. When Camille jilted him, she was devastated. But it was no longer quite the same. When, two years later, Nancy finally got married, her brother (in Italy) was distressingly cool about it.

Nancy didn't marry a banker. But her husband, Camille Pal, was only a degree or two better: he was a lawyer, and he was fifteen years older than she was. In her brother's eyes she had given in and joined the ranks of that stifling bourgeois environment from which she had once struggled so desperately to escape. Back home in Dauphiné, Berlioz writes to Madame Vernet in

Rome about his experiences in the 'judgemental world' of Grenoble, where every second person seems to be occupied with the law and they all insist on holding forth on art and music and poetry: 'to hear them talk of Byron or Goethe or Beethoven you'd think it was some tailor or bootmaker of more than average ability'.[20] He retreats into a morose silence, which makes his sister feel physically ill. 'Not once', she tells Adèle, 'did he come in without a dismal, scowling expression on his face. You will have to forgive them if they take him for a savage and a misanthrope.' Their old alliance was well and truly dead.

In the renewed family hostilities that broke out over his proposed marriage to Harriet Smithson, Nancy sided with her parents. She informed him it that it was just a passing fancy of his, but that if he persisted in marrying a penniless Protestant actress, he might well jeopardise Adèle's chance of making a good match. The breach with the family that followed Berlioz's marriage drew him closer to Adèle – his 'good sister, who doesn't succumb to crass prejudice or play the prude, the dolt, like our honourable sister Nanci, who didn't deign to reply to the letter I was fool enough to send her'.[21] More than two years passed before relations were resumed. We do not have the letter Nancy eventually wrote, in 1836, but Berlioz's answer, while welcoming their reconciliation ('let's be friends again as we used to be'), couldn't resist adding a little homily: 'Our errors of judgment often spring from being applied to matters we know little or nothing of because they are beyond our understanding. Give that a thought'.[22]

Yet, interestingly, in the same letter he writes about Harriet more candidly than he ever does to Adèle: 'she doesn't take enough account of the work I am forced to do, at home and away from the house, which obliges me to leave her on her own'. It is a glimpse of the closer equality of minds that had once made them close – as was the vivid way, in writing to her, he described, frequently and at length, the goings-on in the artistic world of Paris. Later, Nancy would warm his heart by becoming an affectionate and caring aunt to his troubled son Louis.

In the event Adèle was not prevented from making a good match, or at least a happy one. But Nancy's was anything but happy. Nothing suggests that the large, loquacious Camille Pal was an agreeable man, let alone the 'support, guide and protector' Nancy and her brother had agreed a wife had the right to look for. She seems to have spent a good deal of her existence away from him, in their house at Saint-Vincent, north of Grenoble at the foot of the Chartreuse range, which became for her a favourite refuge. Her

20 *Correspondance générale*, Vol. II, p. 21.

21 *Ibid.*, p.167.

22 *Ibid.*, p. 287.

end was cruel: death at the age of 44 from breast cancer after months of unmitigated agony. During that time, as Adèle nursed her, she revealed her inmost thoughts about her life – till then kept to herself – and the aspirations that had come to nothing. The letter Berlioz wrote to Adèle, two weeks after Nancy's death, makes this all too clear:

> My dear, dear sister, your letter, which I was begging for the day before yesterday, has shattered me. I had guessed only too well all the details of our unhappy Nanci's physical torments, but what you tell me of her mental suffering breaks my heart. Added to them, it must have made her torture unendurable. You may be sure she had long made up her mind about the two members of her intimate family [Camille and their daughter Mathilde]. I too had long divined her efforts to delude us as to her private sorrows, her disillusionment, all her disappointed hopes.[23]

In the *Memoirs* Berlioz vehemently attacks the prohibitions imposed by both the law and the church on the use of anaesthetics to put an end to incurable disease. 'My sister herself would probably have rejected that means of escape had it been offered her. "God's will be done" [...] – as if God's will would not have been as well manifested in the release of the patient by a swift and peaceful death as in the prolonging of her pointless and abominable torture.'[24] But his deepest feelings are for Adèle, harrowed and exhausted by weeks of nursing her dying sibling: 'As for you, my poor sister, I can only adore, with tears, the gentle, noble and forceful qualities of your heart'.

[23] *Ibid.*, Vol. III, pp. 713–14.

[24] *Memoirs*, p. 504.

II

APPRENTICESHIP AND FIRST MATURITY

Messe solennelle

The following piece originated as a lecture I gave to a music society in Montpellier. It was later the basis for a talk to the Berlioz Society given in December 1995 and published in the Berlioz Society Bulletin *No. 156 (Winter 1996–97).*

The rediscovery of the *Messe solennelle* has come a bit late for my generation of Berlioz biographers. I was writing my first volume in the mid-1980s, before such a thing was dreamed of and when – apart from a single movement, the 'Resurrexit', which had survived – the work was a blank that one speculated about in a paragraph or two before passing on to solid ground: the *Scène héroïque*, the surviving fragments of *Les Francs-juges*, *La Mort d'Orphée*, *Herminie*, and then the *Huit Scènes de Faust*, where the real Berlioz began.

I must admit that when I heard of it my first reaction was almost one of vexation. The sheer inconvenience of the thing! Why couldn't the admirable Frans Moors, the Flemish organist who came upon the manuscript in the organ loft of his church in Antwerp, where it had been sitting unguessed at for the last hundred years – why couldn't he have made his sensational find ten years earlier? I can see why he couldn't, of course: the chain of circumstances that led him to it was – as he has told – connected with the Mozart bicentenary of 1991. All the same, it was undeniably a bit of a nuisance.

A second and perhaps slightly more reasonable motive for half-wishing the work hadn't turned up was the fear of what it could do to Berlioz's reputation – to the dearly won respectability he had at last begun to acquire. The dedicated enemies of all things Berliozian were a dying race; the old parrot cry that 'he didn't know how to compose' had become no more than a faint, querulous squawk. Was this the moment to rouse it from its slumbers? There was also the matter of the new life the Mass might give to that other ancient *canard*, Berlioz the liar. He said he burned it, and here it was, returned to haunt him. As Tovey remarked, 'in Berlioz's vocabulary "burnt" means carefully preserved'.[1] The press, as expected, enjoyed itself, especially in Paris; the article in *Figaro* describing the discovery was

[1] Donald Tovey, *Essays in Musical Analysis*, Vol. 4, Oxford University Press, London, 1936, p. 74.

headlined 'The lies of a young Romantic: Berlioz claimed he burned it. Like the phoenix it is reborn from its ashes'.[2]

In fact, it is easy to see what happened. But first let me summarise the history of the work. In the spring of 1824 the twenty-year-old Berlioz, who had been studying composition with Le Sueur for about a year and a half, was commissioned by the church of Saint-Roch to write a Mass for the Feast of the Holy Innocents the following December. But on the eve of the great day the performance had to be cancelled, partly because many of the musicians, who were taking part unpaid, failed to appear at the rehearsal, but chiefly because the orchestra and chorus parts, which had been copied by the Saint-Roch choirboys, turned out to be full of mistakes and there was no time to correct them.

Once he had recovered from the blow, the composer set to work to copy them again himself. At the same time he took the opportunity to revise his score. Another date was fixed: 10 July 1825. This time the orchestra was paid (with money he borrowed); the performance took place and was a considerable success. It was the first time a work of his had been heard in public, and the first time he himself had heard any of his large-scale music. His excitement bubbles over in the letters he wrote immediately afterwards. Most of all, it was what his teacher Le Sueur thought that delighted him. As soon as he could he hurried to Le Sueur's house in the rue Saint-Anne, just round the corner from the church (very probably it was Le Sueur, who, knowing Masson, the choirmaster of Saint-Roch, had arranged the commission). Le Sueur's eldest daughter answered the bell. 'Papa – he's here!' And the next moment:

> Let me embrace you. By Jove, you're not going to be a doctor or an apothecary, you're going to be a great composer. You have genius – I say it because it's true. There are too many notes in your Mass, you have let yourself get carried away, but in all this ebullience of ideas not a single intention miscarries, all your pictures are true. The effect is extraordinary. And I want you to know that everybody felt it. I had chosen a seat by myself, in a corner, on purpose to observe the audience, and you can take my word for it that if it hadn't been a church you would have received three or four right royal rounds of applause.[3]

All this heady excitement did not prevent Berlioz from examining the score with a critical eye and doing his best to put right whatever struck him as weak or defective. It may well have been then that he wrote, at the top of the 'Quoniam', 'This frightful fugue must be rewritten, in a completely

[2] 'Les mensonges d'un jeune romantique', *Le Figaro*, 23 November 1992.

[3] *Correspondance générale.*, Vol. I, pp. 96–97.

" Papa le voilà — " Venez que je vous embrasse; morbleu
" vous ne serez ni médecin ni apothicaire, mais un
" grand compositeur; vous avez du génie je vous le dis parceque
" c'est vrai. il y a trop de notes dans votre messe, vous vous
" êtes laissé emporter, mais à travers toute cette pétulance
" d'idées, pas une intention n'est manquée, tous vos tableaux
" sont vrais; c'est d'un effet inconcevable; Et je veux
" que vous sachiez que cet effet a été senti de la multitude;
" car je m'étais placé exprès tout seul dans un coin pour
" observer le public, et je vous répond que si ce n'eut pas été
" dans l'église vous auriez reçu trois ou quatre fameuses
" salves d'applaudissemens.

Mon cher albert j'en reste là, je ne puis tout vous écrire je vous raconterai le plus intéressant. C'est ce qui est arrivé dernièrement à Lesueur à mon sujet au Conservatoire. Sa conversation avec Cherubini et Berton. Les félicitations que je reçus le lendemain de l'exécution de ma messe, à la noce de la fille de Mme Branchu, à laquelle j'étais invité, et où je trouvai à qui parler.

Je n'ai pu avoir l'adresse de Mr Bessault je suis entré dans dix maisons de la rue du Bac et ne le trouvant pas j'ai pris le parti de lui écrire sans numéro; je crains que la lettre ne lui soit pas parvenue, ayez la bonté de le lui faire savoir. Je comptais sur Mr De Montesquiou pour le déterrer, mais je ne sais comment je m'y suis pris, sa propre invitation m'a passé de la tête et je n'y ai songé

Berlioz writes to Albert Du Boys on 20 July 1825,
ten days after the first performance of the Messe solennelle

The façade and interior of the seventeenth-century church of Saint-Roch, in the First Arrondissement of Paris, not far from the Louvre

different style', and it's possible he did. The score we have is probably the Mass as it was in 1825, and, for the performance that took place two years later in another Paris church, Saint-Eustache, a fresh score was made that has not survived.

A few months after the Saint-Eustache concert of 22 November 1827, Berlioz received his initiation into the music of Beethoven at the Conservatoire concerts, and his art took a new direction – at which point he had to recognise that, even revised and corrected, the Mass as a whole no longer represented his inmost thoughts, no longer spoke the language of music as he now understood it. I don't doubt it was then or

soon afterwards that he took the decision to put an end to its existence by the most effective means, the destruction of the performing material, which he had written out with such labour a few years before. Only the 'Resurrexit' was spared, to figure in concerts of his for the next couple of years before being sacrificed in its turn. That he kept the full score of the Mass as a source of ideas for later works doesn't make his decision any less final. Without the chorus and orchestra parts, the Mass, as a work for performance, in effect ceased to exist.

In 1835 he gave the original score to a friend, the Flemish violinist Antoine Bessems, who had played in the orchestra at his concerts that year; Bessems's name is on a list of musicians, in Berlioz's hand, and is among those indicated as playing without a fee. Very likely, Berlioz wanted to give him something as an expression of gratitude, and Bessems asked for the score of the Mass, in whose performance he had presumably taken part eight years before. (Bessems, like Berlioz, enrolled at the Conservatoire in 1826. Part of the orchestra that played the Mass the following year was made up of Conservatoire students.) Bessems recorded the gift by writing at the bottom of the title page: 'The score of this mass, entirely in Berlioz's hand, was given to me as a souvenir of the long-standing friendship that unites us. A. Bessems, Paris, 1835'.

On Bessems' death in 1868, his possessions passed to his brother Joseph, choirmaster at the church of Saint Charles Borromeus in Antwerp. After Joseph died, in 1892, the score remained in its oak chest in the organ loft until Frans Moors found it a hundred years later. I should state here that although Berlioz biography has been plagued by forgeries, and although Mr Moors is a schoolmaster, like the author of the new 'Haydn sonatas' that also caused a furore in the 1990s, his role was confined to discovering the score, which is indeed 'entirely in Berlioz's hand'. It was promptly authenticated by Hugh Macdonald, who on hearing the news rushed from St Louis to Antwerp, and there can be absolutely no doubt that it is the lost Mass of 1824–25.

And it is a real find. The score fills a big gap in the biography of the composer. It is of unquestionable musicological interest. Yet who would have imagined that it could be anything more than that? When Berlioz began to write the Mass it was a mere twenty months since he had started studying composition – starting virtually from scratch. He was twenty. He had arrived in Paris in a state of almost total ignorance, having been brought up in something of a desert, musically speaking, and never having heard an orchestra. He made up for lost time, plunging into the world of opera and immersing himself in the scores of Gluck and Spontini and the others every hour of the 24 that could be spared from his medical studies and some that could not. But the Mass was composed less than two years after he first became a pupil of Le Sueur. How could it possibly be, if not an embarrassment, at least any good, dating from so early in his apprenticeship?

Well, it is no masterpiece, and the success of the CD[4] – Bärenreiter, publisher of the New Berlioz Edition, reported to Hugh Macdonald that it had replaced Górecki's Third Symphony at the top of their bestseller list – is certainly more a commercial than an artistic phenomenon. Nonetheless, the Mass turns out to have intrinsic qualities beyond its musicological significance and way beyond what one could have expected. Berlioz may have disowned it; but, apprentice or not, he was already capable of

[4] Recorded by Donna Brown (soprano), Jean-Luc Viala (tenor), Gilles Cachemaille (bass), The Monteverdi Choir and the Orchestre Romantique et Revolutionnaire, conducted by John Eliot Gardiner, released on Philips 442 137-2 in 1994.

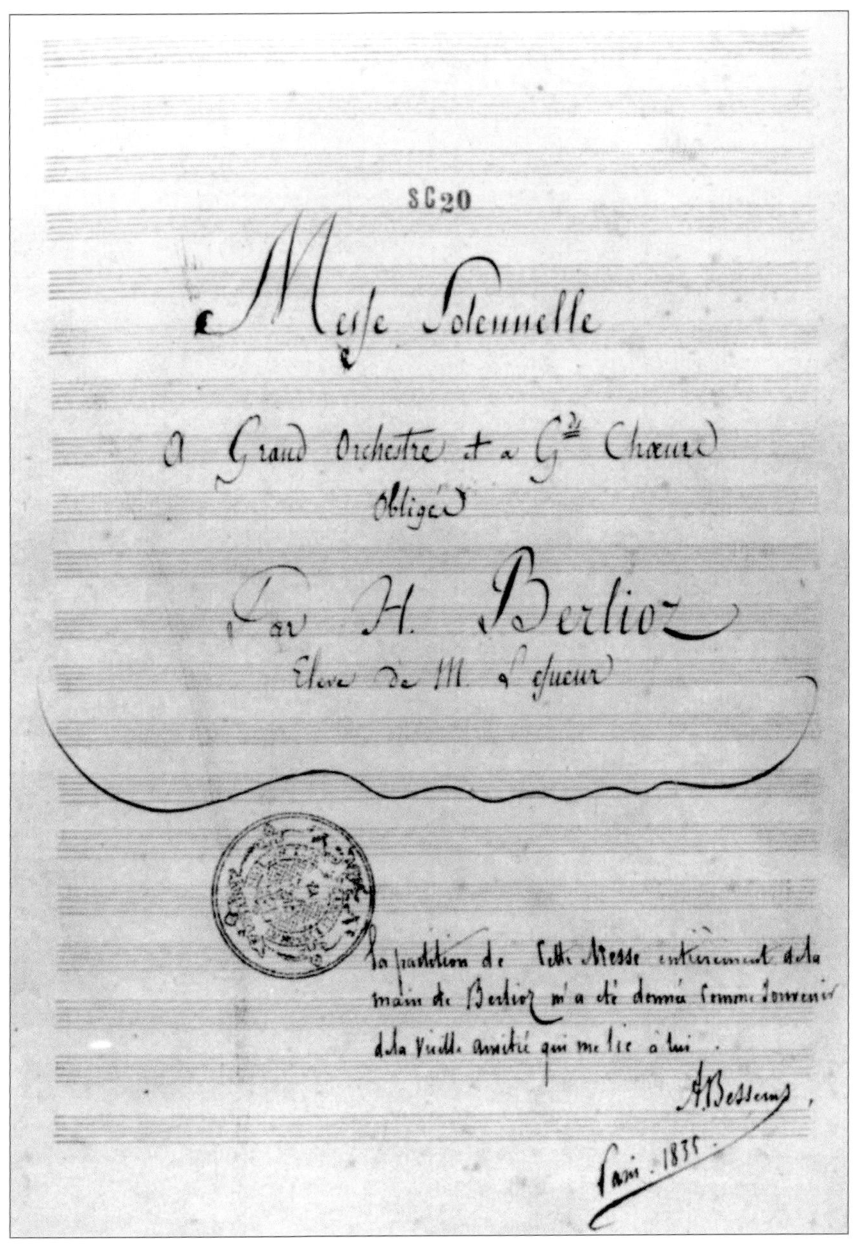

The title page of the Messe solennelle,
with Antoine Bessems' inscription explaining how the score came into his possession

Berlioz's teacher, Jean-François Le Sueur

creating striking ideas – as indeed he recognised by using them in works of his maturity, where they are not disowned.

Because the 'Resurrexit' survived (in the copy Berlioz sent to the Academy as 'evidence' of his hard work in Rome), we have long known about some of them. The most celebrated is the 'Et iterum venturus est', which, much extended and developed, was to become, thirteen years later, the 'Tuba mirum' of the Requiem. In 1824 it had a part for tam-tam, which Berlioz himself played at the premiere, hitting it – he said – with such force that the whole church shook.[5] (The tam-tam was removed in 1827; at the same time the voice part, originally for solo bass, was given to all the chorus basses.) Immediately afterwards in the 'Resurrexit' the

[5] *Correspondance générale*, Vol. I, p. 96.

tempo quickens and the chorus, to the same words, sings a motif that will reappear in the tumultuous carnival scene in *Benvenuto Cellini*, at the point where, Pompeo (in friar's robe) having just been killed by Cellini, the words are 'Assassiner un capucin'. Another tune from the 'Resurrexit' forms the basis of the immense ensemble that concludes the first act of the opera.

As the rest of the Mass now reveals, these are by no means the only examples of later borrowing. Berlioz used to be severely reproached for this kind of thing, either on the grounds that it smacked of cynical opportunism or because it showed him running out of ideas, or both. Such criticism has always seemed to me wide of the mark. It is normal practice for composers to relocate their ideas, and a perfectly reasonable one. Often an idea will fit better in a new setting. Two of the most moving passages in *Fidelio*, the 'Namenlose Freude' duet and the ensemble 'O Gott, welch' ein Augenblick', started life in quite different contexts. Berlioz had the bad luck that several of his rejected works, through no fault of his own, survived. (Brahms was altogether more successful in covering his tracks.) It is no surprise, and no reproach, to find the same thing happening in the Mass.

One of the most startling cases is the 'Gratias agimus'. We have heard it before (in much more developed form), but I see no reason to be dismayed. The slow movement of the *Symphonie fantastique* is by no means devalued by the pre-existence of the tune in the Mass. Aesthetically its re-use makes good sense. The atmosphere of devotion, serene yet tinged with anxiety, translates fittingly from one dramatic context to the other; the difference is that in the first it is devotion before God, in the second devotion before Nature. One can well understand that the idea was destined to find fulfilment in the landscape of the 'Scène aux champs'. The same may be said of the borrowing, or rather transformation, of a theme in the 'Gloria', which turns up near the beginning of the carnival presto in *Benvenuto Cellini*. Though the 'Gloria' is taken, on the Gardiner recording, at a speed that overtaxes even the excellent sopranos of the Monteverdi Choir, I think we can agree that the tune required a different incarnation to find its true nature.

The 'Gratias agimus' is notable not only for the glimpse it gives of the slow movement of the *Fantastique* but as the first known example of something that will recur throughout Berlioz's *œuvre*, the sonority of soprano and alto voices alone, especially, though not exclusively, in a religious context. There are other examples in the Mass. I have no doubt that the predilection goes back to that crucial moment described in the *Memoirs*, when the voices of the young girls of the convent school singing the Eucharistic hymn just as he was taking his first communion left an impression he never forgot. He relived the experience many times.[6] We recognise the influence of that early epiphany in the innocent sounds of 'To Thee all angels cry aloud' in the Te Deum and also in the little-known but charming *Prière du matin*. Given the intensity of what he calls his 'first musical experience' it is no surprise to find the trait already apparent in the *Messe solennelle*. In that respect at least the work is characteristic of the Berlioz we know.

So it is, too, in two other examples that have come to us, like the 'Gratias', absolutely out of the blue. The first is in the opening 'Kyrie', a fugal movement whose D minor theme in $\frac{3}{4}$ time is familiar from its later incarnation in the 'Offertorium' of the Requiem, There it is in common time, the mood less anxious, the fugal texture much richer – the whole thing, in fact, radically reworked. In addition, the repeated two-note chant of the souls in purgatory adds a sense as of the unnumbered generations of the human race that universalises the prayer. But the melody is exactly the same, in its winding contours, its accidentals of E flat, F sharp and G sharp, and the insistent accent on the final beat.

The other example is even more remarkable. That Berlioz was able to reuse ideas from this product of his youthful inexperience – and one can hardly say of him what he said of the young Saint-Saëns, that 'he lacks inexperience'[7] – is not after all so surprising. One could have predicted that even at twenty, with so little study behind him and in spite of his subsequent lack of enthusiasm for the work, it would have contained some inspirations, some *trouvailles*. But that at a period when his true style had yet to be formed, he should have composed an entire movement, the 'Agnus Dei', so characteristic that it could go largely unchanged into one of his grandest scores, the Te Deum – that is astonishing. Apart from a different rhythmic *ostinato* in the string accompaniment, the chords for cornets and trombones in the passage for women's voices are all that are new in the 'Te ergo quesumus' of the Te Deum. At the end Berlioz extended the music by about 40 new bars in G major. Otherwise, it is essentially the same. We can now see the significance of the title 'Agnus de la messe solennelle', which figures in an autograph list of 1845 of manuscripts in his possession that was discovered not long ago. You can well understand why he kept the piece.

Perhaps the most remarkable thing about the Mass is the effectiveness of the music that doesn't sound like Berlioz and that he never made use of

[6] *Memoirs*, p. 6.

[7] Quoted in Jean Bonnerot, *Saint-Saëns*, Durand, Paris, 1922, p. 43: 'Il sait tout, mais il manque d'inexpérience'.

again. He himself wrote disparagingly of the work as a 'clumsy imitation of Le Sueur'.[8] If we knew Le Sueur's music better, we would be in a position to confirm, or not, the accuracy of that judgement. As it is, you can see why, when the revelation of Beethoven's symphonies, of a totally new world of music, forced him to repudiate Le Sueur, he should reject most of what he had written before. There are feeble passages in the Mass, and moments of clumsy writing such as you might expect from someone who had been studying for such a short time, and there are one or two movements, among the fourteen that make up the score, that go through the motions without much conviction. One such is the Offertory motet, which he added to the liturgy on the model of the Cherubini Masses he heard at the Chapel Royal. (Since the text is from the Book of Exodus, where the Israelites' escape from the Egyptians is described, the movement may well have originally belonged to an earlier Berlioz score, *Le Passage de la mer rouge*, which has not survived.) In the opening bars we are back in the eighteenth century, if not the Baroque.

The 'Sanctus', too, though vigorous, is without much interest. As for the 'Quoniam', it attracted the composer's wrath, as we have seen: 'Il faut refaire cette exécrable fugue'; and he goes on to swear that he will 'never write a fugue except when the dramatic situation, in an opera, demands a piece in this form: a chorus of drunkards, or a battle between incarnate devils'. He didn't keep to his oath: there are formal fugues in both the Requiem and the Te Deum; but otherwise he did more or less exactly as he said he would. The drunkards in Auerbach's Cellar in *La Damnation de Faust* sing a fugal Amen, and in the finale of the *Symphonie fantastique* the demons assembled for the Witches' Sabbath take part in a danced fugue. The 'Quoniam' at least has the merit of being extremely short – it lasts a minute and a half on the recording – and it is made bearable, if not redeemed, by its energy, as is generally the case with even the dullest pages of the work.

What strikes one most of all about the Mass is its sense of purpose even when it is least typical of Berlioz's music as we know it. The *Credo* – austere, virile music – is one example of that. It leads to an 'Et incarnatus' of touching gentleness and innocence, in a C major practically pure of accidentals, which again doesn't sound like Berlioz but is impressive. In the graphic music of the 'Crucifixus' we find a Berlioz already in possession of the skills to translate his vision into sound and handle the chromatic harmonies with some assurance. The end of the movement, after the darkness of the tomb, is particularly memorable, with its isolated,

[8] *Memoirs*, p. 29.

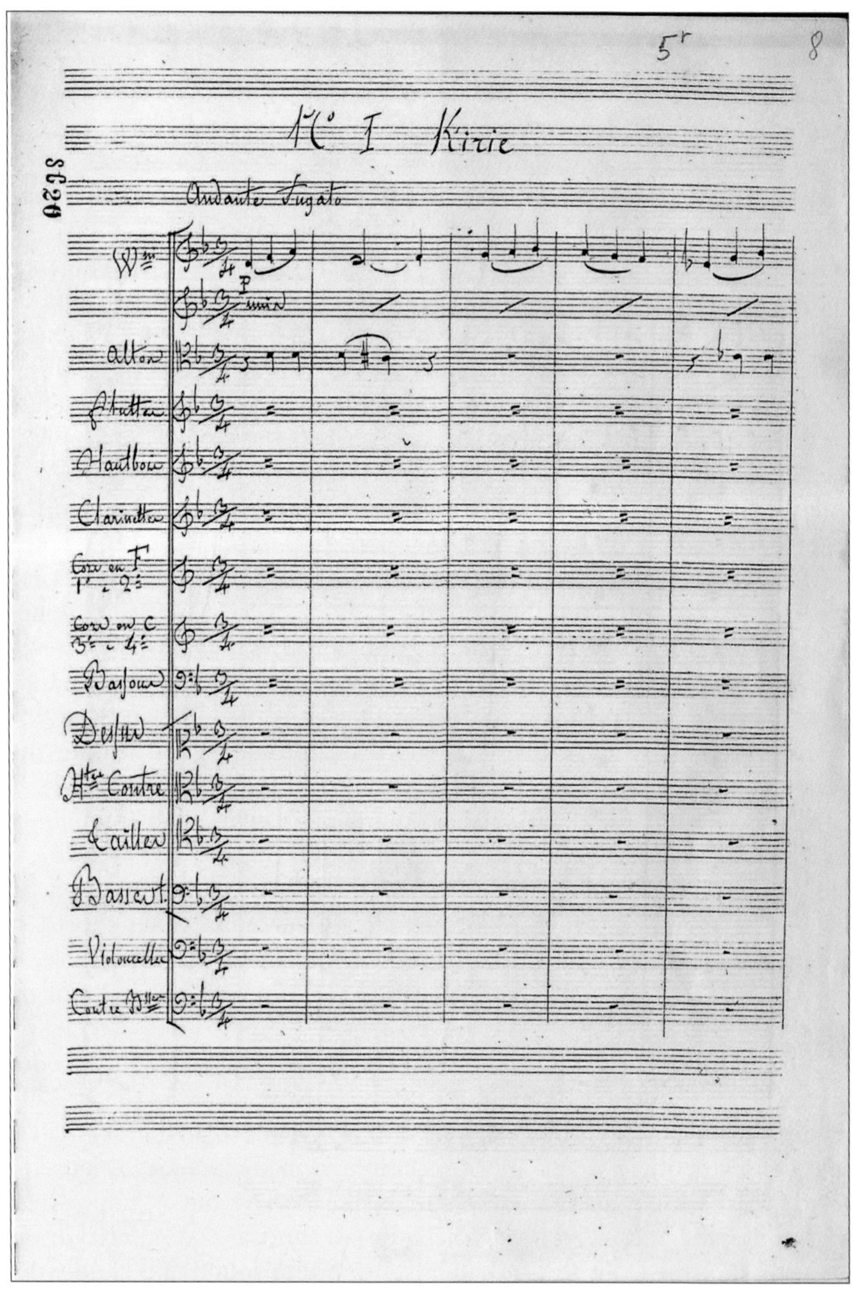

The first pages of the 'Kyrie' of the Messe solennelle *and of the 'Offertoire' of the* Grande Messe des morts

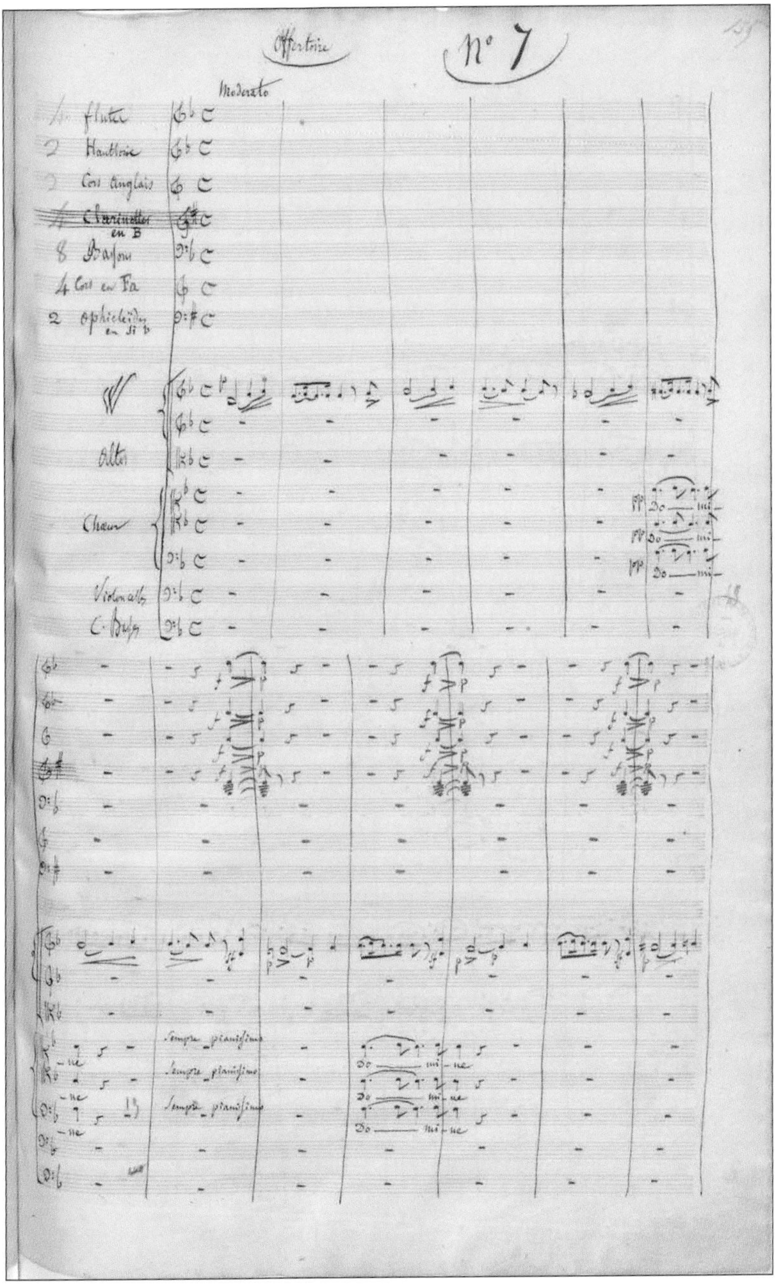
Offertoire
N° 7
Moderato
Cor anglais
en B
Basson
Cors en Fa
en si b
Choeur
Do — mi — ne
Sempre pianissimo

suspenseful horn notes, then the vivid flash (*fortissimo* woodwind and brass, *tremolo* strings and timpani) for the actual moment of Resurrection, followed by the luminous ascent of strings and woodwind. Berlioz the dramatist is suddenly present.

The end of the 'Kyrie', too, again without sounding like him, generates real excitement. The two themes, Kyrie and Christe, are superimposed (it's interesting to see Berlioz already concerned with long-range musical architecture), the tempo accelerates, D minor turns to D major and the brass and the drums (offbeat) come in with thunderous effect as the young composer throws all his forces into the attack. Hugh Macdonald calls it 'a blistering fortissimo',[9] and it is. Writing to his Dauphinois friend Albert Du Boys after the first performance, Berlioz described how he was so stirred by the crescendo and the timpani strokes that he began talking compulsively. 'I don't know what I was saying, but at the end of the movement Valentino, the conductor, said: "My friend, try to keep calm if you don't want me to lose my place".'[10] It's nice that we now know what it was that excited him so much.

The 'Kyrie' is one of the movements that seem most to have impressed the audience. And the 'O salutaris' (another Cherubini-inspired insertion into the Mass) won Berlioz the approval of the formidable Mme Lebrun, singer and celebrated character, who leant over and, grasping his hand, her witchlike features creased in a glittering smile, exclaimed: 'B--- me, my dear child, that's a Salutaris with no flies on it. I bet none of the little f-----rs in the Conservatoire counterpoint classes could write a piece so neat and so damn religious.'[11]

That, in brief, is Berlioz's *Messe solennelle*. Despite its exalted position in what Bärenreiter calls its 'hit list', I cannot see it becoming a repertory work. It is too uneven for that. Nonetheless it is a rather wonderful discovery. It might have turned out an awkward and insignificant piece of prentice work. In fact, it is moving testimony to the twenty-year-old composer's audacity and strength of will, to the confidence with which he takes on a score of this scope and importance less than two years after the beginning of his studies, and to the ability he has acquired in so short a time. Derivative though it may be, in the composer's own estimation, and superseded by his real work, it shows us a young artist dedicated to his vocation, sure of his genius, to a remarkable extent in command of himself and his means – a composer who sees his objective clearly before him and knows he has only to work patiently to achieve

[9] Hugh Macdonald, 'Berlioz's *Messe solennelle*', *19th-Century Music*, XVI/3, Spring 1993, pp. 267–85.
[10] *Memoirs*, p. 95.
[11] 'F and B were her two preferred consonants': *Journal des débats*, 24 October 1857.

it. The *Messe solennelle* alters our picture of Berlioz's apprenticeship; and, inconvenient as it may be for some of us, I don't any longer wish it undiscovered.

Shakespeare – Our Father

'Shakespeare – Our Father' was a talk given at the Berlioz Society Members' Weekend in November 2010, and reproduced in the Berlioz Society Bulletin *No. 185 (April 2011).*

I will begin with texts – lots of texts. Shakespeare is one of the main threads, perhaps the central thread, running through Berlioz's existence as an artist, from 1827, his 24th year, to the end – even, as I shall attempt to show, through his existence as a human being – uniting it, binding it, making sense of it: Shakespeare (with Goethe), as he writes in 1828 to his 'Horatio', Humbert Ferrand, 'the silent confidant of my griefs, the interpreter of my life'.[1] You will know many of these texts, so I must ask you to forgive me for repeating what is already familiar to you: they are necessary to the picture, the argument that I am trying to construct.

First, the *Memoirs*:

> Shakespeare, falling upon me unawares, struck me like a thunderbolt. The lightning flash, the sublime explosion, of that discovery opened before me in an instant the whole heaven of art, illuminating it to its remotest depths. I saw dramatic grandeur, dramatic beauty, dramatic truth in their real form. At the same time I recognised the utter absurdity of the French view of Shakespeare that derives from Voltaire [here Berlioz quotes Victor Hugo], 'that ape of genius, sent among men by Satan to do his work', and the pitiful narrowness of our worn-out, cloistered academic traditions of poetry. I saw, I understood, I felt … that I was alive and that I must arise and walk.[2]

The use of Biblical language – Jesus' words to the centurion's daughter – to evoke the miracle of that momentous revelation was not peculiar to Berlioz: it was common to the young artists transfixed by the performances of the English company at the Odéon. Dumas' 'Imagine a man blind from birth receiving the gift of sight and discovering a world of which he had had no inkling' evokes another of Jesus' acts of healing.[3] Berlioz's instant passion for the actress playing Ophelia may have made it a double revelation. But the whole Romantic movement in France interpreted the coming of Shakespeare in religious terms. It was the earthquake that blew apart their prison gates

[1] *Correspondance générale*, Vol. I, p. 208.

[2] *Memoirs*, pp. 70–71.

[3] *Théâtre complet de Alex. Dumas*, Vol. 1, Michel Lévy Frères, Paris, 1863, pp. 14–15.

un dégré voisin de zéro le thermomètre de l'enthousiasme.
Les magnificences religieuses de La Flûte enchantée m'avaient, il est vrai, rempli d'admiration, mais ce fut dans le Pasticcio des Mystères d'Isis que je les contemplai pour la première fois, et je ne pus que plus tard, à la bibliothèque du Conservatoire, comparer la partition originale à l'odieux pot-pourri français qu'on exécutait à l'opéra.
L'œuvre dramatique de ce grand compositeur m'avait, on le voit, été mal présentée dans son ensemble, et c'est plusieurs années après seulement, que, grâces à des circonstances moins défavorables, je pus en goûter le charme et l'inimitable perfection. ~~Les beautés merveilleuses de ses quatuors, de ses quintettes et de quelques unes de ses Sonates furent les premières à me ramener au culte de l'angélique génie, dont la fréquentation, trop bien constatée, des Italiens et des pédagogues contrepointistes, a peu à peu en quelques endroits altéré la pureté.~~

XVIII (18)

(Apparition de Shakespeare. Léthargie morale. Mon premier concert. Opposition comique de Cherubini. Sa défaite. Premier serpent à sonnettes.)

Je touche ici au plus grand drame de ma vie. Je n'en raconterai point les douloureuses péripéties. Je me bornerai à dire ceci: Un théâtre anglais vint donner à Paris des représentations des drames de Shakespeare alors complètement inconnus au public Français. J'assistai à la première apparition d'Hamlet à l'Odeon. ~~Je vis, dans le rôle d'Ophelia, Henriette Smithson qui, cinq ans après est devenue ma femme. L'effet de son prodigieux talent ou plutôt de son génie dramatique sur mon imagination et sur mon cœur, n'est comparable qu'au ravage exercé sur eux par le poète dont elle était la digne interprète. Je ne puis rien dire de plus~~. Shakespeare en tombant ainsi sur moi à l'improviste me foudroya. Son éclair en m'ouvrant le ciel de l'art avec

In chapter 18 of his Memoirs
Berlioz describes the 'plus grande drame de ma vie' –
his first encounter with Shakespeare

and set them free. We can't exaggerate the extent to which they felt 'cabin'd, cribb'd, confin'd' by the 'narrowness of our worn-out, cloistered academic traditions of poetry' and the joyous sense of liberation Shakespeare brought. It was like a totally new way of conceiving and creating art. Remember the composer Henri Berton – member of the Fine Arts Academy of the Institute and one of the judges in the Prix de Rome competition – giving Berlioz a patronising little homily after his failure with the 1827 cantata *La Mort d'Orphée*, only a few weeks before the Shakespearean *coup de foudre*. 'Novelty in music? It's an illusion, my dear. There's no such thing. The great masters conformed to certain musical procedures, but you don't want to. You think you can do better than them?'[4]

Academic art, wrote Hugo in the preface to his *Odes et ballades* the year before, seeks to impose fixed models on artists, to codify what is permitted and what is not. But art cannot be bound by preordained rules. The spirit of imitation taught in the academies is the negation of true art, for which there can be only one model, nature, and only one guide, truth.

Shakespeare was the answer, the saviour, the bible of the Jeunes-France, as the Romantics styled themselves – in Berlioz's words, 'the voice out of the burning bush'.[5] He *was* drama, wrote Hugo in the manifesto that was the preface to his verse drama *Cromwell*: 'drama that mingles in one and the same breath the grotesque and the sublime, the awe-inspiring and the clownish, Tragedy and Comedy'. Shakespeare's plays depicted human existence as they imagined it, as they lived it. What had that to do with the academicians' good taste? 'Farewell for ever good taste', exulted Delacroix. 'It behoves the Academy to declare all imports of the kind incompatible with public decency'.[6]

If we can't exaggerate the constricting hold of academic rules on the young artists of the time, equally we can't exaggerate the life-giving impact, the exhilarating shock of an art that, in the service of a poetic style of infinite variety and total flexibility, simply ignored the precepts of French Classical drama – the unities of time, place and action, the eternal separation of genres – and whose language freely mixed poetry and prose, the lofty and the colloquial, the grandly rhetorical and the down to earth, and saw nothing wrong in intruding popular forms on a tragic context: the mad Ophelia's bawdy songs, the allusion to phallic flowers in the Queen's account of Ophelia's drowning, the sentry's 'not a mouse stirring' that so offended Voltaire.

[4] *Correspondance générale*, Vol. I, p. 161.

[5] *Memoirs*, p. 509.

[6] *Correspondance générale d'Eugène Delacroix*, Vol. 1, Plon, Paris, 1935, p. 198.

But if Shakespeare's art overthrew the old rules, that didn't mean he didn't have any – on the contrary. Voltaire and his kind thought the plays disorderly. But what was crucial in the lessons to be learned from them, and what Berlioz was not slow to realise, was that they obeyed rules but the rules were their own, made afresh each time in response to the demands of the specific dramatic context and material. I shall come back to this point later.

In identifying particularly with Hamlet, Berlioz was no different from thousands of young people. It was as if Hamlet had been created for them: his longings, his doubts and sufferings, his self-questioning, his angst, held the mirror up to their own souls. But perhaps with Berlioz it went especially deep. Hamlet goes with him all his life. He is his companion in Italy[7] and ever afterwards. It is not a reassuring presence. Desolation is the word he uses in the monologue in *Lélio* invoking and celebrating Shakespeare – Hamlet, 'that profound but bleak creation', 'que de mal tu m'as fait' – what harm it has done him, echoing his own inner torments, playing on, exacerbating them.

Writing to his sister Adèle nearly 30 years later, while composing *Les Troyens*, it is Hamlet again, still Hamlet:

> Yesterday evening I had the misfortune to open a volume – I've three editions of Shakespeare, two in English, one a 'translation'. I chanced on *Hamlet*, and couldn't put it down. I re-read it from end to end. I'm knocked out by it – it's as if my heart were alternately contracting and dilating, at that prodigious and devastating picture of human life, at the awe caused by the contemplation of so huge a genius, at thinking of the causes that still prevent so many people from understanding him, at the crimes of his interpreters and translators – and the poet's indifference to the effect he produces, like the sun, which pours its light on the earth without troubling itself whether the clouds of this puny planet get in the way.[8]

'What a world a masterpiece like that is', he exclaims, after seeing the play in London in 1848:

> How this one above all harrows you, heart and soul! Shakespeare was bent on depicting the nothingness of life, the vanity of human designs, the tyranny of chance, the utter indifference of Fate or God to what we call virtue, crime, beauty, ugliness, love, hate, genius, stupidity. And how cruelly he succeeded.[9]

1848 was the year Berlioz completed the dark *Marche funèbre pour la dernière scène d'Hamlet*, first drafted in 1844 at the time of the breakdown of his marriage, as part of incidental music for a projected production of the play, which in the event didn't take place, and then revised four years later,

[7] *Cf.*, for example, *Correspondance générale*, Vol. I, pp. 418, 443, etc.
[8] *Ibid.*, Vol. V, p. 379.
[9] *Ibid.*, Vol. III, p. 547.

very probably in response to a new loss, the death of his beloved father. The year before, on his way back from Russia, Berlioz sees a performance of *Hamlet* in Riga and, writing to his new Russian friend Count Michael Wielhorsky, cries out: 'As always I was turned upside down by that marvel of the greatest of all human geniuses'.[10]

Hamlet continues to be his gospel. In the mid-1860s he takes to reading it aloud, along with *Coriolanus* and *Othello*, to groups of friends. 'In general he read well', his friend Stephen Heller recalled, 'though often he let himself be carried away by his feelings. At the finest moments tears flowed down his cheeks, but he went on, hastily brushing them aside so as not to interrupt the reading.'[11] These readings would have been in French; but to himself, in his later years at least, he generally read Shakespeare in the original. When in a letter written during the composition of *Les Troyens* he quotes, in French, Lear's 'I am a foolish fond old man… I think this lady to be my child Cordelia', Cordelia's reply – 'and so I am, I am' – is given in English.[12]

The letter – if I may digress for a moment – shows that the ancient French objections to Shakespeare's 'barbarity' were, even then, not dead. 'Have you read the tedious inaugural address of Ponsard [the academician]? Is it *possible*? A parochial Voltairean […] setting up a hullabaloo against Shakespeare's fame?' Thanks to the notes by Hugh Macdonald, editor of Volume V of the *Correspondance générale*, we know what Ponsard ('that noodle, that over-ripe cucumber', as Berlioz calls him) said: 'sublime touches surrounded by bombast and turgidity, profound observations side by side with childish babblings'. It is this that prompts Berlioz to quote the lines from *King Lear* just cited – he has, he says, been reading the play in bed.

He knows his Shakespeare – not just the obvious plays but the whole corpus. Jacques Barzun found that Berlioz alludes to over twenty of the plays in his writings, including even a quotation from *Henry VI* (a calculation that was made in the 1940s, on the basis of far fewer letters and articles than are now available).[13] But *Hamlet* remained his favourite, as is testified by the young musician Louis Bourgault-Ducoudray, winner of the Prix de Rome in 1862, whose encounter with Berlioz that same year at the corner of the Chaussée d'Antin and the boulevard des Italiens and their long walk arm in arm through the streets of Paris is the subject of one of the most vivid pictures we have of Berlioz in his later years. I quote a part of it:

[10] *Ibid.*, Vol. III, p. 433.

[11] *Revue et Gazette Musicale*, March 1879.

[12] *Correspondance générale*, Vol. V, p. 402.

[13] Jacques Barzun, *Berlioz and the Romantic Century*, Columbia University Press, New York, 3rd edn., 1969, Vol. 2, p. 220, note 15.

> That evening Berlioz was in the vein – you could say 'in eruption': his liveliness had something volcanic, his energy overflowed as though from a crater. His mind didn't merely flash, it blazed. What a walk we had! If I live to be a hundred[14] I shall never forget it. His dazzling improvisations were in every key, broached every subject: memories of his youth, intimate outpourings, theories of art, grand musical conflicts, favourite books, historical figures exalted or brought low. Meanwhile we elbowed passers-by, turned round abruptly and retraced our steps, threaded our way through, as if the whirlwind his thoughts revolved in had created a torrential current sweeping us along. […] Before long, amid this swarm of ideas and characters, Shakespeare inevitably made his appearance – Shakespeare his favourite poet […], whose plays were the Bible by which this votary of poetry and art lived. Berlioz admired all Shakespeare, but I think he had a special predilection for *Hamlet*. He had made a written translation of long passages, and dreamed of translating the whole play.[15]

Before we leave *Hamlet* – always a difficult thing to do – I should mention the other completed piece inspired by it, *La Mort d'Ophélie*, the intensely sad *mélodie* that is an elegy not just for the character herself but for the actress whose interpretation had stamped itself on a whole generation in France, and the wife whom Berlioz never ceased to cherish. The identification is made unmistakable by the clear reference in the first nine notes of the vocal line (Ex. 7(a)) to the *idée fixe* of the *Symphonie fantastique* – Harriet's theme (Ex. 7(b)).

Ex. 7

(a)

(b)

[14] He lived to be 70, being born on 2 February 1840, in Nantes, and dying on 4 July 1910, in Vernouillet, to the north-west of Paris.

[15] 'Les Musiciens célèbres: Berlioz, souvenirs intimes', in *Le Conseiller des dames et des demoiselles*, 1 February 1886.

Hamlet, and Ophelia, Berlioz's remote, inaccessible star, had been powerful presences behind the composition of the *Huit Scènes de Faust* in the winter of 1828–29. When he told Ferrand that he was dedicating the published score to the Vicomte de la Rochefoucauld, he added: 'it was not meant for him' – it was meant for *her*.[16] In a resounding declaration of Romanticism, each of the eight numbers carried an epigraph from *Hamlet* or *Romeo and Juliet* – for *Romeo and Juliet* was, of course, the other Shakespeare play that Berlioz saw Smithson perform.

The writer Armand de Pontmartin was there on that memorable night and, without knowing who he was, spotted Berlioz in the pit, sitting further along the same row, and marked his rapt profile, with its distinctive nose, but above all, he said, 'his eyes, of a pale, intense grey, fixed on Juliet with the expression of ecstasy that pre-Renaissance painters gave their saints and angels. Body and soul were totally absorbed in that consuming gaze'.[17]

The impact of *Romeo and Julie*t on Berlioz was as dramatic as that of *Hamlet*, as the *Memoir*s make clear. The contrast between the two works, seen one after the other, overwhelmed him.

> After the melancholy of *Hamlet*, after the agonising griefs, the tragic love, the cruel ironies and black meditations, the heartbreak, the madness, the tears, the bereavements, the disasters and fatal accidents, after Denmark's sombre clouds and icy winds, to be exposed to the fiery sun and balmy nights of Italy, to witness the drama of that passion swift as thought, burning as lava, radiant and pure as an angel's smile, imperious, irresistible, immense, the raging vendettas, the desperate kisses, the frantic strife of love and death – it was more than I could bear. By the third act, scarcely able to breathe, it was as though an iron hand gripped me by the heart. I knew, with utter conviction, that I was lost.[18]

Lost, yes; but the mind was soon active, pondering the lessons of Shakespeare, the profound consequences for his art. Six months later came the complementary revelation of Beethoven, with the *Eroica* and the Fifth at the Conservatoire concerts – complementary, because Beethoven's symphonies taught a similar truth: that each major work is a unique poetic world, for which the right form must be found and forged anew; also that symphony equals drama, a drama every bit as real and vivid as opera, if not more so; for, in Berlioz's words, 'music' – and by that he meant music as revealed by Beethoven – 'has wings too wide to spread fully within the confines of a theatre'.[19]

[16] *Correspondance générale*, Vol. I, p. 245.

[17] Armand de Pontmartin, *Nouveaux samedis*, Paris, 1880, pp. 101–2.

[18] *Memoirs*, pp. 72–73.

[19] *Correspondance générale*, Vol. II, p. 198.

Harriet Smithson as the demented Ophelia in Act 4, scene 5, of Hamlet: *lithograph from 1827 by Achille Devéria (1800–57) and Louis Boulanger (1806–67)*

The 'Dramatic Symphony after Shakespeare's *Romeo and Juliet*' was Berlioz's repayment of his debt to the two supreme creators who had shown him the way.[20] But if I may, I will quote from Berlioz's *feuilleton* in the *Journal des débats* of 13 September 1859 (later incorporated in *À travers chants*), because it shows how deeply the Tomb Scene, in the Garrick version of the play (where Juliet wakes before the poison has killed Romeo), burned itself into his consciousness, so that 32 years later he was still reliving it:

> At the name of 'Romeo', breathed out faintly from the lips of the reviving Juliet, the young Montague stands motionless, riveted. As the voice calls a second time, more tenderly, he turns towards the tomb. He gazes at her. There is movement. He can no longer doubt – she is alive! He flings himself on the funeral couch, snatches up the beloved body, tearing away veils and shrouds, carries it to the front of the stage and holds it upright in his arms. Juliet looks dully about her from sleep-drugged eyes. Romeo calls her name, he clasps

[20] On the occasion when this paper was delivered, *Roméo et Juliette* was the subject of a paper by John Warrack and so is not discussed at length here.

y trouvera peut-être quelques rares sympathies; les cœurs déchirés s'y reconnaitront. Un tel morceau est incompréhensible pour la plupart des Français, et absurde et insensé pour des Italiens.

En sortant de la représentation d'Hamlet, épouvanté de ce que j'y avais ressenti, je m'étais promis formellement de ne pas m'exposer de nouveau à la flamme Shakespearienne. Le lendemain on afficha Romeo and Juliet .... J'avais mes entrées à l'orchestre de l'Odéon; eh bien, dans la crainte que de nouveaux ordres donnés au concierge du théatre ne vinssent m'empêcher de m'y introduire comme à l'ordinaire, aussitôt après avoir vu l'annonce du redoutable Drame, je courus au bureau de location acheter une stalle pour m'assurer ainsi doublement de mon entrée. Il n'en fallait pas tant pour m'achever.

après la mélancolie, les navrantes douleurs, l'amour éploré, les ironies cruelles, les noires méditations, les brisements de cœur, la folie, les larmes, les deuils, les catastrophes, les sinistres hasards d'Hamlet, après les sombres nuages, les vents glacés du Danemarck, m'exposer à l'ardent soleil, aux nuits ~~enivrantes et~~ embaumées de l'Italie, assister au spectacle de cet amour prompt comme la pensée, brulant comme la lave, impérieux, irrésistible, immense, et pur et beau comme le sourire des anges, à ces scènes furieuses de vengeances, à ces étreintes éperdues, à ces luttes désespérées de l'amour et de la mort, c'était trop. aussi, dès le troisième acte, tombant brisé à genoux sur un siège placé devant moi, respirant à peine, et souffrant comme si une main de fer m'eut ~~[illegible]~~ étreint ~~[illegible]~~ le cœur, je me dis avec une entière conviction: ah! je suis perdu. Il faut ajouter que je ne savais pas alors un seul mot d'anglais, que je n'entrevoyais Shakespeare qu'au travers des brouillards de la traduction de Letourneur et que je n'appercevais

Berlioz's Memoirs *on the impact of* Romeo and Juliet

> her in a desperate embrace, parts the hair hiding her pale forehead, covers her face with kisses, laughing convulsively. In his heartrending delight he has forgotten that he is dying. Juliet breathes deeply. Juliet! Juliet! But a stab of agony recalls him: the poison is at work, devouring his vitals. 'O potent poison! Capulet, Capulet, forbear!' He crawls on his knees. Delirious, he imagines he sees Juliet's father come once more to take her from him.

The classicists might inveigh against the violence of Shakespeare's plays and question whether it was really the province of art to portray the detailed physical agonies of a dying man: Berlioz had no doubts. The Tomb Scene is the most extreme music he ever wrote.

The other point I'd like to make about the *Romeo* symphony is that it doesn't come into existence until nearly twelve years after Berlioz sees the play in September 1827. The process is necessarily long drawn out. There is no doubt that from the first the thought of some kind of musical response to the experience was in his mind. As he says in the *Memoirs*, apropos of the Prix de Rome cantata of 1829, *Cléopâtre,* he had 'often in my imagination conceived a musical equivalent of Juliet's wonderful monologue "How if, when I am laid into the tomb", a passage that had something in common, at least in its sense of dread', with the feelings expressed in the doomed queen's 'Grands Pharaons'[21] (he had the temerity to inscribe the line on his manuscript score, followed by the still more provocative 'Shakesp.'). Long before that, he was certainly having musical ideas inspired by the play. At first, before the discovery of Beethoven in early 1828, they would not have been symphonic – a symphony was the last thing he would have thought of writing. But that discovery changed everything. We have the testimony of Émile Deschamps, who was to be the librettist of Berlioz's symphony, that he and Berlioz discussed some such work in 1829.[22] Two years later, there was the conversation with Mendelssohn in the Roman Campagna, about a possible composition based on Mercutio's Queen Mab speech;[23] and, not long after that, the *Romeo* scenario set out in Berlioz's 'Letter from an Enthusiast on the Present State of Music in Italy'.[24]

In terms of practical issues, it was not until Paganini's princely gift of December 1838 that Berlioz had the financial security and the freedom of mind to attempt what was arguably the most demanding challenge of his artistic career until then (a work about which commentators have been arguing ever since). But I think we can nonetheless see a pattern here – that Berlioz, usually, didn't rush into things. He himself said, of the composition

21 *Memoirs*, p. 100.

22 Émile Deschamps, *Œuvres complètes*, Vol. 6, Alphonse Lemerre, Paris, 1874, p. i.

23 *Memoirs*, p. 150.

24 *Revue européenne*, March–May 1832; republished in *Critique musicale*, Vol. 1, 1823–34, ed. H. Robert Cohen and Yves Gérard, Buchet/Chastel, Paris, 1996, pp. 69–83.

of the Thomas Moore song *Élégie*, which he wrote immediately on coming upon his copy of Moore's book open at the poem, after returning from one of his Harriet Smithson-haunted treks over the countryside, that it was 'the sole occasion when I was able to express an emotion of the kind directly in music while still under its active influence'.[25]

One might point out that *La Captive* was also written straight off in comparable conditions. But Berlioz might equally retort that *La Captive* hardly embodies an emotion of the same kind. One might also object that the *King Lear* overture was composed only a week or two after Berlioz read the play for the first time. Those, however, were exceptional circumstances. At that moment he desperately needed the balm of composition, after the trauma of his rejection by Camille Moke. As Horace Vernet said, in the friendly letter that Berlioz received in Nice, the sovereign remedies for an afflicted mind were love of one's art and concentrated hard work.[26]

Generally speaking, it's surely true to say that Berlioz waits and ponders, and lets new influences ferment and germinate and bear fruit in their own time. The process by which his creative imagination absorbed the impact of an unfamiliar style was habitually long and slow; the first composition that sounds at all like Beethoven, the slow movement of the *Symphonie fantastique*, was written a good two years or more after Berlioz discovered his music. One of the most fallacious of the many received ideas about him is that he threw himself heedlessly and recklessly into important projects without first thinking them through.

I am now going to leap forward in time and pass over the *Tempest* Fantasy, the *King Lear* overture and other pieces, and spend the rest of this talk on *Les Troyens*. Of all Berlioz's works that took their time to come to life and that waited for the moment, it is the prime example – written, after 40 years' gestation, to 'satisfy a passion that flamed up in my childhood and that has grown continually since then'.[27]

It is also, I think, the major exemplar of Shakespeare's influence on Berlioz, and by no means only because the love duet in Act 4 of the opera was based on the last act of *The Merchant of Venice*. 'In such a night', Jessica's and Lorenzo's duet – one can really call it that – had long been familiar and dear to Berlioz. He quoted it often, in a variety of contexts: for instance, in the speech made in Strasbourg in 1863, celebrating the new bridge over the Rhine: 'The great poet has said: "The man that has no music in himself/Is fit for treasons, stratagems and spoils –/Let no such man be trusted"'.[28] In 1855

[25] *Memoirs*, p. 71.

[26] *Ibid.*, p. 137.

[27] *Correspondance générale*, Vol. V, p. 548.

[28] *Cf. ibid.*, Vol. VI, p. 464.

he managed to work 'In such a night' into what was supposed to be a review of the latest offering at the Théâtre-Lyrique.[29]

Already, the year before, in 1854, with the idea for an opera on the *Aeneid* more and more pressing on his mind, he paid tribute in a *feuilleton* to the great soprano Henriette Sontag, who had just died: she 'would have been worthy to sing the incomparable love duet in the last act of *The Merchant of Venice*'.[30] Clearly he is already thinking of it as a source for the love duet that would be needed in such an opera; with its references to Dido 'on the wild sea banks', wafting 'her love to come again to Carthage', and to Troilus on the walls of Troy, 'sighing his soul toward the Grecian tents', it is an obvious and necessary source, one might say an unavoidable one.

Berlioz would no doubt have noticed, from his constant reading of Shakespeare, that the poet of the *Aeneid* is a frequent presence in the plays. Dido in particular is a recurring figure: for example, in *A Midsummer Night's Dream*, where Hermia swears she loves Lysander 'by that fire which burn'd the Carthage queen/When the false Trojan under sail was seen' (an image Shakespeare took directly from Virgil, not from Marlowe's *Dido, Queen of Carthage*, where it doesn't appear); in *Antony and Cleopatra*, when the dying Antony refers to her; in *The Merchant of Venice* (as we have seen); and in *The Tempest*, where 'Widow Dido' is bandied about in the conversation of the shipwrecked courtiers. Long before Berlioz knew anything of Shakespeare, when the boy Hector wept at Dido's fate, he was already linked unknowingly with the dramatist who would reveal to him 'a new universe of poetry', and whose 'so potent art' would pervade and shape his Virgilian opera.

'Virgil Shakespeareanised' was his phrase for *Les Troyens*.[31] In the task of reducing his chosen books of the *Aeneid* to the dimensions and demands of opera – of reconciling the conflicting claims of dramatic coherence and the richness, colour and diversity of the Virgilian world – Shakespeare was his guide and the inspiration for much, much more than the text of the love duet. Shakespeare's open form, his free mixing of genres, his genius for achieving coherence by means far subtler and deeper than the unities of time and place and action – all this is manifest in the way Berlioz created his music-drama. From the beginning it was a joint enterprise; he wrote the work – this 'spectacle Virgilio-Shakespearien' – under the aegis of both.[32]

[29] *Journal des débats*, 17 April 1855; republished in *Critique musicale*, Vol. 8, 1852–55, ed. Anne Bongrain and Marie-Hélène Coudroy-Saghaï, Buchet/Chastel, Paris, 2016, p. 485.

[30] *Journal des débats*, 5 October 1854 (republished in *Critique musicale*, Vol. 8, pp. 410–13).

[31] *Correspondance générale*, Vol. VI, p. 477.

[32] *Ibid.*, Vol. V, p. 437.

Shakespearean are the time-differences and the far-flung topography of the action (think of *Othello*, *All's Well That Ends Well*, *Antony and Cleopatra*, *The Winter's Tale*), Shakespearean the infusing of the heroic with the homely (the sentries' duet in Act 5) and with the grotesque and the supernatural, and Shakespearean the resonances that unite widely separate parts of the drama: Andromache recalled in the Act 4 quintet; the vocal line of Dido's 'Pluton semble m'être propice', in Act 5, descending slowly in broken phrases through a whole octave and thus echoing the prophecy of Hector's ghost, in Act 2, that would be the cause of all her woes; the rising chromatic figure that punctuates the refrain of the love duet, echoing, again, the moment in Act 3 where Aeneas tells his son that he can teach him only the virtues of the fighting man and obedience to the gods – how to be happy he will have to learn from others – so that its recurrence in the duet at the height of the lovers' apparent bliss tells us, subliminally, that Aeneas will place duty above his happiness and Dido's. Ian Kemp has pointed out[33] yet another secret correspondence: the semitonal chordal shift heard three times in bars 7–10 of the 'Trojan March' (Act 1 finale) – the future anthem of the triumphal Roman Empire – and which insinuates itself three acts later, near the end of the Septet, quietly undermining its felicity.

Shakespearean, too, is the juxtaposing of sharply contrasted scenes so as to create new perspectives and anchor the epic in human reality: the sentries chatting about how well settled they feel in Carthage, so that the last thing they want to do is to have to leave and travel to Italy, or Hylas' song emphasising what the grand heroic issues mean in terms of the life of a single individual. All this explains and justifies Berlioz's statement, to Liszt and the Princess, that he planned to write a Virgilian opera 'on the Shakespearean plan'.[34]

I could go into this further, but instead I should like to end by considering another aspect of the relationship between Shakespeare and Berlioz, the most intimate and the most personal of all. Twice near the end of his life Berlioz singles out the four creative geniuses who have been the central, crucial presences in his life. He does so, both times, interestingly, in the context of his love for Estelle Fornier/Dubœuf. In a letter to Estelle, he tells her that meeting her again and being able to write to her and see her from time to time has been an 'unbelievable happiness – as if Virgil, Shakespeare, and Gluck and Beethoven returned to this world, all four of them, to say

[33] In conversation with the author; *cf.* also Kemp, *Hector Berlioz. Les Troyens*, Cambridge University Press, Cambridge, 1988, pp. 112 and 159.

[34] *Memoirs*, p. 532. *Cf.* Berlioz's letter to Adolphe Samuel (*Correspondance générale*, Vol. V, p. 637): 'the score was dictated both by Virgil and by Shakespeare'.

"you understood us and loved us. Come here so that we may bless you!"'[35] And on the final page of the *Memoirs* he writes: 'I must be reconciled to her [Estelle] having known me too late, as I am reconciled to not having known Virgil, whom I should have loved, or Gluck or Beethoven – or Shakespeare, who might perhaps have loved me.'[36]

The relationship with all four was – one can only call it – personal. On completing *Les Troyens*, he told his sister Adèle, he felt 'that if Gluck returned to earth he would say of me, when he heard the work, "Truly, this is my son"'. ('Not exactly modest of me, is it?', he adds; 'but at least I have the modesty to admit that lack of modesty is one of my failings.')[37] While composing the opera, he told Émile Deschamps that it was 'as if I knew Virgil, as if he knew how much I love him.'[38] Beethoven he described – in a *feuilleton* on the Bonn festival in 1845 – as 'benefactor and father',[39] and having repaired to the village of Königswinter and written the article and sent it off to the *Journal des débats*, he communed with his mighty mentor and, under his inspiration, embarked – for the first time in years – on the composition of a major work, *La Damnation de Faust*.

But with Shakespeare it was something else as well – Shakespeare, 'who might perhaps have loved me', the closest of all his companions, but also a semi-divine being, watching over him, protecting him, as Venus is always on hand to protect and guide Aeneas. 'The English are absolutely right when they say that, after God, Shakespeare created the most.' But God, for Berlioz, was no more. The faith that had burned bright in his boyhood had failed during his student years and never returned.

I remember, in Paris in the 1970s, going to see Abbé Chapot – then the eldest living descendant of Adèle Berlioz/Suat – and his saying that Berlioz had a profound need to believe, to be able to worship, to adore. Shakespeare answered that need.

In the turmoil of his feelings at the death of Harriet – the guilt, the pity, the heartbreaking sense of the waste of her genius as an artist – Berlioz turned to Shakespeare, whom Harriet Smithson had first revealed to him, changing his life. Shakespeare is the all-seeing, compassionate deity into whose hands he commends her spirit, and his own. 'Thou art our father which art in heaven – if there is a heaven.'[40] I hope that when Berlioz died he found that there is, and that Shakespeare was waiting to greet him.

[35] *Correspondance générale*, Vol. VII, p. 216.

[36] *Memoirs*, p. 570.

[37] *Correspondance générale*, Vol. V, p. 551.

[38] *Ibid.*, p. 502.

[39] *Journal des débats*, 3 September 1845; republished in *Critique musicale*, Vol. 6, 1845–48, ed. Anne Bongrain and Marie-Hélène Coudroy-Saghaï, Buchet/Chastel, Paris, 2008, p. 116.

[40] *Memoirs*, p. 505.

cesse: l'académie m'a nommé, vous
le savez déjà; et l'opéra est à peu
près terminé. J'en suis à la dernière
scène du 5me acte. Je me passionne
pour ce sujet plus que je ne devrais,
et je résiste aux sollicitations que la
musique me fait de temps en temps
pour que je m'occupe d'elle. Je veux
tout bien finir avant d'entreprendre
la partition. Il n'y a pas eu moyen
pourtant, la semaine dernière, de
ne pas écrire le Duo de Shakespeare

« In such a night as this
When the sweet wind did gently kiss the trees
etc

Et la musique de ces litanies de l'amour
est faite.
mais il me faudra bien encore quinze
jours, pour limer et ciseler et polir et
corriger et tordre et redresser tous ces
vers tels quels.
Je vous devais ce compte du travail que

A page from Berlioz's letter of 24 June 1856
to the Princess Carolyne zu Sayn-Wittgenstein

I end with Berlioz's letter of 24 June 1856 to the Princess Carolyne zu Sayn-Wittgenstein:

> A thousand apologies, Princess, for not replying till today to your last two letters. As you will have guessed, the Academy and the *Aeneid* were the cause of the delay – the *Aeneid* much more than the Academy. Every morning as I got into a cab and went on my pilgrimage, I thought not of what I was going to say to the Immortal I was visiting but of what I was going to make my characters say. But now this double preoccupation is at an end. The Academy has elected me, as you know, and the [libretto] is virtually complete – I'm at the final scene of the fifth act. I get more impassioned about the subject than I should, but am resisting the appeals for attention that the music makes from time to time. I want to get everything finished before starting on the score. But last week it simply wasn't possible not to write the Shakespearean duet 'In such a night as this,/When the sweet wind did gently kiss the trees', etc. And the music for that litany of love is done.[41]

[41] *Correspondance générale*, Vol. V, p. 329.

The Mighty Bird

The original version of this essay was written for The Cambridge Companion to Berlioz, *ed. Peter Bloom, Cambridge University Press, Cambridge, 2000.*

In the reminiscences of Berlioz which he addressed to Eduard Hanslick in the *Revue et gazette musicale* ten years after the composer's death, Stephen Heller recalled his friend's response to a performance of Beethoven's E minor Quartet (the second 'Rasumovsky'), which they attended together in the 1860s:

> During the Adagio there was a look of rapture, of ecstasy on his face; it was as if he had experienced a 'transubstantiation'. One or two other fine works still remained to be played at the concert, but we didn't wait for them. I accompanied Berlioz to his door. On the way no word was exchanged between us: we were still hearing the Adagio and its sublime prayer. As I said good-bye he took my hand and said: 'That man had everything … and we have nothing!'[1]

To that anecdote we may add Berlioz's account of a rehearsal of a late Beethoven quartet (perhaps Op. 127), which was in the repertory of the Bohrer Quartet when they played in Paris in February and March 1830:[2]

> To my mind Anton Bohrer feels and understands the popularly supposed eccentric and unintelligible works among Beethoven's output as few men do. I can see him now at quartet rehearsals, with his brother Max (the well-known cellist, now in America), Claudel, second violin, and Urhan, viola, in ardent support. Max, at the strains of this transcendental music, would smile with the sheer pride and delight of playing it; he had the relaxed, contented air that comes from breathing one's native element. Urhan worshipped in silence, eyes averted as though from the radiance of the sun; he seemed to be saying, 'God willed that there should be a man as great as Beethoven, and that we should be allowed to contemplate him. God willed it'. Claudel admired the others for the depth of their admiration. But with Anton Bohrer, the first violin, it was a sublime passion, an ecstasy of love.

[1] *Revue et gazette musicale*, 9 March 1879.

[2] *Cf.* Joël-Marie Fauquet, *Les Sociétés de musique de chambre à Paris*, Aux Amateurs de Livres, Paris, 1986, p. 117.

> One evening, in one of those unearthly Adagios where Beethoven's spirit soars vast and solitary like the mighty bird above the snows of Chimborazo, Bohrer's violin, as it sang the heavenly melody, seemed to become possessed with the divine fire and, suddenly taking on a new force and eloquence of expression, broke into accents unknown even to it, while his face lit up with the light of pure inspiration. We held our breaths, our hearts swelled – when, abruptly, he stopped, put down his bow and ran from the room. Mme Bohrer, worried, went after him; but Max, still smiling, said, 'It's nothing – he couldn't contain his feelings. Leave him to calm down a little, then we'll start again. You must forgive him'. We forgive you – dear great artist.[3]

The image of the bird soaring to unknown heights (taken from the passage on the condor in Alexander von Humboldt's *Tableaux de la nature*) recurs more than once in his writings on Beethoven.[4] For Berlioz, Beethoven's spirit and sovereign art inhabit regions beyond the reach of other composers, even of his beloved Gluck. At times he will seem to place the two on an equal footing.[5] But Beethoven is the greatest. It was the discovery of his music, in the winter and spring of 1828, that set him consciously on a new compositional path, and that would soon inspire him to become one of Beethoven's most dedicated and articulate champions.

The shock of that discovery can be compared only to the experience of hearing the full orchestra and chorus of the Paris Opéra six years earlier, after a boyhood in which the summit of musical life was the band of the local Garde Nationale. But the impact must have been in some ways even more powerful and profound on a sensibility as acute as Berlioz's and on a musician whose musical experiences had been quite circumscribed. There had been a vigorous French tradition of symphonic writing at the turn of the century, but it had petered out by the time he came to Paris in 1821. The French tradition he acquired, in the opera house and the library, was that of Gluck and his lesser followers, and Cherubini and Spontini. (Weber's *Der Freischütz*, at the Odéon throughout 1825, alone suggested perspectives beyond the confines of Classicism.) The occasional Haydn or Mozart symphony, performed without conviction on the bare stage of the Opéra at the Lenten *concerts spirituels*, left little impression. The story of Berlioz exclaiming, after the first night of *Romeo and Juliet* in September 1827, that he would 'write his greatest symphony on the play' (reported in chapter 18 of the *Memoirs*) – a story he himself denied – cannot possibly be true. At that stage, six months before the first Conservatoire concerts, he would not

3 *Memoirs*, pp. 361–62.

4 *Cf.* also pp. 50 and 51, above.

5 *Cf.*, for example, *Correspondance générale*, Vol. V, pp. 244–45.

have thought in those terms. An operatic *Romeo* could have been in his mind: a symphonic *Romeo* would not have occurred to him.

Exactly when Berlioz first became aware of Beethoven is uncertain. In his *Memoirs* he speaks of having seen two of the symphonies in score, and of 'sensing' that Beethoven was a 'sun', though 'a sun obscured by heavy clouds'.[6] It is very likely that he knew of the Beethoven symphony rehearsals going on in the months preceding the inaugural season of the Société des Concerts du Conservatoire – some of the players were friends of his – and that it excited his curiosity. He must have heard echoes of their excitement, beginning with the St Cecilia's Day gathering at the house of the violinist-conductor François-Antoine Habeneck, who invited 30 of the best players to dine with him and bring their instruments for 'a little music', whereupon they found music stands set out with the parts of a work they didn't know (the *Eroica*) and then, after they had rehearsed with a sense of growing wonder, Madame Habeneck entering the room and exclaiming, 'In the name of a grateful Beethoven – *à table!*'[7] Berlioz would have heard these and similar stories, and of the musicians' increasing enthusiasm for music that prejudice had declared obscure, ugly and impossible to play. But nothing can have quite prepared him for the reality, encountered in the flesh in the resonant acoustics and intimate ambience of the Conservatoire Hall – the *Eroica* and the Fifth played by an orchestra of 80 made up of the elite of Paris, diligently prepared and animated by a unique *esprit de corps* and a passionate belief in the holiness of their cause.

By the time he left for Italy three years later he had heard the first eight symphonies, some of them several times, as well as various other works including the *Coriolan* Overture (and the C sharp minor Quartet), had studied the Ninth in the Conservatoire library, and had taken Beethoven to his heart and soul and mind. In Beethoven's music, in the rages and lightning emotions of the Fifth, the pantheistic joys of the *Pastoral*, the *Allegretto* of the Seventh, 'that inconceivable achievement of the great master of sombre and profound meditation',[8] he found the mirror of his own innermost self and the catalyst his creative being had been waiting for.

The revelation was both formal and expressive, or rather an interfusing of the two. It did not make him forswear Gluck or abandon the artistic beliefs by which he had lived (any more than the discovery of Shakespeare turned him against Racine, Corneille, Molière and La Fontaine). That would have been out of character in someone of such tenacious loyalties,

[6] *Memoirs*, p. 51.

[7] Quoted in D. Kern Holoman, *The Société des Concerts du Conservatoire, 1828–1967*, University of California Press, Berkeley, 2004, p. 13.

[8] *Correspondance générale*, Vol. I, p. 238.

and in any case not necessary. He remained a dramatist. But his whole conception of the dramatic was enlarged to include the symphonic, which, he saw at once, had become in Beethoven's hands a medium for dramatic music of a scope and on a scale not encountered before. Berlioz (like Liszt) was wrong when he accused Haydn of slavishly adhering to formal stereotypes in his symphonies; but he was right to see that the Beethovenian revolution was for him a crucial liberation. Beethoven's symphonic dramas were living organisms. Their endless variety of compositional procedures was the musical equivalent of what Shakespeare's plays taught – the formal freedom, after years of French classical drama turned out according to set rules. Form was each individual work's unique response to the poetic idea and material it embodied. Each work – the *Eroica*, the Fifth, the *Pastoral* and the others – was a fresh dramatic utterance, with its own character and colour, its own laws and structure, its own world.

This 'pensée poétique' governing a whole symphony yet subordinate to purely musical logic was for Berlioz one of the revelations of Beethoven. Complementary to it was the revelation of the limitless expressive possibilities of the symphony orchestra. The language of instruments spoke. It was as eloquent as human speech – more so, in fact: when Berlioz wrote his love scene for *Romeo and Juliet*, he entrusted it to the orchestra alone.

The consequence of 1828 was an upheaval in his artistic being. The 'awe-inspiring giant' Beethoven widened not only his idea of what was possible in music but of what he himself could achieve. Like Columbus, Beethoven had discovered a new world. Why should he not be its Cortez or Pizarro? From now on, the Beethovenian symphony – what Berlioz calls the 'genre instrumental expressif'– is at the forefront of his thoughts and ambitions. Already by the end of 1828 the symphony that will become the *Fantastique* is active within him.[9]

The resulting work, and its successors, show us that Beethoven's influence on Berlioz was general rather than specific. Certainly the many detailed innovations – the harmonic freedom, the emancipation of the timpani, the superimposition of different rhythms and metres, and such things as the melodic disintegration at the end of *Coriolan* and the *Eroica* Funeral March, used as an image of the cessation of life – were not lost on him. Particular echoes of Beethoven may strike us in the *Fantastique*, notably in the slow movement, the 'Scène aux champs' – the quail-call on the oboe (the *Pastoral*), the successive *fortissimo* diminished seventh chords of the opening movement of the Fifth, Florestan's ebbing paroxysm in *Fidelio*; and Berlioz has, clearly, learned from what Wilfrid Mellers calls 'Beethoven's

[9] Berlioz, 'Aperçu sur la musique classique et la musique romantique', in *Le Correspondant*, 22 October 1830; republished in *Critique musicale*, Vol. 1, pp. 63–68.

technique of thematic generation and transformation'.[10] But the formal processes are quite different. Berlioz does not follow the Viennese classical tradition exemplified, however radically, by Beethoven's symphonies. The reprise of the *idée fixe* two-thirds of the way through the first movement is in the dominant; it represents not a sonata-form recapitulation but a stage in the continuous evolution of the theme, from monody to its integration with the orchestral *tutti* beginning at bar 410. The structure of the finale is like nothing in Beethoven – nor anyone else: the Witches' Sabbath not having been used as the subject of a symphonic movement before, Berlioz had to invent a form for it.

In short, though Beethoven's influence is paramount, it is a matter of inspiration more than imitation. Beethoven himself may sometimes dispense with orthodox recapitulation (for example, in *Coriolan* and in *Leonore* No. 2, which, as it happens, were Berlioz's favourite Beethoven overtures): Berlioz goes much further. In the opening *Allegro* of his second symphony, *Harold en Italie*, the second theme only hints at the dominant; the movement is soon merging exposition, development and recapitulation in a free-flowing continuum. Even the echo of the finale of the Ninth Symphony – the recall of earlier themes – that begins the finale of *Harold* is adapted to ends opposite to those of Beethoven, as a means not of justifying the introducing of new elements – voices and text – into an instrumental work but of sanctioning the exclusion of elements previously integral to the score, the solo viola and its motto theme.[11]

Similarly, the Dramatic Symphony *Roméo et Juliette* takes Beethoven's Ninth only as its stimulus and starting point. The concept of a symphony with a big choral finale, introduced by instrumental recitative, is extended, if not altered, to one in which the vocal element and the overtly dramatic content are present from the beginning: graphic orchestral depiction of the street battles in Verona, brass recitative leading to a choral prologue which sets out the action, and voices not entirely forgotten even in the central orchestral movements, so that the full-scale choral dénouement will be heard as the natural culmination of the work.

Beethoven, for Berlioz, is a 'benefactor', a tutelary spirit, both household god and 'father'.[12] That is how he describes him in the *Journal des débats* when drafting his report on the Beethoven Festival organised by Liszt in

[10] Mellers, *op. cit.*, p. 762.

[11] Paul Banks was the first to point out this basic difference, in 'Byron, Berlioz and *Harold*', a paper delivered at the annual conference of the Royal Musical Association, in Birmingham, in 1984, and republished in the *Bulletin* of the Berlioz Society (No. 205, June 2018). He seems also to have been the first musicologist to devote intelligent thought to the question rather than simply assuming that it is an example of Berlioz's well-known opportunism.

[12] *Journal des débats*, 3 September 1845; republished in *Critique musicale*, Vol. 6, p. 115.

Bonn in 1845. The decision to write a major work, after six years in which he has produced only small-scale compositions, is taken immediately after the festival, in the solitude of Königswinter, the village where Beethoven used to go as a young man. And the shape of the opening phrase of *La Damnation de Faust* will reflect, consciously or not, in the calm stepwise ascent to the keynote followed by a falling sixth, its Beethovenian inheritance.[13]

By that time Berlioz had been expounding him in print for the past sixteen years.[14] That was not necessarily regarded in France as a respectable thing to do, especially where the works of Beethoven's final period were concerned. Fétis, in the *Revue musicale*, made much of the many false harmonic progressions – some of them no better than schoolboy howlers – in the late quartets (Berlioz's soaring bird, he might have said, had crash-landed); even the Seventh Symphony, in its first and last movements, was 'the improvisation of a gifted composer on an off day'.[15] Adolphe Adam considered Beethoven too flawed to be – as some misguidedly claimed – the leading composer of the century (that honour belonged to Auber). Rellstab, in the *Revue et gazette musicale*, deplored the ruin of Beethoven's once noble genius, as exemplified by the follies of the Ninth Symphony.

Dismissive criticism of the sort, however, had been quite untypical of the *Revue et gazette* under Maurice Schlesinger's editorship. His regular writers worked on the assumption that music of the highest quality by definition challenged the listener and might well not reveal itself immediately. Foremost among composers of such music was Beethoven; and foremost among his advocates was Berlioz. For him, the symphonies – the Ninth above all – were the beginning of modern music. In the 1830s Berlioz published 'critiques admiratives' of all nine. He had first enunciated this idea of criticism in December 1825 when in a letter to *Le Corsaire* he took issue with Castil-Blaze's strictures on Gluck's *Armide*. The critic's duty, he said, was to write a reasoned appreciation of the music he admired, to 'reveal the strokes of genius' in a work, many of which may have 'escaped the notice of a public blinded by the prejudices of the moment'.[16]

This principle, essentially, informs all Berlioz's writings on Beethoven. From time to time his admiration is qualified by a touch of Conservatoire pedantry (such as, ironically, will characterise subsequent French criticism of Berlioz's music). He is not immune to prejudices himself. He fails to

[13] *Cf.* the opening bars of Beethoven's *An die ferne Geliebte*.

[14] His first *feuilleton* for the *Journal des débats* (25 January 1835) included a long analysis of the *Eroica*; his articles in *Le Rénovateur* the previous year frequently extolled and discussed Beethoven; in 1829 he published a three-part biographical essay on the composer (*Le Correspondant*, 4 August, 11 August and 6 October 1829; republished in *Critique musicale*, Vol. 1, pp. 47–61).

[15] *Revue musicale*, V (1829), pp. 131–32 and 235–36.

[16] *Le Corsaire*, 19 December 1825; republished in *Critique musicale*, Vol. 1, p. 9.

respond to the humour of the sudden, brusque conclusion of the Eighth Symphony's *Allegretto scherzando* ('How can this ravishing idyll finish with the commonplace for which Beethoven had the greatest aversion, the Italian cadence? [...] I have never been able to explain this vagary'[17]). Equally mystifying to him, and even more disagreeable, is the dissonance that opens the finale of the Ninth, and which is repeated, still more discordantly, just before the entry of the voice. The bee in his bonnet about 'obligatory' fugues in religious works buzzes so loudly that it deafens him to the glories of 'In Gloria Dei Patris', 'Amen' and 'Et vitam venturi saeculi, Amen' in the *Missa solemnis*; the fugal treatment of 'Amen' is like a red rag to a bull.

Such failures, however, are exceptional. In general he respects what Beethoven does, even when he can't see the reason for it. His account of the C sharp minor Quartet, which he hears in 1830 – a work excoriated by Fétis – is like that of a postulant, a believer, ready as in an Orphic initiation to follow Beethoven wherever he leads. As he says in the Postscript of the *Memoirs*, '[I am] a freethinker in music, or rather I am of the faith of Beethoven, Weber, Gluck, and Spontini, who believe and preach, and prove by their works, that everything is "right" or "wrong" according to the effect produced'.[18] At the end of his long and detailed 'critique admirative' of the *Pastoral*, he concludes:

> After that, can one speak of oddities of style in such a work – of groups of five notes in the cellos opposed to four-note phrases in the double basses without combining into a genuine unison? Does one have to point out the horn-call on an arpeggio of the chord of C while the strings sustain the chord of F? Must one search for the reason for such harmonic anomalies? I confess I am incapable of it. For that, one must be cool and rational – and how can one keep ecstasy at bay when the mind is engaged with such a subject?[19]

Berlioz's method aims to lead the reader/listener into the music by a mixture of the two modes of criticism first defined by E. T. A. Hoffmann, the poetic and pedagogic. He uses literary analogy and evocative imagery seasoned with technical description. A representative example, combining both modes, is this account of the second movement of the Seventh Symphony. Here he takes in his stride the unresolved chord which begins and ends the movement. (Elsewhere he defends the chord against critics, who, failing to see the reason for it, 'point out as a fault one of Beethoven's finest inspirations'.)

[17] *Revue et gazette musicale*, 18 February 1838; republished in *Critique musicale*, Vol. 3, 1837–38, ed. Anne Bongrain and Marie-Hélène Coudroy-Saghaï, Buchet/Chastel, Paris, 2001, p. 400.

[18] *Memoirs*, p. 520.

[19] *Revue et gazette musicale*, 4 February 1838; republished in *Critique musicale*, Vol. 3, p. 388.

> Rhythm – a rhythm as simple as that of the first movement – is again the chief element in the incredible effect produced by the Andante [*Allegretto*]. It consists entirely of a dactyl followed by a spondee, repeated uninterruptedly, now in three parts, now in one, now all together, sometimes as accompaniment, often focusing attention solely on itself, or providing the main subject of a brief double fugue in the stringed instruments. It is heard first on the lower strings of the violas, cellos and double basses, played piano, then repeated shortly afterwards in a mysterious and melancholy pianissimo. From there it passes to the second violins, while the cellos utter a sort of sublime lament, in the minor mode. The rhythmic figure, rising from octave to octave, reaches the first violins which, while making a crescendo, hand it to the wind instruments at the top of the orchestra, where it bursts out with full force. The plaintive melody, now more energetic, becomes a convulsive wailing. Conflicting rhythms clash painfully against each other. We hear tears, sobs, suffering. But a ray of hope shines. The heartrending strains give way to a vaporous melody, gentle, pure, sad yet resigned, 'like patience smiling at grief'. Only the cellos and basses persist with their inexorable rhythm beneath this rainbow-like melodic arc: to borrow once again from English poetry, 'One fatal remembrance, one sorrow that throws /Its bleak shade alike o'er our joys and our woes'.[20]

After further alternations of anguish and resignation, the orchestra, as though exhausted by its struggle, can manage only fragments of the main phrase, before giving up the ghost. The flutes and oboes take up the theme with dying voice but lack the strength to go on; the violins complete it with a few barely audible pizzicato notes – after which, flaring up like the flame of a lamp about to go out, the wind instruments give a deep sigh on an incomplete harmony and… 'the rest is silence'. This plaintive exclamation, with which the *Andante* opens and closes, is produced by a chord, that of the six-four, which normally resolves. In this case the placing of the tonic note in the middle of the chord, while the dominant is above and below it, is the only possible ending, leaving the listener with a sense of incompleteness, and intensifying the dreamlike sadness of the rest of the movement.[21]

Berlioz's analyses of Beethoven symphonies, as we have seen, appeared in the *Revue et gazette musicale* (and subsequently in *Voyage musicale* and *À travers chants*). The *Revue et gazette* had a specialist readership. But he could also treat subscribers to the *Journal des débats* to just as demanding a course of instruction. The long crescendo in the opening movement of

[20] From 'As a beam o'er the face of the waters may glow', Thomas Moore, *Irish Melodies*.

[21] *Revue et gazette musicale*, 11 February 1838; republished in *Critique musicale*, Vol. 3, pp. 393–94. Katharine Ellis points out that the style and structure of Berlioz's account of the *Allegretto* replicate the shape and progress of the music, mirroring 'the effect of cumulative rhythm reaching towards a climax and, finally, dying away as the movement reaches its close'. *Cf.* 'The Criticism' in *The Cambridge Companion to Berlioz*, ed. Peter Bloom, Cambridge University Press, Cambridge, 2000, pp. 159–60.

Eugène Lami's 1840 watercolour L'andante de la symphonie en la – *audience members listening to the second movement of Beethoven's Seventh Symphony*

the Fourth Symphony, which prompted one of his most detailed technical pages, originally appeared in a *feuilleton* in the *Journal des débats*:

> The second part of this same Allegro contains a totally new idea whose first bars seize the attention and which, after carrying one away by its mysterious development, astonishes one by the unexpectedness of its conclusion. This is what happens. After a vigorous tutti the first violins break up the main theme and make a game out of it with the second violins. Their pianissimo dialogue leads to two sustained dominant seventh chords in the key of B natural, each interrupted by two silent bars during which all that is heard is a quiet roll of the drums on B flat, the enharmonic major third of the bass note F sharp. The drums then stop, leaving the strings to murmur other fragments of the theme and then, by a new enharmonic modulation, to arrive on a six-four chord of B flat. The drums, re-entering on the same note, which instead of being a leading tone as it was the first time is now a genuine tonic, go on with their roll for a further twenty bars. The force of the key of B flat, barely perceptible to begin with, becomes stronger and stronger the more the roll continues; and while the drums rumble on, the momentum of the other instruments, scattering fragments of phrase as they go, culminates in a great forte which finally establishes B flat in all its majestic energy.
>
> This prodigious crescendo is one of the most extraordinary inventions in music. To find another like it you have to go to the one that concludes

the famous scherzo of the C minor Symphony; and even then, despite its immense effect, the latter is conceived on a less spacious scale. It starts piano and proceeds straight to its climax, never leaving the main key – whereas the one we have just described starts mezzo forte, sinks down for an instant to a pianissimo coloured by harmonies that remain deliberately imprecise, then reappears with more clearly defined chords, and burst forth only at the moment when the cloud which veiled the modulation is completely dispersed. It is like a river whose calmly flowing stream suddenly goes underground, from where it re-emerges with a roar, as a foaming cascade.[22]

His account of the crescendo in the scherzo of the Fifth is perhaps too well known to be quoted in full, though it provides a further example of his method, and must have delighted the Beethoven-lovers among his readers and astonished those who were yet to be converted: the theme of the trio 'played by cellos and basses with the full force of the bow, whose ponderous gait makes the desks of the whole orchestra shake, and suggests the gambolling of a herd of high-spirited elephants' – as 'the sound of this mad stampeding gradually fades, the motif of the scherzo reappears, pizzicato, the silence deepens and all that is left are a few notes plucked by the violins and the strange gobble of the bassoons, playing high A flat against the jarring juxtaposition of the octave G, the bass note of the dominant minor ninth' – 'the ear hesitates, unsure where this enigmatic harmony will end' – 'the dull pulsation of the drums gradually growing in intensity' – and so on.[23]

Almost his last Beethoven article, the 'critique admirative' of *Fidelio* in the *Journal des débats* of 19 and 22 May 1860, contains some of his most arresting images and at the same time a final declaration of faith:

[*Fidelio*] belongs to that powerful race of maligned works that have the most inconceivable prejudices and the most blatant lies heaped on them, but whose vitality is so intense that nothing can prevail against them – like those sturdy beeches born among rocks and ruins, which end by splitting the stone and breaking through the walls, and rise up proud and verdant, the more solidly rooted for the obstacles they have had to overcome in order to force their way out; whereas the willows that grow without effort on the banks of a river fall into the mud and rot, forgotten.

Its time will come:

Who knows that light may not dawn sooner than one thinks, even for those whose spirits are closed at the moment to this beautiful work of Beethoven's as they are to the marvels of the Ninth Symphony and the last quartets and the

[22] *Journal des débats*, 12 April 1835; republished in *Critique musicale*, Vol. 2, 1835–36, ed. Marie-Hélène Coudroy-Saghaï and Anne Bongrain, Buchet/Chastel, Paris, 1998, pp. 115–16.

[23] *Journal des débats*, 18 April 1835, *Revue et gazette musicale*, 28 January 1838; republished in *Critique musicale*, Vol. 2, pp. 121–22, and Vol. 3, pp. 379–80.

great piano sonatas of that same inspired, incomparable being? Sometimes, when one looks at a particular part of the heaven of art, a veil seems to cover 'the mind's eye' and prevent it from seeing the stars that shine there. Then, all of a sudden, for no apparent reason, the veil is rent, and one sees, and blushes to have been blind so long.

The need to expound Beethoven was for Berlioz the most important *raison d'être* of his work as a critic, and a compensation for the mental and psychological burden that criticism and his financial dependence on it increasingly became. He surely hoped, too, that initiating readers into the mysteries and splendours of Beethoven's music would help to make his own works more intelligible – works that Paganini was not alone among musicians in regarding as inheriting the mantle of Beethoven. But above all he celebrated Beethoven because he had to: he must share his enthusiasm, communicate to others the wonder of the discovery. He could not do otherwise. And it is clear that he often did, verbally and in private. Ernest Legouvé never forgot hearing Berlioz explain to him the Ninth Symphony:

> His articles, admirable as they are, give an imperfect idea of it, for they contain only his opinions. When he spoke, the whole of him was in it. The eloquence of his words was enhanced by his expression, his gestures, tone of voice, tears, exclamations of enthusiasm, and those sudden flashes of inspired imagery which are sparked by the stimulus of a listener hanging on every word. An hour spent in this way taught me more about instrumental music than a whole concert at Conservatoire – or rather, when I went to the Conservatoire the following Sunday, my mind full of Berlioz's commentaries, Beethoven's work suddenly opened before me like a great cathedral flooded with light, the whole design of which I took in at a glance and in which I walked about as though on familiar ground, confidently exploring every recess and corner. Berlioz had given me the key to the sanctuary.[24]

There was, of course, another way of expressing his feelings about Beethoven and of communicating his understanding of the Ninth and the other symphonies to a wider audience: conducting. Berlioz's emergence, in the 1830s, as a conductor of a new school, who beat time with a baton, not with a violin bow, and who rehearsed the orchestra sectionally and with numbered parts, was significant first of all for his own music, which till then he had generally had to hear performed 'approximately' under the bow of Habeneck or Narcisse Girard. But as his renown spread he came to be in demand as a conductor of music other than his own, which to him meant, above all, Beethoven.

[24] Ernest Legouvé, *Soixante ans de souvenirs*, Vol. 1, pp. 306–7.

Opportunities, by modern standards, were admittedly infrequent for someone who, though regarded by many musicians as the finest conductor of the day, was never attached to a permanent concert-promoting body. The first Beethoven symphony he is known to have conducted – the *Pastoral* – was part of a one-off Beethoven programme put on by Liszt at the Paris Conservatoire on 25 April 1841 to raise money for the fund that Liszt had set up to pay for a statue of the composer in his native town, Bonn. (The 'Emperor' Concerto, played by Liszt, the 'Kreutzer' Sonata, with Liszt and Lambert Massart, and the Overture *The Consecration of the House*, were the other works.) In January 1845, at the Cirque Olympique, Berlioz accompanied Charles Hallé in a Beethoven concerto (No. 4 or the 'Emperor': the evidence is conflicting).[25] And in London in December 1847 he opened the inaugural season of Jullien's Grand English Opera, of which he was music director, with *Leonore* No. 2, his somewhat specious excuse being that *Lucia di Lammermoor*, the main item of the evening, did not have a proper overture of its own.

He had more scope in the 1850s, with the founding of the Société Philharmonique, under his leadership, and then of the New Philharmonic Society, created for him by his London admirers. In 1850, in Paris, he gave the Fifth Symphony, and in 1852, with the New Philharmonic, the Fifth, the Triple Concerto, *Leonore* No. 2 again, and two performances of the Ninth, which were reckoned incomparably the best ever given in London, with a first-rate orchestra and a choir far superior to its Parisian counterpart. Of those performances *The Morning Post* wrote:

> The most worthy execution of Beethoven's magnificent symphony, and at the same time the best orchestral performance, ever heard in this country. [...] We never before heard so much accent and true expression from an English orchestra.[26]

And the *Illustrated London News* called it

> the greatest victory ever yet attained in the development of Beethoven's intentions. [...] We heard on Wednesday night professors of no little note, whose sneers and scoffs at the Ninth Symphony years back we had not forgotten, make avowal that it was incomparably the grandest emanation of Beethoven's genius. [...] [H]onour and glory to the gifted conductor, who wielded Prospero's wand and subdued all the combined elements to one harmonious whole. Well did Berlioz earn the ovation bestowed by the moved

[25] According to *Life and Letters of Sir Charles Hallé*, Smith, Elder and Co., London, 1896, p. 68, he played the Fourth Concerto; D. Kern Holoman, *Berlioz*, Harvard University Press, Cambridge, Mass., 1989, p. 618, lists the 'Emperor'.

[26] 13 May 1852.

thousands who filled the hall on this memorable occasion, one to be for ever treasured in our musical annals.[27]

Such revelations were not achieved without much more thorough rehearsal than was customary in London then or for long afterwards. Berlioz had six rehearsals for the Ninth, and it was partly because the cost was higher than the sponsors of the New Philharmonic expected, and also because of the machinations of the mediocre but ambitious conductor Dr Henry Wylde, that Berlioz was not invited back to the orchestra except briefly in 1855. In the late 1850s, owing to ill health and preoccupation with composing and then promoting *Les Troyens*, he virtually gave up conducting, except for the annual gala concert at Baden-Baden (where excerpts from Beethoven figured on some of the programmes). But not long before he died, his career as conductor enjoyed a belated flowering thanks to an invitation to Russia in the winter of 1867–68. Though chronically sick and in pain, he directed six concerts in St Petersburg and two in Moscow. The main content of the programmes was divided among Beethoven, Gluck and his own music. He conducted the *Eroica*, the Fourth, the Fifth, the *Pastoral*, the 'Emperor' and the Violin Concerto. Ill as he was, the experience rejuvenated him. After the series opened he wrote to his uncle Félix Marmion (on 8 December 1867):

> At the first concert I directed Beethoven's Pastoral Symphony, with profound adoration for the poor great man who had the power to create so amazing a poem in music. And how we sang that poetry! What a splendid orchestra! They do what I want, these fine artists.[28]

What were Berlioz's Beethoven performances like? We have no way of knowing for sure. All we have are fleeting indications. The composer and critic César Cui wrote in the *St Petersburg Gazette*:

> What a grasp he has of Beethoven, how exact, how thoughtful his performances are, how effective yet without the slightest concession to the false and the tawdry. I prefer Berlioz as an interpreter of Beethoven to Wagner (who, with all his excellent qualities, is at times affected, introducing sentimental rallentandos). [...] Of all the conductors we have heard in Petersburg, Berlioz is unquestionably the greatest.[29]

[27] 15 May 1852. Berlioz's earlier doubts about the vocal writing in the finale of the Ninth (*cf.* Katharine Ellis, *Music Criticism in Nineteenth-Century France*, Cambridge University Press, Cambridge, 1995, p. 111) may have been allayed by the excellent singing of the New Philharmonic Chorus – far surpassing the usual standard at Paris Conservatoire performances.

[28] *Correspondance générale*, Vol. VII, p. 633.

[29] Quoted in Stasov, *Selected Essays on Music*, *op. cit.*, p. 166.

From Berlioz's and Wagner's comments on each other's conducting, their interpretations and style of music-making seem to have been as different as Toscanini's and Furtwängler's (Berlioz being more like the Italian and Wagner the German). Where his own music was concerned, Berlioz set much store by the metronome, but there is no evidence of how much importance he attached to Beethoven's metronome marks. So far as I know, he never raised the question in his journalistic writings, apart from what he said about Spohr's conducting of the Ninth Symphony at the Bonn Berlioz Festival in 1845: that Spohr's tempos were similar to Habeneck's at the Société des Concerts performances in Paris, except for a much quicker double-bass recitative at the beginning of the finale. Beethoven's metronome mark and written instructions make it perfectly clear that the recitative should be quick (though even now it often isn't) and that Spohr was right and Habeneck wrong; but Berlioz makes no comment. His calling the second movement of the Seventh Symphony (a work he never conducted) *Andante* instead of *Allegretto* may indicate that Habeneck took it more slowly than Beethoven's ♩ = 76, and that, to begin with, he too thought of it like that. On the other hand, Berlioz's *Hamlet* Funeral March, an *Allegretto* in A minor like the Beethoven movement and based on the same rhythmic figure, long–short–short–long–long, has the same metronome mark, 76. Press reports of his performance of the Ninth mention the very rapid tempo of the trio and of the concluding variations – a startling difference from the plodding performances by the Old Philharmonic, thrown on with one rehearsal, which London audiences had had to make do with till then.

All we can say for certain is that Berlioz found joy in repaying something of what he owed to the mighty mentor who, together with Gluck and Shakespeare, had pointed the way for his own music.

The March to the Scaffold

This next piece, and the following one, are taken from the first volume of my biography of Berlioz. I thought it worth including them here. The origins of the Marche au supplice *are still sometimes misunderstood; and the nature and composition (in both senses) of the* Symphonie fantastique *– and in particular the vexed question of Programme Music, both in its alleged and often frowned-on connection with that work and in itself – continue to give rise to doubts and misrepresentations. That being so, I have taken the opportunity to give my convictions another airing. I also felt that, in the chronological arrangement of this part of the book, Berlioz's first large-scale orchestral work – his first considered response to Beethoven's symphonic dramas – demanded extended treatment.*

The *Neuf mélodies* may not have been the only composition of this period originally meant to figure in Berlioz's concert of 1 November 1829: the 'Marche des gardes' from *Les Francs-juges,* the piece that became the fourth movement of the *Symphonie fantastique,* was quite possibly another. Some such conclusion is prompted by the title page of the manuscript score. 'Marche des Gardes/du Franc comte/Dans l'opéra des Francs-juges/musique de/Hector Berlioz': the existence of such a title page, naming the composer and the work from which the music comes, is evidence that the piece in question has been extracted from its context in order to fulfil, however temporarily, a different, independent role – maybe performance at a concert or, if not, as an example of recent work submitted to the Conservatoire.

Exactly when it was composed we don't know; there is no reference to it in the correspondence. All we can say for sure is that it doesn't come straight from the original *Francs-juges* of 1825–26. Everything about the manuscript, and the music, suggests a later date: scoring, for an orchestra much bigger than the forces of the Odéon theatre for which the opera was intended; layout of the score, with the violins in the modern position, beneath the wind and percussion, not at the top of the page (as they are in the manuscript of 1825–26); size and type of paper; handwriting; and style of the music, which has an individuality and power, and richness and virtuosity of scoring, not found in the surviving fragments of the opera.

The provenance of the March was the subject of an internecine feud among French Berlioz scholars at the beginning of the twentieth century, conducted with extraordinary ferocity in the correspondence columns of *Le Ménestrel*, the musical journal in which Julien Tiersot was publishing a series of weekly articles entitled 'Berlioziana'. Tiersot stoutly denied that the 'Marche au supplice' and the 'Marche des gardes' had anything to do with each other. Adolphe Boschot and Charles Malherbe maintained, in increasingly sneering and triumphal tones, that they did, and the argument raged backwards and forwards for several months ('La marche au supplice vient des Francs-juges', 'La marche au supplice ne vient pas des Francs-juges', 'La marche au supplice continue à venir des Francs-juges', etc.). [1]

As it happened, Boschot and Malherbe were in a strong position, as Malherbe owned the manuscript of the symphony, in which the double title page of the fourth movement, 'Marche des gardes' and 'Marche du supplice', is plain to see, and it remains a mystery how Tiersot failed to see it, even during the brief examination of the score Malherbe allowed him – unless Malherbe actually concealed the first title page.

In any case the whole controversy now seems pointless. Modern scholarly work on the fragments of *Les Francs-juges* has confirmed once and for all that there is a musical as well as documentary connection between the 'March to the Scaffold' and the opera; but in today's more enlightened climate that is no longer a fatal admission. Why shouldn't there be? Some of the most sacred, most quintessential passages in *Fidelio* were borrowed from other works, and no one, I take it, thinks the worse of it for that. Though Malherbe and Boschot sought to discredit the *Fantastique* by proving the connection, and Tiersot, and Barzun after him, to vindicate its good name by denying it, it is common enough in the genesis of art for elements of the finished work to have started life in a different context. I doubt very much whether, if we knew nothing about the history of the 'March to the Scaffold', it would occur to us to feel that its inclusion in the symphony is arbitrary. The distant, thudding drums and eerie, hand-stopped horn chords of its opening bars grow out of the ominous drum-rolls and sustained horn of the closing page of the slow movement; the March fits quite naturally into the dramatic and musical progression whereby the dreams of the first three movements become the nightmares of the last two.

In his *Memoirs* Berlioz states that he composed the March in a single night (whereas the slow movement, he says, cost him weeks of labour).[2] Strange to say, it is still necessary to point out that the destination of a piece of music and the time taken to compose it are separate questions, and that Berlioz's statement is not disproved – as Boschot, sneeringly

[1] *Le Ménestrel, Journal du Monde Musical*, Vol. 72, 1906, pp. 153–288.

[2] *Memoirs*, p. 104.

again, supposed – by demonstrating that the March was originally written for the opera, not the symphony. The composition in short score of a 164-bar movement of the character and straightforward form of the March in the course of one night is a remarkable but not an impossible feat, especially if, as was the case, it involved reworking and developing existing material.

The history of the March is complicated by the fact that the surviving libretto of the opera makes no formal provision for it; the nearest it comes is a stage direction in Act 2 which speaks of 'innumerable battalions' passing to the strains of 'grim music' – 'une musique farouche' ('musique farouche' is how Berlioz described the 'Marche au supplice' in a letter to Humbert Ferrand announcing the completion of the symphony[3]). But in Act 3, where the hero falls asleep in the forest, and the orchestra, in a dream sequence, is said to play reminiscences of music from scenes earlier in the opera, one of the scenes recalled is 'la marche des gardes d'Olmerik' (the tyrant-villain of the work and the 'Franc comte' of the title page); and on the torn-off remnants which are all that exist of this part of the manuscript the four notes discernible in the cello and double-bass parts are clearly notes 6 to 9 of the first theme of the 'March to the Scaffold', though the key signature is G major, not the eventual G minor.

The most plausible conclusion is that, making use of thematic material from the earlier, less developed 'musique farouche' of 1826, Berlioz wrote the present March for the grand-opera version of *Les Francs-juges* which he and Ferrand planned when their hopes of a performance at the Odéon (an *opéra-comique* theatre) finally collapsed.

When he did so remains an open question. Ferrand, late as always and having to be prodded by his friend, did not send the revised libretto till April 1829; but the decision to compose a more elaborate and extended march is one that Berlioz could have taken without it. One possible date is January or early February 1829, when, believing that Harriet Smithson was interested in him after all, he felt a surge of confidence in his powers ('Oph's love has multiplied my capabilities a hundredfold');[4] in such an exalted state of mind he could well have sat up all night composing the March in a sustained burst of inspiration. But a later date is equally possible – for instance, September 1829, a month or two before the concert of 1 November, at which he may have planned to perform the March. An alternative which cannot be ruled out is that the March was composed shortly after the concert and was to have been performed at one of the inaugural concerts of the Athénée Musical, the new society at whose soirée on 18 February 1830 two

[3] 16 April 1830; *Correspondance générale*, Vol. I, p. 319.

[4] *Ibid.*, p. 232.

of the *Neuf mélodies* were given, and whose conductor was Berlioz's friend and champion Nathan Bloc.

In either case, the reason for not performing the March was the same. Whatever the precise date of composition, it came into being at a time when a much bigger work was forming itself insistently in Berlioz's mind. The gravitational pull of the *Symphonie fantastique* was too strong, and the March yielded to it.

'Programme Music' and the *Symphonie fantastique*

From the first volume of my biography of Berlioz

The composition of the *Symphonie fantastique* was the culmination of a process traceable in Berlioz's correspondence for more than a year; its genesis goes back at least to the beginning of 1829, very likely further. It is already hinted at in the letter he wrote to Edouard Rocher on 11 January 1829, when the possibility that his passion for Harriet Smithson might have a happy outcome was broached for the first time:

> Oh, if only I didn't suffer so much… So many musical ideas are seething within me… Now that I have broken the chains of routine, I see an immense territory stretching before me, which academic rules forbad me to enter. Now that I have heard that awe-inspiring giant Beethoven I realise what point the art of music has reached; it's a question of taking it up at that point and carrying it further – no, not further, that's impossible, he attained the limits of art, but as far in another direction. There are new things, many new things to be done, I feel it with an intense energy, and I shall do it, have no doubt, if I live. Oh, must my entire destiny be engulfed by this overpowering passion?… If on the other hand it turned out well, everything I've suffered would enhance my musical ideas. I would work non-stop… my powers would be tripled, a whole new world of music would spring fully armed from my brain or rather from my heart, to conquer that which is most precious for an artist, the approval of those capable of appreciating him. Time lies before me, and I am still living; with life and time great events may come to pass.[1]

These are more than prophetic words; they link with the letter written three weeks later to Ferrand – at the high tide of his fond illusions about Harriet – to make it clear that the work that became the *Symphonie fantastique* was already active in him. 'Listen, Ferrand: if I succeed [with Harriet Smithson], I feel certain beyond a shadow of doubt that I shall become a colossus in music. For some time I have had a descriptive symphony on *Faust* in my brain. When I have released it, I mean it to stagger the musical world.'[2] (That the 'Faust symphony' and the *Fantastique*

[1] *Correspondance générale*, Vol. I, p. 229.

[2] Letter of 2 February 1829; *ibid.*, p. 232.

are fundamentally the same work is confirmed by the statement, in the *Memoirs*, that the latter was written 'under the influence of Goethe's poem'.[3]) Early in June 1829 he is still 'meditating an immense instrumental composition', which he hopes to perform in London, thus achieving 'a brilliant success in *her* presence'.[4]

By the beginning of 1830 he is almost ready to begin the actual work of composition. On 30 January he tells his sister Nancy that he has just arranged to give a concert in May, and is preparing a large orchestral work in a new genre, the outlines of which he has had in his head for some time, but he fears it may not be ready: to bind together all the various elements and put the whole thing in good shape requires long and patient labour.[5] The letter echoes the sense of great events impending and unknown territory to be explored that was expressed in the letter to Edouard Rocher twelve months before.[6] Yet a week later (he tells Ferrand) he has not started:

> I have been plunged back into the anguish of an endless, uncontrollable passion without motive, without object. She is still in London, yet I feel her all about me. [...] I was on the point of beginning my big symphony (Episode in the life of an artist), in which the course of my infernal passion is to be depicted, I have the whole thing in my head, but I can write nothing.[7]

The long letter to Dr Berlioz written on 19 February, though not mentioning Harriet Smithson, gives an unusually full and frank account of his state. After describing his efforts to deal with a bad attack of toothache, he goes on:

> I wish I could also find a specific to calm the feverish excitement that so often torments me; but I shall never find it, it comes from the way I am made. In addition, the habit I have got into of constantly observing myself means that no sensation escapes me, and reflection doubles it – I see myself in a mirror. Often I experience the most extraordinary impressions, of which nothing can give an idea; nervous exaltation is no doubt the cause, but the effect is like that of opium. What surprises me is that I can remember having experienced exactly the same thing from the age of twelve; my memory clearly recalls days spent in a continual state of grief without subject or object. Especially on Sundays I see myself at Vespers in the days when you were taking me through Virgil's *Aeneid*. The effect of the calm, unvarying Vespers chant, combined with that of some of the words such as *In exitu Israel*, spoke to me so powerfully of the past that I was seized with an almost desperate sense

3 *Memoirs*, p. 104.

4 *Correspondance générale*, Vol. I, p. 258.

5 *Correspondance générale*, Vol. I, pp. 303–4.

6 11 January 1829; *Correspondance générale*, Vol. I, p. 229.

7 9 February 1830; *Correspondance générale*, Vol. I, p. 306.

J'étais sur le point de commencer ma grande symphonie (Episode de la vie d'un artiste) où le développement de mon infernale passion doit être peint; je l'ai toute dans la tête, mais je ne puis rien écrire .... attendons

Vous recevrez en même temps que ma lettre, deux exemplaires de mes chères mélodies; un artiste du théâtre Italien de Londres vient d'en emporter pour Moore qu'il connaît et à qui nous les avons dédiées. Adolphe Nourrit vient de les adopter pour les chanter aux soirées où il va habituellement.

Il s'agit à présent de les faire connaître. mais je n'ai plus d'activité.

Mon cher ami, écris-moi souvent, et longuement je vous en supplie, je suis séparé de vous, que vos pensées me parviennent du moins; Il m'est insupportable de ne pas vous voir. Faut-il qu'à travers les nuages, chargés de foudres, qui grondent sur ma tête, un seul rayon de l'astre paisible ne puisse venir me consoler!......

Adieu donc j'attends une lettre de vous dans 9 jours; si votre état maladif vous permet d'écrire. Votre fidèle ami H. Berlioz

Gounet sous les yeux duquel je vous écris, me charge de mille choses amicales pour vous.

A page from a letter to Humbert Ferrand, 6 February 1830, where Berlioz states that he has not yet begun work on the score of the Symphonie fantastique, *although 'je l'ai toute dans ma tête'*

> of anguish; my imagination called up around me all my heroes of Troy and Latium [...] and then the flashing weapons that I could see through clouds of dust reflecting the sunlight of Italy, and all that way of life so different from ours, all mixed up with Biblical impressions, ideas about Egypt, and Moses, wrought me into a state of indescribable suffering [...]. This imaginary world ['ce monde fantastique'] is still part of me and has grown by the addition of all the new impressions that I experience as my life goes on [...]. I have found only one way of completely satisfying this immense *appetite for emotion* and that is music. Without it I am certain I couldn't go on living. First and foremost the works of the great *free spirits* make me live from time to time with incredible energy – and then my own music.[8]

Yet the music that was waiting to give form to this 'monde fantastique' still lay locked within him. Two weeks later he is still paralysed by the hopelessness of his passion, the *idée fixe* that is wearing him out. 'Today it is a year since I saw HER for the last time... Unhappy woman, how I loved you! I shudder as I write it – how I *love* you'.[9]

It was the final spasm. Soon afterward he must have set to work, for the next we hear of it, six weeks later, the symphony is written. On 16 April he reports to Ferrand that he has 'sanctioned his resolve with a work that satisfies him completely'. The resolve is nothing less than the abandonment of his passion for Harriet Smithson, in the face of the 'horrible truths' ('affreuses vérités') that he discovered about her, which set him on the road to a recovery that 'will be as complete as the tenacity of my nature allows'.[10]

The letter contains the first draft of the famous programme of the symphony. Its double title – *Fantastic Symphony, Episode in the Life of an Artist* – echoes E. T. A. Hoffmann, whose *Contes fantastiques* included one called *La vie d'artiste*. The scenario, too, has something of the character of a Hoffmann tale in miniature.

> Here is the subject [of the work], which will be set forth in a programme and distributed in the hall on the day of the concert:
> *Episode in the life of an artist* (grand fantastic symphony in five parts).
> FIRST MOVEMENT: in two sections, made up of a short adagio, followed without a break by a fully developed allegro (intimations of passion; aimless daydreams; frenzied passion with all its bursts of tenderness, jealousy, rage, alarm, etc., etc.).
> 2nd MOVEMENT: *Scene in the country* (adagio: thoughts of love and hope, disturbed by dark premonitions). [At that stage the 'Scène aux champs' came before, not after, 'Un bal'.]

[8] *Ibid.*, Vol. I, pp. 309–13.
[9] To Ferdinand Hiller; *ibid.*, Vol. I, p. 314.
[10] *Ibid.*, pp. 318–20.

3rd MOVEMENT: *A ball* (brilliant, stirring music).
4th MOVEMENT: *March to the scaffold* (grim, imposing music).
5th MOVEMENT: *Dream of a witches' sabbath.*

Now, my friend, this is how I have woven my novel, or rather my history, whose hero you will have no difficulty in recognising. I conceive an artist, gifted with a lively imagination, who, in that state of soul which Chateaubriand so admirably depicted in *René*, sees for the first time a woman who realises the ideal of beauty and fascination that his heart has so long invoked, and falls madly in love with her. By a strange quirk, the image of the loved one never appears before his mind's eye without its corresponding musical idea, in which he finds a quality of grace and nobility similar to that which he attributes to the beloved object. This double obsession ['double idée fixe'] pursues him unceasingly. That is the reason for the constant appearance, in every movement of the symphony, of the main melody of the first allegro (No. 1).

After countless agitations he imagines that there is some hope; he believes himself loved. One day, in the country, he hears in the distance two shepherds playing a *ranz des vaches* to one another; their rustic dialogue plunges him into a delightful daydream (No. 2).

The melody reappears for a moment across the themes of the adagio.

He goes to a ball. The tumult of the dance fails to distract him; his *idée fixe* haunts him still, and the cherished melody sets his heart beating during a brilliant waltz (No. 3).

In a fit of despair he poisons himself with opium; but instead of killing him the narcotic induces a horrific vision, in which he believes he has murdered the loved one, has been condemned to death, and witnesses his own execution. March to the scaffold; immense procession of headsmen, soldiers and populace. At the end the *melody* reappears once again, like a last reminder of love, interrupted by the death stroke (No. 4).

The next moment he is surrounded by a hideous throng of demons and sorcerers, gathered to celebrate Sabbath night. They summon from far and wide. At last the *melody* arrives. Till then it had appeared only in a graceful guise, but now it has become a vulgar tavern tune, trivial and base; the beloved object has come to the sabbath to take part in her victim's funeral. She is nothing but a courtesan, fit to figure in the orgy. The ceremony begins; the bells toll, the whole hellish cohort prostrates itself; a chorus chants the plainsong sequence of the dead (*Dies irae*), two other choruses repeat it in a burlesque parody. Finally, the Sabbath round-dance whirls. At its violent climax it mingles with the *Dies irae*, and the vision ends (No. 5).

So there you have it, dear friend; the plan of my immense symphony has been carried out. I have just written the last note. If I can be ready by Whit Sunday, I shall give a concert at the Nouveautés, with an orchestra of 220 [*sic*]; but I'm afraid of not having the parts copied in time. At the moment I feel like an idiot; the fearful effort of concentration that produced my work has

> exhausted my imagination and I should like to be able to rest and sleep the whole time. But if the brain slumbers, the heart is awake, and I am very much aware that I miss you.

It is often suggested that the 'discovery' of Harriet's baseness was what determined the character of the finale, which might otherwise have been quite different: the movement was an act of revenge, a violent gesture in reaction to the traumatic dethroning of the beloved. To my mind, that is to impute far too specific an artistic influence to the immediate events of his personal life. For one thing, it was not his way to put his emotional experiences straight into music (his composition of the *Élégie* in the uncooled heat of the moment was, he pointed out, quite exceptional[11]). For another thing, though the finale took on, in the light of events, the character of an act of revenge, it was 'not written in that spirit', so Berlioz told Ferrand[12] – a friend to whom he was not given to lying. Above all, the documents all indicate that the 'plan of the symphony' had been in existence for some while before the discovery in question, waiting to be given form but frustrated by the too-present, incapacitating intensity of the passions it was to depict. The likelihood – to put it no stronger – is that it included a nightmarish finale, the character of which had its origin in Goethe's *Faust* and in particular the Walpurgis Night scene, combined with the 'Ronde du sabbat' from Hugo's *Odes et ballades*, which Berlioz had read by 1829. The 'affreuses vérités' reported to him in March 1830, and purporting to reveal the pure and spotless Harriet as an all too human and imperfect woman, had a general, not a specific, effect: the revelation, by freeing Berlioz from his thraldom, released his pent-up energies. Its immediate result was to precipitate the most dramatic of all his marathon treks into the country. But though his 'vessel cracked horribly' (he told Ferrand, quoting from Gérard de Nerval's translation of *Faust*), it 'righted itself'. And, as he had predicted would happen once his 'destiny' was no longer 'engulfed by an overpowering and hopeless passion', everything he had suffered served to enhance the force of his musical ideas; 'a whole new world of music sprang fully armed' from him. Once cured, he flung himself into the task of working out and setting down on paper the orchestral composition that had been forming in his mind for more than a year; and within six intense, concentrated weeks it was done. The one substantial change that was made to the scheme of the work after his change of heart about Harriet – the addition of an extra movement, the Waltz, to the original four – had nothing to do with that.

The best place to seek the facts about the *Symphonie fantastique* is the score – the music itself and the autograph manuscript. It is necessary to

[11] *Memoirs*, p. 71.

[12] *Correspondance générale*, Vol. I, p. 328.

insist on this point; for few works in the history of music have been subjected to so much idle theorising, and till recently none was so much talked about and so little studied. The notion that the symphony was no more than an opportunistic patchwork of already existing music had a long run; and its consequences linger on, oozing down through unconsidered programme notes and casual critical asides, even though, as Edward Cone observes, 'the unity of the symphony speaks out clearly' against such a view.[13]

It may be said that none of this pseudo-scholarly finger-wagging has done the work lasting harm; it remained a popular and much-performed piece notwithstanding what experts were saying about it; and its continuing to be controversial is a kind of tribute to its undiminished vitality: that people should still believe it introduced a totally new if not alien and improper element into symphonic composition shows that at least it is in no danger of being taken for granted. But that would be to imply that being controversial is the best that can be hoped for Berlioz and his symphony. And the controversy about the nature and essence of the *Symphonie fantastique* involves wider issues than critical opinion of one particular work: it is central to the ancient and fallacious doctrine of Berlioz the composer unlike any other and, beyond that, to the whole muddled, contentious question or non-question of programme music.

The concept – in the exclusive sense of a fundamentally different kind of music – has been so deeply ingrained in the minds of generations of music historians and amateurs, has set such deep and irresistible torrents of ink flowing, that I suppose it is too late to ask whether after all there is such a thing. But what does it amount to, in any practical and meaningful sense? And what is it based on, except a false distinction: that music which is not programme music is 'pure'? As Wilfrid Mellers has pointed out, it would be hard to find a more 'imbecile notion' than the concept of pure music, 'for the simple reason that although in a sense all music must be programme music, since it is concerned with human emotions, in another sense music, in so far as it *is* music, can never be anything but pure'.[14] The unreality of the distinction becomes disconcertingly evident when, as happens from time to time, a piece of 'absolute music' is revealed to be programmatic after all. Is Berg's *Lyric Suite* somehow made less purely musical by the discovery, 50 years after its first performance, that it embodies the detailed 'programme' of the composer's love affair with Hannah Fuchs-Robettin? For that matter, is Mendelssohn's *Hebrides* Overture less than pure because its musical imagery is dictated by Nature, by the multitudinous sea in all its humours? Is Beethoven's *Pastoral* Symphony experienced differently from

[13] Edward T. Cone (ed.), *Berlioz, Fantastic Symphony*, Norton Critical Scores, New York, 1980, p. 10.

[14] *Scrutiny*, March 1939, p. 480.

the other eight by reason of its movements having titles that unequivocally declare extra-musical associations and point the audience in a specific direction? Is such a work in practice – that is, in its effect on a sensitive listener – different in kind from a Haydn symphony? Or even from a Bach partita?

To go further, is one's experience of opera or song – music attached to and motivated by a text – different *in kind* from one's experience of instrumental music?

The change introduced by the Romantics was a change of degree, a development. Music did not abdicate its prerogative. It remained sovereign. What the Romantics did, and what Liszt meant when he coined the term programme music, was to make explicit what had been implicit before. Taking their lead from Beethoven, they brought the inherent expressivity of music further, so to speak, into the open (a process already begun in the eighteenth century). At the same time they widened its frame of reference (like Beethoven again, in his Ninth Symphony); and, in keeping with the spirit of an age concerned with the unification of the various arts, they blurred the distinction between 'absolute' music and music associated – as most music has been since the beginning of time – with words or an identified situation. Under the inspiration of Beethoven, whose symphonies they perceived as dramas – the *Eroica* and the Fifth no less than the *Pastoral* and the Ninth – they brought the theatre into the concert hall. Berlioz's introductory note to the *Symphonie fantastique* calls it an 'instrumental drama' whose 'outline, lacking the assistance of speech, needs to be explained in advance'. 'The following programme', he goes on, 'should thus be thought of as like the spoken text of an opera, serving to introduce the musical movements, for whose character and expression it provides the motive.' As in an opera, the communicativeness of musical images depends on the listener's being made aware of the reference. In a subsequent article, 'On Imitation in Music', Berlioz pointed out that Weber did not actually 'depict' moonlight in the second act of *Der Freischütz* nor Rossini the movement of oars in *Guillaume Tell*, as they were often considered to have done; rather, they created sounds which the listener, being apprised verbally of the context, accepted as plausible images of moonlight and the movement of oars. For the source of such images to be recognised, the listener had to be notified in some indirect way of the composer's intention.[15]

This is not to deny that the *Fantastique* was an audaciously innovative work. It was typical of Berlioz's freedom of spirit that he should have chosen, in his first major orchestral score, to override the normal categories of

[15] *Revue et gazette musicale*, 8 January 1837; republished in *Critique musicale*, Vol. 3, pp. 12–13.

musical discourse and attempt a mixture, a 'mélange des genres' analogous to what the Romantic dramatists were attempting under the influence of Shakespeare. In fact, he never again used the device of a detailed literary programme in a symphony. His second symphony, *Harold en Italie*, like the *Pastoral*, has movement titles only ('Harold in the mountains – scenes of melancholy, happiness and joy', 'March of pilgrims chanting the evening hymn', and so on); so has his fourth, the *Symphonie funèbre et triomphale*; and in the third, *Roméo et Juliette*, which is subtitled 'Dramatic Symphony', the drama is articulated by means of a text sung by a chorus, which in one form or another appears in four out of the seven movements. Berlioz thus adopted varying solutions to the problem of acquainting the listener with the frame of reference within which the symphonic narrative is to be heard.

One can say that in each case the content of the work dictated its own particular mode of communication; but you could also argue that had Berlioz written the *Symphonie fantastique* ten years later he might have confined himself to movement titles, after the example of *Harold* – a practice which he authorised many years later in a note prepared for a joint performance of the symphony and its sequel *Lélio* when he wrote that 'if the symphony is performed on its own [that is, without *Lélio*] [...] the detailed programme may possibly be dispensed with, only the titles of the five movements being retained, since the symphony can (the author trusts) provide its own musical interest independently of any dramatic intention'.[16] This is in effect what happens whenever a listener who knows the work hears it again: you respond to it as to any other piece of music; to quote Rudolf Reti, 'the music stands its ground, while the programme evaporates into the void'.[17] It may even happen when you hear it for the first time. The programme is not necessarily indispensable for an immediate response to the music – just as there are people who happily listen to *The Ring* without having much idea what is going on.

True; but, rather as understanding the words of an opera or a song adds something essential to our perception of it, the programme of the *Fantastique* – even though, once we have absorbed it, we may well forget about it – is at some stage an integral part of the experience. Berlioz, at the time of composing and first presenting the work, was in no doubt of that.

Some writers, seeking to defend it against the damning associations of 'programme music', have tried to wriggle out of this awkward fact. They explain it by reference to the climate and conditions of the time. Thus, Berlioz in 1830 was introducing music of startling novelty to a public which

[16] When Mahler removed the literary titles originally attached to his early symphonies, he meant that they were no longer necessary, not that they didn't express the intentions behind the music.

[17] Rudolf Reti, *The Thematic Process in Music*, Macmillan, London, 1961, p. 294.

had only lately come into contact with Beethoven's symphonies and was still convulsed and divided by the encounter. Furthermore, literary exegesis was a natural and important weapon for the French Romantic artist, the composer as well as the writer and painter (and this not merely because, as Schumann said, 'to the French, music by itself has no interest'[18]). Artistic manifestos were both fashionable and necessary; they were propaganda in a war of liberation in which, in an atmosphere of the barricades, the artists of Jeune-France strove to free art from the life-denying restraints of academicism and endow it with the beauty of naked unvarnished truth. It was a cause that needed, and wanted, to explain itself publicly; and it was to this fraternity of writers and painters, not to the Parisian composers of the day, that Berlioz naturally belonged. He was also not above exploiting his well-known and fashionably hopeless passion for Harriet Smithson to whip up interest in his symphony. (The mixture of sharp calculation and naïve spontaneity is one of the more disconcerting things about Berlioz. It is not that there aren't thousands of people who experience life and suffer with an equal intensity of emotion. But they don't usually feel free to talk about it, nor do they often combine it with the capacity for detaching themselves from their emotions and observing them with the objectivity of a scientist examining a specimen under a microscope.) It is a fact that the programme, publicised in advance in the press, caused a useful stir and aroused the curiosity of the musical and literary public both because of its known autobiographical connotations and because of the unprecedented degree to which it associated instrumental music with a story.

All this, though undeniable, does not alter the fact that Berlioz himself saw the symphony in autobiographical terms and made no bones about it. 'You will have no difficulty in recognising its hero',[19] he told Ferrand, to whom, while he was still planning the work, he had announced that it was to 'depict the course of his infernal passion'.[20] Even allowing that Berlioz tended to play the role of hyper-Romantic and 'artiste maudit' in his relations with Ferrand, that is a statement which, to say the least, is difficult to get round. But why should we wish to get round it? Once we rid ourselves of the whole concept of programme music as a different (and lowlier) form of the art, there is nothing to apologise for.

To find musical suggestion in non-musical things is far from peculiar to Berlioz. The capacity to do so is, after all, one of the distinguishing marks of a musician. Extra-musical ideas provided the impulse for many more works

[18] From the final section of his essay on the *Symphonie fantastique* in the *Neue Zeitschrift für Musik*, July–August 1835.

[19] *Correspondance générale*, Vol. I, p. 319.

[20] *Ibid.*, p. 306.

of Beethoven than the *Pastoral* – or of Mendelssohn than the *Hebrides*, as the testimony of the Taylor family, with whom Mendelssohn stayed in Wales in 1829, suggests:

> We observed how natural objects seemed to suggest music to him. There was in my sister Honora's garden a pretty creeping plant, new at the time, covered with little trumpet-like flowers. He was struck with it, and played for her the music which (he said) the fairies might play on those trumpets. When he wrote out the piece (called a capriccio in E minor) he drew a little branch of that flower all up the margin of the paper. The piece (an Andante and Allegro) which Mr Mendelssohn wrote for me was suggested by the sight of a bunch of carnations and roses. The carnations that year were very fine with us. He liked them best of all the flowers, would have one often in his buttonhole. We found he intended the arpeggio passage in that composition as a reminder of the sweet scent of the flower rising up.[21]

What matters is not what goes into a work but what comes out. The integrity of the *Symphonie fantastique*, like that of Berg's *Lyric Suite*, is not impugned by demonstrating that the work sprang directly from the turmoil of the composer's emotional life and that a network of personal associations underlies the musical argument. The symphony survives not because it tells the story of its author's obsession with a particular woman but because it expresses, in a musically coherent form and with a vividness of imagery and an originality of sonic and formal invention that remain fresh and vital, the agonies and ardours, the dreams and nightmares, of the youthful imagination. Its power, and its eternal youth, come from its mastery of large-scale musical narrative as well as from the undimmed intensity of recollected emotion that the composer embodied in it.

For Berlioz himself it represented more than the distillation of his passion for Harriet Smithson. Victor Hugo's lines from *Feuilles d'automne,* which he wrote on the title page of the manuscript, speak of 'My heart's book inscribed on every page', 'All I have suffered, all I have attempted', 'The loves, the labours, the bereavements of my youth'. The symphony was the repository of his entire imaginative existence up till then; it was the expression of the 'monde fantastique' of which he spoke to his father shortly before he began to compose the work, and which had been his inner life since boyhood.

One of the tutelary spirits of that world was Chateaubriand; his concept of the 'vague des passions' – that state of dreamlike melancholy in which the young imagination feeds on its own impossible desires and 'one inhabits,

[21] Quoted in Sebastian Hensel (trans. Carl Klingemann), *The Mendelssohn Family (1729–1847) from Letters and Journals*, Vol. 1, Harper & Brothers, London, 1881, pp. 226–27.

with a full heart, an empty world' – is invoked in the introductory note to the symphony.

But the presiding divinity was Estelle. It was her theme – the setting of Florian's 'Je vais donc quitter pour jamais/Mon doux pays, ma douce amie', written in his teens[22] – that Berlioz chose to open the symphony, scoring it for the muted string quartet, with isolated *pizzicato* phrases for the double basses pulsating like the vibrations of a stone dropped into still water, the whole image like a far-off remembered country still 'visible to him across the timeless air', though seen through a veil of tears. The theme, he said, recurred to him when he was planning the symphony, and he adopted it 'because it seemed to me apt for the expression of that overpowering sadness felt by a young heart first tortured by a hopeless love'.[23] Beyond that was the kinship that related the intervals and contours of the theme to the Vespers plainsong whose 'sad persistent chant' (springing to a plangent minor sixth, then sinking back) set off his Virgilian visions in the church at La Côte-Saint-André, and whose influence sounds repeatedly through his music.

The Estelle theme was also very apt in its relationship to the main melody of the work, the *idée fixe* (the melody that had been associated with an ideal, unattainable beloved at least since 1828, when Berlioz used it in his Prix de Rome cantata *Herminie*). Not only is the first phrase echoed in the second part of the *idée fixe*, but, when it is repeated at the same pitch in the relative major – with a rippling accompaniment of flutes and clarinets suggestive of the river in which Némorin gazed at the reflection of Estelle's beauty – the phrase becomes identical with the motif of the sighing fourth, followed by the dejected descent to the leading note, which is the most important element of the *idée fixe*. Thus the Berlioz/Chateaubriand concept of 'rêverie' – creating from its unsatisfied desires their ideal object – was mirrored and embodied in the melodic evolution of the music. Autobiography was absorbed into art.

The other literary sources fed the compositional process in a similar way and were transmuted into the musical images they inspired. We can trace them because of the written programme (as we usually cannot in the case of other works that sprang from comparable extra-musical ideas and experiences, but of which the composers left no record). These sources included, in addition to *René* and *Faust*, Victor Hugo's 'La Ronde du sabbat', from *Odes et ballades*, in which the striking of midnight on a monastery bell precipitates a hideous gathering of witches, demons and grotesque half-human, half-animal creatures who dance a whirling

22 *Cf.* pp. 74–76, above.

23 *Memoirs*, p. 16.

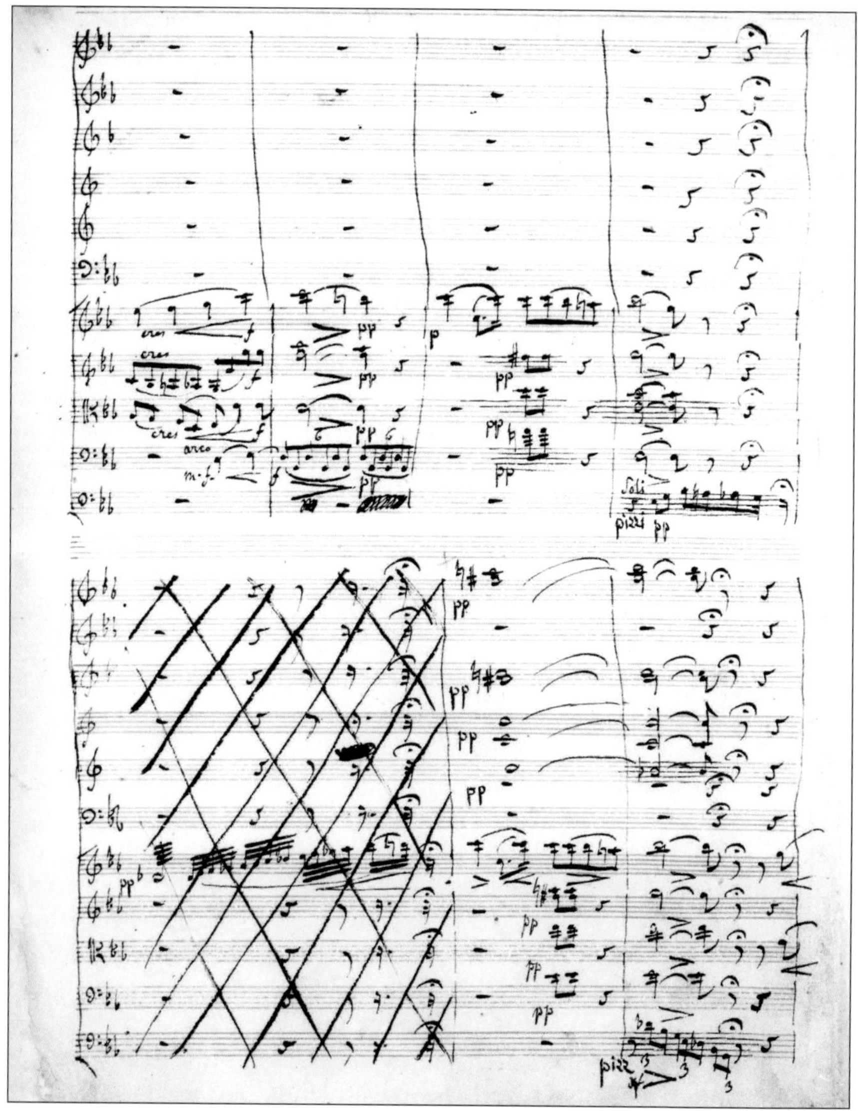

'Estelle's theme' on the second page of the first movement of the Symphonie fantastique

round-dance and perform obscene parodies of church rituals. Hugo's anti-capital-punishment novella *Le Dernier jour d'un condamné*, which Berlioz read in 1829, also contributed ideas and images: not only the general notion of an '*idée fixe* haunting the mind every hour, every moment' but also the picture of the chained convicts in the prison courtyard dancing furiously in a ring while 'the rhythmic clashing of their chains served as orchestra to their raucous song': 'If I were looking for an image of a witches' sabbath', writes Hugo, ' I could not find a better nor a worse one.' In the same passage the convicts catch sight of the condemned man looking down from the window of his cell and give a roar of delight – the same 'rugissement de joie' (Berlioz's programme borrows Hugo's phrase) that is heard in the finale of the symphony when the appearance of the murdered beloved, transmuted into a prostitute (the *idée fixe* trivialised as a vulgar, lewdly cackling tune on the E flat clarinet), is greeted by a roar from the whole orchestra, complete with violent change of key, metre and orchestral colour.

Chateaubriand, again, may have helped to suggest the piping shepherds' call at the beginning of the 'Scène aux champs'. In the same passage that describes René crying out to the mountains and torrents to give him 'the ideal object of his waiting passions', he speaks of 'listening to [the shepherd's] melancholy songs, which reminded me that in all lands man's song is naturally sad, even when it is expressing happiness'. Another source was De Quincey's *Confessions of an English Opium-Eater*, in the French version by Alfred de Musset that came out in 1828. In one of the passages that Musset added to the original, the hero imagines, under the influence of the drug, that he has committed a frightful crime and, in a darkness lit by torches and the gleam of pikes and halberds, hears the sentence of death pronounced on him. Elsewhere he attends a ball one evening when he has not taken opium and catches glimpses of his beloved through the brilliant throng. The scenario of both the 'March to the Scaffold' and the 'Witches' Sabbath' echoes Gretchen's words at the end of *Faust*, Part I, where she imagines the crowd gathering in the square and the funeral bells tolling as she is dragged to the scaffold.

These and no doubt other sources went to the making of Berlioz's instrumental drama. Did he also take opium? Even though, as Nicholas Temperley has said, 'the industry and achievement of Berlioz's life make it certain that he was not a drug addict',[24] it seems likely that he had experimented with it (in the letter to his father, quoted above, he says that the sensations he experiences in his own imaginary world resemble the effect of opium) and, like so many of his contemporaries, knew from personal experience the Goya-esque images – the hags, the Satanic goat-faced deities, the magicians and prostitutes – conjured by the potency of the poppy seed. Whether the 'March to the Scaffold' and the 'Witches'

[24] Nicholas Temperley, in *Symphonie Fantastique*, New Berlioz Edition, Vol. 16, Bärenreiter, Kassel, p. XI.

Sabbath' came from his imagination unaided or were drawn up from its darkest depths by De Quincey's 'subtle and mighty opium' is immaterial. They remain classic visions of nightmare; the enormous developments in orchestral colour and mass since 1830 have not dimmed their power.

The Two Italies

'The Two Italies' began life as a talk given to the Berlioz Society, was then enlarged into a lecture delivered to the Department of Music at the University of California, Davis, in November 2008, and in 2012 was repeated, in French, at the Festival Berlioz in La Côte-Saint-André.

I'm interpreting my title in the widest sense, to include all Berlioz's relationship with Italy, of which his travels form the major part but not the sole part. His views may be summed up in the mingled cry of delight and despair that concludes chapter 37 of the *Memoirs*, where he celebrates the beauties of the Italian landscape: 'O grande et forte Italie! Italie sauvage! insoucieuse de ta sœur, l'Italie artiste, "La belle Juliette au cercueil étendue"'.

This antithesis dominates all his writings on Italy – the *Voyage musical en Allemagne et en Italie* and the *Memoirs*, newspaper articles, letters – and I propose to discuss both Italies as he experienced the one and the other, wild Italy, and the Italy of Art, the once lovely but now dead Juliet, 'stretched upon her bier'.

That is exactly the antithesis we find in a letter of Mendelssohn, written from Rome at the time Berlioz was there: 'Why should Italy still insist on being the land of Art, when it is in reality the land of Nature, delighting every heart?' Mendelssohn had been describing the state of music in Rome; and though his words are more temperate than Berlioz's, the sentiments, and the examples given, are no different:

> The Papal singers are almost all unmusical and don't perform even the most familiar pieces in tune. [...] The orchestras are worse than one would believe possible. [...] The two or three violinists play in quite different styles and come in when they please, the wind instruments are tuned either too high or too low, and they execute flourishes in the subordinate parts like those we are accustomed to hear in the streets, but hardly as good. The whole thing is an absolute caterwauling.[1]

First the Italy of Art. Berlioz had his knife well and truly into contemporary Italian music long before he set foot in Italy. His exclusive cult of French classical opera made him the implacable enemy of the craze for Italian opera

[1] *Letters from Italy and Switzerland*, transl. Lady Wallace, Longman, Green, Longman and Roberts, London, 1862, *passim*.

that swept Paris in the early 1820s. It prevented him – as he admitted – from recognising the greatness of *Il barbiere di Siviglia* or delighting in *Le Comte Ory* (as he later did) or admiring the grandeur of *Guillaume Tell*. Italian opera as embodied in the all-conquering Rossini seemed opposed to everything he believed about dramatic music. Gluck and Spontini were the true gods. The new pagan deity was anathema. The dilettanti exalted Rossini and his imitators to the skies – Rossini was the Michelangelo of music – and sneered at Gluck as outmoded, mere 'plainchant'. They were the enemy. Berlioz's career as critic and proselytiser begins with an attack on them, in the articles published in the *Corsaire* in 1823, when he was nineteen. The idea of blowing up the Théâtre-Italien with all its congregation of false believers might have to be abandoned as too difficult to carry out, but he could conduct his campaign in print. Later, much of his serious professional music criticism will be devoted to combating what he regards as the ridiculous deference paid by French musical opinion to Italian music and Italian musical values – not so much modern Italian music *per se* as its abuses, and its corrupting influence, which even leads French singers to disfigure the vocal line in French operas with ornaments in the Italian mode.

Though his attitude would relax a little and he would come to admire particular works, he would never lose his antipathy to what he considered the anti-dramatic absurdities of Rossini in his cynical and perfunctory mode: the repetition of a single stereotyped cadence formula (parodied in the ophicleide solo in *Benvenuto Cellini*), the inevitable crescendos, the brutalising din of cymbals and bass drum used invariably in tandem as a means of whipping up physical excitement, the mania for vocal display, the tendency for even the most expressive passages to give way suddenly to empty decoration. Here is Ernest Legouvé's account of Berlioz at a performance of Rossini's *Otello*:

> The finale of the second act contains a famous passage in which Desdemona, at her father's feet, cries '*Se il padre m'abandonnà,/Che mai più mi resterà?*' – 'If my father renounces me, what will I have left?' The first line, which is sung twice, expresses Desdemona's grief in a slow and very poignant phrase. Then at the second line, to depict her despair, there is a sudden flurry of scales and roulades. I found them very stirring, but they infuriated Berlioz. At the end of the act he leant over and murmured in my ear, in a voice as expressive as the melody itself: 'If my father renounces me, if my father renounces me'. Then, in a burst of savage laughter and, faithfully reproducing all the coloratura of the score: 'I don't give a damn, I don't give a damn, I don't give a damn'.[2]

[2] Legouvé, *Soixante ans de souvenirs*, Vol. 1, pp. 298–99.

If that was so, how much more detrimental were Rossini's successors and imitators! Berlioz's writings on the subject become less fevered, more laid back than his early fulminations against the dilettanti, but the basic objections remain. Here he is in 1834, reviewing an opera by the minor Italian composer Renato Gabussi in the *Rénovateur*:

> The other day I went to the Théâtre-Italien – something that doesn't often happen to me; but, when all is said, with a new opera and an opera entitled *Ernani* and with Rubini, Tamburini, Santini and Grisi in the cast, a visit to the Favart was clearly in order.
>
> Ye gods! What gilded visions the young composer must have had before his eyes. No doubt he had heard all about the feud generated by Victor Hugo's play. Echoes of the tumult that engulfed the pit at every performance, the sarcastic laughter of the hostile faction, the furious threats and passionate enthusiasm of the supporters of the new school, had reached him and set his heart aglow with noble emulation. 'I shall make Victor Hugo's play into an opera', will have been his response. 'I shall find a way of getting it put on at the Théâtre-Italien in Paris. I shall rekindle the great conflict that the French poet provoked not long ago. There will be confrontations, shouting matches, duels for and against me. And, with a company formed of the finest singers in Europe, I cannot fail to have all my intentions brought out and displayed in the best possible light'.
>
> Poor maestro! What a sad awakening. Nothing could have been cooler and better behaved than the audience at the fourth performance of *Ernani*: no trace of confrontation, not a whisper of an argument, everyone on the contrary in perfect agreement. On the way out we talked of everything but the opera we had just heard. It might have been the hundredth performance of a long-established work. That is cruel for a composer. But in all honesty what can one say of this *Ernani*, which is no more *Ernani* than I am the Pope. Where are the volcanic passions, the fierce vengefulness, the impetuous, consuming love, the pure and noble devotion of Doña Sol, and the other outstanding features that made Victor Hugo's play absurd to some, sublime to others, remarkable to all? The physiognomy of the Italian drama is such that it might just as well be called *Francesco* or *Pietro*; and the music shares this fault. It wants distinctive colour. The cavatinas are tailored to the pattern of every other example of the kind. The ritornellos have the form in use with every other maestro of the Italian school; the same modulation appears at exactly the point where custom decrees it should appear. The tunes have sisters and cousins in every corner of the globe. And this fault, which is a very serious one, to our way of thinking, in any composition, becomes shocking in a subject as extreme as that of *Ernani*.[3]

[3] *Le Rénovateur*, 5 December 1834; republished in *Critique musicale*, Vol. 1, pp. 463–64.

I have to admit that I share these prejudices, if prejudices they are. A good deal of Italian opera of this period is simply not serious. The operas of Donizetti (after Rossini the next conqueror of Paris, with nine playing in Paris in a single year, 1840) are certainly many cuts above Gabussi's *Ernani*, and unquestionably have many fine moments, but at the same time there is so much formula in them, so much that is dramatically unmemorable.

One of the many ironies of Berlioz's life was that to have a chance to get on as a composer he had to win the Prix de Rome and therefore spend time in Italy, when he could have been fostering his career in Paris and building on the successes already achieved there. The Prix de Rome was the occasion of yet more clashes with the musical establishment and what he considered its illogical and often senseless rules and regulations, its discouragement of originality or anything truly dramatic in the cantatas the candidates were set to compose. Berlioz alienated his elders and betters still more by the things he wrote, later, about the organisation of the prize. I have no doubt it was because of his two scurrilous but essentially accurate articles in *L'Europe littéraire* in 1833 that Habeneck decided not to conduct Berlioz's concerts at the Conservatoire, as he had been doing till then.

One of the rules Berlioz objected to was that the competing cantatas, though written for orchestra, were performed to the judges on the piano. It reduced the candidates, the knowledgeable and the ignorant, to the same level. 'The piano, for the orchestral composer, is a guillotine which chops off the aristocrat's head and from which only the poor have nothing to fear.'[4] Another questionable rule was that the music prize was judged not simply by the music section of the Académie des Beaux-Arts but by the architects, painters, sculptors and engravers as well. He made much fun of it in the second of the two articles I mentioned – the account of the old Institute usher, Pingard, who had been a cabin-boy with the French East Indies Company and had been to South-East Asia, the region Berlioz had dreamed of obsessively as a boy when he pored over the big atlas in his father's library – Java, Borneo, Sumatra, the coast of Coromandel:

> When I arrived at the Institute on the evening of Judgment Day to learn my fate and discover if the painters, sculptors and engravers had decreed whether I was a good musician or a bad one, I met Pingard on the stairs.
> 'Oh hello, Berlioz, I've been looking for you'.
> 'What have I got? Honourable mention, first prize, second, or nothing at all?'

[4] *Memoirs*, p. 89.

> 'Look here, I'm feeling quite shaken. Would you believe it, you were only two votes short of first. You've got second all right. Another two votes and you'd have got first. Look here, it's really upset me – because, look here, I'm not a painter or an architect or an engraver of medals so of course I know nothing about music, but I'll be damned if that "God of the Christians" of yours didn't fair churn me up inside. And by thunder, if I'd run into you just then I'd – I'd have stood you a small cup of coffee.'
>
> 'Thanks awfully, Pingard, I admire your taste. Besides, haven't you been on the coast of Coromandel?'
>
> 'I certainly have. Why?'
>
> 'And the isles of Java?'
>
> 'Yes, but – '
>
> 'And Sumatra?'
>
> 'Yes.'
>
> 'Borneo?'
>
> 'Yes.'
>
> 'You knew Levaillant well?'
>
> 'I should say so – hand in glove with him.'
>
> 'You've often talked with Volney?'
>
> 'Count de Volney who wore blue stockings?'
>
> 'That's the one.'
>
> 'Absolutely.'
>
> 'Well then, you're an excellent judge of music.'
>
> 'How's that?'
>
> 'It's obvious – simply that if anyone asks you, "What right have you to judge music? Are you a painter, an engraver, an architect, a sculptor?", you can reply, "No, I'm a – er – a traveller, sailor, friend of Volney and Levaillant. What more do you want?"'[5]

It's a mark of Berlioz's mixture of common sense, clarity of mind and detachment that the fact that he owed his second prize that year precisely to the non-musicians and the mixed voting procedure – the architects and the painters overturned the preliminary vote of the musicians – didn't alter his opinion: it was still a bad principle. In the same way, even though he personally got so much out of the Italian experience, he still thought it made no sense to send budding composers to such a sink of musical mediocrity and worse.

He did his best to get out of going and campaigned to be allowed to draw his Prix de Rome grant in Paris; he got Meyerbeer and Spontini (and Fétis) to write in support, and his doctor, Jules Guérin, who had been a contemporary of his at the École de Médecine, to testify that the hot

[5] *Memoirs*, pp. 93–94 (*L'Europe littéraire*, 19 July 1833, *Critique musicale*, Vol. 1, pp. 107–12). This account refers to 1828, when Berlioz's cantata was *Herminie*.

climate of Rome could be dangerous for someone so highly strung.[6] But to no avail. And as Madame Moke, Camille's mother, had made winning the Prix de Rome one of the conditions of her consenting to his engagement to Camille, he had no choice but to go.

Another irony: once he was safely out of the way, the perfidious Madame Moke arranged for her daughter to marry the piano manufacturer Pleyel. We know Berlioz's response to that, and the circumstances that led to his spending nearly a month in Nice in the spring of 1831, where he recovered from the shock and wrote the *King Lear* Overture – a work whose tense, dry, electric string textures surely reflect what he had recently been through, just as I am certain that the tender, long-drawn-out second theme of the *Allegro* and the way it is systematically destroyed in the coda stand not only for the tragic death of Cordelia but also for the loss of Camille and the annihilation of their love.

We know, too, from the *Memoirs*, what Berlioz thought of the Italian musical life he encountered during his year there. It confirmed all his fondest prejudices. 'I'm forced to live in a country where the god I serve is unknown', he writes to his grandfather Nicolas Marmion.[7] And to Spontini: in Italy he has 'found nothing but childishness, pettiness, servile imitation, and a total lack of grand ideas and genius'.[8] On his way back from Nice he heard from the Florentine monks he travelled with all about the splendours of the coming Corpus Christi procession. But nothing more squalid and devoid of all dignity could be imagined. And as for the music! The monks' 'coro immenso' resolved itself into a handful of out-of-tune castratos, 'sounding like an ensemble of rusty gate-hinges', while the band with its 'quacking clarinets' and 'circus trumpets' would have been apter to Silenus and his satyrs than to the statue of the Blessed Virgin.[9] 'That is how religious festivals are regarded in the capital of the Christian world', he writes to his sister Adèle,

> the city where we are sent 'to admire the masterpieces of the art of music'. [...] How much better it is, the Corpus Christi procession in France – I could never watch it even at La Côte without being moved – and here I feel only disgust.[10]

Secular music, he finds, is almost as bad. The only theatres worth frequenting are the ancient theatres at Pompeii, San Germano and Tusculum, where the wind among the ruins makes a sweeter music than anything heard at the Fondo or the Pergola. His response to a Roman

6 Cairns, *Berlioz,* Vol. 1, pp. 420–21.

7 *Correspondance générale*, Vol. I, p. 483.

8 *Ibid.*, p. 545.

9 *Memoirs*, p. 145.

10 *Correspondance générale*, I, pp. 454–55.

music-dealer who has never heard of Weber, and who instead offers him music by Pacini, is: 'Non avete dunque vergogna, corpo di Dio?' – 'Have you no shame?'[11] The fact that Weber is not known there will be one more nail in Italy's coffin. The *Memoirs* add:

> The names of Weber and Beethoven are virtually unknown. A learned priest of the Sistine Chapel told Mendelssohn that he had heard mention of 'a young man of great promise called Mozart'. It is true that the worthy cleric lives away from the world and has devoted his life to the works of Palestrina. [...] Although Mozart is never performed, there are undeniably quite a number of people who have heard more of him than that he is a young man of great promise. The smarter dilettanti know that he is dead and that, without approaching Donizetti, he wrote one or two remarkable things.[12]

In 1832 Berlioz wrote an essay for the *Revue européenne* in Paris, which he entitled, ironically, 'Letter from an Enthusiast on the Present State of Music in Italy', and in which he contrasted the decay of Art Music with the vigour of the typical Abruzzian serenade – which though primitive is at least fresh and uninhibited – and with the music of the *pifferari*. He concluded:

> And it's there that the French Institute annually sends its prize-winning composers. What exile better calculated to waste their time and dampen their spirits, delay their careers, clip their wings (if they have any) – which one must presume is the objective of those responsible for the regulation, since they stick to it in defiance of common sense and the repeated warnings of impartial witnesses. [...] By all means send painters, sculptors and architects to Rome – but composers! No one laughs more than the Romans themselves.

That is one side of the picture – one of the two Italies. One could multiply the examples I've given many times. Berlioz wasn't exaggerating, as Mendelssohn's independent testimony makes clear. And it was worse, much worse, for him than for Mendelssohn. Berlioz's chief reason for being in Rome – his engagement to Camille Moke – no longer applied. And Rome cut him off from active pursuit of his art and career and, just as bad, from the 'musical joys' (the 'jouissances musicales') that were the condition of his existence ('I'm ill from the need of music')[13] – cut him off from the great things that were going on in Paris: the first performance in France of Beethoven's Ninth Symphony, Paganini's recitals, the advent of a new kind of opera, in Meyerbeer's *Robert le diable*, which might be the longed-for

[11] *Ibid.*, 426.
[12] *Memoirs*, p. 171.
[13] *Correspondance générale*, Vol. I, p. 542.

answer to the frivolities of the Italian school. All this was happening while he chafed in what he called 'that cursed barracks',[14] the Villa Medici.

Mendelssohn could sit in his sunny room in the Piazza di Spagna calmly composing masterpieces like the *Hebrides* Overture and the Italian Symphony; Berlioz's Italian symphony had to wait till he was back in Paris. The atmosphere of Rome, he found, was so deadening that it stifled his creative faculties. He felt devoid of ideas. He might manage to rewrite the 'Scène aux champs' of the *Symphonie fantastique* in Rome. But that was a question of revising and reshaping something that had already been created, somewhere else, if in imperfect form. The one substantial new score of the whole Italian period, the *King Lear* Overture, was composed far from Rome, at Nice, in his head as he walked on the seashore. There, ideas flowed. In Rome there were almost none. Only once, in the *Méditation religieuse*, written 'one day when the spleen was killing me', was he able to turn the ennui of Rome to positive account.[15] Otherwise, he could only lie on Mendelssohn's sofa, listening to his new friend play from his latest scores or play music they both admired, like Iphigénie's 'D'une image, hélas, trop chérie', which Mendelssohn accompanied while Berlioz sang.

Mendelssohn liked Berlioz but couldn't understand how someone who had such an acute feeling for art and such sensible opinions about it should write such dreadful music and have no idea that he was doing so. The score of the *Symphonie fantastique*, he told his family, filled him with such horror and depressed him so deeply that he couldn't work for two whole days.[16] Berlioz wasn't the only one with prejudices – or perhaps Mendelssohn was afraid of what he saw, a new music not dreamed of in his philosophy.

One other musical pleasure was the impromptu operatic sessions Berlioz sometimes held round the fountain in the portico of the Villa Medici overlooking the gardens, when he would gather a few chosen spirits from among his fellow inmates and hum favourite numbers or whole acts of *Der Freischütz* or *La Vestale* or *Don Giovanni*, while he played his guitar.

> There were four or five of us, sitting in the moonlight round the little fountain above the steps that lead down to the garden. We drew lots for who should go and fetch my guitar; and as the audience was composed of the small number of inmates whom I can stand I needed no urging to sing. As I was beginning an aria from *Iphigénie en Tauride*, Carle Vernet appeared. Within a minute or two he started weeping, sobbing out loud, then, unable to bear any more, took refuge in his son's drawing-room,

[14] *Ibid.*, p. 457.

[15] *Ibid.*, p. 516.

[16] *Briefe einer Reise durch Deutschland, Italien und die Schweiz*, Max Niehans Verlag, Zürich, 1958, pp. 119–20.

'D'une image, hélas, trop chérie' from Gluck's Iphigénie en Tauride, *in Berlioz's hand*

The Villa Medici in Rome, with St Peter's in the background

crying in a choking voice: 'Horace, Horace, come here!' – 'What is it, what is it?' – 'We're all in tears.' 'Why – what's happened?' 'It's Monsieur Berlioz, he's singing us Gluck. Yes (turning to me), as you say, sir, it makes you want to go on your knees. Believe me, I know you, you're a melancholic character, there are some people who....' He couldn't finish. Yet no one laughed. The fact is, we were all moved. I felt in the mood, it was night, there was nothing to inhibit me beneath that echoing portico, and I let myself go as if I had been on my own.[17]

But the sovereign remedy for the boredom and uncongenial atmosphere of Rome was to shake off the dust of it and head for the plains and hills, for Tivoli, Subiaco and beyond, into the Abruzzi – 'l'Italie sauvage'. The song that became such a hit at the Villa Medici, until Horace Vernet had to beg people to stop whistling it and forbad his new valet to utter a note of it on pain of instant dismissal – *La Captive* – was composed not in Rome but in Subiaco.

In spite of all of Berlioz's gripes about the absurdity of sending musicians to a country that had no musical life worthy of the name, you have only to read his accounts of his wanderings in Italy to see how deep the experience went, how much he enjoyed himself there, and what an incalculable benefit

[17] *Memoirs*, p. 494.

it was for him. In chapters 37 and 38 of the *Memoirs* his writing takes wing. I will quote only a little, since it is so familiar:

> the rows of shrines to the Madonna along the tops of the high hills where, at evening, returning late from the plains, the reapers pass, chanting their litanies, while from somewhere comes the sad jangle of a monastery bell – pine forests resounding to the rustic tunes of the *pifferari* – great girls with raven hair and swarthy skin and raucous laughs whose passion for dancing so often taxed the patience and the fingers *di questo signore che suona la chitarra francese* – the traditional tambourine beating time to my improvised saltarellos – the carabinieris' insistence on forcing their way in and joining our tavern ball – indignation of the dancers, French and Abruzzian – Flacheron's prodigious fists flailing – humiliating expulsion of the soldiers of the Pope – dark threats of ambuscades and long knives – Flacheron, without a word to any of us, slipping off to his midnight tryst armed only with a stick – total absence of carabinieri – wild delight of Crispino. And then Albano, Castelgondolfo, [...] the lake of Gabia, the marsh where I slept at midday without thought of fever, the remains of the gardens where Zenobia lived, beautiful dethroned queen of Palmyra, the long lines of ancient aqueducts melting into the distance.[18]

Interestingly, Berlioz was more positive about the Italian experience in what he wrote soon after returning from Italy than he was in the later *Voyage musical* and his *Memoirs*. With all the frustration, it was, he acknowledged, a blessing, and a blessing only partly in disguise. The musical life of Italy, he says, may be hopeless but 'it is in this regard only that I find the Italian journey a nonsense for a musician. In every other, it is bound to have a powerful influence on lively and poetic imaginations'.[19]

It certainly did on his. *Sur les alpes, ah! quel délice*: the sentiments of the Swiss song – and Berlioz can't resist a dig at Italian music ('Is there an Italian musician anywhere who could have thought of this *ranz de vaches*'[20]) – become a motif of his year in Italy. Like the 'chamois-hunter' of the text he is 'drawn to the hills' where, his 'heart unburdened and void of care', 'o'er leaping boulder and torrent', he walks huge distances and roves freely under the span of heaven. It's one more irony, as Michel Austin puts it, that it was in Italy where, forced by the regulations of the Prix de Rome to go there, Berlioz discovered liberty.[21] He recognised it himself: 'Thanks to my exile in Italy – my very isolation, the loss of the joys of my art, the rarefaction of my

[18] *Ibid.*, pp. 157–58.

[19] *Gazette musicale*, 2 February 1834; republished in *Critique musicale*, Vol. 1, p. 160.

[20] *Correspondance générale*, Vol. I, p. 463.

[21] Michel Austin, 'De Nice à Naples, le voyage du compositeur', in Chantal Spillemaecker and Antoine Troncy (eds.), *Berlioz et l'Italie, voyage musical*, Éditions Libel, La Côte-Saint-André, 2012, p. 62.

Corot, Roman Campagna with Claudian aqueduct, *1826*

intellectual environment – I have been thrown on the life of wild Italy and have come to feel all the delight of absolute physical liberty'.[22]

The benefits of this carefree existence were, first and crucially, in the realm of health, physical and mental. After the shocks and tensions and hyperactivity of his life in Paris, it gave his nervous system a badly needed rest, a necessary time to do nothing – just relax and absorb. It sweated the previous ten years out of him. Secondly, and no less important, was the influence of wild Italy on his music, on his art, both direct and indirect.

The two influences – the holiday from the Parisian vortex, the effect of the luminous landscapes – arguably lie behind the greater roundness and richness of sonority in Berlioz's music, if we compare the *Fantastique* with *Roméo et Juliette*. This distinction can't be proved, of course, nor can we say whether the revised 'Scène aux champs' and its sense of space and wide, gleaming distances show the effect of those influences: the original version of the movement, performed in 1830, hasn't survived. But the traces of Italian folk music in *Harold en Italie* and *Benvenuto Cellini*, and the scenes of Italian popular life celebrated in both works, are obvious examples. Berlioz's friend Crispino and his serenade accompanied by mandolin and triangle reappear, transmuted, in the melancholy song of the foundry workers, 'Bienheureux les matelots', in *Benvenuto Cellini*. The whole liberating experience of the

[22] *Correspondance générale*, Vol. I, p. 536.

hills and the improvised saltarellos of Subiaco lies behind the rhythmic exuberance and vivid colours of both *Benvenuto* and *Harold*.

Although Berlioz doesn't spell it out, we can find pre-echoes, as it were, of the *Harold* symphony in the experiences he writes about. The first movement, 'Harold aux montagnes, scènes de mélancolie, de bonheur et de joie' – here without doubt, it seems to me, we have a direct translation of a visual and atmospheric experience such as any walker in the mountains will have had: the moment when the clouds suddenly give way and the sun bursts through and parts the curtain to reveal the whole landscape.

There's no need to search for sources of the third movement. It was inspired by the *pifferari*, the strolling wind-players whom Berlioz described in detail in the 'Lettre d'un Enthousiaste' (*La Revue musicale*, 1832), and then in *Voyage musical* and the *Memoirs*:

> In Rome I was struck by one type of music only, [...] the folk music of the *pifferari*. These are strolling musicians who, towards Christmas, come down from the mountains in groups of four or five, armed with bagpipes and *pifferi* (a sort of oboe) to play in pious homage before the statues of the Madonna. They are generally dressed in large brown woollen coats and the pointed hats that brigands sport, and their whole appearance is instinct with a sort of mystic savagery that is most striking. I spent hours at a time watching them in the streets of Rome as they stood, heads inclined to one side, bright eyes alight with faith and fixed adoringly on the Holy Mother, almost as still as the image they worshipped. The bagpipe sustains a harmony of two or three notes, supported by a large *piffero* doubling the lowest; above it a double *piffero* of medium size gives out the melody, and above that two very small *pifferi* played by children from twelve to fifteen years of age execute trills and rhythmic figures, drenching the rustic tune in a shower of the weirdest ornamentation. After a lot of lively, cheerful tunes, which they repeat over and over again, the concert concludes with a slow, grave piece like a prayer, deeply felt, full of solemn, patriarchal dignity. [...] If I was impressed by them in Rome, you may imagine what I felt when I encountered them in the mountains of the Abruzzi. Volcanic rocks and dark pine forests are the natural setting and complement of such primordial music. When the scene included some great Cyclopean mass of masonry, monument of a vanished age, and a few shepherds dressed in rough sheepskins with the whole fleece worn outside, I could believe myself back in the time of the ancient peoples among whom Evander the Arcadian settled, the liberal host of Aeneas.[23]

Most Italian of all, in the sense I'm speaking of, is the 'Pilgrims' March'. The passage in the *Memoirs* that I quoted earlier brings it instantly to mind: 'the reapers, at evening, chanting their litanies, while from somewhere

[23] *Memoirs*, pp. 171–72.

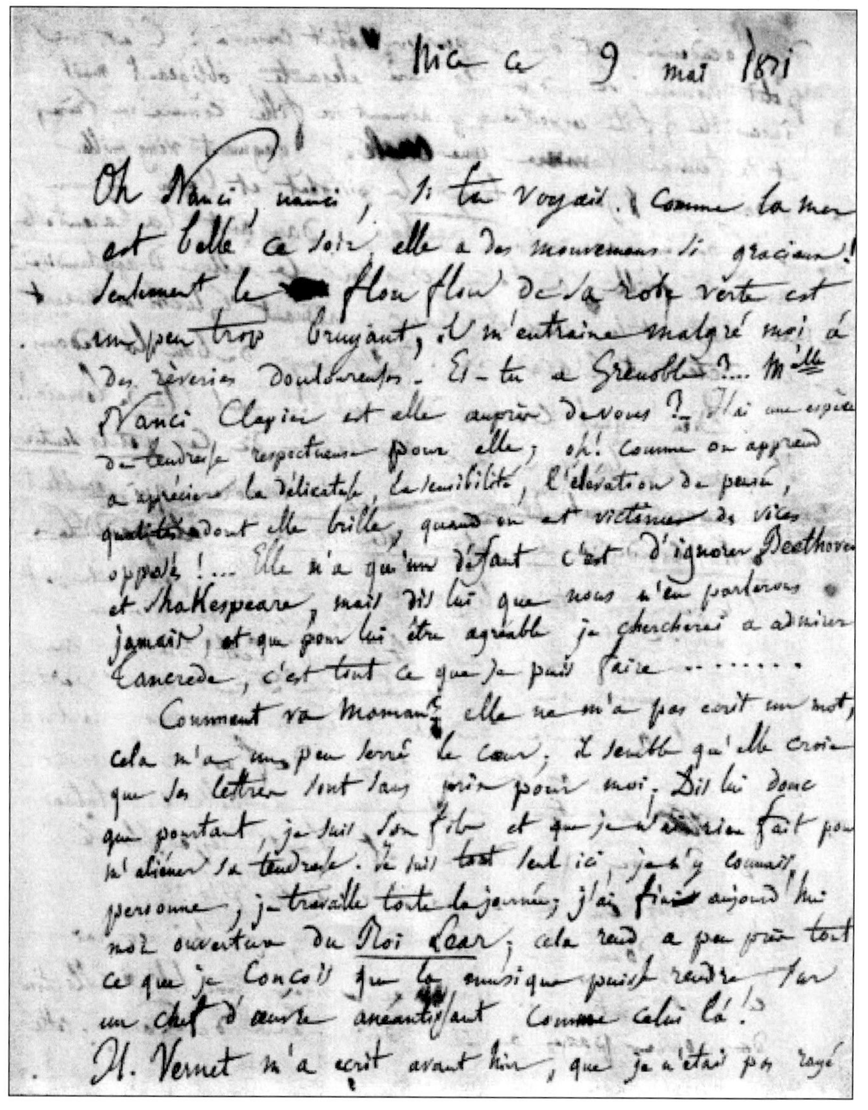

Nice ce 9 mai 1831

Oh Nanci, nanci, si tu voyais comme la mer est belle ce soir, elle a des mouvemens si gracieux! Seulement le flou flou de sa robe verte est un peu trop bruyant, il m'entraine malgré moi à des rêveries douloureuses. Es-tu à Grenoble?... Mlle Nanci Clappier est elle auprès de vous? J'ai une espèce de tendresse respectueuse pour elle; oh! comme on apprend à apprécier la délicatesse, la sensibilité, l'élévation de pensée, qualités dont elle brille, quand on est victime des vices opposés!... Elle n'a qu'un défaut c'est d'ignorer Beethoven et Shakespeare, mais dis lui que nous n'en parlerons jamais, et que pour lui être agréable je chercherai à admirer Tancrède, c'est tout ce que je puis faire.......

Comment va Maman? elle ne m'a pas écrit un mot, cela m'a un peu serré le cœur; il semble qu'elle croie que ses lettres sont sans prix pour moi. Dis lui donc que pourtant je suis son fils et que je n'ai rien fait pour m'aliéner sa tendresse. Je suis tout seul ici, je n'y connais personne, je travaille toute la journée; j'ai fini aujourd'hui mon ouverture du Roi Lear; cela rend à peu près tout ce que je conçois que la musique puisse rendre par un chef d'œuvre anéantissant comme celui là!

H. Vernet m'a écrit avant hier, que je n'étais pas rayé

A letter from Berlioz to his sister Nancy, 9 May 1831

comes the sound of a monastery bell' – that for the repeated high B on harp and woodwind. For the booming C natural we can turn to that other passage in the *Memoirs*, where Berlioz, standing on one of the hillocks that dot the Roman plain, listens to the sound of the bell of St Peter's.

The mention of Aeneas' host, Evander the Arcadian, brings me to the work which above all others grew, in part at least, out of the Italian experience. I'm thinking first of the strange vision that came to Berlioz as he stood on Mount Posilippo on a celestial October evening in 1831, after a day full of Virgilian associations, and suddenly *saw* the coast below swarming with the heroes of the *Aeneid*, the demigods with whom, he later wrote, he had spent his life.[24] I'm thinking also of those other excursions described in the *Memoirs*, when, in the Campagna or the mountains, 'some passage from the *Aeneid*, dormant in my memory since childhood, would come back to me, set off by the character of the country I had wandered into' and, singing to his guitar, he would 'improvise a strange recitative to still stranger harmony'.[25] It's a different 'étrange récitatif' and no doubt different 'étrange harmonie', but it's hard not to think of Dido's 'Dieux immortels! Il part'.

I'm thinking too of the Villa Mecena, which Berlioz visited and where he imagined 'the melancholy voice of Virgil reciting [...] some splendid fragment from his country poems'[26] – a voice we hear in the music for the 'Entrée des Laboureurs' in the third act of *Les Troyens*: those who practise what Dido celebrates as 'the greatest of the arts, the art that nourishes men', music which we would not otherwise expect to be so melancholy, so elegiac. And could Berlioz have written the septet in the fourth act if he had never seen the Mediterranean – the deep impression which gave rise to the 'passion for the sea that will be one of the most lasting memories of his Italian journey'?[27]

Beyond any particular work, it is the influence of the whole Italian experience that is so profound. I believe it is second only to his childhood and adolescence in the richness of suggestion it stored in his creative imagination. So many of his subsequent works were born, or – if already implanted in his mind – nurtured, in Italy: not only *Harold* or *Les Troyens* but *Roméo*, which began to take shape 'beneath the stars of Italy',[28] and *Benvenuto*, that exuberant celebration of Renaissance Rome inspired, by inversion, by the decadence and lassitude of its modern counterpart, which he had had to endure. By inversion too, the Berliozian concept of monumental church music as the 'soul' of the building, proportionate to its size, receives a vital stimulus from his discovery that the local musical response to the majesty of St Peter's is a choir of eighteen and a small organ on wheels.

[24] *Correspondance générale*, Vol. I, p. 523.

[25] *Memoirs*, pp. 154–55.

[26] *Ibid.*, p. 189.

[27] Michel Austin, *loc. cit.*, p. 62.

[28] *Memoirs*, p. 473.

The pifferari *in Rome, playing before an image of the Virgin Mary – chalk lithograph after a painting by Sir David Wilkie (1785-1841)*

By the time he crosses the Alps into France in May 1832 a large part of the work of his remaining 30 years is already laid down. I think we can conclude that for Berlioz – whatever he may have said about it – the virtues of wild Italy outweighed the vices of its hapless sister.

Harold en Italie, the Viola and the Stage Directions in the Score

This piece is reprinted from the Berlioz Society Bulletin No. 184 *(December 2010).*

Mary Anderson, a violist, wrote to the Berlioz Society asking for advice about (1) 'where to stand', and (2) 'when to walk off into the distance', when she played the viola solo in a concert in Alderley Edge, Cheshire.

On (1), Berlioz's instructions are clear and explicit: the viola soloist should be placed separate from and in front of the orchestra; furthermore, the harp should be placed 'near the soloist'. As to (2) – the point near the end of the finale where the reminiscence of the 'Pilgrims' March' breaks in on the 'Brigands' Orgy' – there are no instructions for the viola to move: on the contrary, the soloist is not meant to walk off and join the two violins and cello playing offstage ('dans la coulisse'), but stays put. The composer's intention – even if often ignored – is surely quite unambiguous: Harold (viola) is recalling in his imagination the sounds of the 'Pilgrims' March', represented by the three offstage string-players (a characteristically Berliozian effect). Remaining where he is, he responds to them (*ppp*, swelling to *sf*, then subsiding, then *p diminuendo*), before his nostalgic musings are swallowed up in the sound of the full orchestra resuming the 'Orgy'. The poetic idea is achieved precisely by the physical separation between the soloist, still in front of the orchestra, and the string trio in the wings.

PS. At the 2018 Festival Berlioz, at La-Côte-Saint-André, in a performance of *Harold* given on 31 August by John Eliot Gardiner and the Orchestre Révolutionnaire et Romantique, the solo viola, Antoine Tamestit, instead of remaining at the front, moved continually around the orchestra – in emulation of the Byronic hero wandering through the Italian landscape – and, at the end, joined the three string-players at the back and played with them. This was by no means what the composer asks for, but it was very effective and, arguably, true to the spirit of the work. This 'staging' was repeated when the same performers performed the work at the BBC Proms in the Royal Albert Hall, London, on 5 September.

III

THE 1830s

The Journalist, the Writer

It was in the early 1830s that journalism began to take over much of Berlioz's professional life, and so I decided to place the next two pieces at this point in the chronology of the book, between Harold en Italie *and* Benvenuto Cellini. *The* Critique Musicale d'Hector Berlioz, 1823–1863 *will, when complete, run to ten volumes and more than five thousand pages. Reading them, one is not only struck by the sheer number of words he poured out in those forty years: they also remind us that there are still things we don't know about Berlioz. His own published collections of reviews give only a partial idea of the scope of his journalistic writings and the wide range of topics they discuss: to take one example, his at first sight surprising interest in what is now called 'Early Music', including Handel, and the lasting influence exerted on him by the great choral director and educator Alexandre Choron.*

Berlioz and the Music of the Past

This article is reprinted from Berlioz Society Bulletin *No. 207 (March 2019).*

Reading the transcript of David Charlton's ground-breaking 'Berlioz and earlier Italian music' has prompted the following thoughts. First, that though it seems a strange and even glaring omission, perhaps we shouldn't be surprised that Alexandre Choron – an important and highly regarded musician in Berlioz's life in the 1820s and early 1830s – doesn't appear at all in the *Memoirs*.

In his Preface Berlioz states that he will tell only what he wishes to tell. His intention is 'to give a clear idea of the difficulties confronting those who try to be composers at the present time and to offer them a few useful hints'. The book, explicitly, doesn't set out to present a full account of his life (thus, by being confessedly incomplete, providing biographers with a convenient pretext for filling the gaps). That being so, maybe we can understand why the record of his career – his struggles to get his music adopted in his native land, the hostile conditions which forced him to spend much of his time as a journalist, his proselytising campaigns in Germany, Russia and England – has little room for the past: why, as Charlton says, Berlioz excluded from his

Memoirs 'much thought and action directed towards earlier music, pieces that he heard, liked and conducted', and which 'a different autobiography' might well have included.

True, Gluck plays a part in the narrative; but, for Berlioz, Gluck 'was a Romantic', as he wrote in an 1830 article, not a figure from the past. (Two decades later, while he composed *The Trojans*, he felt Gluck as a living presence.) The *Memoirs*, combative, didactic, deal with the present, and the future. Given its overriding purpose, the book necessarily excludes the past. Palestrina, Clari, Marcello are not relevant to the tale of a modern musician's life and his beliefs and innovations, the enmity they provoked, the victories they won. Palestrina is mentioned briefly, but in such a way that you wouldn't guess that Berlioz admired him.

Similarly, the three collections he made of his journalistic writings, *Les Soirées de l'orchestre, Les Grotesques de la musique* and *À travers chants*, are mainly contemporary and forward-looking. It is only thanks to the many volumes of reviews and articles assembled in the *Critique musicale* that we realise how interested he was in the music of the past, and that, as Charlton says, 'our image of the composer Berlioz becomes every day more subtle and complex'.

Selected Letters of Berlioz[1]

The following review is a fuller version of one that appeared in the books section of The Sunday Times *on 23 July 1995.*

During his lifetime Berlioz's music was overshadowed in his own country by the reputation he enjoyed as a writer. When, in 1856, he finally became a member of the Institut de France, one of his enemies objected that instead of electing a composer they had elected a journalist.

This was a well-worn gibe: the absence of anything by Delacroix at the 1846 Salon was explained by his being 'a journalist, not a painter'. (A hundred years later, General Weygand's comment on de Gaulle's appointment as Under-Secretary for Defence in 1940 was: 'more a journalist than a soldier'.) But with Berlioz the accusation, to the Parisian mind, had an irresistible logic. Of the great nineteenth-century composers he was the only one who scribbled for a living. Schumann, despite his years as editor of the influential *Neue Zeitschrift für Musik*, was best known as a composer, and Wagner, though his theorising covered mountains of paper, was never seriously mistaken for anything else; but Berlioz throughout the thirty years of his active career earned most of his income in France as a critic, and it was as a critic, fluent, amusing, widely read and feared, that he most impinged on his fellow citizens. Being so obviously good at it, how could he also be good at writing music (any more than a pianist of Liszt's brilliance could ever be considered a genuine composer)? It was the perfect pretext for ignoring the challenge of his radically innovative compositions. Once Paris had tired of the Romantic excitements of the 1830s, Berlioz could make money from his music only outside France.

Even before that, criticism constantly got in the way of composition. One article begins:

> Oh the brutal, brainless profession of reviewer! Then why do it?, I will be asked. What a question! Why do you, sir, who are a banker, spend your day calculating figures, when you have splendid horses pawing your stable floor and you could be pacing the woods and enjoying the last rays of the autumn sun? Why do you, doctor, who have sensibility and taste, consume your existence in the infected air of the demonstration room and amid the

[1] *Selected Letters of Berlioz*, ed. Hugh Macdonald, transl. Roger Nichols, Faber, London, 1995.

sufferings of a hospital, listening not to beautiful music but to the cries of pain and as often as not, for all your skill, the death rattle of the dying? For the same reason that I all-complainingly write articles which use up time that could be far, far better employed.[2]

He was, besides, all too conscious of being hindered by considerations of diplomacy or censorship from saying what he really thought. Often his letters warn their recipient not to believe what a review of his has said in praise of such and such a work or performance. Letters, by contrast, were a precious outlet for anger or scorn held back in his public utterances; his pen could go where his mind led it. Letters could reveal his innermost thoughts and chart the course of his creative life. They were also an indispensable method of communication for someone leading the hectically busy life of concert organiser, conductor and touring musician, and beyond that a vital daily channel for conversing with his intimates.

Berlioz loved writing letters and wrote an extraordinary number, even by the standards of the age. I think Hugh Macdonald, in his very welcome edition (the first in English since Humphrey Searle's long-out-of-print collection of 30 years ago[3]), might have included more that show him involved in the minutiae of practical music-making – for instance, advising Liszt what to do if the Weimar orchestra doesn't have a third and fourth bassoon for *Benvenuto Cellini* – and also perhaps more of the high-spirited, swift-moving letters he could write to sympathetic friends and relations when he was in the mood. But, with so complex and mercurial a personality, not even a selection as generous as this can reflect everything.

As it is, we have his account of visiting the bed-ridden Heine, 'at death's door but still mentally alive – he gives the impression of standing at the window of his tomb so that he can continue to look out at this world of which he is no longer a part, and mock it'.[4] We see him, while working on *Les Troyens* (the crowning achievement of his life and the composition most fully documented in the correspondence), refusing the offer of an American tour:

> I should be in a fine mess if I'd accepted. The talk there is all of bankruptcies; their theatres and concerts are heading for the Niagara Falls. Ours are in no such danger: there's no cataract here – there's no current. We drift about on a placid pond full of frogs and toads, enlivened by the quacking and flapping

[2] *Le Rénovateur*, 5 October 1835 (*Critique musicale*, Vol. 2, p. 305).

[3] *Hector Berlioz: A Selection from his Letters, selected, edited and translated by Humphrey Searle*, Gollancz, London, 1966.

[4] *Correspondance générale*, Vol. IV, p. 44.

> of the occasional duck. [...] But I live in my score, like La Fontaine's rat in his cheese – if you will pardon the comparison.[5]

And we find him, a dying man, standing out against the wickedness of a world where he is asked to 'say nice things about a German musician, things I do in fact believe, but on condition that I say nasty things about a Russian musician whom they want to replace with the German'. This, he says, he 'will not do'.[6]

In quoting the above examples I have modified Roger Nichols' rendering of the French here and there. But translation can only be a personal matter (as well as never being more than approximate). On the whole Nichols has done his job well; he has caught the mixture of enthusiasm, mockery, prejudice, spleen, black rage, naïve optimism, tenderness and love accurately enough.

By the end, exhausted by chronic illness, Berlioz admits failure in his lifelong struggle to establish himself comfortably as a composer in France. There is a poignant letter here in which, by now over 50, he confesses to still 'hankering after the sort of studio painters and sculptors have, untidy but large, echoing and isolated – I've always more or less written on my knee, on pedestal tables, on the ends of things so to speak, in cafés, in the street, on trains or steamboats'. The book, inevitably, is the record of defeat. But it was a heroic defeat, and the world has begun to make amends for it.

[5] *Ibid.*, Vol. V, p. 509.
[6] *Ibid.*, Vol. VII, p. 709.

Evenings in the Orchestra, Memoirs

This is a shortened and edited version of the first extended piece I wrote on Berlioz (in 1962), the introduction to Evenings in the Orchestra, *published by Peregrine.*[1]

If we believe that Berlioz is a composer of the first rank – and this is now beginning to be widely accepted – then his career is one of tragic irony. He, among the most original musicians that ever lived, had the imprudence to be born a Frenchman and to live and work during one of the most impoverished periods of a grandiose but convention-ridden musical culture.

At first his works cause a certain stir in Paris. Arriving there from Dauphiné in 1821, not yet eighteen, he makes a name as the musical representative of a new movement for freedom of expression in the arts. It is the high tide of Romanticism in France, the Paris of Victor Hugo, Eugène Delacroix, the newly discovered Shakespeare, the first French translations of Goethe's *Faust*. The works of Berlioz's first maturity – 1829–1840 – are controversial, and disliked by many, but they are heard. Articles are written defending and explaining him. He is commissioned by the government to write a full-scale Requiem. Liszt, already at nineteen a virtuoso of European fame, hears the *Symphonie fantastique* and hails its author as a genius. Paganini mounts the platform at the end of a Berlioz concert and kneels in homage to the 'successor of Beethoven' and follows it with a cheque for 20,000 francs.

Then gradually the scene darkens. Romanticism loses impetus. Bourgeois values, apparently swept away by the 1830 Revolution, again predominate. Public taste is unshakeably for the familiar and the flattering – Meyerbeer at the Opéra, at the Opéra-Comique Auber and Adolphe Adam. Berlioz becomes a cartoon stereotype, a figure of fun, the butt of Rossini and the boulevard wags when they have nothing more amusing to be witty about. He takes to travelling – in Germany, Austria, Hungary, Bohemia, Russia, England – and, everywhere, finds audiences responsive to his music. But always he is drawn back to Paris, 'that electrifying city [...] to which one must forever return if one has lived there and above all if one is French.'[2]

[1] Hector Berlioz, *Evenings in the Orchestra*, transl. C. R. Fortescue, Peregrine/Penguin Books, London, 1963.

[2] *Correspondance générale*, Vol. III, p. 366.

And always (except once, when the success of *L'Enfance du Christ*, judged to have been written in a 'new style' by a reformed Berlioz, implicitly damns his other works), he returns to find the same situation: a musical economy centred on opera (from which his reputation for unorthodoxy debars him) and not organised for concert-giving. His performances have a core of enthusiastic support but it is not enough to make them more than spasmodically profitable, and after 1843 he is denied use of the Conservatoire, the one decent hall in Paris, where most of his concerts had been given up till then. The symbol of his Parisian career in the last twenty years of his life is the ruinous failure of *La Damnation de Faust*, heard by a few hundred people in the theatre that in the same month resounded to the applause of packed houses for Clapisson's *Gibby la cornemuse*. He dies, with half his greatest work, *Les Troyens*, unheard and the other half put on 'approximately' in a theatre too small to reveal more than a shadow of its grandeur.

In all this the irony had an added twist. Berlioz was obliged to rub his nose in his own humiliation: he earned his living as a reviewer. Not only did Clapisson, Adam and the others condition Paris to a taste that could not stomach Berlioz: they forced him to spend time and energy on their music that should have been spent on his own. He was at least as renowned for his articles as he was for his compositions. When Berlioz was finally elected to the Institute (after being passed over several times, once in favour of Clapisson), Scudo, that prince of critics, the man who announced that Gounod's *Faust* was German music devoid of melody, commented: 'They were supposed to elect a musician – they have elected a journalist'.[3] Berlioz was obviously much too intelligent to be a good composer. His reviews in the *Journal des débats* were read and chuckled over by people who knew nothing about his music except that it was tuneless and very loud. A typical cartoon of the time shows a cab-driver bawling through cupped hands into the ear of a dazed citizen who is emerging from a concert hall. 'Does Monsieur want a cab?' 'My friend, I see that you are addressing me but I have just come from a Berlioz concert and I cannot understand a word you are saying.'

For Berlioz, journalism could not be other than servitude. His relief at election to the Institute is strictly practical: 'This will give me a stipend of 1,500 francs a year – fifteen fewer articles to do!'[4] And in 1864 the proceeds of the truncated *Troyens* finally enable him to give up his post on the *Journal des débats* for good, after more than 30 years of music criticism (his last article is a friendly review of Bizet's *Les Pêcheurs de perles*).

[3] Quoted in Adolphe Boschot, *Le Crépuscule d'un Romantique*, Plon, Paris, 1912, p. 309.

[4] *Correspondance générale*, Vol. V, p. 331.

Feuilleton du Journal des Débats

DU 24 MAI 1846.

THÉATRE DE L'OPÉRA.

Débuts.

Un jour sur ses longs pieds, allait je ne sais où
Le héron au long bec, emmanché d'un long cou.

L'Opéra, ce grand théâtre avec son grand orchestre, ses grands chœurs, sa grande subvention, son long titre, ses immenses décorations, imite en plus d'un point le piteux oiseau de la fable. Je l'ai laissé, il y a six mois, *dormant sur une patte*, le voilà qui chemine maintenant, et va on ne sait où, cherchant pâture dans les plus minces ruisseaux, et ne faisant point fi du goujon qu'il dédaignait naguère, et dont le nom seul irritait sa gastronomique fierté. Mais le pauvre oiseau est blessé dans l'aile; il marche et ne peut voler, et ses enjambées, si précipitées qu'elles soient, le conduiront d'autant moins au but de son voyage, qu'il ne sait pas lui-même vers quel point de l'horizon il doit se diriger.

L'Opéra voudrait, comme le veulent tous les théâtres, de l'argent et des honneurs, il voudrait gloire et fortune. Les grands succès donnent l'une et l'autre; les beaux ouvrages obtiennent quelquefois les grands succès; les grands compositeurs et les auteurs habiles font seuls de beaux ouvrages. Ces œuvres où rayonnent l'intelligence et le génie ne paraissent vivantes et belles qu'au moyen d'une exécution vivante et belle aussi, et chaleureuse, et délicate, et fidèle, et grandiose, et brillante, et animée. L'excellence de l'exécution dépend non seulement du choix des exécutans, mais de l'esprit qui les anime; cet esprit pourrait être bon si tous n'avaient fait depuis longtemps une découverte qui, en les décourageant, a amené chez eux l'indifférence et à sa suite l'ennui et le dégoût. Ils ont découvert qu'une passion profonde dominait tous les penchans, enchaînait toutes les ambitions et absorbait toutes les pensées de l'Opéra; que l'Opéra enfin était amoureux fou de la médiocrité. Pour posséder, établir chez lui, choyer, honorer et glorifier la médiocrité, il n'est rien qu'il ne fasse, pas de sacrifice devant lequel il recule, pas de labeur qu'il ne s'impose avec transport. Avec les meilleures intentions, de la meilleure foi du monde, il s'anime jusqu'à l'enthousiasme pour la platitude, il rougit d'admiration pour la pâleur, il brûle, il bouillonne pour la tiédeur, il deviendrait poëte pour chanter la prose. Comme il a remarqué d'ailleurs que le public avait à peu près donné sa démission, qu'il s'était depuis longtemps résigné à tout ce qu'on voudrait lui présenter, et qu'il venait cependant tout voir, tout entendre sans rien approuver ni blâmer, l'Opéra a conclu avec raison qu'il était maître chez lui et qu'il pouvait sans crainte se livrer à tous les emportemens de sa fougueuse passion et adorer, sur le piédestal où il l'encense, la médiocrité.

Le hasard fait que, dans un concert récemment donné sur son théâtre, des fragmens d'un immortel ouvrage de l'ancien répertoire soient entendus. Les exécutans, qui accomplissent cette fois une tâche bien différente de celle qui leur fait si tristement gagner leur pain quotidien, électrisés en outre par les magnificences de l'œuvre, s'élèvent au niveau de l'inspiration du maître; l'effet produit est immense, inouï, foudroyant; l'assemblée entière, bouleversée, présente un aspect jusqu'à ce jour inconnu. Il n'y a pas de claqueurs, et trois mille mains applaudissent; les hâbleurs de l'amphithéâtre, émus eux-mêmes jusqu'aux larmes, n'osent se moquer que de leur propre émotion. On fait recommencer le finale tout entier; l'auteur, aperçu dans une loge, est forcé de s'avancer pour recevoir en personne ces manifestations d'un enthousiasme qui déborde; tout brûle, tout frissonne, la splendide fleur de l'art, cette fleur si rare, vient de s'épanouir avec explosion, et ses parfums enivrans remplissent la salle étonnée. Tout autre que l'Opéra, en le supposant même capable d'ignorer jusqu'à ce moment les merveilles de la partition illustre, s'empresserait de supplier humblement le compositeur de lui permettre de la représenter. Il mettrait aux ordres du grand maître toutes les ressources vocales et instrumentales de l'art musical, toutes celles de la danse, de la peinture et de la mise en scène. Mais lui déclare formellement qu'il ne partage point cet engouement et que *La Vestale* ne sera pas rendue à la scène.

— « Allons donc, plaisantez-vous? qu'ai-je à faire de pareils ouvrages? et comment trouver place là-dedans pour ma médiocrité? Nous avons autre chose en tête, vous verrez dans peu une production autrement conçue et qui certes calmera la fièvre ridicule qui vous agite! » — Pour obtenir un si beau résultat, il a *médiocrisé* tout ce qu'il a pu dans sa troupe.

Aidé par ceux de ses ministres dont l'heureux naturel ne demande que d'être abandonné à lui-même, il a tellement lassé, blasé, entravé, englué, tous ses artistes, que plusieurs, suspendant leurs harpes aux saules du rivage, se sont arrêtés et ont pleuré. « Que pouvions-nous faire? disent-ils maintenant; *illic stetimus et flevimus!* »

D'autres se sont indignés et ont pris en haine leur tâche, beaucoup se sont endormis; les philosophes touchent leurs appointemens et parodient en riant le mot de Mazarin: « L'Opéra ne chante pas, mais il paie. » L'orchestre seul a donné quelque peine à l'Opéra pour le réduire. La plupart de ses membres, étant des virtuoses de premier ordre, font partie du célèbre orchestre du Conservatoire; ils se trouvent ainsi naturellement en contact avec l'art le plus pur et un public d'élite; de là les idées qu'ils ont conservées si longtemps et la résistance qu'ils ont opposée aux efforts qui tendaient à les asservir. Mais avec du temps et de mauvais ouvrages, il n'y a pas d'organisation musicale dont on ne parvienne à briser l'élan, à éteindre le feu, à détruire la vigueur, à ralentir la fière allure. « Ah! vous raillez mes chanteurs, leur a dit l'Opéra, vous vous moquez de mes partitions nouvelles, Messieurs les habiles! Je saurai bien vous mettre à la raison; tenez, voici un ouvrage en une foule d'actes dont vous allez savourer les beautés. Trois répétitions générales suffiraient pour le monter, c'est du style d'antichambre, vous en ferez douze ou quinze; j'aime qu'on se hâte lentement. Vous le jouerez une dixaine de fois, c'est-à-dire jusqu'à ce qu'il n'attire plus personne, et nous passerons à un autre du même genre et d'un mérite égal. Ah! vous trouvez cela fade, commun, froid et plat! J'ai l'honneur de vous présenter un opéra plein de galops et fait en poste, que vous voudrez bien étudier avec le même amour que le précédent, et dans quelque temps vous en aurez un autre d'un compositeur qui n'a jamais rien composé, et qui vous déplaira, je l'espère, bien davantage encore. Vous

Journal des débats, *24 May 1846: the beginnings of Berlioz's front-page article where he likens the Opéra in its present feeble state to the hard-to-please heron in Book VII of La Fontaine's* Fables

His letters are full of complaints that journalism is eating into the time that should be given to composition: 'I want so much to work, but am forced to drudge for a living' is a constant cry. In 1835 the Opéra agrees to stage *Benvenuto Cellini*; but 'I cannot yet begin on the music – like my hero, I'm short of metal'.[5] While writing the libretto of *Les Troyens* he exclaims:

> I think of little else, and if I only had time to work at it, in two months the whole mosaic would be complete. But how to find the time? [...] Those infernal articles to write, on debutants male and female, revivals of antiquated operas, first performances of antiquated operas, end-of-season concerts which go off between my legs like forgotten squibs at the end of a firework display that singe the beards of the passers-by.[6]

There is that *cri du cœur* in the *Memoirs*:

> To be always at it! Let them only give me scores to write, orchestras to conduct, rehearsals to take! Let me stand eight or ten hours at a time, baton in hand, training choirs without any accompaniment, singing the leads myself. Let me carry desks, double-basses and harps, let me remove steps or nail planks, like a commissionaire or a carpenter, and all night, by way of a rest, correct the mistakes of engravers and copyists. I have done it, I do it, I will do it. It is part of my life as a musician and I bear it without a murmur, without even a thought, as a sportsman endures the thousand fatigues of the chase. But eternally to write articles for a living! To write nothing about nothings, to bestow lukewarm praise on unbearable insipidities! To speak one evening of a great master and the next of a fool, in the same serious manner, the same language! To spend one's time, one's intelligence, one's courage and patience on this toil, with the certainty that even then one has not been able to serve art by abolishing a few abuses, enlightening opinion, purifying the public's taste, and putting men and things in their true place and perspective – oh, that is the very depth of humiliation.[7]

Berlioz, perforce, became an unrivalled authority on the musical life of a nation that largely ignored his music – to scrutinise under a microscope the pullulating infusoria of the Parisian scene: the swarming operetta composers, the imbecile impresarios, the rapacious divas, the tenors, the claques, the hack musicians, the toiling chorus singers and orchestral musicians, the whole ephemeral army of parasites running to and fro over the art of Gluck and Beethoven. He insisted that, whereas musical composition came naturally to him, prose-writing was a labour. Most writers-to-order can echo from their own experience his description of himself at work on an article that will not come: elbows on table and

[5] *Ibid.*, Vol. II, p. 263.
[6] *Ibid.*, Vol. V, pp. 300–1.
[7] *Memoirs*, p. 375.

head in hands; striding up and down 'like a sentry on duty in twenty-five degrees of frost'; standing by the window staring out on the neighbouring gardens, his thoughts miles away; turning back to the blank sheet of paper on the desk waiting for the words to cover it.[8] But this was more than the common psychological inability of the journalist to begin. He had the most urgent reasons – creative reasons – for hating it. The boredom of struggling against the grain to write about a new comic opera whose very existence he would have forgotten a week later filled him with disgust. It was to relieve this disgust, and divert his readers, that he would resort to the tactical evasions displayed in his review of Adam's *Giralda* (included in *Evenings in the Orchestra* under a false name, *Diletta*), which is largely devoted to two long and bizarre anecdotes with nothing to do with the opera, discussion of which is continually sidestepped.

Yet, when all is said, the fact remains that he was a born writer. Reading his books or his letters, it is impossible to doubt that he enjoyed the act of expressing himself in words. When the pressure of ideas was strong, he wrote with fire and humour and imagination. The style of his prose and of his music have affinities. At its best his writing has the 'combination of irresistible élan and the utmost precision', the 'controlled vehemence' that he believed were essential to faithful performance of his music.[9] The mixture of vivacity, wit, sadness, panache, dreamy exaltation, fierce partisanship, objectivity, frankness, generous indignation and hauteur is characteristically Berliozian; so are the quick transitions from one mood to another and the sense of form and the careful workmanship and joinery so often denied by his detractors. And always the heat is tempered by his admirable irony. His sense of the absurd embraces himself. The account of his time as a Prix de Rome student in Italy is full of passages like this, at the same time exalted and self-quizzical:

> Sometimes, when I had my guitar with me instead of my gun, I would station myself in the midst of a landscape in harmony with my mood, and some passage from the *Aeneid*, dormant in my memory since childhood, would come back to me, set off by the character of the country into which I had wandered. Then, improvising a strange recitative to still stranger harmony, I would sing of Pallas's death and the despair of the good Evander, the young warrior's funeral procession, his horse Aethon, unharnessed and with flowing mane and great tears, following the body, the terror of good King Latinus, the siege of Latium (whose dust I trod), Amata's sad end and the cruel death of Lavinia's noble betrothed. Under the combined influence of poetry, music and association, I would work myself up into an incredible state of excitement.

8 *Ibid.*, p. 376.

9 *Ibid.*, p. 526.

> The triple intoxication always ended in floods of tears and uncontrollable sobbing. What was most curious was that I took note of my tears. I wept for poor Turnus, robbed by the hypocrite Aeneas of kingdom, mistress and life; I wept for the beautiful and pathetic Lavinia, forced to wed an unknown brigand with her lover's blood fresh on him. I longed for those poetic days when the heroes, sons of the gods, walked the earth in glittering armour, casting delicate javelins, their points set in a ring of gleaming gold. Then, quitting the past for the present, I wept for my private griefs, my uncertain future, my interrupted career; until, collapsing amid this maelstrom of poetry and murmuring snatches of Shakespeare, Virgil and Dante – *Nessun maggior dolore... che ricordarsi... Oh poor Ophelia... Good night, sweet ladies... Vitaque cum gemitu... fugit indignata... sub umbras* – I fell asleep.[10]

Later in his life, even when he rails against the world, he retains his dignity:

> And now, if not at the end of my career, I am at any rate on the steep slope that leads with ever-increasing swiftness to the end; burnt up yet still on fire and filled with an energy that sometimes flares up with terrifying force. I begin to know French, to be able to write a decent page of music, of verse or prose. I can direct an orchestra and give it life. I worship art in all its forms. But I belong to a nation that has ceased to be interested in the higher manifestations of the mind; whose only god is the golden calf. [...] I am conscious of what I could do in dramatic music, but to attempt it is as futile as it is dangerous. [...] For the last three years I have been tormented by the idea for a vast opera, for which I would write the words and the music, as I have just done for my sacred trilogy *The Childhood of Christ*. I am resisting the temptation to carry out this project [*The Trojans*] and shall, I trust, resist to the end. To me the subject seems grand, magnificent and deeply moving – guarantee that Parisians would find it flat and tedious.[11]

He can describe the enforced removal of his first wife's body, to the cemetery where his second wife has lately been buried, with a dramatic sense that avoids sensationalism and a pathos free of self-pity:

> I gave the necessary instructions at the two cemeteries and one morning in overcast weather went alone to the burial ground. A municipal officer, who had orders to witness the exhumation, was waiting for me. A gravedigger had already opened the grave. On my arrival he jumped down into it. The coffin, though ten years in the ground, was still intact; only the lid had decayed, from damp. Instead of lifting out the whole coffin, he wrenched at the rotting planks, which came away with a hideous crack, exposing the coffin's contents. The gravedigger bent down and with his two hands picked up the head, already parted from the body – the ungarlanded, withered, hairless head of 'poor Ophelia' – and placed it in a new coffin prepared for it at the edge of

[10] *Ibid*., pp. 154–55.

[11] *Ibid*., pp. 509–12.

> the grave. Then, bending down again, with difficulty he gathered in his arms the headless trunk and limbs, a blackish mass that the shroud still clung to, like a damp sack with a lump of pitch in it. It came away, with a dull sound, and a smell. The municipal officer stood a few yards off, watching what was going on. Seeing me leaning back against a cypress tree, he called out, 'Don't stay there, Monsieur Berlioz, come here, come here!' And as if the grotesque must also have its part in this grim scene, he added (getting the word wrong), 'Ah, poor inhumanity!' A few moments later we followed the hearse and its sad contents down the hill to the larger Montmartre cemetery, where the new vault stood ready, gaping open. Harriet's remains were laid in it. The two dead women lie there now peacefully, awaiting the time when I shall bring my share of corruption to the same charnel-house.[12]

Berlioz's writing shows a gift for imagery. He has an eye for detail and an ear for dialogue. Staying for a few weeks' convalescence in Nice, in 1831, he is interrogated by the Italian[13] police on suspicion of being a revolutionary:

> 'What are you doing here?'
> 'Recovering from a painful illness. I compose, I dream, I thank God for creating this glorious sun, this beautiful sea and these great green hills.'
> 'You're not a painter?'
> 'No.'
> 'Yet you are seen everywhere, and always drawing in a notebook. Are you by any chance making plans?'
> 'Yes, I'm making plans for an overture on King Lear. That is to say, I have made the plan – the form and the instrumentation are complete. I believe it will cause a real stir when it appears.'
> 'Appears? Who is this King Lear?'
> 'Alas, a poor old devil of an English king.'
> 'English!'
> 'Yes, according to Shakespeare he lived about 1,800 years ago and was foolish enough to divide his kingdom between two wicked daughters who kicked him out when he had nothing more to give them. You will realise that few kings – '
> 'Never mind the king. This word instrumentation?'
> 'It's a musical term.'
> 'The same excuse again. Now, sir, you know perfectly well that it is not possible to compose music like that without a piano, just wandering about on the beach with nothing but a notebook and a pencil. Tell me where you wish to go and your passport will be made. You can't stay in Nice any longer.'

[12] *Memoirs*, pp. 547–48.

[13] Nice finally became French only in 1860, having been shuffled between the House of Savoy and France no fewer than seven times in the preceding 169 years.

'Very well, I will return to Rome, and by your leave continue to compose without a piano.'[14]

In his letters his humour is constantly at the ready. Writing to Princess Wittgenstein to tell her of his election to the Institute, he ends: 'Forgive the coldness and triviality of this letter. Can it be that already I…? But no – my official uniform has not even been ordered'.[15] In another letter he writes of the pains of his intestinal neuralgia, which make him 'suffer like a demon forced to take a hip bath in a stoup of holy water'.[16]

The drudgery of a reviewer, writing whether he wanted to or not, was another matter. But even journalism had its rewards. There was 'the scope it gives to my passion for the true, the great, the beautiful, wherever they exist'.[17] Though the severity of his articles and their power of ridicule made life even more difficult because of the animosity they aroused ('I make my way in Paris like a red-hot cannon ball, hissing and laying waste'[18]), journalism was necessary for him, a vent for enthusiasm as well as for spleen. He needed it as a platform on which to campaign for his ideals and explain his practice of them. The detailed programme originally attached to the *Symphonie fantastique*, and the rolling manifestos of its sequel, the extravagant *Lélio*, were natural accompaniments of a new and revolutionary kind of music. It was the age of the articulate musician – Schumann, Liszt, Wagner, Berlioz. Composers felt themselves part of the same movement as poets and painters, championing the same causes and bound by the same obligation to preach by word as well as by example. Throughout his career Berlioz fought in print for his ideals. The essays he wrote on Gluck's *Orphée*, *Alceste* and *Iphigénie en Tauride*, Beethoven's *Fidelio* and his symphonies, trios and sonatas, and Weber's *Freischütz* and *Oberon*, were an essential part of the struggle for acceptance of music as a free, noble, expressive and dramatic art.

In 1852 Berlioz was in London for a few months to conduct concerts for the recently formed New Philharmonic Society. He seems to have been preoccupied with making a permanent literary record of his life and beliefs. Four years earlier he had begun compiling his *Memoirs*, and now, in between rehearsals and performances, he went through the files of his articles and, selecting a few from them and from his *Voyage musical en Allemagne et en Italie* (by then out of print), combined them into a book. He described its

[14] *Memoirs*, pp. 138–39.

[15] *Correspondance générale*, Vol. V, p. 330.

[16] *Ibid.*, p. 506.

[17] *Memoirs*, p. 231.

[18] *Correspondance générale*, Vol. III, p. 366.

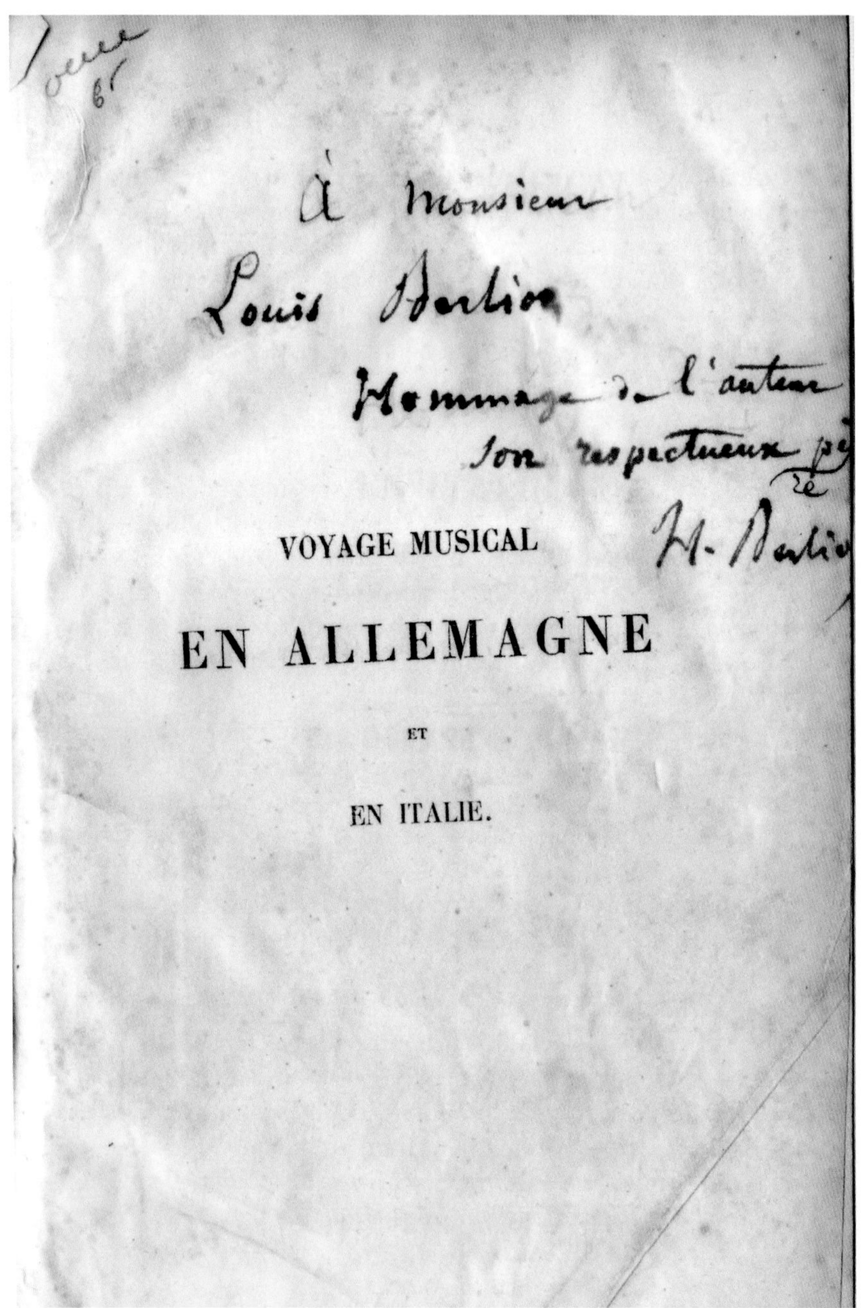

À Monsieur
Louis Berlioz
Hommage de l'auteur
son respectueux père
H. Berlioz

VOYAGE MUSICAL

EN ALLEMAGNE

ET

EN ITALIE.

The title page of Berlioz's Voyage musical, *with an inscription to his son, Louis*

scheme in a letter to his friend the musicologist Joseph d'Ortigue. He is, he says, just finishing a book

> called *Tales of the Orchestra*, comprising short stories, anecdotes, novellas, cracks of the whip, critiques and arguments (in which music is treated only incidentally, and not theoretically), biographical sketches, conversations, carried on or read or recounted by the musicians of an unnamed orchestra *during the performance of bad operas*. They attend seriously to their part only when a masterpiece is being played. The work is accordingly divided into 'evenings'. Most of them are literary and begin with the words: 'A very dull French or Italian or German opera is being given. While the side-drum and the bass-drum get on with it, the rest of the orchestra listens to such-and-such a reader or speaker', etc. When an evening begins with the words: '*Don Juan* is being performed', or *Iphigénie en Tauride* or *Le Barbier* or *La Vestale* or *Fidelio*, the orchestra bends with zeal to its task and no one reads or speaks; the evening consists just of a few words on the performance of the masterpiece. As you may imagine, such evenings are rare. The others give rise to endless scathing ironies and jests, in addition to stories whose interest is purely in the romance of the tale.[19]

Evenings in the Orchestra (*Les Soirées de l'orchestre*) appeared later the same year. It covers virtually the whole of Berlioz's journalistic career up to the time of publication. The earliest piece, 'Vincenza' (First Evening), dates from the beginning of the 1830s; the account of London (Twenty-first Evening) was written in 1851, the year of the Great Exhibition, which Berlioz attended as a member of the French delegation of the international jury on musical instruments. After the *Memoirs,* it is the fullest expression of his artistic principles and practice. The tone is predominantly whimsical or satirical, but the humour is founded on harsh experience and solid fact. Certain themes recur: the economics of opera and concert organisation, the hardships of the great composers, the perennial, depressing contrast between the highest achievements of the art and the inadequacy of so many of the people involved in it. On claques, puffs, tenors, choruses and the idiosyncrasies of that strange beast the orchestral player, the book has left little to be said.

Any bitterness it contains would be easy to understand. But in fact gaiety is the prevailing mood; irritation is quickly relieved in satire or sublimated in fantasy (of which a characteristic example is the tale – one of those in the Eighteenth Evening that keep postponing discussion of Adam's *Giralda* – of the Pleyel piano which, having had Mendelssohn's G minor concerto played on it 30 times in a Conservatoire competition, goes on playing it by itself and can be stopped only by being chopped

[19] *Ibid.*, Vol. IV, p. 151.

to pieces). As Ernest Newman says, Berlioz was able to 'stand at a distance from the cause of his sufferings and see them objectively as subjects for the art of letters, to universalise them, and to sprinkle them with the salt of an irony that has kept them fresh.'[20] It is the same objective attitude to his own passions ('I took note of my tears') that makes him, for all his obvious Romanticism, a Classical composer.

Much of the book describes his own experiences, which are related by the narrator or put into the mouth of Corsino, a first violin in the orchestra. Berlioz in the *Evenings* is certainly a good hater and can store up a nice revenge. The grocer's assistant who hisses Agathe's Act 2 aria in *Der Freischütz* duly turns up fifteen years later in the same opera, as a skeleton lit up by Bengal lights at the climax of the Wolf's Glen (Fourth Evening). Alfonso, the young Florentine composer (First Evening), waits till the city that once spurned his innovations is at his feet before exacting a ferocious punishment.

Only when he comes to the Twenty-fifth Evening ('Euphonia, or the Musical City') does Berlioz lose his detachment. The (thinly disguised) heroine of this curious sci-fi fantasy is the famous pianist Marie Pleyel, the former Camille Moke with whom as a young man Berlioz had a passionate and serious affair that led to their engagement. Like Xilef in the story, he had gone off to Italy apparently secure in the love of his 'Ariel', only to hear nothing until the sudden news that she was getting married. In real life he went no further than Nice, on the road from Florence to Paris (where he had planned to shoot Camille, her husband and her mother, and then himself). In fiction he was more persistent. Camille's fascinating but frivolous character had already been depicted in the *Evenings*, as Hortense, the heroine of the Twelfth Evening ('Suicide through Enthusiasm'), who wounds the hero to the heart by speaking scornfully of *La Vestale*. In 'Euphonia' Berlioz took a full, grotesque and public revenge. Mina (the first published version of the story called her Ellimac – Camille backwards), the woman who sings gloriously but without a deep understanding of music, who finds Beethoven's adagios boring, and who flits from one man to another, is polished off in circumstances of Edgar Allan Poe-like horror and depravity.

There is also something naïvely utopian and at the same time stifling about this city, totally organised for the solemn ritual performance of monumental music. For the first time the Berliozian irony is absent, autobiography has not been refined into art, frustrated idealism has sought overcompensation. But Euphonia, with its ideal public, is an understandable wish-fulfilment. It

[20] From the introduction to *Evenings in the Orchestra*, transl. Charles E. Roche, Alfred A. Knopf, New York, 1929, quoted in Barzun, *Berlioz and the Romantic Century*, *op. cit.*, Vol. 2, p. 55.

must be set against Berlioz's Parisian struggles and the glimpses of a saner musical order in the courts of Austro-Germany and Russia. When he wrote the story (1844), he already knew how much could be expected from the bourgeois audiences of the day, and his scepticism would be vindicated, first by the *Faust* debacle and then by the mutilation of *Les Troyens*, of which he never heard the first two acts complete, although the work had been in existence for ten years by the time he died.

'Euphonia' is the one pipe-dream he allows himself in the book (even in Germany Wagner was forced to create, at Bayreuth, his own special conditions for the realisation of his operatic ideals – which remained less than fully realised). Otherwise the *Evenings*, underneath the deliberate exaggerations and the *blague*, provide an anatomy of the European musical scene. They are also an anatomy of Berlioz's musical personality – his enthusiasms, his intolerances, his extravagances, his refinement, his clear-sighted attention to practical realities and details of organisation and performance, his common sense, his defeats, his vision. They can help us to understand the man and what he was trying to achieve, they can send us back to the works with warmer sympathy and clearer insight. Some people's first reaction to Berlioz's music is an inability to find sense or melody in it. In that case it may be in his writings that the initial contact comes. To read *Evenings in the Orchestra*, or the *Memoirs*, is to find oneself on his side. And then it becomes clear that the energy and sweat he expended on journalism was not after all wholly wasted.

Benvenuto Cellini

Before it figured in chapter 5 of the second volume of my biography of Berlioz, this passage was part of a private Festschrift *sent to Jacques Barzun in 1994 in celebration of his 90th birthday. It begins with a quotation from Berlioz's* Memoirs.

> I was plunged in gloomy thoughts, when Ernest Legouvé came to visit me.
> 'How are you getting on with your opera?', he asked.
> 'I haven't finished the first act yet. I can't get time to work on it.'
> 'Supposing you had time?'
> 'Don't – I would write from dawn till dusk.'
> 'What would you need to make you independent?'
> 'Two thousand francs – which I haven't got.'
> 'And if someone… supposing you were… come on, help me.'
> 'What? What do you mean?'
> 'All right – supposing a friend of yours lent it to you?'
> 'What friend could I possibly ask to lend me such an amount?'
> 'You don't have to ask. I'm offering it to you.'[1]

The sum was 1,000 francs, not 2,000 (the other 1,000 was lent two years later), but it was still the equivalent of ten *feuilletons* in the *Journal des débats*, and enough to relieve the pressure. Berlioz sent Legouvé a signed IOU and thanked him for 'having the best heart of anyone I have met in my whole life; if there is anything superior to your goodness, it's your delicacy',[2] and flung himself into his opera. Winter was over, and with it the muddy lanes that isolated them from their friends and the bitter winds that made it so hard to keep warm in their draughty apartment on the northern slope of the village (Montmartre). It was spring. A summer of composition lay before him.

What the money gained above all was the sense that he now had time to devote to sustained work. He might not be entirely free from journalism; but what was crucial was the end, for the moment, of his oppressive dependence on it. Psychologically, it liberated him. Whenever Berlioz *felt* free and able to give his mind and all his creative attention to composing, he wrote quickly, with concentrated intensity. By the beginning of July half

[1] *Memoirs*, p. 239.
[2] *Correspondance générale*, Vol. II, p. 451.

the opera was done: the scene between Balducci the papal treasurer and the maskers under his window; the first version of the aria for Balducci's daughter Teresa; her duet with Cellini and the captivating trio in which their plan to elope during the revels in the Piazza Colonna is overheard by Fieramosca, official papal sculptor and rival for Teresa's hand; Fieramosca's drubbing by the female inhabitants of the quartier; the big choral scene in the tavern on the edge of the piazza, where Cellini and his metalworkers carouse and celebrate the glories of the goldsmith's art; and the huge carnival finale in which, as Liszt said, 'for the first time in opera the crowd speaks with its great roaring voice'.[3]

It was once again like their first Montmartre summer two years before, when he was completing *Harold en Italie*; in fact, the goldsmiths' chorus, at that stage the opening scene of the opera, had been drafted immediately after *Harold*, in the flush of his enthusiasm for the project and in the same bright 'Italian' G major which the opera shares with the symphony. But *Benvenuto* takes *Harold*'s already audacious rhythmic freedom and brilliance of colour much further.

The opera had been often in his thoughts since then. We catch an oblique glimpse of it in the *Journal des débats* article of 27 September 1835 on *Zampa*, where he contrasts Hérold's mish-mash of an overture with Weber's overtures to *Der Freischütz* and the others. Weber, he says, like Hérold, fashioned them out of themes taken from the opera; but unlike Herold he succeeded in shaping them into a unified whole. Then (in an allusion to the casting of Cellini's Perseus that will form the climax of Berlioz's opera): 'He threw silver, copper and gold into the melting-pot but was able to combine them into a single alloy, and when the statue emerged from the mould its sombre hue displayed but one metal, bronze'.[4] Yet, apart from the little *Chansonette de M. de Wailly*, written in August 1835 to words by one of Berlioz's librettists and used for the offstage serenade in scene 1, no work on the score seems to have been done during the twenty-odd months between autumn 1834 and spring 1836. Now that the signal was given, the pent-up music poured out of him, as it had done two years before, when his Italian experiences were transmuted into the music of *Harold*.

Only, it was a different Italy this time: except for Crispino's rustic serenade, used for the foundry-workers' song in the final scene, not the 'wild Italy' where he had taken refuge from the deadness of modern Rome but the eternal city in its burgeoning Renaissance heyday, an Italy where Art, no longer 'Juliet stretched upon her bier', was once again vitally alive and an issue of public importance. The subject seized his imagination; and, having

[3] *Neue Zeitschrift für Musik*, Vol. 483, quoted in Barzun, *Berlioz and the Romantic Century*, Vol. 1, p. 304.

[4] *Journal des débats*, 27 September 1835; republished in *Critique musicale*, Vol. 2, p. 289.

exorcised, in an article in the *Revue et gazette musicale*,[5] his memories of the present-day carnival and its squalid barbarities, he turned to the task of re-creating its one-time counterpart with all the resources at his command. The work would be a historical opera with modern connotations, a passionate comedy designed both to evoke the exuberance of sixteenth-century Italy and to show the triumph of the unorthodox, innovatory artist over his sceptical conservative opponents.

The libretto he eventually set had gone through several stages, the exact sequence and history of which remain unclear. Starting as an *opéra-comique* – of which we know nothing for sure except that it began with the goldsmiths' chorus – it was upgraded, with the Opéra in mind, into a much grander work (which apparently featured the Siege of Rome and the killing of the Constable of Bourbon, based on the account of them in Cellini's autobiography), before becoming the two-act, four-tableau 'opera semi-seria' that Duponchel was induced, with Meyerbeer's aid, to accept for production. In this form it owed almost as much to E. T. A. Hoffmann's story 'Signor Formica' as it did to the autobiography. Cellini's *Memoirs* supplied the sculptor's battles with officialdom, many of the character's names (though some of them were given different identities), the three cannon-shots from the Castel Sant'Angelo that mark the end of carnival, and the casting of the Perseus – in Rome instead of in Florence and commissioned by Pope Clement VII, not by Cosimo de' Medici. Most of the personal drama, on the other hand, derived from the Hoffmann story, in which Salvator Rosa (an artist-bandit in the Cellini mould, much admired by the Romantics) helped a fellow painter serenade the niece of a Balducci-like miser with guitars beneath her window and then elope with her under cover of darkness during an open-air performance on the last night of the carnival.

The resulting text, criticised at the time and since, does not succeed in 'combining into a single alloy' the disparate elements of the drama, the heterogeneous character of which was at least partly the consequence of the different stages the project had gone through. The would-be serious theme of the embattled artist-hero is fundamentally at odds, not with a comic context *per se* but with this particular one, in which farce keeps rearing its grinning head. It is like an *Ariadne auf Naxos* without the rationale for juxtaposing *commedia dell'arte* and high romance – or like *Don Giovanni* as it appears to those opera-lovers to whom its mixture of deadly seriousness with farce at its crudest has been a stumbling block from 1787 to the present day. Rather as the superhero of Mozart's opera is permitted to rise to his full stature only at the end – till then the situations have been constantly making fun of him – so it is not till the final scene of Berlioz's opera that the

[5] *Revue et gazette musicale*, 21 February 1836; republished in *Critique musicale*, Vol. 2, pp. 407–11.

focus is at last on Cellini at grips, however melodramatically, with his art, and not on the operatic lover enmeshed in the conventional complications of an amorous intrigue. It is true that Cellini takes part, in the second tableau, in the goldsmiths' hymn to the mystery and greatness of their craft, which is the conceptual core of the work; but he does so as the leader of the guild, *primus inter pares*: the song is a collective utterance. It is also true that Berlioz treats the essentially Italianate plot in a subversively un-Italian way. The fact remains that when the libretto (the 1836 version, that is) does eventually give Cellini a moment to himself for reflection, he uses it to fantasise about escaping from it all and embracing the shepherd's simple life – an understandable human reaction in someone about to face the supreme crisis of his existence, and the cue for a noble piece of pastoral music, but not quite what one was hoping for.

In both operas, however, the score transcends the limitations of the libretto when it doesn't also transform its character. The overmastering virility of Don Giovanni's music contradicts the literal fact that he fails, seemingly, to make any fresh conquests. Similarly, Cellini's creative energy and audacity are not demonstrated only in the casting scene but are incarnate in the music of the opera as a whole – music so exuberantly inventive that a good production can sweep away the best-founded objections, as happened at the Lyon Berlioz Festival in 1988, when you were made to forget that *Benvenuto Cellini* had ever been a problem opera.

The libretto gave Berlioz what he wanted, a subject he could identify with in a setting that offered an exceptionally wide range of moods and situations, serious and comic: love songs, guild hymns, crowd scenes, prayers, solitary communing with nature, massive choral ensembles, parody. It was the opportunity he had been waiting for. Cellini's challenge to the establishment would be matched by his own; he would show Paris what the typecast symphonist whose place was in the concert hall could do in the opera house. After the months of compositional fast, he gorged himself on music.

In a long score – at its full length, getting on for three hours of music – there are few failures. One is the Teresa/Cellini duet in Act 2 (despite some attractive phrases in the first section). Another is Cellini's 'La gloire était ma seule idole', written late on so that Duprez could have another aria, and eminently removable (allowing the second tableau to begin, as planned, with the panache and high good humour of the goldsmiths' scene). Otherwise the composer's verdict stands. Having read through the score twelve years later 'with the strictest impartiality', he could not 'help recognising' that it contained 'a variety of ideas, a vitality and zest and a brilliance of musical colour such as I shall perhaps not find again'.[6]

[6] *Memoirs*, p. 238.

La Damnation de Faust, his only dramatic work of comparable brilliance (if you can compare two such different works and worlds), may be much more tautly constructed and have a surer sense of direction, a greater coherence and depth of idea and mastery of ends and means; but Berlioz was right: the zest and abundance of *Benvenuto Cellini* is unique in his output, let alone in the music of his time – above all in terms of rhythm, including the rhythm of contrasting timbres. The constantly changing pulse, the continual syncopation of instrumental colour, the sheer pace at which things happen, make it still, after a century and a half, an extremely demanding score to play and sing and an astonishing one for its date. Although the influence of Meyerbeer is negligible – and if anything it is *Robert le diable*, not *Les Huguenots*, that we catch echoes of, comic echoes – the work is also a kind of encyclopaedia (as Berlioz said of *Les Huguenots*), an encyclopaedia of the Berlioz style, excluding only the austere monumentalism of what he called his architectural works. That would very soon be heard in the *Grande Messe des morts*, but it had no place here. *Benvenuto* was a celebration of life; and to that end he summoned his utmost vitality and virtuosity.

Like the women in the carnival crowd with their compulsive chatter (whose babbling thirds make a ludicrous yet strangely beautiful accompaniment to Harlequin's song), he could not stop himself. He had to give everything, all his inventiveness as melodist and harmonist, all his rhythmic energy and high spirits and his sensitivity to orchestral colour. Nothing must escape commentary. Every detail must be registered, from the single coin that is Harlequin's derisory consolation prize in the singing contest, or the lava torrent of woodwind semiquavers that streams out as Fieramosca compares his feelings to Vesuvius in eruption, to the heaving, clanking rhythm of the bellows in the foundry as the statue is about to be cast.

Benvenuto Cellini is an opera of memorable sound vignettes: the innkeeper's whining recital of the bill, with its pungent Musorgsky-like modal harmonies and droll offbeat chords for bassoons and horns; the lampoon on musical philistinism and platitude as Midas-Balducci beats out of time to the ass-eared Pasquarello's parody cavatina for ophicleide and bass drum and the grotesquely prolonged final cadence that carries off the prize (a passage, as Robert Craft remarks, that 'would have delighted the composer of the bombardon part in *Wozzeck* as well as softened the anti-Berlioz prejudice of the creator of the Bear's music in *Petrushka*'[7]); the monks' procession chanting its 'Rosa purpurea, Maria sancta mater ora pro nobis' in harsh fifths against the softly luminous sound of solo soprano and mezzo and their

[7] Robert Craft, *Prejudices in Disguise: Articles, Essays, Reviews*, Alfred A. Knopf, New York, 1974, p. 155.

accompanying flutes and clarinets and cor anglais, joined by muted strings – a jewel of a duet, with its tender, rapt melodic line and its deftly managed yet seemingly natural series of modulations that make it cadence successively on D, G, E, C and F before finally returning to the home key of E major.

Harmony as well as rhythm plays a part, too, in the rapidity of motion that is such a feature of the score, as the music slips in and out of keys in its headlong course: a trait not uncommon in Berlioz's fast music, when one thinks of the 'Queen Mab' scherzo and the 'Ride to the Abyss', two other movements, like the elopement trio in the opera, where quicksilver harmonic change contributes to the sense of speed.

Liszt characterised the music of *Benvenuto Cellini* as 'at once gorgeous metalwork and vital and original sculpture'.[8] The charm of the vignettes is equalled by the power of the scenes that are constructed on a large scale, most obviously the carnival, but also the casting scene: Cellini's men, when the metal gives out, passing goblets and bowls and statuettes from hand to hand, the huge shining Perseus rising from the ground and the people of Rome pouring in to gape and cheer. When well performed, they are as exhilarating as anything in opera.

The goldsmiths' scene in Act 1 and (in its uncut form) the sextet in which Cellini confronts the Pope are further examples of the assured handling of varied choral and vocal ensemble as well as of a gift for comedy that must have surprised anyone who listened with an open mind. The sextet is in its way as central to the spirit of the work as is the sextet in *Don Giovanni* to the strange fusion of opposites that is Mozart's opera. In its mixture of grandeur and levity, the musical treatment of the Pope epitomises the score. His grave, unctuous trombone theme, with punctuating swish on the cymbals, as he enters Cellini's studio dispensing indulgence with practised hand, befits the dignity of his exalted office yet is compromised by a barely concealed twinkle. This hint of complicity comes out fully in his second theme, the roguish, swinging $\frac{6}{8}$ melody to which he inquires impatiently after his statue. He is an ambiguous figure, at once awesome and profoundly cynical, though with the redeeming grace that he places supreme value on art: a *buffo* character with the power of life and death. When he informs Cellini that if the statue is not cast that day he will hang, the horror-struck repeated 'Pendu!' of the bystanders is undercut by Cellini's ironic 'So that is your indulgence for my sins!', sung to the opening phrases of the first papal theme in the silences between each 'Pendu!' and echoed by the harp on the offbeat. The passage sums up Berlioz's 'opera semi-seria'.

Typical of the score, too, are the transformations that both papal themes undergo. The jovial second theme is slowed to a shocked *pianissimo* when

[8] *Revue et gazette musicale*, 4 April 1852.

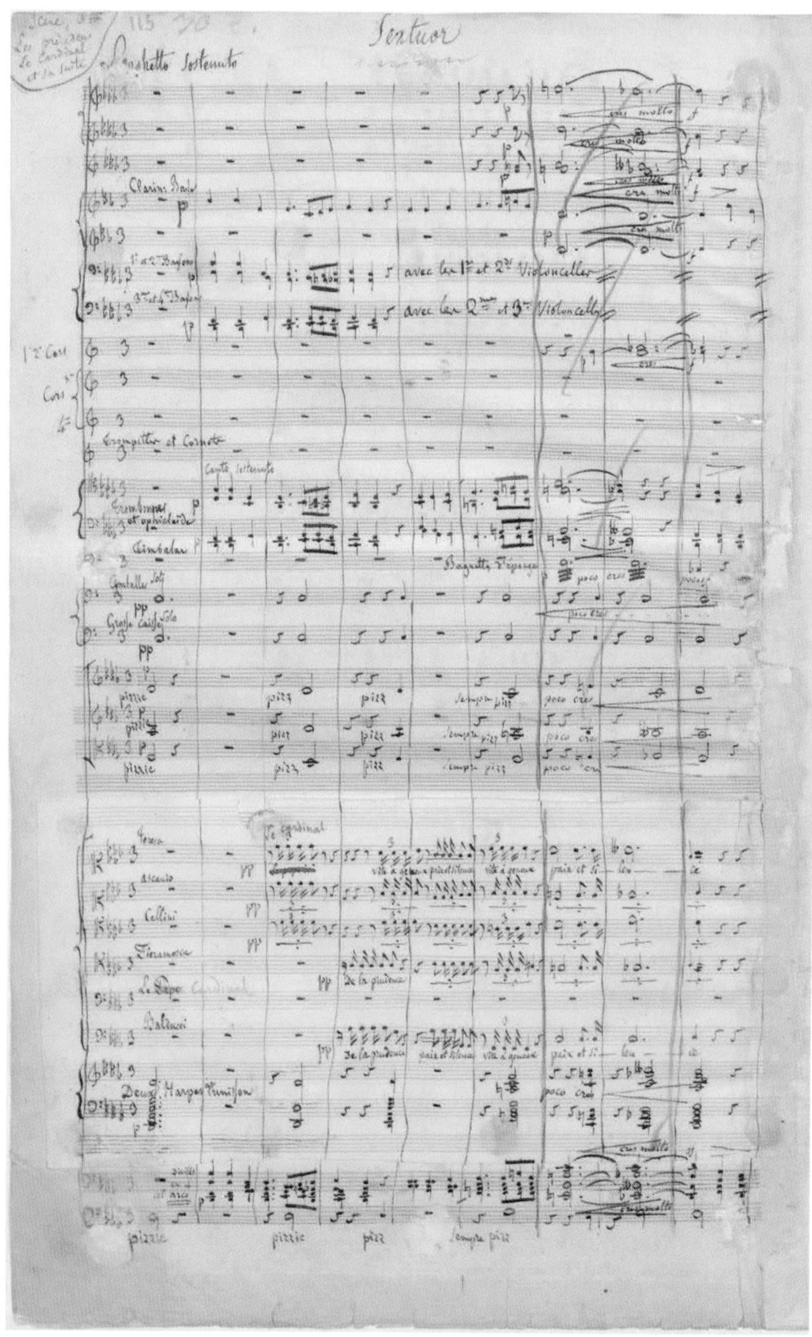

The Sextet from Act 2 of Benvenuto Cellini *in the autograph full score*

Cellini threatens to smash the model if the guards lay a finger on him, and then galvanised into a galloping *presto* for the final ensemble (a movement of Rossinian effrontery further enlivened by bars in $\frac{3}{4}$ and $\frac{4}{4}$ that go off like firecrackers under its prevailing $\frac{6}{8}$). *Benvenuto Cellini* abounds in such thematic alterations and allusions. The first papal theme is prefigured many scenes before, when Ascanio jogs his master's memory about the statue, commissioned by the Pope, which all Italy awaits. A memory of the goldsmiths' genial G major song prefaces the third tableau, but now in an ominous E minor, scored for brass alone, with soft insistent trumpet thirds in each pause in the tune, echoed by the same rhythm on the drums. The fourth tableau is introduced by a reminiscence of the mock-pompous E major music to which Ascanio exacted Cellini's promise to complete the Perseus, tune and accompaniment now hardly recognisable in a spectral D minor: the statue has still to be cast and time is running out. Fieramosca's fencing aria is recalled, no longer boastful and thrusting but limping, abject on Prokofiev-like solo bassoon accompanied by awkward staccato cellos, as the humiliated papal sculptor is forced to don a worker's apron and help in the foundry.

A moment later another transformation occurs, when the angry, vehement music of the workers' revolt, changed from duple to triple time and from *Allegro* to *Allegretto*, reappears in a veiled F minor, and a sudden hush descends as everyone awaits the supreme moment of the casting. And at intervals in the score a chromatic bass figure, heaving up sometimes comically, sometimes menacingly, serves as a recurring motif and heightens the tension: most obviously in the final section of the carnival music, where the dense crowd sways and struggles like a vast pulsating organism that is only half human – a scene which in its quite different way rivals the depiction of mob violence at the end of the second act of *Die Meistersinger*.

Not only in the carnival but in the opera as a whole rhythm plays a role it will hardly play again until Stravinsky. As David Charlton says, 'probably no score since the Renaissance' had been composed more determinedly against the bar-line.[9] The principle is established at the opening of the overture, where the time signature, *alla breve*, is immediately subjected to metrical ambiguity: is this music in $\frac{2}{2}$ or $\frac{3}{4}$? The goldsmiths' hymn constantly cuts across the bar and the three beats of its notation. In Teresa's aria (second version) cross-rhythms enhance the insolent verve of a piece which without them and without its piquant orchestration might seem commonplace. Fieramosca practising his swordsmanship, and imagining Cellini already

[9] 'Romantic Opera, 1830–1850', in Gerald Abraham (ed.), *Romanticism, 1830–1890*, New Oxford History of Music, Vol. IX, Oxford University Press, 1990, p. 111.

transfixed on his blade, is accompanied by orchestral phrases successively in seven, six and five beats.

Or take the very characteristic passage in the opening scene where Teresa comes upon a bouquet among the flowers that the maskers have thrown through the window and, concealed in the bouquet, a letter. Her pleasure at the flowers, followed by her discovery of the note and her progressive alarm as she finds it's from Cellini and he is about to pay her a visit, are conveyed in a recitative as lifelike as it is unconventional: the sustained woodwind notes rising by semitones punctuated by breathless violin figures, the rests between the snatched vocal phrases getting shorter each time and the tempo quicker, and then, with the realisation that her father has gone out and the coast is clear, the music expanding into half ecstatic, half anxious *arioso* on Berlioz's favourite cellos (whose role throughout the opera as bearers of expressive melody amounts almost to that of an *obbligato* instrument). The passage catches perfectly the mood and actions of the character, but it is also, you feel, written out of an overflowing delight in the possibilities of music as a language of comedy. It is typical both of the realism of the score and of the high degree of skill it expects of singers, orchestra and conductor.

In terms of orchestral forces *Benvenuto Cellini* is quite modest by the standards of the Paris Opéra of the day. There are guitars in a couple of scenes – contrasted, in one of them, with the tangy, juicy sound of trumpets – and tambourines for the carnival music (and in one scene the timpanist is directed to play a roll on a tambourine placed on one of the drumheads), but no stage band and, apart from an offstage anvil in the final tableau, no unusual instruments – nothing like the multiple bells and saxhorns in Meyerbeer's *Le Prophète*. Where its demands are exceptional and indeed unprecedented is in the dexterity and rhythmic alertness required of every section of the orchestra. They presuppose a conductor of the new type, such as Berlioz was in the process of becoming, not an old-style violinist-conductor like Habeneck, who would be in charge of the performance.

Even the numbers that do not make a special feature of cross-rhythms are far from playing themselves. Least of all the Act 1 trio 'Ah! mourir, chère belle… Demain soir, mardi gras', where Cellini tells Teresa of his plan for their elopement, and Fieramosca, hidden behind an armchair, strains to overhear their hurried exchange. Berlioz never wrote anything more scintillating than this gleeful piece, which goes like the wind yet finds room for some of the most beautiful music in the score. In the original version the reprise of the whole first section of the trio, flashing $\frac{9}{8}$ and lyrical $\frac{3}{4}$, is motivated dramatically as well as musically; only when Cellini goes over his instructions a second time does Fieramosca, who has managed

A caricature of Berlioz by 'Benjamin' (Benjamin Roubaud, 1811–47), the first in a series called La Caricature provisoire, *published on 1 November 1838*

Recording Benvenuto Cellini, *Wembley Town Hall, July 1972. Seated, left to right: David Cairns, Erik Smith (producer), Colin Davis (conductor), Christiane Eda-Pierre (Teresa); standing, right: Nicolai Gedda (Benvenuto Cellini). Jacques Barzun is just visible, seated far left.*

to creep closer, succeed in hearing what is being said: the first time round, he catches just the final syllable of each *sotto voce* phrase, which he repeats uncomprehendingly. This complication, of course, requires the singer of the role to master two different forms of a part hard enough to get right once, while the other singers must learn to accommodate to them, and all at a galloping tempo, mostly in offbeat interjections executed with the lightest possible touch while the pulse that gives them the beat is articulated *pianissimo* by an orchestra of woodwind and muted strings.

In the garden room at Montmartre that summer, intoxicated with the composition of his score, it was as if Berlioz had forgotten who he was writing it for. *Benvenuto Cellini* imagines a Paris Opéra as it might be in an ideal or at any rate a very different musical commonwealth, peopled with sympathetic, dedicated singers, with a chorus all of whose members spare no pains to learn the music and get their tongues round syllabic choral writing moving at the equivalent of four hundred quavers a minute, an eager virtuoso orchestra, a conductor to marshal and inspire them, and a management and backstage staff who give the work their enthusiastic and unstinting support. The Opéra, as it was, was quite another story.

The Dramatic Symphony *Roméo et Juliette*

The failure of Benvenuto Cellini, *following 'as the night the day', in effect ended Berlioz's hope of gaining a foothold at the Opéra. Nonetheless, I doubt if its fate influenced his choice of medium for the work he had long thought of writing in response to Shakespeare's* Romeo and Juliet. *Even if he had succeeded in the theatre and had been encouraged to compose other operas, the dramatic concert work inspired by the example of Beethoven was always going to be a central preoccupation of his career. What happened to* Benvenuto Cellini – Malvenuto Cellini, *the cartoonists duly christened it – only confirmed a decision already taken. 'Music has wings too wide to spread fully within the confines of a theatre.' And this particular theatre was no place for so holy an enterprise. Given the 'bazaar' the Académie Royale de Musique had become, it would be a 'profanation' – the word he used in reply to a correspondent who said it was time the Opéra revived Gluck: 'you have no idea what atrocities are committed there. Music and drama are dragged through the mud'.*[1] *Besides, to do justice to the play and all that he felt about it, his wings must suffer no let or hindrance. By its 'very sublimity', he would later write, the passion of the young lovers and their utterances – the heart and* raison d'être *of the work – had to be expressed in 'the language of instruments, a language richer, more varied and by its very impreciseness incomparably more potent' in such a context.*[2]

The following piece is an amalgam of articles written, at different times, for the London Symphony Orchestra, the Orchestra of the Age of Enlightenment, The Guardian, the *Financial Times and the American magazine* Symphony.

Paul Scudo, the vitriolic and mendacious French music critic who was a scourge of both Berlioz and Wagner and who, appropriately, ended his life in a lunatic asylum, described the two men as enemy brothers sprung from Beethoven's demented old age.[3] The notion that the music of Beethoven's last years was the music of a once-remarkable composer who had lost his wits was still quite common at the time. Naturally, neither Wagner nor

[1] *Correspondance générale*, Vol. II, p. 545.

[2] Preface to the vocal score published in 1858.

[3] *L'Année musicale – deuxième année*, Paris, Hachette, 1861, p. 151.

Berlioz thought so. But Scudo's *mot* had a grain of truth in it. For both of them, Beethoven's Ninth Symphony was the beginning of modern music. Berlioz proclaimed this belief in what he wrote about Beethoven, and in London in 1852 he conducted performances of the work that were hailed by many musicians and music-lovers as revelatory, converting those who had previously been puzzled by it or had openly scoffed. Wagner (though feeling an irresistible need to improve its orchestration) wrote eloquently about its greatness and its dramatic qualities; and in 1872, in an act rich in symbolism, he conducted the symphony at the laying of the foundation stone of the Bayreuth Festival Theatre.

In the event the future belonged to Wagner, not to Berlioz. But both were heirs to that dramatic moment at the premiere of the Ninth Symphony in Vienna in 1824, when a singer rose to his feet among the musicians of the orchestra and declaimed 'Friends, not these sounds' and, in doing so, opened the future and changed the history of music.

If not those sounds, what then? For Wagner the answer was blindingly obvious. By calling on words and voices to resolve the conflicts generated in the previous movements Beethoven had in effect acknowledged that the symphony as an art form had reached its ultimate end, could go no further and must merge in a new kind of drama. And in Paris, as early as 1839, around the time when he heard Berlioz's 'Dramatic Symphony after Shakespeare's *Romeo and Juliet*' and recognised in it 'a new world of music', he outlined his convictions in a short story published in the *Revue et gazette musicale* – 'A Pilgrimage to Beethoven' – in which a young German musician calls on the master and hears these truths from the lips of the composer himself.[4]

For Berlioz, on the contrary, the Ninth proclaimed the final emancipation of the form from its eighteenth-century restrictions. The Beethovenian orchestra, he wrote, was 'the most complete manifestation of what is meant by music today'.[5] Anything was now possible, including a symphonic reworking of a play. It must have been this that he meant when, early in his initiation, having studied and lived the score of the Ninth in the Conservatoire Library (it had not yet been performed in Paris), he spoke of taking the art of music as transformed by Beethoven 'in another direction'.[6] 'Music is free and does what it wants – without permission'.[7] Even before his discovery of Beethoven he had already been thinking of some kind of

[4] *Revue et gazette musicale*, 19, 22 and 29 November and 3 December 1840.

[5] *Memoirs*, p. 400.

[6] *Correspondance générale*, Vol. I, p. 229.

[7] Quoted in Peter Bloom, '*Berlioz à l'Institut* Revisited', *Acta Musicologica*, Vol. 53, 1981, p. 197 (session of the Academy of Sciences, 30 October 1865).

musical response to the play which, in the autumn of 1827, had seized his imagination and stirred him to the depths of his being. Once symphonic music and its immense dramatic and expressive possibilities had been revealed to him, such ideas began to take clearer shape. According to the poet Émile Deschamps (who would write the sung text of the symphony), two years after the epiphany at the Odéon Berlioz discussed with him what kind of work it should be. And in 1832, in an article on the state of music in Italy written for a Paris journal, and under the spur of his disgust at Bellini's *I Capuleti e i Montecchi*, he sketched a scenario for a dramatic work that, unlike the Italian opera, would be faithful to Shakespeare:

> To begin with, the dazzling ball at the Capulets, where amid a whirling cloud of beauties young Montague first sets eyes on 'sweet Juliet' whose constant love will cost her her life; then the furious battles in the streets of Verona, the 'fiery Tybalt' presiding like the very spirit of rage and revenge; the indescribable night scene on Juliet's balcony, the lovers' voices 'like softest music to attending ears', uttering a love as pure and radiant as the smiling moon that shines its benediction upon them; the dazzling Mercutio and his sharp-tongued, fantastical humour; the naïve old cackling nurse; the stately hermit, striving in vain to calm the storm of love and hate whose tumult has carried even to his lowly cell; and then the catastrophe, extremes of ecstasy and despair contending for mastery, passion's sighs turned to choking death; and, at the last, the solemn oath sworn by the warring houses, too late, on the bodies of their star-crossed children, to abjure the hatred through which so much blood, so many tears were shed.[8]

Much of this will feature in the symphony. The play that Berlioz saw in 1827 was the Garrick version (itself truncated), in which Juliet wakes from her drug-induced sleep while the dying Romeo is still alive. But it is clear that in the intervening four years, between the evening at the Odéon and the writing of the article, he had read and absorbed the Shakespearean original. The 'cackling nurse' doesn't appear in Garrick's *Romeo* as given in Paris. Nor does the oath sworn by the warring houses (Garrick's version ends with the lovers' death); it figures only briefly in Shakespeare – clearly, too, Berlioz is thinking in terms of a big final scene which, in whatever form the work takes, will bring the tragic events to a fitting close. And by the time Paganini's gift makes it possible for him to compose and himself promote and perform a work on a grand scale, the choice has been made. It can only be a symphony, the medium that Beethoven revealed and where Shakespeare's drama belongs.

[8] 'Lettre d'un enthousiaste sur l'état actuel de la musique en Italie', *Revue européenne*, Vol. III, No. 7, March–May 1832, and in *La Revue musicale*, 31 March and 9 April 1832; republished in *Critique musicale*, Vol. 1, pp. 69–83, and reproduced in *Memoirs*, p. 141.

The choice has been much disputed – first of all by Wagner, who thought the form of the work was as wrong-headed as the music was inspired (Berlioz was one of the elite, but 'only the drama' – that is, Wagnerian music-drama – 'can save him', he told Liszt).[9] Interestingly, the mixed form of *Roméo et Juliette* – so troublesome to generations of music critics and commentators – doesn't seem to have been a problem for more than a minority of listeners when the work was first heard, in 1839 and the 1840s. Genre was not then so sacred a concept as it would be later. It was only in the second half of the nineteenth century – when the Austro-German tradition became the mainstream, genres were more fixed, 'absolute music' was in the ascendant and musical opinion was polarised between Wagner and Brahms – that Berlioz's symphony was dismissed as a freak and only the middle three instrumental movements allowed.

If the official critical reaction to Mahler's so-called symphonies was deeply hostile, how much more so to a 'queer hybrid' like *Roméo*, as Donald Tovey called it?[10] Until recently, Berlioz's dramatic symphony was the least esteemed of his large-scale compositions, as well as one of the least often performed. Even Wilfrid Mellers, author of the brilliant essay on Berlioz in *Man and His Music* (1961), called it 'a curious, not entirely convincing compromise between symphonic and operatic techniques'.[11]

Since then, the enormous popularity of Mahler's multi-movement, mixed-media works and their acceptance as symphonies has helped to clear the way for a more perceptive approach (the composer Hugh Wood has pointed out the 'deeply Berliozian' conception of Mahler's second, 'Resurrection', symphony[12]). Is it too much to believe that the time has finally come when not only its beauties but its formal coherence may be accepted? If Tovey had taken the trouble to examine it properly, he could have seen that the scheme of the work, far from being 'incoherent and unwieldy', is strictly logical, and the mixing of elements – the legacy of Shakespeare and Beethoven – precisely gauged. *Roméo et Juliette* shows its composer's habitual concern for proportion, for linkage, for flow, for context. Berlioz was certainly being ironic when he wrote, in a preface to a later edition, 'There will doubtless be no mistake as to the genre of the work'. Yet (as he went on), 'although voices are frequently employed, it is

[9] Stuart Spencer and Barry Middleton (transl. and ed.), *Selected Letters of Richard Wagner*, J. M. Dent & Sons, London, 1987, p. 268.

[10] Donald Tovey, *Essays in Musical Analysis*, Vol. 4, Oxford University Press, London, 1936, pp. 86–87.

[11] Harman and Mellers, *Man and his Music*, p. 765.

[12] Review of Hugh Macdonald's *Berlioz's Orchestration Treatise, A Translation and Commentary* (Cambridge University Press, Cambridge, 2002), *The Times Literary Supplement*, 7 March 2003.

neither a concert opera nor a cantata but a choral symphony'.[13] That is what it is.

True to this description, the symphony, beginning with a fugal introduction that depicts the fury of the two warring houses and establishes the principle of dramatically explicit orchestral music, then crosses over into vocal music, using the bridge of instrumental recitative (as in the finale of the Ninth). A choral prologue states the argument (which the choral finale will resolve) and prepares the listener for the themes, dramatic and musical, that will be treated in the main body of the symphony. In addition, the two least overtly dramatic movements, the *Adagio* and the Scherzo, are prefigured and emphasised, the one in a contralto solo celebrating first love, the other in a 'Scherzetto' for tenor and semi-chorus that introduces the mischievous Mab. At the end of the work the finale brings the drama fully into the open in an extended choral movement that culminates in the abjuring of the hatreds depicted orchestrally at the outset of the work.

At the heart of the symphony, structurally and emotionally, is the wordless love scene, for orchestra alone. But voices are never forgotten. They are used enough to keep them before the listener's attention, in preparation for their full deployment in the finale. After the choral prologue comes the orchestral 'Roméo seul – grande fête chez Capulet'. Then, in the following love scene, the songs of revellers on their way home from the ball float across the stillness of the Capulets' garden. Two movements later, in the funeral procession, the Capulets are heard chanting their 'Jetez des fleurs' to the orchestral fugato, before taking it over and making it fully choral. The use of the chorus thus follows what Berlioz, in an essay on the Ninth Symphony, called 'the law of crescendo'.[14] The law also operates dramatically: the voices, having begun as onlookers, become full participants, just as the anonymous contralto of the prologue, and Mercutio-like tenor, give way to an identified human personality, Friar Laurence. At the same time, the two movements preceding the finale take on an increasingly descriptive character, the funeral dirge merging into an insistent bell-like tolling and the tomb scene taking the work still nearer to narrative, in such a way that the oratorio-like finale is made to evolve out of what has gone before.

In the same concern with structure and unity, resemblances and echoes link the different sections; the score is a network of thematic cross-reference, anticipation and recall. The brass recitative in the introduction, representing the Prince's rebuke to the feuding families, is formed from the notes of their angry fugato, lengthened, 'mastered'; the ball music is

[13] *Cf.* 'Avant-propos de l'auteur', *Roméo et Juliette*, ed. D. Kern Holoman, New Berlioz Edition, Bärenreiter, Kassel, Vol. 18.

[14] *Revue et gazette musicale*, 4 March 1838; republished in *Critique musicale*, Vol. 3, p. 404.

transformed to give the departing guests their dreamlike song; in the tomb scene Juliet (clarinet) wakes to the identical rising cor anglais phrase from the opening section of the love scene, and this recall is followed by the love theme itself, now blurred and torn apart as the dying Romeo relives it in distorted flashback; and in the finale, as the families' vendetta breaks out again over the bodies of their children, the return of the introductory fugato unites the two extremes of the vast score. The principle is active to the end: the theme of Friar Laurence's oath of reconciliation takes as its point of departure the B minor feud motif of the introduction, reborn in a broad, magnanimous B major.

Motivically close-knit, the work is a rich treasure-house of musical invention. No Berlioz score is more abundant in lyric poetry, in a sense of the magic and brevity of love, in 'sounds and sweet airs' of so many kinds: the flickering, fleet-footed scherzo, which stands not only for Mercutio's Queen Mab speech but for the whole nimble-witted, comic-fantastical, fatally irrational element in the play, and in which strings and wind seem caught up in some gleeful, menacing game; the swell of the grand extended melody that grows out of the questioning phrases of 'Roméo seul'; the awesome unison of cor anglais, horn and four bassoons for Romeo in the Capulets' tomb; the haunting beauty of Juliet's funeral procession; the long, exalted lines for flute and clarinet in the friar's noble 'Pauvres enfants'; the deep-toned harmonies and spellbound melodic arcs of the *Adagio*, conjuring the moonlit garden and the wonder and intensity of the passion flowering in it.

'Oh, the ardent existence I lived during the time of its composition', wrote Berlioz in the *Memoirs*.

> I struck out boldly across that great ocean of poetry, caressed by the wild, sweet breeze of fancy, under the fiery sun of love that Shakespeare kindled. I felt within me the strength to reach the enchanted isle where the temple of pure art stands serene under a clear sky.[15]

That was lofty. But then he adds: 'It is not for me to determine whether I succeeded'. What are we to make of that?

Berlioz was a diligent reviser (if not an obsessive one, like Mendelssohn). He frequently made changes to his compositions in the light of performances he heard or himself conducted; as the pragmatic and self-critical musician he was, he waited to judge the effect of a new piece, and the process could last a long time. The autograph score of the *Symphonie fantastique* is a battleground of alterations, crossings-out, colettes, whole pages replaced, textures lightened or enriched, orchestration modified, all done during the fifteen years that separated composition and publication. This *Fantastique*

[15] *Memoirs*, p. 244.

was no doubt an extreme case: he had written nothing like it before – nor had anyone else – and he was venturing into unknown territory. But that had always been his practice, from the beginning. ('When I want to know if a thing of mine is good', the 21-year-old student writes to his sister Nancy, 'I put it on one side once it's finished and give myself time to recover from the excitement that composition always produces in my system. Then when I am calm again I read my work as if it were not by me'.[16]) He was still revising the *Grande Messe des morts* (for a new edition) nearly 30 years after its premiere.

Roméo et Juliette is no exception. In the eight years before it was published (1847), the work was subjected to many changes, major changes as well as changes of detail. The choral prologue was revised and – because of the removal of the second prologue that originally came between the scherzo and the funeral procession and prefigured the tragic dénouement – its ending was rewritten to supply the want. A substantial cut was made in Friar Laurence's narration and the rather abrupt conclusion of the Scherzo replaced by a longer and better proportioned ending.

What is unusual about *Roméo* is the composer's defensive attitude to it. After describing (in the *Memoirs*) the changes he made, he goes on:

> If there are other blemishes that I have missed, at least I have tried sincerely and with what judgement I possess to detect them. After which, what can a composer do but admit candidly that he has done his best, and resign himself to the work's imperfections?[17]

I can't think of another work of his maturity that he is so ambivalent about. Admittedly, the apologia comes in the context of a swipe at the 'pundits' who, after the premiere, 'pronounced for or against the work' – 'none of whom deigned to point out a single one of its specific faults, which I corrected later as and when I recognised them'.[18]

How should we regard Berlioz's implied strictures on *Roméo et Juliette*? Do they authorise us to judge it a flawed masterpiece, a noble endeavour that could only fail in the attempt (assuming, that is, that we don't agree with the Toveys of this world that it is simply a mistake)? If Berlioz was dissatisfied with it, don't we have every right to be?

I think we should seek to understand his uncertainties and to place them in perspective. After all, composers are uniquely well placed to criticise their works, knowing them better than anyone and having lived through the struggle of bringing them to life. They are their most exacting critics.

[16] *Correspondance générale*, Vol. I, p. 101.

[17] *Memoirs*, p. 246.

[18] *Ibid.*, p. 245.

A lithograph of Charles Kemble and Harriet Smithson in the tomb scene from Romeo and Juliet, *by Francis, 1827*

Think of Verdi on the press notices of *Aida*: 'Stupid criticisms, and still more stupid praise'.[19] Berlioz's 'doubts', and his scorn for the pundits, are echoed by Benjamin Britten, speaking of his own music: 'I can say with honesty that in every piece I have written, in spite of hard work there are still passages where I have not quite solved problems. Not once have these passages been noticed, nor of course suggestions made as to how I could have improved them'.[20]

In *Roméo et Juliette* Berlioz was trying something he had never tried before: instrumental, non-verbal music that enacted a dramatic text. Not even the *Symphonie fantastique* was such a leap into the unknown. (As it is, you can see why they are the two whose autograph scores show the most revision.) He was attempting to put so much – an entire Shakespeare play – and so much that was central to his innermost feelings and convictions into a structural plan that was without precedent. One problem was that it moved him so deeply (as he recalled twenty years later during the composition of *Les Troyens*, 'One must strive to do the most fiery things coolly. That was what held me up so long when I was writing the Adagio of *Roméo et Juliette* and the final scene of reconciliation'[21]). Another was the crucial problem of finding the just balance between dramatic narration and symphonic design. That was why he worked and reworked it and kept on having second thoughts, and why in the end he still had doubts.

They focused on the tomb scene. Here surely is the source of the anxieties expressed in the *Memoirs*. In the original scheme of the work there was a second prologue (in emulation of Shakespeare) which introduced and explained the tomb scene and prepared the listener for the events the music dramatised. By removing it (in the interests of balance and continuity), he created fresh difficulties for himself; the revision tightened the structure of the work but left the uninitiated without an idea of what the music – the most avant-garde he ever wrote – was saying. So worried was he that he added a despairing note to the score, calling for the suppression of the movement whenever the work was performed before an audience that was not exceptionally sensitive and thoroughly familiar with the Garrick version of the scene – that is, he said, 'ninety-nine times out of a hundred'.[22]

Extreme though the solution is, you can see why he felt as he did. The tomb scene was too sacred to be listened to casually, without understanding of its agonising import, too vital to be thrown away on an idle audience that

[19] Letter to Tito Ricordi, 3 January 1873, in Gaetano Cesari and Alessandro Luzio (eds.), *I copialettere di Giuseppe Verdi*, Comune de Milano, Milan, 1913, p. 280.

[20] Benjamin Britten, 'Variations on a Critical Theme', *Opera*, Vol. 3, No. 3, March 1952, pp. 144–46.

[21] *Correspondance générale*, Vol. V, p. 353.

[22] Handwritten note in the autograph full score.

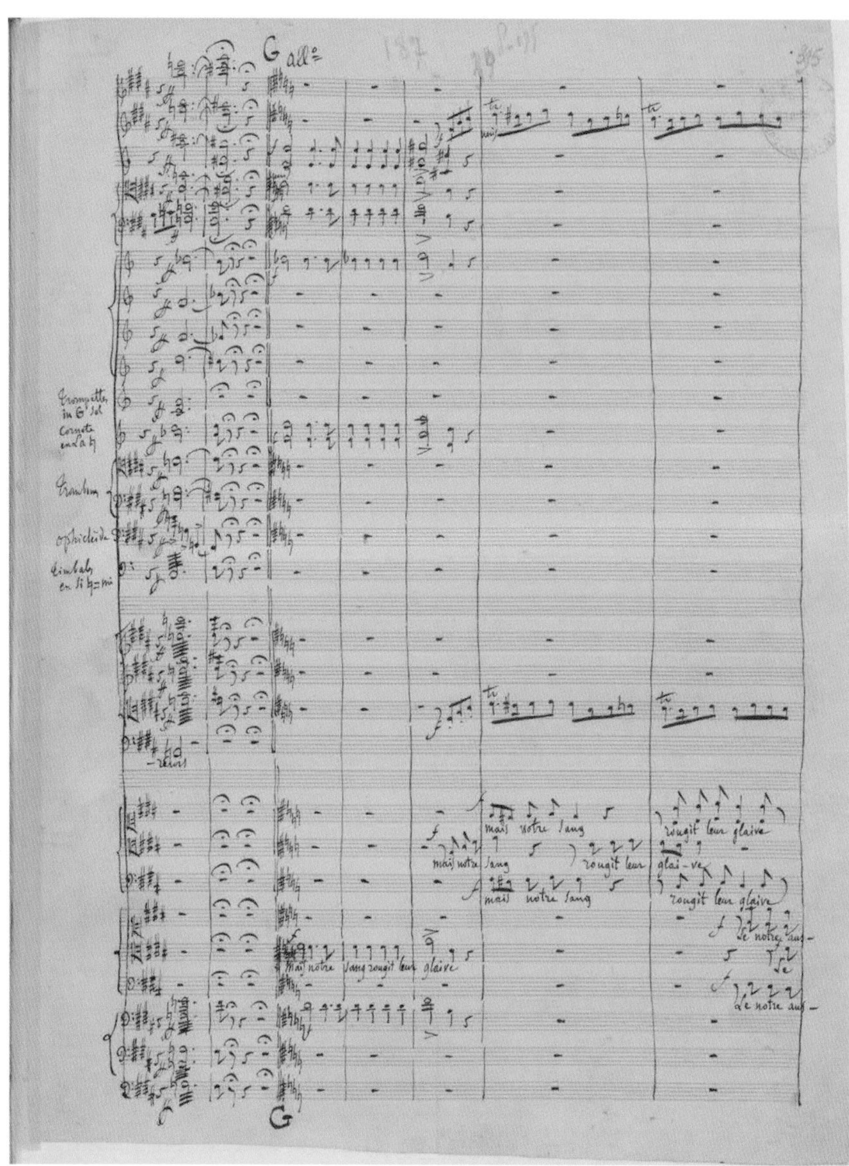

Autograph full score of Roméo et Juliette, *finale*

might only at best be startled, if not shocked, by the music's ultra-modern sounds and gestures. That was more than he could bear.

But that was a century and a half ago. Perhaps today the issue has lost its sting, and we can follow the scene, comprehend it, and experience to the full its extraordinary music and, in doing so, appreciate how essential it is to a work at whose heart is the vision of young love, all-embracing but fatal because the world can only destroy it. In the radiant light of the love scene, the physical disintegration and destruction of that love is as poignant and riveting as anything in the music of the nineteenth century.

Some would say that of the whole work. If Berlioz's dramatic symphony has regularly perplexed commentators and fallen foul of impatient critics accustomed to making snap judgements and in need of pigeonholing works in conveniently defined categories, there are others, conductors as well as music-lovers, who cherish it above all his scores and who feel for it, as the composer felt, a special passionately protective love (as Beethoven felt for *Fidelio*: 'Of all my children, this was born in greatest labour'). For them, *Roméo et Juliette* poses no problems. They could say of it what the great nineteenth-century conductor Felix Mottl, champion of Berlioz and of Wagner, said in answer to anyone who found fault with Berlioz: 'There is no *but*...'[23]

[23] Quoted in Georges de Massougnes, *Hector Berlioz: son œuvre*, Calmann-Lévy, Paris, 1919, p. 138.

Roméo et Juliette: An Alternative Reading

The first two paragraphs of this piece are reprinted from the Berlioz Society Bulletin No. 185 *(April 2011), the third from No. 186 (August 2011).*

The page from the autograph of *Roméo et Juliette* (finale) reproduced on p. 228 shows an afterthought of the composer's, duly incorporated in the published edition of the full score (1847): the two-and-half-bar phrase for clarinets, bassoons, first horn, cornets and Montague tenors ('Mais notre sang rougit leur glaive') – minim, dotted crotchet, quaver, four crotchets, minim, crotchet (half-note, dotted quarter-note, eighth-note, four quarter-notes, half-note, quarter-note) – that comes between the fermata which closes Friar Laurence's 'Oubliez vos propres fureurs' and the reprise of the introductory B minor fugato.

The change was made during Berlioz's revision of the work, after the performance of 1846 in Prague. It is what we invariably hear when *Roméo et Juliette* is performed; but Ian Kemp maintains that there is a good argument for omitting it. In his view, it was added almost certainly as a safety measure, Berlioz having found that choruses had difficulty coming straight in on the offbeat, after the fermata, and needed the two-and-a-half bars of preparation in the new metre and (much faster) tempo. Modern choruses, on the other hand, would have no problem with it; so why not revert to what Berlioz originally wrote? Will any conductor who happens to read this please take up the challenge?

While on the subject of *Roméo et Juliette*, may I also suggest to the putative conductor of the work that he or she consider observing Berlioz's notation of the trombone and ophicleide (tuba) parts six bars from the end (New Berlioz Edition, Vol. 18, p. 361, bar 452), which means that those instruments sustain the B major chord for its full value, across the whole bar, instead of releasing it before the end of the bar, as all the other instruments and the voices are required to do. It is absolutely clear, from the autograph as well as from the published score, that this is not a slip of the pen but is intended. It would be nice to hear it, for once, as written.

IV

THE 1840s

The *Grand Traité*: Origins and Genesis

This essay first appeared in the Berlioz Society Bulletin *No. 196 (April 2015).*

Berlioz's *Grand Traité d'instrumentation et d'orchestration modernes* was published in 1844, when the composer was 40. But the story begins long before that. The trail goes back past the great innovatory works of the 1830s, the *Fantastique, Harold en Italie, Benvenuto Cellini,* the *Grande Messe des morts, Roméo*; past Berlioz's exuberant letter of January 1830 to his sister Nancy describing how he approaches the challenge and excitement of composing for large orchestra; past the revelatory Beethoven concerts at the Conservatoire; past the immersion in Weber's *Der Freischütz* at the Odéon; past the *Messe solennelle*; past the buttonholing and questioning of orchestral musicians about the technical and expressive nature and possibilities of their instruments; past the hours spent in the Conservatoire Library poring over Gluck's scores and copying them out by hand; past the sermons preached to his fellow Gluckists as they wait in the pit for the three loud knocks that signal that the performance is about to begin; past the earliest momentous encounters with the Opéra, when the boy from the provinces hears an orchestra for the first time – past all that, to his childhood.

Like so much else in his life and career, the *Traité* and the experiences and preoccupations and beliefs that went into it are explained by and rooted in what happened in those early years in the remote seclusion of La Côte-Saint-André.

In chapter 2 of the *Memoirs* he recounts what he calls 'an apparently trivial incident' and the sudden 'flash of illumination' it precipitated:

> I had never seen a full score. The only pieces of music I knew were *solfèges* with figured bass, flute solos, or excerpts from operas with piano accompaniment. One day I came across a piece of paper with twenty-four staves ruled on it. The moment I saw that great array of lines I became aware of what a multitude of instrumental and vocal combinations lay open to an ingenious hand, and I exclaimed: 'What an orchestra one could write down on that!'[1]

[1] *Memoirs*, p. 17.

When the Bibliothèque nationale in Paris was planning its major bicentenary exhibition in 2003, Cécile Reynaud, with the help of Richard Macnutt, had the brilliant idea of showing just such an object, alone in a glass case, to commemorate a crucial moment in the composer's boyhood – the symbolic moment, one might call it, when the creator of the modern orchestra was introduced to his *métier* by a blank sheet of music paper.

How was it that the incident had such a profound effect? What lay behind that flash of illumination, what made it so dazzling? Everything, it is hardly an exaggeration to say: everything in his inheritance, his nature, his upbringing. Let me try to analyse the different elements – though they can't really be separated. First, the power of an exceptionally vivid, all-encompassing imagination – inborn, one must suppose, but fostered and brought to the highest degree by his upbringing. Berlioz doesn't go, except briefly, to the local seminary, so escapes the constrictions of conventional schooling. He is educated at home by his father, a tolerant man with a wide-ranging mind, varied interests and quick sympathies, who leaves him to make his own discoveries, or at least to pursue them himself, but at the same time communicates to his son his natural curiosity, his instinct for innovation, for scientific enquiry, for seeking answers to questions that it doesn't occur to others to think of.

The teenage Berlioz was left free to read, which he did, avidly. He had the run of his father's well-stocked library, where in addition to Virgil, Chateaubriand, La Fontaine, Cervantes, Plutarch, Rousseau, and Humboldt and Volney and other travel writers, all of whom had an influence on his budding imagination, he read Michaud's *Biographie universelle*, to which his father subscribed. This encyclopaedia, arranged alphabetically, started coming out in 1811, and appeared at the rate of three or four volumes a year. It included long entries on composers, and Berlioz devoured them. Sometimes what he found seemed to chime uncannily with his own fraught situation and his secret hopes: Dalayrac's vocation opposed by his father, who intended him for the bar and at first would not let him play the violin, but in the end was won over by his persistence; Haydn's long struggle for recognition, his childhood in an obscure village where, like Berlioz, he played the drum on feast-days.

Above all, the long Gluck entry captivated him. He read and re-read it till he had it by heart: more than 40 years later, an essay he wrote on *Alceste* reproduced phrases first found in Michaud. Berlioz is a Gluckist before he has heard a note of his music, before he has had a chance to read any of it (apart from an extract or two from *Orfeo* with guitar accompaniment among his father's papers). The ideas he encounters in the Gluck article will become his ideas. It could be Berlioz himself speaking: how Gluck set himself

accompagnées d'une basse chiffrée (en solos de Flûte,) ou en fragments d'opéras avec accompagnement
de Piano. Or, un jour, une feuille de papier reglé à 24 portées me tomba
sous la main. En apercevant cette grande quantité de lignes, je
compris aussitôt à quelle multitude de combinaisons instrumentales et
vocales leur emploi ingénieux pouvait donner lieu; et je m'écriai :
«quel orchestre on doit pouvoir écrire là dessus!» à partir de ce moment
la fermentation musicale de ma tête ne fit que croître et mon aversion
pour la médecine redoubla. J'avais de mes parents une trop grande
crainte, toutefois, pour rien oser avouer de mes audacieuses pensées; quand
mon père, à la faveur même de la musique, en vint à un coup d'état
pour détruire ce qu'il appelait mes puériles antipathies et me faire
commencer les études médicales. afin de me familiariser instantanément
avec les objets que je devais bientôt avoir constamment sous les yeux,
il avait étalé dans son cabinet l'énorme traité d'ostéologie de Munro,
ouvert, et contenant des gravures de grandeur naturelle où les diverses
parties de la charpente humaine sont reproduites très fidèlement.
« Voilà un ouvrage, me dit-il, que tu vas avoir à étudier. Je ne pense
pas que tu persistes dans tes idées hostiles à la médecine; elles ne sont
ni raisonnables ni fondées sur quoi que ce soit. Et si, au contraire, tu
veux me promettre d'entreprendre sérieusement ton cours d'ostéologie,
je ferai venir de Lyon pour toi une Flûte magnifique garnie de
toutes les nouvelles clefs.» Cet instrument était depuis longtemps
l'objet de mon ambition. que répondre?... la solennité de la proposition,
le respect mêlé de crainte que m'inspirait mon père malgré toute sa
bonté, et la force de la tentation, me troublèrent au dernier point.
Je laissai échapper un <u>oui</u> bien faible et rentrai dans ma chambre
où je me jetai sur mon lit accablé de [struck through] chagrin.
Être médecin! étudier l'anatomie! disséquer! assister à d'horribles

In chapter 4 of his Memoirs *Berlioz recounts the moment when, having discovered blank music-paper with 24 staves, 'my head was in a state of ever-increasing ferment, and my aversion to medicine grew accordingly'.*

to abandon 'the beaten track of prejudice and routine' and emancipate himself from the vain and frivolous conventions of Italian opera; how he pioneered a new and grander art based on the sacred principle of fidelity of dramatic expression, and believed that the only rule that can never be broken is dramatic truth; how when Orestes in *Iphigénie en Tauride* utters the words 'peace returns to my heart', the orchestra contradicts him, and how, at a rehearsal of the passage, when Gluck was asked, 'why then these muttering cellos, these snapping violins [actually violas], the great man answered: "He's lying – he murdered his mother"'. And how, when someone complained about the repetition of a single note at 'Charon calls thee', in *Alceste*, Gluck replied, 'My dear fellow, in Hades passion dies down and the voice loses its inflection'.[2] Dramatic truth is paramount.

It was the Gluck article that first gave Berlioz his conception, his vision, of the orchestra. At that stage in his life he had heard nothing more substantial than the band of the local National Guard playing on the Esplanade at La Côte or processing through the streets, producing sounds that made Nancy Berlioz and her friend Elise Rocher stuff their fingers in their ears. But he could imagine an orchestra by reading Michaud:

> Who has made the instruments speak as powerfully as Gluck? [...] It is in his orchestra that you will find the solemn rites of sacrifice, the horrors of war, the force of the winds, the howl of the storm, the thunder's roar, the cry that recalls the lovesick Renaud to glory, the awesome depiction of hell, the lamenting dead, the baying of Cerberus, and the eternal peace of the Elysian Fields.

When the seventeen-year-old Berlioz takes the mail-coach to Paris in October 1821, what reconciles him to the dread prospect of studying medicine is that not only the School of Medicine awaits him but also the Opéra, where he will be able at last to hear the music he has been dreaming about with his whole soul.

In short, he is ready for the initiation that will in due course make him master of the orchestra. I have mentioned, on the one hand, the growth and development of a super-abundant imagination, a capacity to imagine and inhabit different poetic worlds, each with its own climate and atmosphere, and on the other hand the acquisition of a scientific, analytical cast of mind – two faculties that will combine to give the *Traité* its special and unique character. When he finally hears an orchestra, his response will be that of both poet and scientist.

There is one more childhood event, or rather non-event, that will be of profound and priceless importance. Berlioz is not taught the piano.

[2] Michaud, *op. cit.*

A 1775 portrait of Gluck by the French painter Joseph Duplessis (now held in the Kunsthistorisches Museum in Vienna)

The instruments he learns to play are the flute (very well) and the guitar (passably). He will be blamed for not knowing the piano, traditionally regarded as essential to a composer's training, the indispensable means to correct composition. But, as he remarks in the *Memoirs*, it was in fact his very good fortune to have been 'saved from the tyranny of keyboard habits, so dangerous to thought, and from the lure of conventional sonorities, to which all composers are to a greater or lesser degree prone'.[3] This is not the place to discuss the influence of the piano, and the development of the instrument, on nineteenth-century music and the more complex harmonic language it fostered, which helped to make Berlioz's, with its linear style and separation of timbres, the exception. What is important here is that, unlike so many of his contemporaries, who approached the orchestra through the piano, Berlioz went straight to it, without intermediary. Its colours and textures struck him directly, fresh, unfiltered, new minted. In composing he would think automatically, instinctively, in orchestral terms. And we may add, in parenthesis, that because for him each imagined experience was so vivid and so complete that he lived in it as if it were real, he would tend to give each new work its particular orchestral colour, so that each one inhabited a different sound-world. In the *Ouverture de la Tempête* of 1830 (incorporated into *Retour à la vie/Lélio*) he uses the piano as an orchestral instrument – no one had done that before, but, innovator that he is, he sees no reason not to. But he never does so again. There is no subsequent poetic conception that demands that sound.

A few weeks after his arrival in Paris he hears *Iphigénie en Tauride*. Soon after, he tries to give Nancy an idea of the wonder of the experience: 'Imagine, to begin with, an orchestra of eighty who perform with such precision you'd think it was a single instrument'. Then, having expatiated on the staging, he continues:

> I can't begin to describe to you the sense of horror one feels when Orestes, overcome, sinks to the ground and says, 'Peace returns to my breast'. He dozes, and then you see the ghost of his mother, whom he killed, gliding round him, with various spirits holding an infernal torch in each hand and brandishing them about him. And the orchestra! It's all in the orchestra. If you could hear how every situation is depicted in it, above all when Orestes appears to have grown calm – well, the violins hold a long note, very soft, which suggests tranquillity; but below it you hear the cellos murmuring, like the remorse which despite his apparent calm still sounds in the depths of the matricide's heart.[4]

[3] *Memoirs*, p. 15.

[4] *Correspondance générale*, Vol. I, p. 37.

Here you have the dutiful student of Michaud. But once the overwhelming emotion has subsided, his mind will be busy playing through in his memory what he has heard, analysing it, working out how it was achieved. In the ensuing period – say, seven years, from the summer of 1822 to the autumn of 1828 – Berlioz will be subjecting himself to a private course in orchestration. He will learn little if anything about the subject from his teachers. It is not on the curriculum of the Conservatoire. But it is on his curriculum. The discovery, probably in the summer of 1822 and probably from some fellow *habitué* of the pit at the Opéra, where Berlioz is now a regular – the discovery that the Conservatoire library is open to the public is like a gift of the gods. From now on he can study the full scores of the operas he has just heard, he can find out what produced the sounds he heard and still hears, in his head.

As time goes on, he makes friends with musicians in the various Paris theatre orchestras and gets them to try out things for him. Having written the trombone passage at the beginning of the *Francs-juges* Overture in the key of D flat, he checks with one of the Opéra trombonists that it will go all right. If we are to believe the Irish composer George Osborne, who knew Berlioz well,

> It was his constant habit to go into the orchestras and sit with the different performers watching them and turning over the pages for them. In this way he learned the capacity of each instrument. Besides which, he got several instrumentalists to come to his house where they played together little things which he wrote for them to see what they could accomplish.[5]

Ferdinand Hiller recalled him 'following the performance score in hand'.[6] Such testimonies corroborate Berlioz's own account in chapter 13 of the *Memoirs*, where we read of him taking the score with him to performances, and thus beginning to understand the character and tone of voice of the instruments and to 'appreciate the subtle connection between musical expression and the technique of instrumentation'.[7] We can build up a picture of Berlioz's sustained and systematic first-hand practical study of how an orchestra functions, how it is made up, what are the particular strengths and weaknesses of this or that instrument, what it does well, what it fails to do, and what are the abilities or otherwise of the individual players; a picture, too, of his friendships with the younger players and the high regard that some of them have for him – when he begins to organise concerts of his

5 George Osborne, 'Berlioz', *Proceedings of the Musical Association*, Vol. 5, No. 1 (1878–79), pp. 60–75.

6 Hiller, *Künstlerleben*, p. 103.

7 *Memoirs*, p. 47.

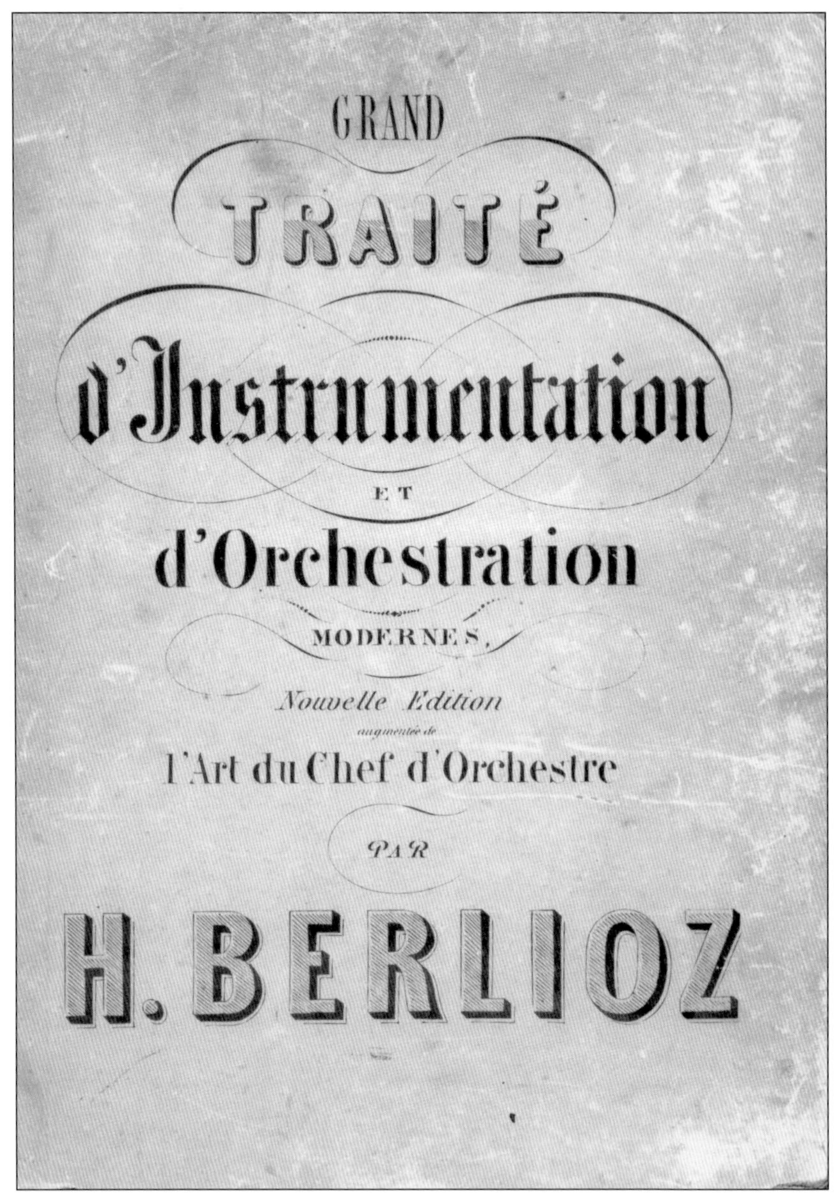

The title page of the Grand Traité, *revised edition*

music, in the late 1820s, and has to put together an orchestra, some of them will give their services. They are on his side.

The account, in chapter 15 of the *Memoirs*, of evenings at the Opéra – with Berlioz rallying his young acolytes and lecturing them on what they are about to hear – though written in a deliberately humorous vein bears witness to the same overriding preoccupations, the same ongoing campaign. We see him finding out in what part of the pit a particular work or passage sounds best, and stationing his troupe accordingly – he has tried out all of them acoustically. And we see him commenting on individual players, as the orchestra assembles:

> There's Baillot. Unlike some solo violinists he doesn't save himself for the ballets, he doesn't consider it beneath his dignity to accompany an opera by Gluck. In a moment you'll hear him play a passage on the G string that sounds right through the orchestra.
>
> That big red-faced man there is the first double bass, old Chénié. A very lively old boy despite his age. He's as good as four normal basses, and you may be sure his part will be played exactly as the composer wrote it – he's not one of your simplifiers.
>
> The conductor should keep an eye on Guillou, the first flute, who's coming in now. He takes extraordinary liberties with Gluck: the sacred march in *Alceste*, for instance, where the composer has written for the bottom register of the flutes, precisely because he wants the special effect of their lowest notes. That doesn't suit Guillou. He has to dominate, his part has to be heard – so he transposes the flute up an octave, thus destroying the composer's intention and turning an imaginative idea into something feeble and obvious.[8]

Incidentally, the bass player Chénié's name appears on the list of people receiving complimentary tickets for Berlioz's concert at the Conservatoire on 1 November 1829.

Alceste was revived at the Opéra in 1825. Four years later, in 1829, when a German opera company came to Paris for a season at the Théâtre-Italien – by which time Berlioz had started on the fatal path of music criticism – he wrote a detailed and unsparing anatomy of the mediocre local band for a Berlin journal, taking advantage of anonymity to say exactly what he thought.[9] It's not a reassuring reckoning: the violins saved from total incompetence only by four young men from the Conservatoire who know how to play the instrument; one adequate viola; one excellent cello out of three (the other two being given more to nodding off than to

[8] *Memoirs*, pp. 55–56.

[9] *Berliner Allgemeine Musikalische Zeitung*, 27 June 1829; republished in *Critique musicale*, Vol. 1, p. 25.

playing); weak double basses; good flute and clarinet but dreadful oboe and bassoon; one first-rate horn, who unfortunately is playing the third part; and the timpanist quite strong but more devoted to ogling the ladies in the audience than to counting his rests. And this wretched orchestra, with all its imperfections on its head, was presuming to present to the public a work as sacred as *Der Freischütz*! One can scarcely imagine what he must have suffered as he listened to them.

The singling out of the virtues and vices of the musicians cited by Berlioz in that passage from the *Memoirs* just quoted is pertinent to the argument of this talk. Musicians like Baillot or Chénié who play what the composer has written are good. Those like Guillou who don't, who simplify or actually alter, are bad. The sanctity of the written score is axiomatic. It is typical of the young Berlioz's originality of mind – the mixture of idealism and simple logic – that he should have conceived so modern an idea as fidelity to the composer's intentions, an idea obvious to us today but not to the musical culture of the 1820s.

It was a matter of principle but also of practice – of fidelity not only to the notes but to their instrumental colour. The catalogue of crimes and misdemeanours shows Berlioz and his friend Augustin de Pons protesting publicly against changes in the orchestration of works performed at the Opéra – for example, adding cymbals to the B minor Scythian dance in *Iphigénie en Tauride*, which impels Berlioz to rise in his wrath and yell 'Who has dared to correct Gluck?', or leaving out trombones in Orestes' Act 3 recitative, or simply cutting out the ballet in the first act of Sacchini's *Œdipe à Colone* and replacing it with solos for horn and cello.[10] (I still regret that when *Les Troyens* was given at Salzburg in 2003 and in the second scene of Act 1 the 'Combat de ceste' was cut, I didn't have the nerve to stand up and shout: 'Et le ballet?'.) Even if Legouvé's story of Berlioz at a performance of *Der Freischütz* shouting out 'Not two flutes, you idiots – two piccolos!' during Caspar's drinking song is apocryphal, it is symbolically true.[11] *Der Freischütz* and his other favourite scores had been absorbed into his inmost being, had become part of him body and soul, so that any tampering with them was a physical blow as well as an outrage to his cherished beliefs. The particular, individual instrumental colour was integral to each moment in the score.

I have thought of Berlioz's private course in orchestration as lasting from 1822 to 1828, when it reaches its spectacular culmination. In 1828 comes the discovery of Beethoven, of the symphony as a dramatic medium as quintessential as opera if not more so, and, not least, the revelation of what

[10] *Memoirs*, pp. 56–57.

[11] Legouvé, *Soixante ans de souvenirs*, Vol. 1, p. 290.

an orchestra can do on its own when mastered by 'an ingenious hand'.[12] The consequences to his own music are fundamental. The Berlioz scores of the mid-1820s, in particular *Les Francs-juges* or what survives of it, show a composer steeped in the music of Spontini and Méhul, using the French classical orchestra resourcefully and with innovative touches, but still part of what, in a letter of 1825, he calls 'our tradition'.[13] Given Berlioz's musical experiences up to then, we can only dimly imagine the effect of the *Eroica* and the Fifth Symphony, played by a thoroughly rehearsed orchestra made up of the best players in Paris, in a small, resonant concert hall, on a musical sensibility like Berlioz's.

His conception of the orchestra and what it can do is revolutionised. And not long afterwards he begins work on the first score that we can say is pure Berlioz, the *Huit Scènes de Faust*. (Maybe that accolade should belong to the overture to *Les Francs-juges*, first completed in 1826 – except that because the autograph hasn't survived and the work published in 1836 is scored for much larger orchestra than was available at the Odéon, the theatre for which the opera was originally intended, we don't know exactly what in that remarkable piece was originally there and what dates from a later revision. The *coup de poignard*, or dagger's stroke, achieved by combining cymbals and piccolos in the introduction to the overture, and already present in June 1828, when Berlioz quotes it in a letter to his friend Ferrand,[14] comes from the ballet music Spontini added to Salieri's *Les Danaïdes*, the first opera Berlioz heard after arriving in Paris in 1821. In the *Traité* he will speak of 'the strange sympathy' between 'two instruments so different', an effect, he says, that can be intensified if one adds a *staccato* stroke by the timpani and a short chord by the rest of the orchestra.) As it is, it's the *Huit Scènes* that first show the composer writing for orchestra to the manner born, knowing what he is doing, playing with it, using the instruments in a way that for him is new: evoking Brander's frantic rat with burbling, grunting bassoons and scrabbling strings, making the violins skip and hop for Mephistopheles' fleas, choosing the dusky tone of a solo viola for the dreamlike sadness of Marguerite's Thulé song and the richer expressiveness of the cor anglais for the anguish of the *Romance*.

A year later he composes the *Symphonie fantastique* – a new orchestral world. Let me quote in full the passage in the letter of January 1830 to Nancy that I mentioned above:

[12] *Memoirs*, p. 17.

[13] *Correspondance générale*, Vol. I, p. 81.

[14] *Ibid.*, p. 199.

> Ah, my sister, you can't imagine what pleasure a composer feels who writes freely in response to his own will alone. When I have drawn the first accolade of my score, when my instruments are ranked in battle array, when I think of the virgin lands that academic prejudice has left untouched till now and that since my emancipation I regard as my domain, I rush forward with a kind of fury to cultivate it. Sometimes I address a few words to my troops: 'You uncouth fellow who up to now have only been able to swear, come here and let me teach you how to speak properly. You delicate little sprites, who've been confined to the dusty closets of learned theoreticians, come and dance for me and show me you're good for something better than acoustical experiments. Above all (I tell my army), you must forget barrack-room songs and the habits of the parade-ground'.[15]

We have here a kind of anticipation of the *Grand Traité*. If the 'acoustical experiments' are possibly a covert reference to Berlioz's teacher Antoine Reicha, that intrepid experimentalist, the uncouth fellow who has been taught only to swear is surely the trombone, an instrument Berlioz venerated and whose abuse by contemporary opera composers roused him to particular indignation when he began to write the articles that led to the *Traité*.

During the nearly two years in 1831 and 1832 when he was away from Paris, mostly in Italy but also in La Côte-Saint-André, there were few if any orchestras worthy of the name to study and none to praise; but once he is back in Paris, and now beginning to write regularly for newspapers and journals, the preoccupation is again predominant. In Paris, too, there is no lack of abuses to castigate, and Berlioz's *feuilletons* in the mid- and late 1830s are alive with admonitions, rebukes, admirations, instructions. He also begins to make practical use of his knowledge of the orchestra by taking up conducting, an activity that extends and deepens that knowledge and at the same time doubly benefits him as a composer – not only to ensure more faithful performances of his music but also in terms of useful experience: to quote Pierre Boulez, 'to have to […] conduct one's own works and face their difficulties of execution' is excellent training for a composer and crucial 'to an understanding of how to write for large orchestra'.[16] Among other things, the experience inspires him to continue revising the *Symphonie fantastique* in the light of what he has learnt in rehearsing and performing it.

Just as watching Habeneck and Girard conduct his music and knowing that he could conduct it better made him realise that, as he was already doing the work of organising his concerts himself, it was only sensible that

[15] *Ibid.*, pp. 303–4.

[16] In William Glock, *Notes in Advance*, Oxford University Press, Oxford, 1991, p. 133, and as reported in David Cairns, 'How the Past makes the Present take note', *The Sunday Times*, 3 December 1989.

the performance too should be in his hands, so the *Treatise* is the logical conclusion of what he had been thinking and arguing and preaching over the years. The spur may have been the two works published in 1837 and 1839 by his friend, Georges Kastner, the *General Treatise on Instrumentation* and the *Course in Instrumentation considered in relation to the Poetic and Philosophical Aspects of the Art*. But it's hard to believe that even without that stimulus he would not have felt impelled to set down his own conclusions in book form. He knew he was the supreme authority on the subject, and he was conscious of an obligation to communicate all he had learned, for that betterment of musical standards that was a constant aim of his music criticism – as he put it, the mission to 'abolish abuses, eradicate prejudice, enlighten opinion, refine public taste and put men and things in their true place and perspective'.[17]

In his review of Kastner's two treatises, which appears in the *Journal des débats* on 2 October 1839, he seizes the opportunity to point out the common misuse of the orchestra, the common ignorance of the range of certain instruments – found not only in many of the mediocre new operas he reviews as a critic but even in the work of some leading composers – which makes them tend to stick nervously to the middle range for fear of writing notes that the instrument can't play, and also the extent to which the spirit of routine that rules in music conservatoires constricts what should be the freedom of the art. 'When a teacher tells his student not to employ such and such an instrumental layout and, when the pupil asks why not?, he answers, because it's never done, that teacher is an ass.' There is nothing sacrosanct (he goes on) about the so-called hierarchy of instruments in the orchestra, as Weber showed in the introduction to his *Oberon* overture, when he gave the cellos the tune and made the clarinets play the bass; and yet many so-called authorities would say it was wrong. The review praises Kastner but concludes that there is more to be said on the subject:

> Instrumentation, [Kastner] says, is the 'art of applying appropriate kinds of instruments to a given melodic line'. Indeed it is. But it is also much more than that: it's the art of using instruments to colour the harmony and the rhythm and, even more, the art of moving the listener by the choice of timbres, independent of any effect of melody, rhythm or harmony.

Berlioz's *Treatise* is already visible above the horizon, and it will deal with instrumentation – the science and art of each instrument – and with orchestration, the science and art of combining them.

Two years later he finally put pen to paper. In the meantime he had been studying the numerous instrumental 'Methods' increasingly put on

[17] *Memoirs*, p. 375.

sale, and checking details with musician friends. He had also just given a sovereign demonstration of his skill by orchestrating Weber's piano piece *Invitation to the Dance* for the obligatory ballet in the Opéra's production of *Der Freischütz.* On 21 November 1841 the first of sixteen articles entitled 'De l'instrumentation' appeared in the *Revue et gazette musicale*, the series continuing till the following May. The entries in the finished *Traité* of 1843–44 are not identical to the original series, which necessarily lacked the copious musical examples in full score which illuminate the book and the technical analysis of each instrument, with detailed graphs and diagrams. But the bulk of the written matter is the same – eloquent with Berlioz's inimitable style and tone of voice. No one else could have written it.

The justification, the need for such sermons, was only too evident. Parisian practice, or rather malpractice, supplied daily examples: a revival of *Don Juan* (*Don Giovanni*) at the Opéra in which Mozart's mandolin accompaniment to the Act 2 serenade was entrusted to two guitars, and trombones played where they shouldn't, and indeed everywhere the gross abuse to which the trombone was subjected. 'The craze for the bass drum', writes Berlioz in the *Journal des débats* on 14 December 1841,

> seems to have abated but the craze for the trombone is growing. While we are admiring the magnificent orchestration of *Der Freischütz*, where Weber has put in the trombones in only three or four places – and with what restraint! – at the Opéra-Comique those dogs are shouting and barking and howling in a love duet or in the middle of a comic scene.

Composers are using it indiscriminately without regard to its special character and in hopelessly inappropriate contexts: 'At the Opéra-Comique an old buffer is upset, he's lost his snuffbox – three trombones! He's happy again because he's found it – three trombones!'

For Berlioz the trombone is a noble instrument and its misuse a personal injury to him. We know that when the trombonist Dieppo began giving classes at the Conservatoire, Berlioz took the trouble to sit in on them. The long trombone entry in the *Treatise*, illustrated by musical examples taken from his own Requiem (*Hostias*), and from *Alceste* ('Divinités du Styx'), *Iphigénie en Tauride* (the chorus 'Vengeons et la nature'), the *Symphonie funèbre et triomphale* (opening of the finale), *Die Zauberflöte* (priests' chorus) and *La Vestale* (funeral march), ends with this passionate tirade, as if he himself has been mortally insulted:

> Gluck, Beethoven, Mozart, Weber, Spontini and one or two others have fully understood the importance of the role of the trombone, they have applied with perfect intelligence to the depiction of human passions and the representation

> of the sounds of nature the varied aspects of this noble instrument, and in doing so have maintained its power, dignity and poetic character. But to force it, as so many composers do nowadays, to yell, in a Credo, brutal phrases more suited to a tavern than to a holy place, to solemnise a dancer's pirouette as if it were Alexander entering Babylon, to bang out tonic and dominant chords under a tune that requires no more than a guitar accompaniment, to mingle its Olympian voice with the pitiful strains of a vaudeville duet or with a contredanse's trivial thump or, in the tutti of a concerto, to use it to herald the triumphal arrival of a flute or oboe solo – this is to cheapen and degrade its magnificent individuality, to turn a hero into a slave and a clown, it is to discolour the orchestra, to undermine and nullify all reasonable progress in instrumental composition, it is to destroy art's past, present and future, it is to commit a knowing act of vandalism or to show a lack of feeling for expression bordering on inanity.

I have no space to give more than a very general idea of this remarkable book or say anything about the long chapter on the art of conducting added to the second edition published in 1855, or the prophetic passage on the orchestra, where his dream of gigantic forces will be fulfilled by Mahler in his 'Symphony of a Thousand'. What I can say is that that phrase 'feeling for expression', in the piece about the trombone just quoted, is central to the *Grand Traité*. The book is written with the same fusion of the objectively technical and the subjectively poetic as his music criticism. The soul of each instrument, as well as the body, is evoked and described. The entry on the clarinet is typical: a table of trills and their varying difficulties, and other technical details, followed by a warning to players to use the instrument specified by the composer and not lazily accommodate everything to the B flat clarinet, then a description of the tone qualities of the different registers (including the sinister effect of sustained low notes, discovered by Weber), advice to composers, who wish to employ the piercing top register, to allow the player to come in on a chord of the full orchestra and establish a steady tone before embarking on his solo, a tribute to the unequalled capacity of the clarinet for dynamic nuance, controlled *diminuendo*, 'echoes, echoes of echoes, a twilight sound', and then an expansive paean to the clarinet as an epic instrument, the voice of heroic love, and how its feminine quality moves him in the same way as reading the epic poetry of the ancient world.

Not surprisingly – think of Dido's 'Adieu, fière cité' – the viola, and its regrettable neglect by composers, inspires his particular zeal. Orestes' 'Le calme rentre dans mon cœur' is, naturally, prominent; it owes its unfailing fascination, he says,

> chiefly to the viola part, to the tone quality of its third string and the syncopated rhythm, and to the strange kind of unison that results from its

syncopated A being brusquely cut across, amidships, by the A of the double bass in a different rhythm.

Most quotable of all, perhaps, is the passage on the 'Dance of the Blessed Spirits' in the flute section of the chapter on 'Wind Instruments without Reeds'. Berlioz has been speaking of the neutral tone-colour of the flute in the middle and upper registers compared with that of the oboe and the clarinet, and the general rather than specific role it is given:

> Yet when you study it closely you realise that it has its own expressiveness and an aptness for rendering certain feelings that no other instrument can challenge. For example, if it is a question of giving a sad melody a desolate yet at the same time humble, resigned character, the soft notes of the flute's middle register, especially in the keys of C minor and D minor, will produce just the nuance required. To my mind only one composer has taken full advantage of this pale colouring, and that is Gluck. When you listen to the pantomime music in D minor that he wrote for the scene in the Elysian Fields in *Orphée* you see at once that only the flute could have played the melody. An oboe would have been too childlike and its tone would not have seemed pure enough; the cor anglais is too deep; a clarinet would no doubt have been less inappropriate but some of its notes would have been too loud and none of its softest notes could fine themselves down to the thin, veiled sonority of the F natural in the middle register or the B flat above the stave which lends the flute its profound sense of sadness in this key of D minor, where they frequently occur. Nor, finally, would the violin, the viola or the cello, solo or as a section, have been able to convey the infinite, sublimely sad lament of a suffering, despairing shade. It required the instrument the composer chose. And Gluck's melody is so conceived that the flute lends itself to every troubled movement of that timeless grief, still instinct with the passions of earthly life.

Not for nothing is Gluck given the largest number of musical examples in the *Treatise*, more even than Beethoven, five of whose symphonies are illustrated, plus *Fidelio* (the gravedigging duet, in the entry on the double bass), and the slow movement of the 'Emperor' Concerto in the chapter on the piano. The viola example from *Iphigénie* has precedence over the slow movement of the Fifth Symphony (cited to show how violas doubling cellos can 'give the cello sonority more roundness and purity' while it remains the dominant tone-colour). The opening chapter of the *Traité* starts with the famous avant-garde, indeed twentieth-century, proclamation: 'Any sound-producing body utilised by the composer is a musical instrument' – a forward-looking manifesto if there ever was one. Yet there is no real contradiction in Gluck's being given pride of place. Gluck can predominate in a treatise on modern orchestration because for Berlioz he remains modern. 'Gluck was a Romantic', he stated in an article in *Le Correspondant* of 22 October

153

Les tons de *Ré, Sol, Ut, Fa, La, Mi* ♮, *Si* ♭, *Mi* ♭, et leurs relatifs mineurs, sont les tons favoris de la flûte, les autres sont beaucoup plus difficiles. Sur la flûte de Boëhm au contraire, on joue en Ré♭ presque aussi aisément qu'en *Ré naturel.*

La sonorité de cet instrument est douce dans le médium, assez perçante à l'aigu, très caractérisée au grave. Le timbre du médium et celui du haut n'ont pas d'expression spéciale bien tranchée. On peut les employer pour des mélodies ou des accents de caractères divers, mais sans qu'ils puissent égaler cependant la gaite naïve du hautbois ou la noble tendresse de la clarinette. Il semble donc que la flûte soit un instrument à peu près dépourvu d'expression, qu'on est libre d'introduire partout et dans tout, à cause de sa facilité à exécuter les groupes de notes rapides, et à soutenir les sons elevés utiles à l'orchestre pour le complément des harmonies aigües. En général cela est vrai; pourtant en l'étudiant bien, on reconnait en elle une expression qui lui est propre, et une aptitude à rendre certains sentiments qu'aucun autre instrument ne pourrait lui disputer. S'il s'agit par exemple, de donner à un chant triste un accent désolé, mais humble et résigné en même tems, les sons faibles du médium de la flûte, dans les tons *d'Ut* mineur et de *Ré* mineur surtout, produiront certainement la nuance nécessaire. Un seul maitre me parait avoir su tirer grand parti de ce pâle coloris: c'est Gluck. En écoutant l'air pantomime en *Ré* mineur qu'il a placé dans la scène des champs-Elysées d'Orphée, on voit tout de suite qu'une flûte devait seule en faire entendre le chant. Un hautbois eut été trop enfantin et sa voix n'eut pas semblé assez pure; le cor anglais est trop grave; une clarinette aurait mieux convenu sans doute, mais certains sons eussent été trop forts, et aucune des notes les plus douces n'eut pu se réduire à la sonorité faible, effacée, voilée *du Fa naturel* du médium, et du premier *Si bémol* au dessus des lignes, qui donnent tant de tristesse à la flûte dans ce ton de *Ré* mineur, où ils se présentent fréquemment. Enfin, ni le violon, ni l'alto, ni le violoncelle, traités en solos ou en masses, ne convenaient à l'expression de ce gémissement mille fois sublime d'une ombre souffrante et désespérée; il fallait précisément l'instrument choisi par l'auteur. Et la mélodie de Gluck est conçue de telle sorte que la flûte se prête à tous les mouvements inquiets de cette douleur éternelle, encore empreinte de l'accent des passions de la terrestre vie. C'est d'abord une voix à peine perceptible qui semble craindre d'être entendue; puis elle gémit doucement, s'élève à l'accent du reproche, à celui de la douleur profonde, au cri d'un coeur déchiré d'incurables blessures, et retombe peu à peu à la plainte, au gémissement, au murmure chagrin d'une âme résignée..... quel poëte !...

The Grand Traité *on the flute*

1830 entitled 'A Summary of Classical Music and Romantic Music'.[18] For him, Gluck was not a figure from a vanished century but a living presence. So Berlioz could compose his most advanced score, *Les Troyens*, under the aegis of the great Chevalier and see no paradox. It was Gluck, 40 years

[18] *Critique musicale*, Vol. 1, pp. 63–68.

before, who showed him the meaning of dramatic music – Gluck, whom the entry in Michaud's encyclopaedia called 'the greatest composer of whom the lyric stage can boast' – and in the *Treatise* Berlioz, loyal as ever to his first affections, pays tribute and repays his debt.

Holy Germany, a Nation of Musicians

'Holy Germany, a Nation of Musicians' was the opening talk at the conference held in Bayreuth in 2001 and hosted by the University of Bayreuth – part of a series of conferences organised by the Paris-based committee 'Berlioz 2003' in the years leading up to the bicentenary of Berlioz's birth. It was published in Sieghart Döhring, Arnold Jacobshagen and Gunther Braam (eds.), Berlioz, Wagner und die Deutschen, *Verlag Dohr, Cologne, 2003, pp. 13–24, and in the* Berlioz Society Bulletin *No. 193 (April 2014).*

It's an honour to have been invited to give the opening talk at this conference, to speak to you about Berlioz and Germany on German soil. I only wish I could return the compliment and give it in German. But though my grasp of the language is superior to Berlioz's – he told his sister Nancy that his German extended only so far as being able to say 'Yes, No, Once again gentlemen, one, two, three, four, five, six, a pause, all the timpani, what the hell'[1] – mine is the German of *Die Zauberflöte*, *Fidelio* and *Der Freischütz*. I can say 'herrlich! himmlisch! göttlich!' when drinking German wine, and 'Mir beben meine Glieder' when confronting an audience of experts like you (not to mention 'Dank, Samiel'), and I did several times appear in *Die Meistersinger* at Covent Garden in the 1950s, as a *Schneider*, and could sing you 'Als Nürnberg belagert war'; but beyond that I would be floundering in deep waters.

Not only am I speaking on German soil but in Bayreuth, of all places. If this is an irony, I hope it's a fruitful one. We live in a time when the old disputes, the polarisations that divided nineteenth-century music, have lost their force and have retreated to the margins of history. It's no longer a case of Wagner versus the rest, or of Wagner or Berlioz – rather, Wagner and Berlioz. This is not the place to consider the intriguing events taking place behind the scenes up there on the *grünen Hügel*. But one radical suggestion thrown up from the welter of conflicting passions and ideas is worth pausing over for a moment: the notion that the Festspielhaus should become home not only to the early, non-canonical works of Wagner himself

[1] *Correspondance générale*, Vol. III, p. 329.

but to operas by other composers – even, audaciously, those of Meyerbeer. And if Meyerbeer, whom Wagner came to despise, why not Berlioz, whose *Roméo et Juliette*, Wagner said, revealed to him 'a new world of music'? I dare say the older among us won't live to see a production of *Les Troyens* here. But such an event would wonderfully signal the peaceful ending of an ideological conflict that has long ceased to have any real relevance or meaning.

I have been speaking of ironies. The title of my talk, however, contains no ironical implications. It's true that Berlioz was sadly mistaken when at the Festival of the Lower Rhine in Strasbourg in June 1863 he saluted the power of music to 'efface national hatreds', and spoke of the love of art that had brought France and Germany together and which, he prophesied, would do more even than the new Kehl bridge and all the other means of rapid communication to unite them.[2] Within seven years the two countries would be at each other's throats. But Berlioz did not live to see the shattering of these no doubt naïve hopes; by the year 1870 he was dead. Germany, to him, was 'Holy Germany' – 'la sainte Allemagne' – 'where the worship of art still burns pure and strong'.[3]

In this he was not alone. Madame de Staël's *De l'Allemagne*, published in 1813, had implanted an exalted notion of German culture in the French imagination – what Bernard Shaw, writing nearly a century later in a review of *Lohengrin*, would call 'the grand calm of the ideal Germany'.[4]

Berlioz imbibed these ideas. The older statesmen of the Paris intelligentsia, the members of the Institute, the *perruques*, might regard with pious horror anything coming from beyond the Rhine – and it was part of the conservative case against Berlioz that he had let himself be corrupted and perverted by Germanic influences – but he looked eastward with hope, and was not disappointed. Germany was where music was honoured and musical life properly organised. Not for nothing did he place Euphonia, the science-fiction city dedicated to ideal performances of monumental works, in Germany.

Above all, Germany was the cradle of the greatest composers. In the 1820s, while still a student, he had the revelations of Weber and of Beethoven to confirm his expectations. When his friend Pingard, the Institute usher, asked him 'Who is this Mister Beethoven? He's not a member of the Institute', he could reply, most emphatically, 'No, he's not!'[5] His desire to go to Germany, to experience German musical life for himself and take his

[2] Quoted in Cairns, *Berlioz*, Vol. 2, p. 695.

[3] *Memoirs*, p. 518.

[4] 'A Butchered Lohengrin', *The Star*, 31 May 1889; republished in *Shaw's Music*, *op. cit.*, Vol. 1, p. 648.

[5] *Memoirs*, p. 95.

own music there, was intense and unequivocal. The fact that in the event it wasn't till the end of 1842 that he did so indicates no ambivalence on his part, as has sometimes been suggested. He would have gone to Germany in 1834 – as indeed he was supposed to, as a Prix de Rome – had his wife not been pregnant. In 1837, in a letter to Schumann explaining why he had not yet published his symphonies – they were, he said, 'still too young to travel without me' – he wrote that 'the approbation of Germany, that fatherland of music ['cette patrie de la musique'], has too great a value in my eyes, and will be too hard to win – if I win it at all – for me not to wait until I can go there myself and as a pilgrim lay my modest offerings at its feet'.[6]

He was all set to do so in 1840 – letter after letter, from late 1838 and throughout 1839, speaks of his determination that the following year he will undertake this journey so long cherished and planned. If he then put it off for another two years, that was, I am sure, because of the passionate opposition of his wife, Harriet. When he did finally go, he had to smuggle his scores and orchestral parts out of the house and leave a scribbled note on the kitchen table. (His domestic life shows nothing like the boldness and decisiveness that mark his career as composer and performing musician. As I say in my biography of Berlioz, 'it was as if, fighting on so many other fronts, he had too little energy or moral courage left for the home front. He lacked ruthlessness'.[7])

I am illustrating my talk with two likenesses – Prinzhofer's lithograph made in 1846 in Vienna, and Lauchert's portrait painted in Weimar nine years later, whose discovery we owe to Gunther Braam – because in my view they convey a fundamental truth. I apologise to those people – I know there are some – who dislike the Lauchert portrait and think it a sentimentalisation of Berlioz, if not a chocolate-box representation of the man. But I am showing it, and the Prinzhofer, because they are perhaps the two most stress-free, least tormented images of him that we have, and that for a very simple reason. They tell us something crucial – that Berlioz was happier in Austro-Germany than anywhere else: he felt himself there, he was able to be himself and do what he wanted to do. Even in those later years when his health was wretched and the so-called intestinal neuralgia – very probably the condition known today as Crohn's Disease – had him in its painful grip, he had only to be there to feel better. That was so during the annual visits to Baden-Baden in the late 1850s and early 1860s, and it was the same in Weimar in 1863, where he arrived in a terrible state but was so restored by his time there, and in Loewenberg, that for a brief period he imagined himself cured of the disease, so strong was the effect of what he

[6] *Correspondance générale*, Vol. II, p. 331.

[7] Cairns, *Berlioz*, Vol. 2, p. 245.

A pencil sketch by August Prinzhofer for the well-known lithograph of November/December 1845. Berlioz thought it a good likeness but said it 'dandified' him by giving him rings and a cane, which he 'never sported'. Prinzhofer's second lithograph (right) was made a month or two later.

Prinzhofer 1846.
Hector Berlioz
VERLAG U. EIGENTHUM VON H.F. MÜLLER'S KUNSTHANDLUNG IN WIEN.

called 'this month of pure musical intoxication'.[8] As late as 1867, in Cologne, when he was in dire health and, according to his old friend Ferdinand Hiller, hardly able to drag himself to rehearsals, he became a different person the moment he mounted the rostrum and stood in front of the orchestra; 'vital, energetic, bubbling with life', Hiller said.[9] Germany made him feel alive.

Earlier, back in Paris from Prague and Vienna in May 1846, he cannot reconcile himself to the return of the old frustrations.

> I miss the great orchestras, with their splendid warmth and responsiveness, and choirs, which I would willingly conduct every day of my life, I miss even the fatigue of the long rehearsals, [...] I miss the intense emotion of directing a grand concert, the sensation of speaking to the multitude through the many-tongued medium of instruments and voices, I miss being able to study the varying impressions produced on an unprejudiced public by the latest experiments in modern art.[10]

These were experiences that in Paris were possible only intermittently and then only at constant risk and with a huge expenditure of physical and moral energy.

This is a leitmotiv of his career. After his first tour of Germany, in 1842–43, he pictures himself springing out of bed in the morning, half asleep, and getting dressed, under the distinct impression that he is late and the orchestra is waiting for him. Then reality breaks in. 'What orchestra? I am in Paris, where they order things differently and it's the orchestra that keeps you waiting'.[11] In September 1843 he tells his sister Nancy that the visit of an acquaintance from Dresden, bringing news of friends left behind in Saxony, has made him feel positively ill – 'I so long to be back there'.[12]

Ten years later it is the same: the realisation that by being in Germany he has failed to get his application for membership of the Académie des Beaux-Arts submitted in time concerns him not a bit. 'My thoughts were elsewhere – I was making music, which doesn't tend to direct one's mind towards academies and academicians'.[13] He is in his natural element: 'I'm like a fish in water'.[14] It is in Germany, immediately after the Beethoven festival in Bonn, that he makes the momentous decision to end the relative dearth of the past five years and commit himself to large-scale composition again, and *La Damnation de Faust*, the great representative score of his

[8] *Correspondance générale*, Vol. IV, p. 433.

[9] Hiller, *Künstlerleben*, p. 95.

[10] *Memoirs*, p. 390.

[11] *Ibid.*, p. 259.

[12] *Correspondance générale*, Vol. III, p. 112.

[13] *Ibid.*, Vol. IV, p. 401.

[14] *Ibid.*, p. 387.

mid-career, first begins to take shape; and under the stimulus of Germany, in the midst of busy music-making and journeys all over central Europe, a good half of the work, music and text, is written. The symbolism of the opening bars' Beethovenian reminiscence, whether conscious or not, is surely not to be missed.

'Me voilà, comme le poisson dans l'eau.' That remark, and another – 'décidément ces allemands sont des musiciens'[15] – says it all. Germany was the right environment for him. First of all, it was not Paris: on tour in Germany he was out of reach of the intrigues and banalities that beset him at home – 'à l'abri des intrigues, des lâchetés et des platitudes de Paris'.[16] Second, it was a *milieu sympathique*, a truly musical environment, where everything was possible and there were abundant opportunities for him to make music.

Berlioz's best-known reports on Germany are the letters first published in the *Journal des débats* – 'dispatches from the Grande Armée', he Napoleonically called them[17] – and later incorporated in his *Memoirs*, and after that his voluminous correspondence. It could be argued that, so far as the reception of his music in Germany is concerned, both these sources tended to put a somewhat euphoric gloss on the reality – he was, after all, writing with an eye to opinion at home, in the hope that news of his successes abroad would have a beneficial effect on his position in his own country. That could apply as well to the letters he addressed to friends like Auguste Morel, Gemmy Brandus or the cellist Jean-Émile Desmarest, who would all be expected to relay what he told them to the press. On the other hand, there is ample testimony to the excitement generated in musical circles in Germany by Berlioz's music and personality – for example, in what Hanslick, Hans von Bülow and Cornelius wrote about his visits to Prague, Dresden, and Weimar and Vienna respectively (to name only three of the many witnesses). Even in his published reports Berlioz does not attempt to minimise the failures during the first tour – in Frankfurt, in Mannheim and in Hanover – and he makes no bones about the difficulty of getting some of the orchestras he encountered to cope with music so different from anything they had had to play before. I shall return to the question of *Berlioz-Rezeption* in a moment.

The standard of playing in Germany improved demonstrably during the quarter of a century spanned by Berlioz's first and last visits, stimulated by the highly demanding music that he himself, and Wagner and Liszt, required the orchestras to play. To begin with, the standard was often pretty

[15] *Ibid.*, Vol. VI, p. 426.

[16] *Memoirs*, p. 258.

[17] For example, in the *Correspondance générale*, Vol. III, p. 80.

Berlioz in the 1855 painting by Richard Lauchert

low, especially in some of the smaller centres Berlioz visited, as Wagner and Liszt testified but as Berlioz generally was too diplomatic to do more than hint at. (Even so, he got into hot water with the first flute of the Berlin orchestra for daring to state in print that nowhere in the world was the flute so well played as in Paris.)

That he was able to achieve the results he did on his first tour was due, I don't doubt, to his genius as a conductor – the mysterious gift of communication, which overrode the language barrier and spoke directly to the players – and all the varied qualities that contributed to it: his musicianship, his knowledge, his super-acute ear, his powers of leadership, his sense of rhythm, his experience of rehearsing in so many different situations, his organising ability. Also, surely, the appeal of his personality. In this respect it's significant, I think, given his reputation for acerbity, sarcasm and general irritability, that critics should have singled out his friendliness towards orchestral musicians, contrasting it with the hauteur and arrogance of other conductors. In London, James Davison in *The Musical World* wrote of 'his polished and courteous manners', his affability in front of an orchestra;[18] and Edward Holmes said he possessed 'the art of engaging their best efforts in his behalf, perhaps beyond any composer of our time', because his manner was 'free from airs of superiority or any assumption of the great man'. 'We have seen him', Holmes adds, 'on occasions that would, in one of the irritable race, have almost justified a fit of anger, mild, considerate and good-humoured'.[19] As a result of all these qualities, orchestras under his baton found themselves playing better than they thought they could.

Berlioz discovered that some things in Germany were less good than he had expected: theatre choruses, for one thing, and the general standard of opera singers, also the condition of percussion instruments and, among the woodwinds, of the bassoons. The brass instruments, on the other hand, were markedly superior in workmanship and tone-quality, and the military bands 'of such splendour beside anything France can boast that French national pride can only feel abased by the comparison'.[20]

As a whole, above and beyond observations of detail, Germany fulfilled his expectations. If no single orchestra equalled the Paris Conservatoire band at its best, that was a Pyrrhic victory for France. Paris had the richer resources, but with rare exceptions it failed to make the most of them or squandered them mindlessly. And France had only Paris to offer in reply to Germany's wealth of musical establishments, the consequence of the country's division into different autonomous principalities, each with

[18] Quoted in Cairns, *Berlioz*, Vol. 2, p. 407.

[19] *Ibid.*

[20] *Memoirs*, p. 333.

its own musical corps, usually directed by a composer of distinction. (In parenthesis, it should be noted that German musicians sometimes came to Paris to study, drawn by the prestige of the Conservatoire, and their presence in some of the orchestras Berlioz faced also helped to ease the language problem.)

The third main source of Berlioz's opinions on Germany is the report on German musical institutions that he was commissioned to make for the Minister of the Interior in Paris on his first tour – a document the discovery of which, like so much else, we owe to Peter Bloom.[21] Here Berlioz was writing not for the public prints – not for an audience – but for the Minister's eyes alone. In the report he emphasised that it was the sheer quantity of musicians even more than their quality that made the German lands exceptional. Some of them, of course, were of the highest quality. But what distinguished them from their French counterparts was not only organisation, crucially important though that was, but attitude. 'These Germans really are musicians.' Among them you found the attentiveness, the seriousness, the openness to the new, that were so lacking in the mass of French musicians. By and large there was none of that cynicism nor that individualism carried to excess that, even in modern times, till quite recently made it hard for the French to combine in large musical ensembles with any conviction.[22] This was a quality in his fellow countrymen that entertained Berlioz in general but that in musical contexts he found exasperating. When, in one of his *feuilletons*, he dreams of being rich enough to buy the plains of Troy, build a concert hall there and transport a crack orchestra to play the *Eroica*, he singles out, among the alien intruders who will have to be expelled before the grand musical solemnity can be fittingly performed, 'roving Frenchmen – sneering Voltairean sceptics with no imagination, no responsiveness, no enthusiasm, no heart'.[23]

With few exceptions, Berlioz met none of that in Germany. He might encounter hostile critics – though they rarely if ever descended to the depths of vulgar abuse plumbed by some of their Parisian opposite numbers – but among musicians he generally found interest and a spirit of cooperation. Like Lindpaintner in Stuttgart, they were not going to let him go without performing some of his works, 'which we are so curious to know'.[24] Interest in Berlioz had been growing for several years before he first went to Germany, fostered by the frequent appearance of his *Débats* articles, translated, in the

[21] Peter Bloom, 'La mission de Berlioz en Allemagne: un document inédit', in *Revue de musicologie*, Vol. 66, No. 1, 1980, pp. 70–85.

[22] Since this essay was written, the whole culture of French orchestral performance has been transformed and has won the admiration of the musical world.

[23] *Revue et gazette musicale*, 28 January 1841; republished in *Critique musicale*, Vol. 4, pp. 437–38.

[24] *Memoirs*, p. 274.

Neue Zeitschrift für Musik, by performances of some of his overtures, and by appraising and positive reviews by Schumann, the composer and critic J. C. Lobe, and others. They were ready to meet him at first hand.

Berlioz drank up all this interest with avidity. Yet the report that he delivered to the Minister in December 1843 is notably even-handed. As I have said, it is not indiscriminately in favour of all things German. The conclusions, however, are overwhelmingly positive: strengths of organisation that far outweigh weaknesses; the central role of music in church and state; and the feeling for music found throughout the population, the consequence of widely diffused basic musical education. In his *Memoirs* Berlioz refers to Martin Luther only as the man under whose 'lourde incubation' Lutheranism was hatched[25] – a schism that he, Berlioz, had had the good fortune not to be born into. But the report submitted to the Minister traces to the great heresiarch the general taste for part-singing (of which we hear a resounding echo in the opening scene of *Die Meistersinger*) and all that followed from it, including the summer festivals which all over Germany united hundreds of amateur musicians in splendid communal celebrations. (Berlioz's concert in the Hall of Industry in Paris in August 1844 was directly inspired by the example of Germany.)

No less important, the high status of musicians, and, at the top of the musical hierarchy, of composers, was reflected in their economic position. I quote from the report: 'A pensions system is in force for all artists in all German courts. [...] Instrumentalists and choristers derive their livelihood from their salaries; they enjoy a security that ours do not'. (The baneful necessity for Paris instrumentalists and choristers to augment their income in other ways is a frequent theme of Berlioz's *feuilletons*.) The report goes on: 'The composer-kapellmeister can produce or ponder his works undistracted. He does not compose in order to live; the sovereign on whom he depends has put him in a position to live in order to compose'.[26] In a roughly contemporary letter to his father, Berlioz remarks that 'if I had been born in Saxony or Prussia I should now have a salary of ten or twelve thousand francs for life, with a guaranteed pension for my family after my death. In France I have... a liberal constitution, the liberality of which does not extend to bothering about the men who could bring honour to their country'.[27]

For many of Berlioz's supporters in Germany, he should have been born there. It was almost as if he had been. 'Why don't you speak German?', demanded the ladies of the Leipziger Singakademie; 'it should be your

25 *Ibid.*, p. 5.

26 Bloom, 'La mission de Berlioz en Allemagne', *loc. cit.*, p. 83.

27 *Correspondance générale*, Vol. III, p. 98.

language – you *are* German'.[28] Berlioz, Cornelius declared, was spiritually a German; there was German blood in his veins; he had been 'nourished on German milk'.[29] Griepenkerl's pamphlet *Ritter Berlioz in Braunschweig* argued that so far from being wanting in the qualities that Germans valued in a composer, as some of his critics charged, Berlioz had penetrated 'the depths of the German spirit'; his gift for humour and for placing opposing moods in dramatic juxtaposition linked his style not only with Shakespeare but, even more, with the Beethoven of the late works, which many critics still rejected because of those very qualities.[30] Cornelius, Bülow and other supporters wanted Berlioz, even if he hadn't been born in Germany, at least to come and live and work among them.

I will consider Berlioz's response to these claims and appeals shortly. For the moment, having considered his view of Germany, let me try to answer the question: what was Germany's general view of Berlioz?

Clearly there can be no simple reply. Whom shall we choose, even just among musicians, to represent the huge range of opinion? Of course, there were reactionaries who spat blood at the very mention of his name. But there always are such people, everywhere, in all ages. As late as the beginning of the twentieth century, twenty years after Wagner's death, the Berlin Conservatoire was refusing to allow Wagner's music on the syllabus. When Hanslick heard Mahler's Second Symphony he exclaimed: 'One of us is mad, and it isn't me!'[31] For the German conservatives of the mid-nineteenth century Berlioz was part of a larger problem, a bigger menace – the menace of modernism. The struggle was for the soul of German music. Berlioz was one of that devilish trinity, Liszt-Wagner-Berlioz, which was threatening to destroy it. There was no lack of critics to give his music the thumbs down – for example, Karl Banck in Dresden, in Frankfurt Anton Schindler, who ridiculed the notion of Berlioz as Beethoven's successor, and Bernhard Gutt in Prague, or, among conductors, Karl August Krebs, the Hamburg kapellmeister, who later turned up in Dresden, and who told Berlioz that it would have been better for the art of music if he had never been born.[32] (Gutt, by the way, is an interesting footnote in music history. As the Canadian musicologist Geoffrey Payzant has shown in his pioneering book *Eduard Hanslick and Ritter Berlioz in Prague*,[33] it was directly under

[28] *Ibid.*, Vol. IV, p. 425.

[29] Peter Cornelius, *Literarische Werke*, Breitkopf und Härtel, Leipzig, 1904–5.

[30] Wolfgang Robert Griepenkerl, *Ritter Berlioz in Braunschweig: zur Charakteristik dieses Tondichters*, Brunswick, 1843.

[31] *Neue Freie Presse*, 20 November 1900, p. 7.

[32] *Memoirs*, p. 325.

[33] Geoffrey Payzant, *Eduard Hanslick and Ritter Berlioz in Prague*, University of Calgary Press, Calgary, 1991.

Peter Cornelius

Gutt's influence that Hanslick recanted his youthful enthusiasm for both Berlioz's and Wagner's music and developed the curious philosophy of music as an essentially non-referential art.)

Admirers of Berlioz should no doubt be on their guard against exaggerating the extent of his acceptance in Germany. We are so conscious that it was there that he was most consistently successful, we are so grateful to Germany for giving him what Paris generally denied him, a serious musical environment that took a lively interest in his doings, that we may be in danger of oversimplifying the picture. The opposition to Berlioz was strong enough to prevent his being appointed *Hofkapellmeister* in Dresden in 1854 – Dresden, where he had just given four of the most brilliant concerts of his career and where the intendant Baron von Lüttichau came near to offering him the post. The reason, I believe, was connected with the opposition to Liszt and his so-called Futurist party, of which Berlioz was seen as a senior member. If Liszt, who was extending his pernicious ideas all over Germany, with Bülow active in Berlin and Franz Brendel in charge of the *Neue Zeitschrift für Musik* – if Liszt had to be stopped, then it followed that Berlioz must be, too: for a position as powerful as the Dresden kapellmeistership to be occupied by one of that gang of non-musicians, and a foreigner too, was not to be thought of.

Further examples of anti-Berliozian sentiment in Germany could be cited. Yet his strong and lasting impact on progressive circles is incontrovertible. Hanslick himself confirmed it: 'Whoever lived and cheered, as I did, at the time of Berlioz's concerts in Germany can testify that never was any dazzling musical phenomenon greeted with such excitement'.[34] Though Weimar was to become the standard-bearer – Weimar where Liszt in the 1850s put on three successive 'Berlioz Weeks' and staged *Benvenuto Cellini* – the excitement was by no means confined to it. It was the same in Vienna, in Pesth, in Prague – where his arrival in January 1846 answered a longing that had been growing for the last three years, ever since news of his presence in Dresden had set the hearts of radical young Prague musicians impatiently aglow and they had played Liszt's piano transcription of the *Fantastique* again and again, and read and found out everything they could about this extraordinary figure, 'a Frenchman who wrote symphonies and whose gods were Beethoven and Shakespeare'.[35]

Nor was it only the avant-garde that responded to him. We may wonder whether Berlioz's own exhilarated accounts, in his letters, should be treated with a dash of caution; but newspaper reports frequently spoke in the same vein, of triumphs without precedent, of whole audiences caught up in the music, listening in rapt silence and at the end breaking into thunderous applause. Hans von Bülow, after the Dresden concerts of 1854, described the 'wild applause [...] not heard in Dresden since before Wagner's flight'. As for the performers, 'the whole orchestra and singers', Bülow said,

> are head over ears with enthusiasm. They are overjoyed that they can now rate their talents and capabilities as they deserve, thanks to this incomparable conductor who has made them feel the shame and sterility of the last five or six years.[36]

[34] Quoted in Barzun, *Berlioz and the Romantic Century*, Vol. 1, p. 399.

[35] Quoted in Payzant, *Eduard Hanslick and Ritter Berlioz*, p. 107.

[36] La Mara (ed.), *Briefwechsel zwischen Franz Liszt und Hans von Bülow*, Breitkopf und Härtel, Leipzig, 1898, pp. 76–78.

For many more than a mere handful of people in Germany, Berlioz was 'one of us'. And though Hanslick would liken him to a meteor, he remained a star. More than anything it was the faith of German musicians, German conductors – Bülow, Richter, Mottl, Mahler, Weingartner, Nikisch – that kept his music alive in the half century after his death.

What of Berlioz? Did he feel one of *them*? There, as Hamlet would say, was the rub. That his music was praised and championed in Germany was a joy to him and an honour he could never prize too highly. His gratitude knew no bounds. Liszt and his eager young disciples, the warmth of the welcome at the Villa Altenberg, the banquets, the deputations that saw him off at the train station with choruses from *Cellini,* the whole heady atmosphere – where else but in Germany could he find such blessings? He was one of them in the sense that they were musicians who felt as he did and made music with him with heart and soul. But blood, or for that matter milk, didn't come into it. Germany was where Beethoven and Gluck and Weber came from. It was 'cette patrie de la musique', the country where music was accorded unique importance. That was all. That was surely enough. In terms of art – the thing that in all the world mattered most, the only thing that could reconcile one to life – in terms of art, his nationality, anyone's, was an irrelevance. In terms of art he was not a Frenchman any more than he was a non-German: he was a musician. To the Germans who wanted to claim him as their own flesh and blood he was as resistant, if politely so, as he was to the Hanover critic who complained that the praise Berlioz was receiving in Germany exceeded what the far superior German composers, Beethoven, Mozart and Weber, ever received in their lifetime.[37] When, in his *Memoirs,* he comments on German criticism of his *Faust* for its modifications of Goethe, and asks why, in that case, the same critics have never blamed him for the libretto of his *Roméo et Juliette* symphony, he answers, 'No doubt because Shakespeare *was not a German*', then bursts out scornfully: 'Patriotisme! Fétichisme! Crétinisme!'[38]

Here, too, we can see, Berlioz stood apart from his age – an age in which nationalism was increasingly the rallying cry and the focus of consuming rivalries and disputes, and whole peoples were struggling to achieve nationhood and self-identification. Though he understood and sympathised, he could not respond. He was a citizen of the world. (I am aware that he held what we would call politically incorrect views on such

[37] *Cf. Correspondance générale,* Vol. IV, p. 400.

[38] *Memoirs*, p. 450. However, a school of thought emerged in Germany that maintained that Shakespeare *was* German (a claim aired during the conversation between Leslie Howard and Francis L. Sullivan at the British Embassy in Berlin in the film *Pimpernel Smith*).

ethnic matters as Chinese music. Nonetheless I think the description holds good.)

Nor – and this was even more the rub – could he subscribe to a specific school or movement. It was not in his nature or his beliefs. What Liszt was doing for him ('you are in every way a man apart', wrote Berlioz in January 1854[39]), the chords of human fellow-feeling the neo-Weimarians struck in him – for that he could only be profoundly and eternally grateful. It had brightened his life and enhanced his career immeasurably. The letter Liszt wrote to his agent Belloni in January 1852 announcing his intention of staging *Cellini* and then performing Berlioz's other major works in turn, together with the memorable phrase 'I consider myself honour bound to create for his works, one by one, the position they deserve in Germany, it is for me a matter of art and of personal conviction' – this letter was certainly seen by Berlioz and treasured ever after (I found it in the family archives).[40] But, however much he was indebted to Liszt, to become a fully paid-up member of the Futurists was impossible. When he and Litolff had words with Liszt after a performance of *Lohengrin* in Weimar in February 1856, Litolff took the elegant cane he had brought as a present for his host and snapped it in two, saying 'I am breaking with your party just as I break this cane'.[41] Berlioz reacted less rudely but no less decidedly – or rather, there was no cause for him to break with Liszt's party: he had never really belonged to it. In Jacques Barzun's words, he, being who he was, could not 'bind himself or anyone else' to a single artistic creed.[42] He must remain independent, owing allegiance to no group or doctrine.

By in effect sidelining himself, Berlioz ran the risk of isolating himself, as he realised, and as indeed happened. The conflicts and issues of the late nineteenth century – Wagner *v.* Brahms, Brahms *v.* Bruckner, programme music *v.* absolute music – largely ignored him. He who had been an innovator of central importance to the German progressive movement became a peripheral figure in the history of music, with consequences to his standing as a composer that lasted well into the twentieth century. But, as it seemed to him in Weimar in 1856, a creed was what one was being invited, even pressed, to join, and he couldn't. In an important sense, in his own mind at least, he had always been on the fringes of the Futurists, but the fact had not been evident. Now the whole question was brought into sharp and urgent focus and made inescapable by the issue of Wagner and of

[39] *Correspondance générale*, Vol. IV, p. 453.

[40] 14 January 1852.

[41] Reported in *La France musicale*, 20 April 1856.

[42] Barzun, *Berlioz and the Romantic Century*, Vol. 2, p. 74. *Cf.* also Berlioz's open letter to J. C. Lobe in *Fliegende Blätter für Musik*, in *Correspondance générale*, Vol. IV, pp. 403–5.

Franz Liszt in 1858, six years after he conducted the revival of Benvenuto Cellini *in Weimar*

Liszt's growing commitment to Wagner's ideas. I don't believe that Berlioz was motivated by jealousy or even resentment at Liszt's devotion to Wagner. Liszt after all was championing him, too. It was Wagnerism rather than Wagner that, for Berlioz, was the stumbling block: that is (whether or not he actually understood it), the doctrine – or rather the very idea of a doctrine, a right way which music must follow if it was to be saved: a doctrine, too, that appeared to relegate Beethoven and Weber to the status of forerunners. For Berlioz, if there was anything that could be called 'German music', they were it.

All this was anathema. To him, such a doctrine didn't open up the future, it narrowed it, and in the name of a theory. As the French writer Jean Pavans remarks, Berlioz's reservations about Wagner – some of whose music he admired, so far as he knew it – 'resulted from a profound aversion to anything that might obstruct the future.'[43] Pluralism was the only -ism that he could admit. A year before, in London, at a time when the two men came nearest to being friends – even as their musical destinies were about to diverge furthest, towards *Tristan* and *Les Troyens* – Berlioz told Liszt that in his opinion Wagner was

> wrong not to regard the puritan Mendelssohn as a real, richly individual talent. When a master is a master and when that master has invariably honoured and respected art, one must honour and respect him too, *however different from ours the path he follows* [italics added].[44]

Wagner's racially based argument for seeing Mendelssohn as necessarily inferior would have struck Berlioz as quite mad. Indeed, in a review of the book *Beethoven et ses trois styles* by his friend Wilhelm von Lenz, he categorically rejected Lenz's suggestion that Mendelssohn's music could never become widely popular because of its 'Hebraic elements'.[45]

The relationship, personal and artistic, between Berlioz and Wagner is too complex to be examined here (I have tried to do so in my biography of Berlioz[46]). Certainly there was a deal of misunderstanding, on both sides. Certainly Berlioz felt bitter resentment at *Tannhaüser* being staged at the Opéra when *Les Troyens* was ignored – as who would not, in the circumstances. Yet what remains striking is that even after all his public

[43] Jean Pavans, 'Hector Berlioz: un art de la fiction', in *Cahiers de la différence*, 9/10, January–June 1990, Paris, p. 23.

[44] *Correspondance générale*, V, pp. 117–18.

[45] *Journal des débats*, 11 August 1852; reprinted in *Les Soirées de l'orchestre*, Deuxième Epilogue, and republished in *Critique musicale*, Vol. 8, pp. 92–93.

[46] Cairns, *Berlioz*, Vol. 2, pp. 205, 285–86, 568–75, 587–89, 628–29, 649–63 and 690.

attacks on Berlioz, and despite his exasperated conviction that Berlioz was following the wrong path, Wagner could still regard him as a genius.

It is a nice irony that the conductors who championed Berlioz in Germany after his death were Wagnerians almost to a man. It is also a pointer to us today. We can admire and love both composers, both men, as they did. We don't have to keep going over the old battles. If Wagner, almost by definition, will never cease to arouse controversy, Wagnerism the cult – I don't think it is too much to claim, even in Bayreuth – has receded. This has nothing to do with the greatness and perennial fascination of Wagner's achievement, and only to do with the exclusive claims made for it. Though Wagner may want us to believe he is the supreme master – the culmination to which all music has been leading – we can fully appreciate his mighty music-dramas without falling for that.

Therefore, with interest in Berlioz in Germany now again somewhere near the intensity of the 1880s and 1890s, when *Benvenuto Cellini* was staged in 21 different German cities and the young Mahler conducted the *Symphonie fantastique* so often that its linear style and open textures rubbed off on his own music, can we not say that there is something symbolic in the choice of Bayreuth for a Berlioz conference, and that the composer whom Wagner numbered, with all his wrongheadedness, among the elite, is once again being taken to its heart by 'cette patrie de la musique'?

La Damnation de Faust

The next four pieces are an amalgam of articles that appeared in the Berlioz Society Bulletin.

Germany and *The Damnation*

Berlioz, in his *Memoirs*, is scathing about the German critics who took violent exception to *La Damnation de Faust* and what they regarded as its profanation of their sacred text – 'as if', he writes,

> no other Faust but Goethe's existed (Marlowe's, for instance, or Spohr's opera) […], and as if in any case it were possible to set such a poem to music complete and unchanged.

The hostility of the reviews of the Berlin performance in 1847 clearly distressed him. Berlin was the city of which, visiting four years earlier, he had written that music, there, was 'part of the air you breathe; you absorb it through the very pores of your skin'.[1] Yet here it was rejecting him out of hand, and finding not a shred of melody in it (a score which Sir Thomas Beecham would later describe, with reason, as 'a bunch of the loveliest tunes in existence'[2]). The best the reviewers could say was that he should be seen as a presage of better things to come, pointing the way forward for composers who would have the genius and skill and taste he so sadly lacked. This judgement, of course, was a commonplace of nineteenth-century criticism. Beethoven's later works would be still, for a long time to come, regular recipients of the same kind of helpful comment. I am reminded of Fétis' patronising disposal of Beethoven's C sharp minor String Quartet, where its composer was acknowledged – all praise to him – to have attempted to widen the boundaries of musical expression and form but to have failed disastrously, his efforts ruined by a mass of errors from which a more thorough schooling might have saved him. So it was not only Berlioz who had not been properly taught. To adapt his exasperated exclamation in the *Memoirs* about singers and their presumptions: 'Critics – what a race!'

All the same, you can understand the adverse response to his treatment of their national heritage. Young German musicians such as Peter Cornelius

[1] *Memoirs*, p. 344.

[2] *The Daily Telegraph*, 27 May 1933.

and Hans von Bülow might be bowled over by the work; but the average critic can hardly be blamed for his hostile reaction, beginning with anger at the deeply offensive title. Before a note had been heard, it was a desecration, by a blasphemous foreigner, of a revered German monument. How could they approve of it? They were thinking of a totally different Faust. To them, Faust was above all the aspiring, idealistic, redeemed hero of Part 2 of Goethe's drama, purged of the sins and follies committed, in Part 1, in his reckless quest for experience, and scaling the heights of greatness. Redemption was the consummation to which it had always been moving.

To Berlioz, on the other hand, as to his fellow French Romantics who read and re-read Gérard de Nerval's translation of Part 1, Faust, like the flawed hero of the old legend and of Marlowe's play, was marked for damnation, not salvation. As Madame de Staël said in her influential book *De l'Allemagne* (1813), '[Goethe's] intention is evidently that Marguerite shall perish but that God shall pardon her, and that Faust's life will be saved but his soul will be lost'. This was the Faust that Berlioz lived with, for years, before Part 2 was published in France, and that he identified with. His Faust is from the first in thrall to Mephistopheles – in fact, from the sixth bar of the work, when the B flat in the violas, the flattened sixth, the 'worm i'the bud' in Faust's imagined felicity, forms a hidden augmented fourth with the preceding E.

Here, for Berlioz, was the perfect hero for a drama – semi-autobiographical, there can be no doubt – in which the ruling power is Mephisto the mocker, the malignant force who turns every aspiration, every positive impulse – towards nature, learning, companionship, faith, love, everything – to dust. This is the governing idea of the *Damnation*: Mephistopheles as mastermind of the action, Faust's eternal shadow, the devil that Faust carries within himself (the same spirit in which Delacroix, in one of his lithographs published just as Berlioz was coming under the spell of Goethe, pictures Faust as almost indistinguishable from his satanic companion). No wonder the Berliners took such exception to it.

Mephisto – the devil it is!

Was the tritone F–B, the medieval 'devil in music' which is a central motif of *La Damnation de Faust*, part of the original conception? It may not have been. Julian Rushton, editor of the score in the New Berlioz Edition, points out that the transposition of Marguerite's ballad 'The King of Thule' from its key in the *Huit Scènes de Faust*, G, to F, in which key its first two notes are F and B, was made very late on, and that Berlioz seems at first to have thought of F and G as alternative keys, the choice depending on whether Marguerite was being sung by a mezzo or by a soprano.[3] Perhaps. But

[3] New Berlioz Edition, Vol. 8b, Bärenreiter, Kassel, 1986, p. 504.

Faust and Mephistopheles in one of a series of seventeen lithographs by Eugène Delacroix, begun in 1825, to illustrate one of the first French translations of Goethe's Faust, *Part I, published in 1828*

we tend to forget how pragmatic composers are and how down-to-earth they can be about their works, doing things to them that would horrify their admirers: for example, Beethoven sanctioning cuts in the *Adagio* of the 'Hammerklavier' Sonata, Elgar agreeing to a recording of his Violin Concerto in a version that reduced it by more than a third, Verdi blithely altering the key of an aria to accommodate a particular singer, though it upset his carefully planned key-scheme. Likewise Berlioz: eminently practical musician that he was, he would no doubt have been prepared for the possibility of a soprano Marguerite singing the piece in G. And what if he grasped the crucial role of the *diabolus in musica* only quite late in the process? (The key of Mephistopheles' serenade, E in the *Huit Scènes*, was first changed to C before it finally settled in B.) Composers aren't always immediately aware of what they are doing, of what it is that impels them, of its full implications. In the end Berlioz did. That is what matters. F–B is demonstratively there, bestriding the work, from Mephisto's first rasping entry in B major after the tentative F major cadence of Faust's imagined recovery of belief, to the opening of the gates of pandemonium – *was* there, you could say, from the beginning, in the interval of the augmented fourth which defines Marguerite's ballad, that original germ of the *Damnation* which in its definitive form tells us that Marguerite herself is Mephisto's creature. She escapes him in the end. But, for this Faust, there is no escape. The demon of denial has him in his claws, and does not let go.

Berlioz, *The Damnation of Faust* and the Critics

The low standard of Berlioz criticism in Britain lasted well into the twentieth century. Even otherwise conscientious critics seemed to take leave of their senses when dealing with him. Ernest Newman himself, one of the few who took him seriously and could write cogently and eloquently about his music, was capable of abandoning his usual rigour and lapsing into the same ignorant assumptions that he was fond of castigating in other journalists, his judgements veering as wildly, though with less excuse, as those of Wagner himself – Wagner for whom Berlioz was a composer whose music lacked any sense of beauty and who was at the same time one of the elite, of the true lineage.

In an article of 1933 on *La Damnation de Faust* Newman belabours 'the academics [who] still feel it safe to speak of [Berlioz] with the mixture of pity and impertinence that has been characteristic of the academic mind, in all epochs, towards whatever is different from, and better than, anything it is able to produce itself'. Yet in the same piece he can claim that 'not the least curious thing' about the work is its title, and that 'there is nothing in the previous portraiture of Faust' to suggest that Berlioz has been 'leading up to' his damnation.[4] In another article, sixteen years later, he is still saying that 'there is no overriding design' in the work – all that Berlioz did in 1846 was to 'take up again the amazing *Eight Scenes from Goethe's Faust* of 1829 and tack others on to them'.[5] How could a critic of his formidable intelligence fail to recognise the *Damnation*'s manifest overriding design, unless he simply neglected to examine it and fell back on the old stereotype of Berlioz the unthinking artist, the fascinated slave of his immediate impressions, who 'plunged into the subject without having thought it all out organically'?

I remember, years ago, an echo of the old image of Berlioz the rebel, the compulsive breaker of rules, the composer like no one else, in a review of the *Damnation* by David Drew. (The performance that prompted Drew's *New Statesman* review had been graced by John Warrack's ground-breaking programme note, which his fellow critics rightly praised while maintaining that it overvalued the work.) Drew wagged his finger, half humorously, half reproachfully, at the 'curious way' Berlioz joins the end of Marguerite's Romance, in F, to the beginning of Faust's 'Nature immense', in C sharp minor, via the minor third of F, A flat, treated as the dominant, G sharp, of the new key – Berlioz 'diving into his new tonic key like a seagull which has suddenly sighted a fish'. There was, he added, 'no use complaining about the absence of a Beethovenian transition'.[6] Quite apart from the dubious ornithology – gannets and terns dive for fish, gulls don't – what was the normally judicious and indeed exceptionally intelligent David Drew thinking of? There is no composer whose 'transitions' can be on occasion more abrupt, more rule-breaking, than Beethoven's. (Think of the coda of the first movement of the Seventh Symphony, the end of the slow movement of the 'Emperor' Concerto.) Why single out Berlioz?

Little by little such preconceptions have been fading away. But, received ideas being so tenacious in music history, we should not be unprepared to find them lingering on, and even being passionately espoused by eminent musicians. A friend tells me that when, a few years ago, he was interviewing a celebrated Baroque specialist and happened to remark that a passage in one of Rameau's operas was prophetic of Berlioz, the man reacted so angrily – dismissing Berlioz out of hand as a worthless, marginal figure – that he nearly walked out of the interview. That recalls to me Ernő Dohnányi's response to Robert Simpson (as recounted by the latter) when,

[4] *The Sunday Times*, 28 May 1933; republished in Peter Heyworth (ed.), *Berlioz, Romantic and Classic: Writings by Ernest Newman*, Gollancz, London, 1972, pp. 186-87 and 175.

[5] *The Sunday Times*, 5 June 1949; republished in *ibid.*, p. 188.

[6] *New Statesman and Nation*, No. 66, 1963, p. 264.

on their discussing the necessity of composing at the piano and Simpson's remarking that Berlioz didn't, Dohnányi replied, 'Berlioz is not a composer'.[7]

Perhaps I am being morbidly sensitive; but it is sad to see a specialist in French music as distinguished as Roger Nichols (who really should know better) coming up with the following, in a sleeve note to a recording of the César Franck and Fauré string quartets: those composers, he writes, were not 'flashy orchestrators in the Berlioz or Rimsky tradition'.[8] Rimsky, perhaps, though even that strikes me as gratuitously derogatory; but Berlioz? *L'Enfance du Christ* flashy? *Les Nuits d'été*? Large parts of the *Requiem*? Nichols goes on: 'Both [Franck and Fauré] cultivated what the French call *intériorité,* which one could translate as "intimacy", though this loses the sense of deep reflection, even of transcendence, immanent in the French term' – the implication being that it is a quality not found in Berlioz.

Again, in an essay by Benjamin Perl that appeared in a recent compendium,[9] we read that Berlioz, who 'never mastered an instrument' (*please*!), owed his ambivalent attitude to Mozart partly to the sense of his own inferiority. (What composer contemplating Mozart has not felt inferior?) 'Despite the apologetic discourse of Barzun and other Berliozians, his shortcomings in harmony, counterpoint and formal organisation are unmistakable even in his mature works'. Berlioz the composer who never mastered his *métier* (or an instrument) – is that ancient *canard* still alive and quacking? In that case – if one is still allowed to quote Barzun – what he advocated ('Ceaseless vigilance') is still the order of the day. But Dr Perl should read the writings of Jean-Pierre Bartoli on Berlioz's radical and purposeful treatment of harmony and its anticipations of Messiaen and Mahler – a French professor, no less, whose analyses have been an important part of the radical change taking place, in France itself, in the perception of the composer.

True, Berlioz the non-instrumentalist is not the most damaging of the myths that have dogged his reputation. It surfaced again recently in the programme note for a concert by the Orchestra of the Age of Enlightenment, entitled 'French Connections' and featuring a performance of *Cléopâtre* and works by Cherubini, Méhul and Mozart: 'Intriguingly, Berlioz remains perhaps the only major composer never to have mastered a musical instrument'. At least, it seems, he was a major composeér. But he was also, by his late teens, an accomplished flautist, able to get his fingers

7 Letter to Colin Mawby, dated 2 May 1988, quoted in Donald Macauley, *The Power of Robert Simpson: A Biography*, self-published via XLibris, Bloomington, 2013, p. 176.

8 Booklet essay for a recording by the Dante Quartet on Hyperion CDA67664, released in August 2008.

9 'Mozartian Undercurrents in Berlioz', in Barbara L. Kelly and Kerry Murphy (eds.), *Berlioz and Debussy: Sources, Contexts and Legacies: Essays in honour of François Lesure*, Ashgate, Aldershot, 2007, pp. 19–34.

round the virtuoso concertos of Louis Drouet (court flautist to Napoleon, first flute in Louis XVIII's Chapel Royal orchestra, and a composer whose music made a speciality of rapid scale-passages, arpeggios and double-tonguing), and he kept up his flute-playing in Paris in the 1820s and was proficient enough to apply for a position in the orchestra of the Nouveautés (the new vaudeville theatre which opened in 1827), but the post was no longer vacant. According to a posthumous account of his life, he played a flute concerto in public about the same time.[10]

Ceaseless Vigilance

Ceaseless vigilance is a recurring theme in Jacques Barzun's writings on Berlioz in the last years of his long life. He warns us against complacency; we cannot afford to sit back in the comfortable belief that the war has been won. He was surely wise to do so. We Berliozians may blithely assume that Berlioz is now in the mainstream of musical history, where he belongs; but there are still people out there who consider him no more than a peripheral figure, when they think of him at all. How often, for instance, does one fail to find any mention of him in biographies of musicians who, as it happens, were admirers and proselytisers of his music? The last time I consulted a modern life of Busoni, Berlioz's name was conspicuous by its absence – Busoni, who said that Berlioz 'pointed the way for untold generations'.[11] Until Gunther Braam gave me chapter and verse, I had had no idea that Bruckner admired Berlioz. When do you ever see that stated?

Some years ago, at a party at the British Library given in honour of Chris Banks (Secretary of the New Berlioz Edition, who was leaving the library to take up a senior post at the University of Aberdeen), the composer Robert Saxton told me that Elizabeth Lutyens, whom he had known well in her last years, was passionate about Berlioz and forever talking about him; but I am not aware that this important allegiance of her life came up during the recent celebrations of the centenary of her birth. At the same party Julian Anderson described Thomas Adès' delight when a fellow composer said that a passage in a new work of his reminded him powerfully of Berlioz. It will be interesting to see how frequently Berlioz is mentioned in discussions of Adès' music.

The sixth edition of *Grove's Dictionary* published in 1980 – *The New Grove* – bore out Barzun's warning. It was almost as if omission of Berlioz had been a guiding editorial principle. The Berlioz entry did him full and splendid justice – it was written by Hugh Macdonald – but elsewhere he

[10] Reported by Émile Mathieu de Monter in 'Études biographiques et critiques: Hector Berlioz', *Revue et gazette musicale*, 27 June 1869: 'a fine flute concerto performed one evening on the stage of the Théâtre de Belleville'.

[11] Quoted in Barzun, *Berlioz and the Romantic Century*, Vol. 2, p. 287.

Jacques Barzun

was often too marginal to register. In the entry on John Ella, the English violinist, conductor and critic, we read that Ella 'cultivated a wide circle of acquaintance among foreign musicians', including Meyerbeer, Thalberg and Wagner but not apparently including Berlioz. That *La Fuite en Égypte* was dedicated to Ella, that he was one of the small group of friends at Berlioz's wedding to Marie Recio, that his congratulatory letter on Berlioz's election to the Institute is one of the most wholehearted and enthusiastic of the many the composer received ('Mon cher, bon Berlioz, ce jour sera, je pense, le plus brilliant de ma vie, [...] [j'ai] le bonheur de vous féliciter pour la justice que la France a rendue [...] à l'un des hommes que j'aime le plus')[12] – all this evidently cut no ice with the contributor. Again, under 'Rouget de Lisle', we were informed that 'with the July Revolution in 1830 the *Marseillaise* regained acceptability', and yet there was no word about Berlioz's setting of it composed that year. This was, to say the least, odd, especially as the

[12] *Correspondance générale*, Vol. V, p. 323.

entry was written by Frédéric Robert, who edited the second volume of the complete Berlioz correspondence.

It was the same when one turned to, of all entries, 'Weimar'. The roster of those who 'frequented' Liszt's home, the Villa Altenberg, included 'such musicians as Wagner, Raff, Brahms, Cornelius, Smetana, Borodin, Glazunov, Rubinstein and Bülow', but not the musician whom Liszt regarded as, after Wagner, the most important composer of the day, in whose honour he put on several 'Berlioz Weeks' and who was one of the two non-German members of the New Weimar Association. Under 'Cornelius, Peter' one looked in vain for the composer whose powerful influence Cornelius openly acknowledged – *Der Barbier von Bagdad*, he told Berlioz, would 'show you that you have a disciple in Germany and that *Cellini* has offspring'[13] – and whose *Damnation de Faust* Cornelius called 'one of our great musical masterpieces'.

Admittedly, these and other errors were put right in the next edition of *Grove* (and perhaps not only as a result of the protests they inspired). There has certainly been progress, significant progress, in the quarter-century since *The New Grove* was published. Berlioz is continually making converts. Some of the defective articles referred to were the work of German musicologists. They were a measure of the status, or lack of it, that Berlioz was accorded in Germany at the time. That is different now. The influence of Bärenreiter's New Berlioz Edition, the crusading zeal of Colin Davis in Dresden and Munich, and productions of *Les Troyens* in German theatres large and small, have borne fruit in a fundamentally new attitude.

Apropos conversions, here is a tale of justice, poetic and actual, told me by Jacques Barzun. Some years ago he sent me a copy of a letter from a friend, a professor of music at an American university, who, on the point of retirement, wrote that to his joy his final seminars were being devoted to Berlioz's Te Deum. 'What a way to go!', he said. The irony of this communication was that many years before, when the young Barzun was at work on *Berlioz and the Romantic Century*, he was taken to task at a dinner party and attacked in violent terms by that same professor of music, who poured scorn on the project and told him that his reputation as a serious scholar would never recover if he persisted in devoting himself to such a disreputable apology for a composer. This particular story had a happy ending. But we would do well not to forget that prejudice still exists and is not always so gratifyingly repented of.

Perhaps Berlioz's music will never lose its capacity to unsettle, to disturb and to alarm. But we have lived to experience a change – even a sea change

[13] *Ibid.*, Vol. VI, pp. 175–76.

(to use that overworked image) into something rich but strange no longer. I was reminded of it afresh when reading Andrew Huth's programme note for the recent performance of the *Symphonie fantastique*, by the National Youth Orchestra, at the Proms:[14] 'Although [the symphony] may end in a depiction of delirium, disintegration and madness, it is also shaped by a keen intellect, with a formal unity that exists on many levels.' Berlioz's written programme 'has often led commentators in the past to focus on the colourful legends surrounding the symphony at the expense of its musical integrity, as though the music were in some way devalued by its personal and literary associations.' 'Recent decades', Huth concludes, 'have seen a full rediscovery and appreciation of Berlioz in all his variety and colour, his unique passion and yearning, his sharp brilliance and deep human insights.'

Not so long ago, would one have expected to read such a ringing affirmation?

[14] The National Youth Orchestra of Great Britain was conducted by Semyon Bychkov on 7 August 2010; the *Symphonie fantastique* was preceded by Dukas' *The Sorcerer's Apprentice* and Julian Anderson's *Fantasias*.

The Damnation on Disc

The following review is extracted from the chapter 'The Operas of Berlioz', which appeared in Opera on Record *2, edited by Alan Blyth and published by Hutchinson in 1983.*

La Damnation de Faust remains the most recorded of Berlioz's dramatic works. There are eight complete versions, as well as two sets of extracts and a host of recordings of single numbers. Yet, whereas a first-rate version exists of the three operas, there is no entirely satisfactory *Damnation* on disc. One contributory factor is that so many of them use non-Francophone singers. Not that the presence of French singers is by itself a guarantee of excellence. But in no other Berlioz work, not even *Les Nuits d'été*, is it so important that the sung text is delivered by singers capable of pointing and stressing and colouring the words in an idiomatic and characteristic way. It is not enough to be able to get by in French; one must be thoroughly at home in it. Of the five most recent recordings, however, two have no French-speaking singers at all in the principal roles and the other three have only one each. The 'decline of French singing' seems to be accepted by most record companies as a fact. No one bothers to find out if it is true, and as a result good French singers are ignored: Pierre Thau, for example, a fine Mephistopheles, appears only as Brander, on the Prêtre recording.

Another reason that the perfect *Damnation* is so tricky is simply the enormously demanding orchestral score, its exceptional range, concision and mercurial changes of mood, style and texture. The musicians have to know 'the intention of every orchestral touch', as Bernard Shaw observed when reviewing a performance under Hallé in which the music 'came to life in the hands of players who understand every bar of it'. Successful Berlioz performances, Shaw goes on, are 'soldiers' victories, not generals'.[1] He overstates the case: the soldiers' understanding derives ultimately from their general, and without a sagacious and far-sighted general, no amount of prowess on their part will win the day. But the reverse is no less true: the most perceptive view of the work will remain earthbound if the conductor doesn't succeed in communicating to his players 'the intention of every orchestral touch'. Add that the large part for male chorus demands, ideally,

[1] 'The Absence of Orchestras', *The World*, 13 January 1892; republished in *Shaw's Music*, Vol. 2, p. 520.

to be sung by professional tenors and basses but is nearly always entrusted to amateurs.

None of the recordings gets everything right, though one or two come close. The earliest, issued by Columbia on fifteen 78s and transferred to LP by American Columbia, is not strictly a complete version; as in the Markevich recording, there are sizable cuts in Parts 3 and 4. Jean Fournet begins promisingly, with a nice lyrical flow in the opening Pastoral Symphony. But the 'Hungarian March' is destroyed by a blatant acceleration three-quarters of the way through. Thereafter, good things – a stealthy, atmospheric opening to Part 2, a crisp and glittering 'Minuet' – alternate with others that show less insight. The French Radio Orchestra and the Émile Passani Chorus are generally punctilious and lively. All the singers are French, though none is particularly distinguished. Paul Cabanel's Mephisto has a strong, bright voice (with rapid vibrato), clear diction and a commanding manner, but not a lot to say. Mona Laurena's Marguerite is sloppy in 'Le roi de Thulé' and, though better in the Romance, inclined to sing flat. The best of the soloists is Georges Jouatte, the Faust. His 'Le vieil hiver', sung with a keen sense of line and phrase, is a powerful lyric statement. Jouatte also captures the hushed rapture of 'Merci, doux crépuscule'. He avoids the high C sharps in the duet, and in the trio is not entirely comfortable even on A. Nonetheless, his 'Nature immense' comes as a disappointment, inaccurate in note-values and peppered with intrusive aspirates and, worse still, constantly anticipating the beat, so that what begins as a tempo of unhurried grandeur, appropriate to this hymn to vast, indifferent Nature, finishes by being rushed off its feet.

Charles Munch recorded the *Damnation* in 1954 (RCA) with the Boston Symphony, with whom he often performed the work. Though ritually invoked by French critics as the last word in Berlioz interpretation, Munch had a wilful streak that could lead him wildly astray, but this is one of his most authoritative and convincing performances. From the first phrase on the violas, played quietly but with a decisive spring, the score comes vividly to life. The miscalculations and errors are few (a hurried and accelerating March, an over-quick Minuet, an earthbound 'Ciel', some painfully strident cornet and trumpet tone). Again and again Munch finds the touch and colour and dynamic to characterise the music: the yearning melodic lines in the Easter Hymn, the sizzling *strettissimo* of violins and violas at Mephistopheles' first entrance, the plangent tone of the solo cornet in 'Voici des roses', the magical drifting fall of the choral harmonies at the end of the Sylphs' scene, the glee of the scampering will-o'-the-wisps in answer to their master's summons, the sense of a monstrous, clattering guitar in the *pizzicato* accompaniment to the Serenade. Munch has perhaps the best

Faust in David Poleri – not French but at home in the language and style and, if not the subtlest interpreter of the music, a refreshingly forceful one, with a feeling for its large melodic line and ardent lyrical utterance ('Adieu donc, belle nuit' in the finale to Part 3 is gloriously sung). The Marguerite of Suzanne Danco, too, is unusually fine. Berlioz specified a mezzo (having first thought of it as a soprano role) and it's true that Danco's voice is not quite weighty enough for the climax of the Romance. But her gem-like concentration of tone, musical phrasing, sensitive use of words and general intelligence give continual pleasure. The weakness of the set is Martial Singher's prosaic Mephisto, stolid as a policeman and devoid of humour or menace. One would hardly know he is French, so unidiomatic is his performance. But for this, I should be tempted to overlook the substitution of trombones for tubas in the drinking and Amen choruses (an error of the old Breitkopf edition) and call it the most authentic of the recorded versions.

The version by Georges Prêtre, the other French conductor to record the work (EMI, 1969), is authentic only in its conformity to the worst traditions of perfunctoriness and routine. Some of the ensemble is all over the place, notably in 'Le vieil hiver' (where, in addition, flute and clarinet miss an entry altogether), the Peasants' Chorus and Marguerite's Apotheosis. At other times a sleepy competence settles over the proceedings. Yet there are enough flashes of vitality and insight to show what it could have been if some trouble had been taken. The Paris Opéra Chorus of that epoch was in a bad way but the orchestra knew the score backwards, and here and there they cannot prevent themselves from playing it well. Nicolai Gedda is not the artist to thrive in this sort of atmosphere. His Faust keeps threatening to become interesting but in the end it founders in a thoroughly undisciplined 'Nature immense'. Gabriel Bacquier's Mephistopheles is more effective. His first entry, with Prêtre and the strings rousing themselves briefly to a crackling accompaniment, is excellent – amused, taunting, yet frighteningly menacing. It is clear what a fine Mephisto he could be. After that his performance declines into mediocrity. By far the best is Janet Baker. True, her voice lacks power in the duet and trio, and her opening phrases ('Que l'air est étouffant', etc.) are sung in a 'little girl' tone that sounds self-conscious. But she is the only Marguerite to hit exactly the right manner for the 'Roi de Thulé', that of a song sung with only half the singer's mind on it, while she is doing something else (in this case, braiding her hair). Her Romance has a sense of heartbreak equalled by few other singers, and it inspires the cor anglais player to richly expressive tone and phrasing. The enumeration of Faust's qualities ('sa marche que j'admire', etc.) is beautifully done. At the climax she observes the crescendo at 'retenir' and links the note to the next phrase, 'O caresses de flamme', with telling effect; and her final 'Hélas' breathes a wonderful sense of quiet desolation. She alone, in this shoddy performance, is able to create an artistic ambience.

After Prêtre, to listen to Markevitch (Deutsche Grammophon, 1960) is a tonic. The vital, singing line of the Lamoureux Orchestra in 'Le vieil hiver' gives the performance a lively start, and the sweet tone and natural phrasing of the French-Canadian tenor Richard Verreau confirm the good impression. Verreau's singing is not very varied and at times, gliding too easily over the notes, suggests an abstracted, thoughtless Faust; but he achieves a ringing climax to 'Nature immense'. By that time, however, Markevitch has thrown away his advantage. It's not only that, presumably to fit the work onto four sides, he countenances a number of cuts (some large, like the first half of the Easter Hymn and a big chunk of the Minuet, others small and fiddly). The interpretation as a whole acquires a slightly hysterical sense of haste from the accumulation of fast tempos: the March, the double chorus, the Minuet (what's left of it), the duet. Verreau, though not ideal, is the best of the soloists. Consuelo Rubio's Marguerite, never very convincing, becomes blowsy in the duet and the Romance; her rich, dark voice spreads badly under pressure in the higher register. Michel Roux, the Mephistopheles, does his best to turn his vocal limitations to account, and at first his slightly camp, aging manservant is not ineffective; but it soon palls. He is weakest in the Evocation, the Serenade and the climax of the Ride to the Abyss (where he loses his place), at his most appealing and suggestive in the final recitative, 'À la voûte azurée'; a pity that Markevitch chose to make a large cut in it.

The second Deutsche Grammophon recording (1974) is conducted by Seiji Ozawa. It has a dream orchestra, the Boston Symphony. This is the best playing of the score on disc. The soldiers, in fact, are magnificent. It is their general I have doubts about. Ozawa secures a brilliant performance from the orchestra and good work from the Tanglewood Festival Chorus, and in music in which precision, perfectly balanced textures and a just tempo lead by themselves to the right expression he is admirable. The final numbers, where personal feeling is not present, are superlatively well done. There is a prodigious climax to the Ride, a Pandemonium of awesome power, and an Apotheosis irradiated with a luminous serenity such as none of the other versions comes near equalling. Elsewhere, however, Ozawa sounds fatally uninvolved. His interpretation moves with superb assurance over the surface of the score, getting the details in place but ignoring the human emotions that animate it. A stronger cast might have kindled his interest. But Stuart Burrows, overparted as Faust even on a recording, makes a feeble impression (though it's to his credit that unlike many tenors he doesn't speed up during 'Nature immense'); and Donald McIntyre, the Mephistopheles, though he works hard and has moments of authority, is handicapped by a language and style unfamiliar to him. Edith Mathis comes out the best of the three. Her rather light soprano cannot command the sustained tone or the strong lower notes required in the Romance, nor does she manage much of a high B flat in the trio, but from the first she is responsive to the dramatic character of the music. The long opening recitative sounds a note both of timidity and of exaltation, and the Romance, especially the latter half, has a keen sense of pathos.

It might have been expected that Colin Davis' recording (Philips, 1973), following his masterly *Troyens* and *Benvenuto Cellini*, would give us something like a definitive version of this familiar but elusive work. It has Gedda, Veasey, Bastin and the London Symphony Orchestra and Chorus – if not ideal participants, on paper at least unusually strong ones. But the performance is uncharacteristically laboured. Davis' interpretation exhibits many fine intentions. He sets some unusually broad tempos, in principle very welcome, as the movements concerned – Faust's 'Sans regrets', the double chorus, the duet, 'Nature immense' – often glide by too glibly. But in practice they don't quite take off, because the playing has insufficient 'lift'. 'Le vieil hiver', the opening number, is symptomatic: a grand conception, but weighed down by pedestrian phrasing; the strings of the LSO sound – for them – in unresponsive, lacklustre mood, the violins especially. The same is true of the LSO Chorus; their tone lacks body and warmth, and the tenors are particularly weak. As Faust, Gedda gives a far more considered and artistic performance than on the Prêtre recording, but there is a sense of effort and a lack of bloom that are evidence of advancing years, though 'Merci, doux crépuscule' is elegantly done and his *pianissimo* high C sharp in the duet still leaves all other recorded Fausts far behind. Like many Marguerites, Veasey finds the 'Roi de Thulé' harder to bring off than the Romance: her singing of it lacks natural flow and suffers from a slight flatness of pitch (and from an undistinguished viola obbligato). In the Romance, inspired by sensitive cor anglais playing, she gains in eloquence as the music proceeds, rising to a wild grief in the *più mosso* and a sense of passionate abandonment in 'voir s'exhaler mon âme dans ses baisers d'amour'.

The best of the soloists, however, is Jules Bastin. No other Mephisto declaims the text as powerfully and subtly, none finds so much nuance and colour in it or rolls it round his tongue with such sardonic relish or quiet meaningfulness. There are certainly more beautiful 'Voici des roses', but his headlong, brilliant 'Flea' is a *tour de force*, at once brutal and whimsical, and 'A la voûte azurée' is a masterpiece of chilling irony. Indeed, there are passages in the performance that go just as one would wish. The whole scene in Auerbach's cellar, where orchestral finesse is less important and the chorus is safely doubled by brass and woodwind, has splendid panache. Here Richard Van Allan's Brander makes a strong contribution. It is good, too, to hear the tubas booming away in the accompaniment to the choruses, leaving the trombones to Mephisto, whose instruments they are.

Daniel Barenboim's *Damnation* – Deutsche Grammophon's third (1978) – comes tantalisingly close to answering the need for a first-rate recording. It has, in the Orchestre de Paris, a group of French musicians who respond to Berlioz's music as to their natural heritage. The chorus, the Chœurs de l'Orchestre de Paris, is the best on record, trained to a near-professional sonority and exactitude by Arthur Oldham (who was much less successful five years earlier with the LSO Chorus). Barenboim understands the score and knows that, to make it spark, it is not necessary to set fast tempos. The opening, taken at an almost ambling pace, is intensely spring-like in feeling, the double chorus moves unhurriedly but with a powerful swagger, the *moderato* tempo of the Minuet brings out the ritual element in that witty, disturbing piece. The quicker speed adopted in the reprise of the duet is a rare example of Barenboim not giving the music space. It is the casting that lets the performance down. Plácido Domingo is an imaginative choice for Faust and, tenors capable of singing Berlioz being in short supply, a valuable recruit; but here he is still feeling his way. The enunciation of the French text causes him problems: in the Easter Hymn 'Sur l'aile de ces chants vas-tu voler aux cieux?' is a gabble, and in 'Le vieil hiver' the unfamiliarity of the music betrays him into rhythmically imprecise singing, to the detriment of the ensemble. But there are thrilling sounds in the duet and in 'Nature immense'. With more experience of the part and some hard work on his French he could be an impressive Faust.

If Domingo is unstylish but exciting, Yvonne Minton's Marguerite is disappointingly dull – characterless in 'Le roi de Thulé', better, yet curiously unmoving, in the Romance. Bastin makes a predictable pungent Brander. But the surprise star of the cast is the Mephisto of Fischer-Dieskau. The very sophistication that can make his lieder-singing sound contrived is an asset in the role of the prince of illusionists and master of calculation. Fischer-Dieskau holds sway over the part from his first entry. His sinister joviality as the cynical 'spirit of life' is spine-chilling. There is no 'Voici des roses' more atmospheric than his and in the trio he achieves a truly demonic energy. Only his 'Flea' lacks savour.

It's hard to say why the Solti recording (Decca) is slightly disappointing. Up to a point it is remarkably good. It has a magnificent orchestra (Chicago Symphony), an adequate choir (Chicago SO Chorus) and a better-than-average cast. The American tenor Kenneth Riegel sounds slightly constricted in tone, and in the duet he adopts a jerky, over-emphatic style that breaks up the vocal line, but this is untypical. Elsewhere his singing is both virile and musical, with arrestingly bright timbre, well-shaped phrasing and keen dramatic involvement, and he rises to the challenge of 'Nature immense', responding to the grandeur and desperation of the music. Frederica von Stade, the Marguerite, sings with much more understanding, variety and passion than her earlier recital recording of the Romance led me to expect, and the beauty of her voice is a constant pleasure, marred only by her oddly genteel way of pronouncing the vowel 'ou'. The Belgian bass-baritone José van Dam's Mephisto is one of the most convincing and finely sung on disc. 'Voici des roses' is a model of suavity and quiet power, and his domination over Faust in Part 4 is conveyed with impressive force and authority. Solti paces the score well – there are few tempos that don't seem right. His reading abounds in telling dramatic details: jagged, violent double-bass phrases at the end of the duet, piquant, debonair violins in the 'Flea'; the exquisite lament of the cor anglais in the Romance, the menacing cornet solo in 'Voici des roses', the prodigious string crescendos in 'Nature immense' and the rumbling, rolling bass line in the same piece, the wild, distracted oboe in the Ride to the Abyss – such examples could be multiplied. The Chicago players, apart from an occasional untidiness of ensemble and one very strange trombone chord in 'Voici des roses', make the most of their opportunities. Yet in comparison with their Boston rivals or the Orchestre de Paris they do not have the music in their bloodstream. Their playing sounds like the product of skill and application but not of instinctive understanding – the sense of 'the intention of every orchestral touch'. With all its formidable qualities the performance, to my mind, lacks the vital spark.

The ten-78 set issued in 1933 under Piero Coppola (HMV) comes somewhere between the complete (or near-complete) versions and the highlights and single numbers. This was the first recorded *Damnation*. It has some good points. Coppola brings out nice touches in the orchestra (the Orchestre des Concerts Pasdeloup) that modern recordings often manage to obscure. The choral singing (Chorus Saint Gervais) is well drilled and sensitive; the Sylphs' Chorus, with its gently flowing tempo and transparent textures, is just about the best version on disc. José de Trevi is a competent Faust. Mireille Berthon has one of those neat, no-nonsense French soprano voices, bright and hard as a new pin: 'Tout s'efface', sings Marguerite at the moment of her seduction; but this one remains thoroughly in control, not a stocking rumpled or a hair out of place. Charles Panzéra's Mephistopheles begins with some polite if well-articulated singing in Auerbach's cellar (the first encounter with Faust is cut), then produces a 'Voici des roses' as fine as any. This is a model of bel canto used in the service of dramatic expression: velvet tone and phrasing, with the hint of an iron hand. 'Où glissera sur toi plus d'un baiser vermeil' is sung in a beautifully veiled, mysterious *pianissimo*, the high Ds at 'Ecoute' with a masterly use of head voice. The whole song becomes a thing of magical deception, with an undercurrent of immortal longings.

A few of the delicate touches of the Coppola recording would not have come amiss in the disc of highlights issued in 1960 under André Cluytens (EMI). The Paris Opéra Orchestra is at an even lower ebb than on the Prêtre recording and the Chorus is lamentable. The soloists promise good things but achieve them only intermittently. Gérard Souzay brings to the 'Flea' song and the Serenade his usual care for diction and inflection, but try as he will, it goes against the grain: this is Mephistopheles in a frock-coat, ineluctably respectable. Gedda is sluggish in 'Le vieil hiver' (this is at least partly the fault of the orchestra), better in 'Merci, doux crépuscule', and better still in 'Nature immense': his voice is in its prime, and the interpretation grand and spacious, and, for once, Cluytens and the orchestra rise to the occasion. After a heavy accompaniment to the 'Roi de Thulé' they also rouse themselves in the Romance, where the dark, glowing tone of the cor anglais matches the beauty of Rita Gorr's tone and her passionately sensuous phrasing. Gorr's voice, inappropriately sumptuous in the ballad, is heard to fine effect here, except for some ominously strained notes above the stave.

In the survey of single-number recordings that followed, the singers who stood out included Georges Thill, Paul Franz (Faust), Vanni Marcoux (Mephistopheles), and Germaine Martinelli, Shirley Verrett and Maria Callas (Marguerite). The article ended:

The ideal cast? A disciplined Thill, or Franz, or Poleri; Vanni Marcoux, Bastin, van Dam (perhaps even Fischer-Dieskau); Callas, Verrett, Martinelli or Baker; the choir of the Orchestre de Paris or the present-day rejuvenated Opéra Chorus; the Boston Symphony under an amalgam of Munch, Davis, Solti and Barenboim, with Ozawa for the final scenes. One day we may get a complete *Damnation* that leaves nothing to be desired. Or maybe that is a will-o'-the-wisp – as Mephistopheles would say, *sancta simplicitas*!

That was written in 1983. Since then there have been fine recordings under John Eliot Gardiner and Kent Nagano, among others, and Monteux's 1962 Royal Festival Hall performance, with André Turp, Michel Roux and Régine Crespin, was issued by BBC Music in 1998. But the search goes on.

Les Nuits d'été

This article appeared in the Berlioz Society Bulletin *No. 182 (April 2010).*

Listening recently, at the Berlioz Society's Members Weekend, to Terry Barfoot's presentation on 'Interpretations of *Les Nuits d'été*', I was reminded again of the problems that beset this enchanting work. Admittedly, they do not prevent it from being one of Berlioz's most highly regarded and frequently programmed compositions. Yet how often do we hear a really satisfying account of all six songs? Rarely, it must be said. The songs make such severe, and different, demands that a single singer, even the finest, is hard put to it to master all of them.

It can happen. The American soprano Eleanor Steber made a beautiful recording in 1954. So, recently, did the mezzo, Lorraine Hunt Lieberson. And in January this year [2010], in Belfast, the young soprano Elizabeth Watts, with the Ulster Orchestra under the Japanese conductor Takuo Yuasa, gave one of the best performances I have ever heard. Watts, one of the prizewinners at the Cardiff Singer of the World competition in 2006 (when she endeared herself to Berliozians by singing, as one of her prepared pieces, Hero's aria from Act 1 of *Béatrice et Bénédict*), had a strong vocal grasp of each song and an understanding of them remarkable in one so young. I thought her account of the work far surpassed the one given by Felicity Lott at Cadogan Hall in 2008. Singing it in the keys of the original voice-and-piano version – A, D, G minor, F sharp, D, F – she sounded thoroughly at home in each of them. We were spared the blight of downward transposition in the first, fourth and fifth songs (where the orchestral version preserves the original keys), which can be so damaging to colour and character.

Of course, even this choice of keys involves a compromise. When Berlioz orchestrated the work (mostly in the 1850s), he changed the keys of the second and third songs, 'Le Spectre de la rose' and 'Sur les lagunes', from, respectively, D to B and G minor to F minor. Especially with the first of these two songs in its orchestral form, to sing it a minor third higher – in D major, not B major – to some extent falsifies the composer's intentions.

At least the higher keys, D and G minor, have a kind of sanction in the original (piano) score, whereas the transposition of 'Villanelle' down from

A to F has none and alters the nature of the song, robbing it of its pristine brightness. With all her artistry – and few singers have understood the cycle so well – Janet Baker could not make 'Villanelle' sound other than muddy in F. Similarly, 'Absence' belongs unequivocally to the bright key of F sharp major, and yet mezzo-sopranos often lower it, though with less excuse, since the vocal line does not lie particularly high – unlike the tessitura of 'Villanelle' or, even more, of the D major 'Au cimetière', cruelly high and sometimes transposed as low as B flat, in which key you may even hear the second clarinet replaced by a bassoon. It should be made illegal to transpose it. But we don't live in Berlioz's imaginary Euphonia (see *Les Soirées de l'orchestre*), unfortunately – in this respect, at least.

What was Berlioz's intention when he published the full score, in 1856, specifying three different singers – mezzo, contralto, tenor – or four, if you add his preferred voice for 'Sur les lagunes', baritone? A performance with three or four singers would have been more normal in the nineteenth century than now – the only time in my experience that it has ever been given like that at a concert was in the Queen Elizabeth Hall, London, in the centenary year, 1969, under Colin Davis (the basis of the subsequent Philips recording). For whatever reason, Berlioz never included the complete work in the few remaining concerts that he conducted between 1856 and 1868. Yet *Les Nuits d'été* is, emphatically, a cycle, not a collection of six separate songs, as Julian Rushton convincingly argues,[1] and Berlioz surely thought of it that way. That is how it is composed: as a dreamlike anatomy of romantic love, beginning in a playful springtime idyll faintly shadowed with uncertainty, progressing through the anguish of loss and separation to obsessive intimations of mortality, to return at the end to the illusion that love may after all be there, waiting, if it could only be found.

So, what form, ideally, should a performance take? Or perhaps the word ideal can't apply. The arguments for several singers are in the realm of the ideal, not the practical. By definition, such a solution can only be very rare. We are left with a compromise. It is undeniable that one has only to hear 'Sur les lagunes' and 'Au cimetière' sung by male singers to understand why Berlioz preferred a baritone for the one and specifically demanded a tenor for the other, and why, in dedicating each song to a different singer, he was not merely expressing his gratitude to artists who had helped him on his visits to Germany. As I wrote in Alan Blyth's *Song on Record* [2], a baritone

[1] '*Les Nuits d'été*: cycle or collection?', in *Berlioz Studies*, ed. Peter Bloom, Cambridge University Press, Cambridge, 1992, pp. 112–35.

[2] *Song on Record*, 2, ed. Alan Blyth, Cambridge University Press, Cambridge, 1988, p. 6.

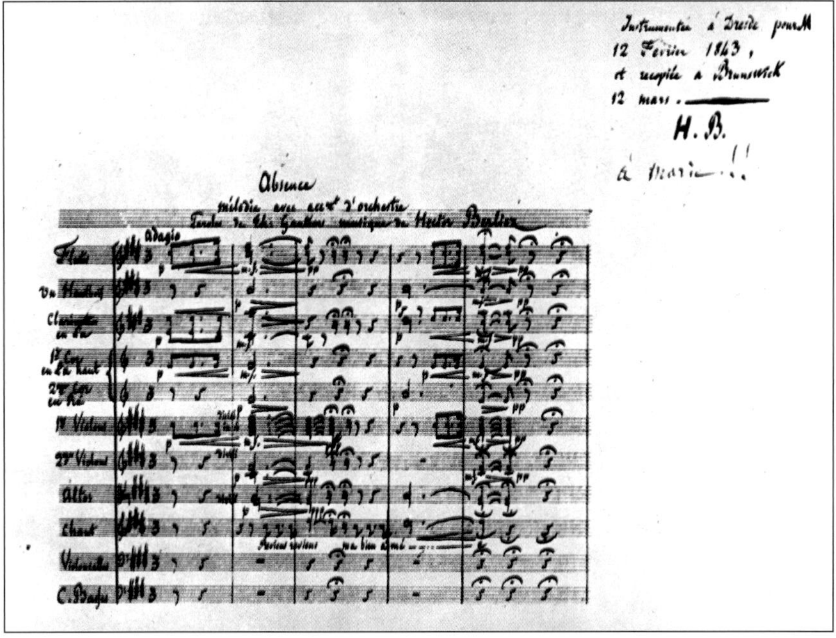

First page of the autograph score of 'Absence'

> fits [the F minor] 'Sur les lagunes' like a glove and brings out its dark, passionate colour. In 'Au cimetière' something of the essential trance-like, hermetic feeling of the music is lost if the vocal line is detached from the muted strings of the accompaniment by being raised an octave [...]. The most veiled, mysterious mezza voce of a soprano or mezzo can't give the effect of a tenor moving with and among the orchestra like a sleepwalker [...].

Yet, because it is a cycle, from instinct as well as habit we want to hear it sung by one singer. The answer must be that, unless we settle for a tenor (and the work's association with the female voice makes that, if not impossible, very difficult), *Les Nuits d'été* should be sung either by a soprano, in the original keys, or by a mezzo with a good range who can comfortably sing the first, fourth and fifth songs at the correct pitches (A, F sharp, D), while also – if that is not utopian – being able to manage the second and third at the pitch of the orchestral version. Even then, of course, it will be a compromise: in both versions of 'Au cimetière' – the original piano score of 1841 and the orchestral score of 1856 – the composer allows no alternative; it is a tenor song, *tout court*. Berlioz never makes things easy.

V

BERLIOZ AND POLITICS

The Reluctant Conservative

This is the text of a talk given to the Berlioz Society Members' Weekend in 2012 and published in the Society Bulletin *No. 191 (September 2013).*

When, a few years ago, there was a serious possibility that Berlioz's remains would be moved from the Montmartre cemetery and, like Dumas', re-interred with full public honours in the Panthéon, loud objections were voiced. How could it be right for a sworn enemy of the French Republic to find a place in the sacred citadel of Republicanism? Victor Hugo had been entombed there not as a great poet nor as the writer of *Les Misérables* but for his services to the Republican cause, as the man who went into exile in protest against Napoleon III and who returned to serve the Republic as a senator.

This was not the first time that Berlioz's anti-Republican sentiments, expressed with his customary trenchancy, had caused pain to his admirers. Julien Tiersot, Romain Rolland and Odilon Redon among others found it hard to come to terms with his criticism of the Republic of 1848 and his acceptance of Napoleon III, as revealed in the letters that began to be published under the Third Republic, when Berlioz's fame was on the rise. What was their hero doing failing to side with the forces of democracy and playing into the hands of the reactionaries? Vladimir Stasov, the patriarch of Russian musical life and a champion of Berlioz, observed ruefully that such jibes enabled the reactionaries 'to make their peace with Berlioz the reformer, Berlioz the bold Titan, who all his life toppled lies and falsehoods from their age-old pedestals. He stumbled – they instantly applauded and burst into song'.[1]

In the first volume of Tiersot's collection of Berlioz's letters, published in 1904, the quotations from the *Livre de Raison* of Berlioz's father systematically expunge all anti-republican sentiments. In the passage dealing with the lawyer Louis-Joseph Berlioz, Dr Berlioz's father, 'he was never a partisan of the revolutionaries' and 'he detested the revolutionary maxims that led to the fall of the Monarchy' are simply omitted. Tiersot evidently couldn't bear to think of the composer's grandfather as a reactionary. Even the homilies of the moderate conservative Dr Berlioz – whom Adolphe Boschot quite

[1] Stasov, *Selected Essays on Music*, p. 53.

wrongly portrayed as a rightist – are bowdlerised by Tiersot. 'Never in any circumstances in life seek public office […] but accept it when you believe you can fulfil it in a manner useful to your country and to your sovereign.' As the sentence appears in Tiersot, 'and to your sovereign' is deleted.[2]

I shall attempt here to show that the truth is more nuanced and that Berlioz's social and political ideas and beliefs were less clear-cut, more ambivalent than Tiersot and the other indignant defenders of the Republic supposed. Reviewing Berlioz's career in relation to the social and political movements of the time, it's hard to see how they could have been anything else. Stasov was right: he may have 'stumbled', but he was also, at times, 'the reformer, the bold Titan, who toppled falsehoods from their age-old pedestals' – the falsehoods of both sides of the ideological spectrum. His is the classic dilemma of the reformer who abhors violence and recoils from the destruction that revolution involves – who would abolish privilege but not the artistic achievements it makes possible (a dilemma explored in Henry James' novel *The Princess Casamassima*). I believe the title of this talk sums up a highly complex situation as accurately as is possible. Berlioz was indeed a reluctant conservative.

He inherited and acquired from his father a profound scepticism as to the likely benefits of drastic political action: 'it is rarely', writes Dr Berlioz, 'that the people gain from a change of government'. The good doctor had not thought like that in his young days. 'All the fine talk about liberty and equality which rang in my ears, the triumphs of our armies, the memory of Athens and Rome, went to my head, as it did to many others.' His son's opinions, broadly speaking, follow a similar trajectory. After the first heady days of the July Revolution of 1830, it will not be so very long before his fond expectations will be confounded and he will come to feel cynical about revolutions and the good that is assumed to come from them. (As Théophile Gautier remarks in the preface to *Les Jeunes-France*, 'the grass grows more luxuriantly next spring – a hero makes excellent *petits pois*. […] It hardly seems worth disturbing so many harmless paving-stones'.) But at the time his enthusiasm is unequivocal and his hopes high. A few days later, writing to his father, he reports that 'the admirable order that reigned throughout this magical three-day revolution is being maintained and confirmed: no stealing, not an offence of any kind. The people are sublime.'[3] Shortly after that, to his sister Nancy:

[2] Julien Tiersot (ed.), *Hector Berlioz, Les Années romantiques*, Calmann-Lévy, Paris, 1904, p. xl.

[3] *Correspondance générale*, Vol. I, p. 346.

*Berlioz's Russian champion Vladimir Vasilievich Stasov (1824–1906),
the most important Russian critic of his day,
in a painting from 1883 by Ilya Repin*

> If you could only see the poor women weeping for a son or husband or father or brother by the black cross set up in front of the Louvre to mark the grave of the National Guardsmen – it's a heartbreaking sight. But the spirit of the people is so fine!

The letter goes on:

> Last night at the Opéra the Marseillaise was called for. Adolphe Nourrit sang it, tricolour in hand, backed by the full chorus and orchestra. You can't imagine the effect. Immediately afterwards a note was thrown onto the stage and, on being read out, informed the audience that the author of that sublime hymn, Rouget de Lisle, was living in poverty; it proposed that a collection be taken for him. At that everyone streamed out into the foyer and a large sum was raised for the modern Tyrtaeus.[4]

Fired by the evening at the Opéra but noting, amid his emotions, that something more could be done with the *Marseillaise*, Berlioz immediately composed his own arrangement of all six verses of the hymn, scoring it for double chorus and an orchestra without oboes but with six trumpets and with a large force of drums used to formidable effect at 'Marchons, marchons' to suggest the tramp of multitudes. Soon afterwards he was reminded of that stirring exhortation by an incident – described later in the *Memoirs* – when, in the courtyard of the Palais Royal, he came upon a group of young men singing his 'Chant guerrier' from the recently published *Neuf mélodies*. Berlioz joins them, a crowd gathers, some National Guardsmen make an impromptu collection in their shakos for the wounded of the Revolution, and as the audience grows larger and larger the singers take refuge in the Galerie Colbert. Berlioz's account continues:

> There, surrounded and hemmed in like bears at a fair, we were invited to resume our singing. A haberdasher, whose shop opened off the glass-covered central area of the arcade, asked us up to the first floor, where we could 'rain down our music on our admirers' without risk of being suffocated. The offer was accepted and we struck up the Marseillaise. Almost at once the seething mass at our feet grew quiet and a holy stillness fell upon them. It was like the silence in St Peter's Square when the Pope gives his blessing, *urbi et orbi*, from the pontifical balcony. At the end of the second verse, at the point where the refrain enters, there was again a profound silence. It was the same after the third. This was not at all what I had expected. On beholding that vast concourse of people I recalled that I had just arranged Rouget de Lisle's song for double chorus and full orchestra and that where one normally writes 'tenors and basses' I had written, instead, 'Everyone with

[4] *Ibid.*, pp. 347–48.

a voice, a soul, and blood in his veins'. Here was just the occasion for it; so it was all the more mortifying to be met with a stubborn silence. The fourth time, unable to contain myself, I yelled: 'Confound it all – sing!' And the great crowd launched into 'Aux armes, citoyens!' with the energy and precision of a trained choir. Picture it: the arcade leading to the rue Vivienne full of people, as was the arcade that gives on to the rue Neuve-des-Petits-Champs and the central area beneath the dome, and those four or five thousand voices crammed into a reverberant space bounded to right and left by the clapboard of the shops' shutters, overhead by the glass roof and beneath by the resonant paving-stones, and most of them moreover, men, women and children, still throbbing with the emotions of the recent struggle – and then imagine the effect of that stupendous refrain. I literally sank to the floor; and our little band, awestruck at the explosion, stood dumbfounded, silent as birds after a thunderclap.[5]

Ten years later disillusionment will have replaced the high hopes of 1830, and the victims of the July days will no longer be sublime but 'plus ou moins héroïques' – more or less heroic.[6] Yet Berlioz will still remember that stirring time, and in the finale of the *Symphonie funèbre et triomphale*, where the voices enter in a low register, he will recall Barbier's lines celebrating the July Revolution that he quotes in chapter 29 of the *Memoirs*: 'Through Paris an awakened people's roar/Was like the sound of an approaching sea'.

Without doubt one of the blessings Berlioz, like most artists young and old, looked for from the July Revolution was an end to privilege and to antediluvian rules and restrictions and bureaucratic interference with and obstruction of the arts. 'Now I can paint anything without fear of censorship', exclaimed Horace Vernet, director of the French Academy in Rome when Berlioz was an inmate there.[7] Such hopes would soon be dashed, as it became clear that the main beneficiaries were the bankers, the industrialists and the politicians, and that the revolution had done little for the artists and nothing for the workers. I think it's important to emphasise this last point. Berlioz's interest in the abolition of privilege was not exclusively artistic and personal. Even as late as 1848, when writing from London about the abortive Chartist movement to his sister Nancy – who had become by then a proponent of Law and Order – he could speak of 'the insolent English aristocracy' who refuse to 'yield an inch of their territory and think it perfectly natural that they should have everything and the poor nothing'.[8]

[5] *Memoirs*, pp. 110–11.

[6] *Ibid.*, p. 247.

[7] Quoted in Barzun, *Berlioz and the Romantic Century*, Vol. 1, p. 202.

[8] *Correspondance générale*, Vol. III, p. 534.

If we examine Berlioz's choice of subjects for his compositions, we see, especially though not solely in the first part of his career, strong populist leanings and hostility to oppression: think of his opera *Les Francs-juges*, his cantata *Scène héroïque (La Révolution grecque)*, the Brigands' Song in *Lélio* and *Benvenuto Cellini*, but also *L'Enfance du Christ* and, as I shall argue later, *Les Troyens*.

Berlioz's feeling for the exploited reappears, perhaps rather surprisingly, in the final scenes of *Benvenuto Cellini*, where Cellini's foundrymen are shown singing their melancholy 'Bienheureux les matelots' as they toil at their work, and then downing tools furiously as Cellini is lured away by Fieramosca to fight a duel, leaving them, as they protest, overworked and unpaid. It's one of the earliest expressions of trade unionism in music.

In 1830, the year of the July Revolution, he began to be seriously interested in the ideas of radical social reform associated with the Saint-Simonian movement. We might be largely unaware of this interest if a letter from Berlioz in Rome to Charles Duveyrier, a lawyer on the staff of the Saint-Simonian newspaper *Le Globe*, had not been intercepted by the Austrian censorship and passed to Metternich in Vienna. When Berlioz met the Austrian chancellor fifteen years later, it was as a revolutionary whose subversive activities were confined to music – Metternich asked him if he was the fellow who 'wrote for an orchestra of five hundred', to which Berlioz replied that he 'sometimes used only four hundred and fifty'.[9] But the letter shows Berlioz, in 1831, actively interested in what he calls 'the political reorganisation of society' and 'the betterment of the largest and poorest class', and eagerly reading back numbers of *Le Globe* lent him by the architect François-Alexandre Cendrier, then in Rome, whom he describes as 'one of *ours*'. Berlioz confesses to being resistant to the mystical side of Saint-Simon's teaching, but he is otherwise convinced, and he asks Duveyrier – 'my dear friend, or rather my dear father' – to 'write to me, and I'll answer and give you my ideas on how I might be used musically to further the Great Work when I'm back in Paris'.[10] This is sound Saint-Simonian doctrine – the artist as the regenerator of society, the priest of the new social order.

The scenario of Berlioz's projected opera/oratorio *Le Dernier jour du monde*, which occupied him around this time, has a distinct Saint-Simonian flavour – a corrupt, unjust society opposed by a small band of the faithful. Nothing came of it, and his article in the *Journal des débats* four years later, describing his missionary 'Evenings at the Opera' in the 1820s, has an ironic tone as he recalls rallying his more faint-hearted Gluckist companions 'with

[9] *Memoirs*, p. 528.

[10] *Correspondance générale*, Vol. I, pp. 476–78.

sermons worthy of the disciples of Saint-Simon'.[11] Yet his writings during the 1830s also reveal a marked sympathy with the many amelioristic social projects that were in the air at the time: 'la haute popularisation' embodied in the educational ideas of people such as Adolphe Nourrit and Guillaume-Louis Wilhem – Nourrit's notion of 'Art for the people and by the people', Wilhem's male-voice-choir movement – and also Abbé Mainzer's choral classes for workers, and Liszt's 1830s utopian manifesto set out in a series of articles in the *Revue et gazette musicale* calling, 'in the name of all musicians, of art and social progress', for wholesale public investment in music, including musical instruction in primary schools. This is Berlioz responding with the idealism that was part of his nature, even if the sceptic in him knows what is all too likely to happen in practice to these noble impulses.

Given that ambivalence, it's not surprising to find him responding contradictorily, at different times, to the manifestations of social unrest that disturbed French society in these years, and also to the whole question of political power and the use of it. You can see this ambivalence – just to digress for a moment – in his complex, if not confused, attitude to Napoleon. Berlioz is not unlike Beethoven in this respect. Beethoven was disillusioned when Napoleon made his concordat with the Pope and still more when he crowned himself emperor, 'trampling', Beethoven said, 'the rights of man under foot'. Yet he continued to be fascinated by him, by his astonishing rise from such humble beginning to such heroic heights, and his overturning of oppressive relics of the past. Berlioz, despite his ever-growing repugnance to the imbecility and brutality of war and the futility of conquest, never entirely shook off the spell of Bonaparte that had taken possession of him as a boy as he listened to the tales of his uncle, the cavalry captain Félix Marmion, and drank in the whole Napoleonic legend – in Jacques Barzun's words, 'that mixture of recklessness, rapid motion and obsession with glory [...] which men as different as Balzac, Vigny and [...] Stendhal [...] found so gripping and so rich in artistic suggestion'.[12] Increasingly as he grew older, Berlioz the humanist, the anti-nationalist, came to deplore all that such figures stood for. 'Those pathetic little gangsters known as great men', he writes in a letter of 1866, 'arouse in me only disgust – Caesar, Augustus, Antony, Alexander, Philip, Peter [the Great] and all the other glorified brigands.'[13] But, significantly, he doesn't include Napoleon in the list.

Scepticism, disillusionment, disenchantment war in Berlioz's soul with idealism. More and more he was driven to see the futility of revolutionary

[11] *Memoirs*, p. 53.

[12] Barzun, *Berlioz and the Romantic Century*, Vol. 1, p. 28.

[13] *Correspondance générale*, Vol. VII, p. 438.

action. Yet he continued to feel for the social misery that inspired it. His comments in letters to friends on the riots in Lyon in 1832 veer between a lively sympathy with the plight of the 'largest and poorest class' and revulsion from the violence and physical disturbance that revolution entails. This revulsion could blind him to the inhumanity, the horror of the revenge the powers-that-be took on those who presumed to rebel against them. There's a letter of 1834 to his sister Adèle that rightly appals those who love Berlioz and believe in him, where, in best Law and Order mode, he sneers at the rioters brutally shot down by government forces in the rue Transnonain – an atrocity immortalised by the art of Daumier. We don't know exactly what was in Berlioz's mind at the time. Harriet was five months pregnant; perhaps he was anxious for her; but it's a blot on his honour.[14]

Not that he generally had any illusions about what governments get up to, about how the world is run, about the haves and the have-nots. More characteristic of him is his comment on the outcome of the Chartist meeting on Kennington Common in 1848:

> The cannon, those eloquent orators and formidable logicians whose arguments appeal so powerfully to the masses, were in the chair. [...] Their presence was enough to persuade everyone of the inexpediency of revolution, and the Chartists dispersed in perfect order.

He adds: 'My poor friends, you know as much about starting a riot as the Italians about writing a symphony.'[15]

Or take his ironic remarks which begin the 'Letter from Pesth' in the *Journal des débats* describing his musical voyage of 1846, where he tells of visiting the major cities of Austria – Vienna, Budapest and Prague. 'Some perverse minds, it is true, insist that Pesth is in Hungary and Prague in Bohemia, but these two states are nonetheless integral parts of the Austrian Empire, attached and devoted to it body and soul and estate, much as Ireland is devoted to England or Poland to Russia or Algeria to France, as subject peoples have in all ages been attached to their conquerors.'[16]

Yet the opening paragraphs of the *Memoirs*, written in London in March 1848, soon after the February Revolution in Paris and the abdication of Louis-Philippe, are pretty unequivocal. 'The juggernaut of Republicanism is rolling across Europe, the art of music, long since dying, is now quite dead.' He is deafened by the 'clamour of sovereign peoples crowning themselves king.'[17] This is not rational. But it is understandable. With Jullien's

[14] *Ibid.*, Vol. II, pp. 175–76.

[15] *Memoirs*, p. 19.

[16] *Ibid.*, p. 409.

[17] *Ibid.*, pp. 3–4.

bankruptcy and the collapse of the Grand English Opera from which he had hoped so much, Berlioz recognised that his life had reached a crisis. He could earn a living neither in Paris nor in London. His plan to return to Prague – of all cities of Europe the one that responded most positively to his music – and perform *La Damnation de Faust* was set at naught by the upheavals there. He has, in his own words, 'the certainty of being *de trop* in this world'.[18] It's not only a profound and total disenchantment with politics and political action: it's a disgust with so-called civilisation itself. 'Poor father', he writes – again that strong sense of kinship with the old man – 'he sees the affairs of this ridiculous world of ours with too clear an eye to have the least illusion about anything.'[19] Berlioz can dream only of voyages. 'The sea, the sea! A good ship and a favourable wind! Fly the old continent, go among simple, primordial savages, and hear no more of our systematically brutal, corrupt savages!'[20] For the moment he really is the American Indian he likens himself to in another letter, moving homeless over the earth.[21] It is no mere affectation.

Six years later, recalling the death from cancer of his sister Nancy after weeks of agony, he burst out at the barbarity of the law that forbad the use of chloroform to put an end to terminal illness: 'Savages are more intelligent and more humane'.[22]

His hostility to the Second Republic is, as I've suggested, more nuanced than his disapproving admirers supposed. Back in Paris, in 1848, as France prepares for its first election under universal (i.e., universal male) suffrage, and Paris grows more calm, he writes to his friend Morel in Marseille: 'God grant it lasts, and the Assembly is a true representation of the country – then one might actually hope for something important to come of it'.[23] His mood and attitude fluctuate according to whom he is writing. To the reactionary Lenz in St Petersburg he says:

> You must be making fun of us, with our 'advanced' ideas [...]. And you're still thinking about music, barbarians that you are. [...] Instead of working for the great cause, the root and branch abolition of family, property, intelligence, civilisation, life, humanity, you bury yourself in the works of Beethoven![24]

These are the ravings of the extreme right – at the opposite pole to the Great Cause of 1831, the betterment of the largest and poorest class. Yet a few

18 *Correspondance générale*, Vol. III, p. 543.
19 *Ibid.*, p. 534.
20 *Ibid.*, p. 644.
21 *Ibid.*, pp. 546–47.
22 *Memoirs*, pp. 503–4.
23 *Correspondance générale*, Vol. III, p. 536.
24 *Ibid.*, pp. 597–98.

months earlier, to Liszt, he remarks that men like the directors of the Opéra are 'a thousand times more our enemies than the unhappy people who kill on the barricades'.[25] And to Nancy, in the letter already mentioned about the rapacity of the English upper classes who 'have everything and the poor nothing', he quotes Don Basilio in Beaumarchais's *Le Barbier de Séville*: 'What's worth seizing is worth hanging on to'.[26]

Berlioz's scepticism about universal suffrage was not class-based: the bourgeoisie were hardly less unfit to vote responsibly and intelligently than the working man. Replying, in 1858, to Princess Wittgenstein, who had written to him about the disappointing reception of a performance of Gluck's *Alceste* at the Weimar opera, he remarks:

> The only thing that surprises me is that the bourgeois are allowed into the theatre when such works are being given. If I were the Grand Duke I'd send each of these fine fellows a ham and two bottles of beer, with a request that they spend the evening at home.

Later, in the same letter:

> Oh the bourgeois! The beer-drinkers, the eaters of ham! Who allowed them to come and hear, or rather listen to, that? [...] There are things the mob shouldn't be allowed to see. The three goddesses may have unveiled before Paris on Mount Ida, but Paris was a handsome young prince. I don't imagine the immortal trio would have revealed themselves to Thersites.[27]

The mob – Horace's *profanum vulgus*, the rabble defied by Berlioz's admired Coriolanus – is by no means confined to the underprivileged.

Berlioz, in other words, was what would be called today, disparagingly or perhaps admiringly, an elitist – but an elitist whose idealistic standards were constantly brought up sharp against, frustrated by, what in another modern coinage is known as 'the real world'. All his life there is this contradiction, this conflict within him – the conflict between his dreams and the facts. That is what happens to his vision of social renewal and social justice, glimpsed in the letter to Duveyrier. A writer can live up to his ideals and take a stand against tyranny and oppression and go into exile, as Victor Hugo did. For a composer, a worker in the art most dependent on practical circumstances for its existence – particularly a composer who writes on a grand scale – it's not so easy. Berlioz seems to have gone off the doctrines of the Saint-Simonians partly because, just as he was becoming attracted to them, the leadership was moving away from its plans for social amelioration

25 *Ibid.*, p. 564.
26 *Ibid.*, p. 534.
27 *Ibid.*, Vol. V, pp. 542–43.

towards a quasi-religious mysticism that was totally alien to him. But the chief reason was surely a practical one. The conversation with Metternich explains it. He was an artist whose ideas commonly required large forces for their realisation, and whose nature rejected compromise. His art came first. The social reformer's dream of a society remade in the interests of the people was submerged in the composer's struggle to make his way.

In the end harsh necessity forced him to the conclusion that, for a creative artist striving to have his works performed, and performed worthily, the political systems that provided the best conditions were not democratic republics or even constitutional monarchies but despotisms. His visit to Germany in 1843 only underlined the unsatisfactory status of musicians in France. In Germany they were looked after. 'If I had been born in Saxony or Prussia I should now have a salary of ten or twelve thousand francs for life, with a guaranteed pension for my family after my death.'[28]

Berlioz saw all too clearly what the upheavals of 1848 did to fellow musicians and friends: for example, to Charles Hallé, whose 'Oh damnable Revolution' was the cry of a man who saw the life he had built for himself in Paris destroyed. Even Wagner the revolutionary ended up depending on the patronage of a distinctly non-constitutional monarch; his vision of a popular theatre, where the people could see *Der Ring des Nibelungen* free, yielded to the expensive exclusivities of Bayreuth. Similarly, Berlioz's position is summed up in the letter he wrote to General Lvov in Russia while in London, preparing for his first concert. He has, he says, yet to have a full complement of players at a single rehearsal – the musicians come and go as they please. 'That is how discipline is understood in this country'. Only the choristers show him a dedication comparable to what he experienced in St Petersburg. 'Oh Russia!', he exclaims, remembering 'the organisation of its theatres and its chapel – the clear, exact, unyielding organisation without which, in music as in many other things, nothing good, nothing beautiful, is attainable'.[29] But surely, he is saying, most of all in music.

The same implacable imperatives bedevilled that other cherished vision of his, of music as a truly popular art, open to all. It had taken root in him in boyhood, as his willing imagination feasted on tales of the grand festivals in Athens and the Temple of Solomon. When he came to Paris the vision took clearer form in his conversations with his teacher Le Sueur, who thrilled him with stories of the heroic days of the Republic, of the Revolution and the Consulate, when the legendary celebrations of the ancient world were reborn and became alive and palpable. He never forgot what Le Sueur told him of the mighty ceremonies in the Champ de Mars, and how the

[28] *Ibid.*, Vol. III, p. 98.

[29] *Ibid.*, p. 513.

composers held public rehearsals in the streets of Paris, standing on carts and teaching the people the tunes which the multitude would then sing on special festal days – the whole community united in a solemn act of praise and thanksgiving. Berlioz remembered it more than 30 years later when he wrote the scene in Act 3 of *Les Troyens* where the select semi-chorus sings the tune and the people repeat it.

The vision of the musician as mentor of the people remained with him all his life. Several of his grandest compositions – the *Grande Messe des morts*, the *Symphonie funèbre*, the Te Deum – address the nation at large, the ideal community, in the populist tradition of the composers of the French Revolution, but universalising it into the whole human race. Berlioz continued to dream of the truly musical city and the celebrations attended there by whole populations of initiates. But 'initiates' is the crucial word. Euphonia the utopian city could only be located in Germany – Germany where, he writes in the *Memoirs*, 'the worship of art still burns pure and strong'[30] – certainly not in Paris. Yet in Germany too there were many like the ham-eating bourgeois of Weimar, let alone in Paris. Even among musicians and music-lovers, how many were there who felt music as he did? Even at the hallowed Conservatoire concerts there were people who went only because it was the thing. Alas, music as he knew and lived it and understood it couldn't be 'brought within the grasp of everybody', as his adversary Fétis insisted it could: Fétis himself was the living disproof of it, Beethoven's greatest works – the Ninth Symphony, the late quartets – being beyond his grasp.

Lost illusions, the defeat of the imagination, the implacability of facts, these were increasingly the realities of Berlioz's life. Yet one of the inspiring things about the *Memoirs*, with all its sadness and bitterness, is that it shows a great artist broken by his fate yet refusing to give up his ideals. Political action is a chimera, the musical city a mirage, but pity for the sufferings of human beings still pierces to the heart. He feels intensely for Mary and Joseph and the child as they toil through the desert and knock unavailingly on the doors of Saïs.

It is surely no accident, no mere pragmatic choice – a response to pressure to shorten the work – that made Berlioz decide to change the denouement of *Les Troyens* and leave out the extended triumphal celebration of the future Roman Empire with which it originally ended. Dido, her grief, her pain, her nobility, her courage, were what counted, not the deluded cause that destroyed her – Dido, and Cassandra, whose despair Berlioz understood, because it was the mirror image of himself, the prophet whose inspired words went unheeded.

[30] *Memoirs*, p. 518.

Berlioz and Napoleon III

The following piece appeared in the Berlioz Society Bulletin *No. 192 (December 2013), in response to Peter Bloom's article in the same issue of the* Bulletin, *'The political implications of the original ending of* Les Troyens*'.*

For anyone who would rather not think of Berlioz as the supporter of a dictatorship with blood on its hands, Peter Bloom's fascinating article in this issue makes uncomfortable reading. With the best will in the world, one looks in vain for a trace of Berliozian irony in his description of Louis-Napoleon's brutal coup of December 1851: 'this coup d'état is a stroke of genius, a complete masterpiece'.[1] There is no arguing away the evidence. But I think there is scope for an alternative interpretation of it, one not so much political or ideological as artistic and nostalgic, and that is what I should like to offer.

Taking a deep breath, I stand by what I wrote about Berlioz's ambivalent, often contradictory, attitude to government and to state authority, and about what I see as the fundamental reasons for his courting the powers-that-be.

He was a composer who commonly wrote on a large scale. Harsh experience taught him that to have his works put on, and performed fittingly, the political systems most likely to oblige were not democratic republics but monarchies, or even despotisms. Wagner found the same; for all his reformist ardour and the risking of his life in the cause of revolution, he ended up depending on – indeed, being saved by – the patronage of King Ludwig II of Bavaria.

The *Grande Messe des morts* was brought into being by a commission from King Louis-Philippe's government. In 1852, when Louis-Napoleon became emperor, Berlioz's Te Deum had been waiting more than two years for a performance. What more natural than that he should hope that a national ceremony – thanksgiving for the plebiscite, Napoleon III's coronation, his marriage – should be the occasion for it, and that he should lobby to make it happen?

However naïve, however much of a delusion it would prove to be, how could he – or a part of him at least – not nourish the wish that Napoleon III would be to him what Napoleon had been to his teacher Le Sueur,

[1] *Correspondance générale*, Vol. IV, p. 92.

a patron, a benefactor, an enlightened authority overriding jealous opposition and cutting through obstacles – for example, by making him director of a revived imperial chapel, as Napoleon I had made Le Sueur, or even, a decade later, ordering his personal fiefdom, the Opéra, to put on *Les Troyens*, as Napoleon I had done for Le Sueur's opera *Ossian, ou Les Bardes*? I don't think we can exaggerate the hold that Le Sueur's stories, told and retold 30 years before, exerted on his young pupil's imagination – the effect of the old man's passionate devotion to the person and the very idea of Napoleon, relived in their conversations at the rue St Anne and in the Tuileries Gardens, on a mind already nurtured on his uncle Félix Marmion's tales of the great days of the Grande Armée.

He discovered soon enough how groundless such hopes were and what a deep-dyed incorrigible philistine the emperor was, at least so far as music was concerned. But in any case I cannot see Berlioz as, in Peter Bloom's phrase, a lifelong admirer of authoritarianism. He may have become one; but, if so, by this stage of his life it was essentially because of artistic imperatives. His art comes first. The creative ego has to take precedence. The score's the thing. 'I live in my score', he writes to the Princess Wittgenstein, during the composition of *Les Troyens*.[2] That seems to me a crucial statement. Attempts, made from time to time and recently become quite fashionable, to formulate a sub-text for the opera – colonialist, imperialist or whatever – founder on that. It was all that counted. The music came first, last, and always.

For the same reasons, I can't see flattery of the emperor as a driving force behind the work, or the original ending – the grandiose vision of imperial Rome - as a deliberate mirror image of France's nascent Second Empire. If it ever had been, if at first he toyed with the idea, it was abandoned decisively, like the prophecy of French dominion in North Africa. *The Trojans* was not that kind of opera. That must have been why he changed it. The fate of Dido, burned into his heart of hearts in boyhood and never forgotten, eclipses the triumphs of all empires, modern and ancient.

[2] *Ibid.*, Vol. V, p. 509.

VI

THE 1850s
AND *LES TROYENS*

Les Troyens and the *Aeneid*

The following essay originated as a talk given in May 1969 to the Royal Musical Association and published, in shortened form, in its journal. It then figured, in full, in my book Responses *(1973). Excerpts from it were included in the Cambridge opera guide on* Les Troyens *(1988, edited by Ian Kemp). What follows is the complete version.*

Tristram Shandy's father, who knew the power of names, would have approved the notion – put forward by I forget which French critic – that, by calling him Hector, Dr Berlioz determined his son's fate: from the first the name marked him out for glory and tragedy, heroic deeds and the bitterness of failure and mutilation. The more one considers Berlioz's life, the more it seems almost mystically inevitable that his crowning work should be an epic on the Trojan war and its aftermath, the wanderings of Aeneas and the myth of the founding of Rome, and the more one comes to see his discovery of Virgil during boyhood and his precocious response to the passion and tenderness of the *Aeneid* as one of the two most important events of his imaginative existence (the other being the discovery of Shakespeare). No less inevitably, such a work was bound to bring defeat and misery on its creator in the cultural climate of Second-Empire Paris. As Gounod justly remarked, Berlioz, like his famous namesake, died beneath the walls of Troy;[1] for the final blow in a lifetime's struggles against a hostile musical environment was the rejection of the work that he knew to be his culminating achievement and artistic justification.

The conviction of its supreme significance in his life pervades the letters that he wrote during the two years of composition. In their mood of exhilaration and their sense of destiny fulfilled, they recall the passage at the end of *The Gathering Storm*, where Churchill describes his emotions on taking power in May 1940: 'I felt […] that all my past life had been but a preparation for this hour and for this trial'.[2] *Les Troyens* is the summing up of Berlioz's existence. It marks the furthest point in the development of his musical style; and in it the characteristics of most of his previous works – the electric energy of the *Symphonie fantastique*, the ceremonial

[1] In his Preface to *Berlioz, Lettres intimes*, Calmann Lévy, Paris, 1882, p. vii.

[2] Winston S. Churchill, *The Second World War*, Vol. 1, *The Gathering Storm*, Cassell, London, 1948, pp. 526–27.

splendours and terrors of the Requiem, the exaltation and sensuous beauty of *Roméo et Juliette,* the massive grandeur of the Te Deum, the sweetness and archaic simplicity of *L'Enfance du Christ,* the refinement of *Les Nuits d'été* – are united.

The determination to write a grand opera on the *Aeneid* crystallised in the early 1850s. In 1854 Berlioz confessed that the idea had been 'tormenting' him for the last three years.[3] His writings around this time are full of allusions, comic and serious, to Virgil. In *Evenings in the Orchestra* (published in 1852) the narrator, asked by his friends to tell them about the Paris Opéra, answers in the ominous words with which Aeneas begins his account of the catastrophe of Troy: *Si tantus amor casus cognoscere nostros.*[4] Later in the same book, modern music torn by conflicting ideologies is likened to Cassandra, 'prophetic virgin fought over by Greeks and Trojans, whose inspired words go unheeded, who lifts her burning eyes to heaven – her eyes alone, for chains bind her hands' (*Aeneid*, II, 405–6). In a letter to Hans von Bülow written in 1854, Berlioz humorously attributes the misfortunes suffered by *Benvenuto Cellini* to the workings of the 'destiny of the ancients', and compares the successive resurrections and collapses of the opera to the wounded Dido 'thrice raising herself upon her elbow, thrice falling back'; then, unable to contain his admiration, he bursts out, 'What a great composer Virgil is! What a melodist, what a harmonist! *He* could have made the deathbed remark *Qualis artifex pereo,* not that humbug Nero, who was gifted with only one bright idea in his life, the night he had all Rome set on fire'.[5] By this time, although he was still fighting against it, the ambition to write a Virgilian opera was fully acknowledged.

It is hard to believe he had not dreamed of it much earlier. *Les Troyens,* planted in boyhood, casts its giant shadow over the years between. The conscious decision to compose it was like the emergence of an underground river to the surface. With hindsight we can see the work pursuing a secret subterranean course during the years when its composer is taken up with other, quite different preoccupations. Even in a jocular context it pops up, reminding us of its future existence – as when, describing his hurried departure from the island of Nisida under threat of a storm, he likens the Neapolitan fisherman in charge of their coracle to Aeneas cutting his vessel's cables and putting out from the port of Carthage on his destined journey to Italy *(Voyage musical,* 1844, later incorporated in the *Memoirs*[6]). Earlier, in 1836, he looks back, with a quizzical eye, on his bouts of musical

3 *Memoirs*, p. 512.

4 'If you are so eager to learn of our misfortunes.'

5 *Correspondance générale*, Vol IV, p. 574.

6 *Memoirs*, pp. 179–80.

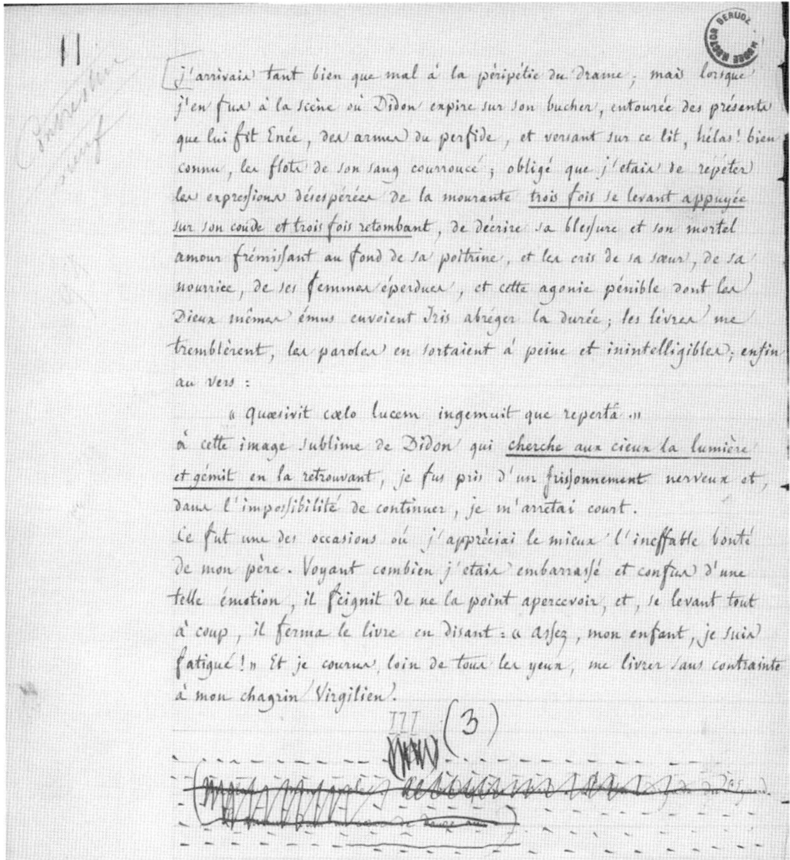

11

J'arrivais tant bien que mal à la péripétie du drame ; mais lorsque j'en fus à la scène où Didon expire sur son bucher, entourée des présents que lui fit Enée, des armes du perfide, et versant sur ce lit, hélas ! bien connu, les flots de son sang courroucé ; obligé que j'étais de répéter les expressions désespérées de la mourante trois fois se levant appuyée sur son coude et trois fois retombant, de décrire sa blessure et son mortel amour frémissant au fond de sa poitrine, et les cris de sa sœur, de sa nourrice, de ses femmes éperdues, et cette agonie pénible dont les Dieux mêmes émus envoient Iris abréger la durée ; les lèvres me tremblèrent, les paroles en sortaient à peine et inintelligibles ; enfin au vers :

« quaesivit coelo lucem ingemuitque reperta »

à cette image sublime de Didon qui cherche aux cieux la lumière et gémit en la retrouvant, je fus pris d'un frissonnement nerveux et, dans l'impossibilité de continuer, je m'arrêtai court.
Ce fut une des occasions où j'appréciai le mieux l'ineffable bonté de mon père. Voyant combien j'étais embarrassé et confus d'une telle émotion, il feignit de ne la point apercevoir, et, se levant tout à coup, il ferma le livre en disant : « Assez, mon enfant, je suis fatigué ! » Et je courus, loin de tous les yeux, me livrer sans contrainte à mon chagrin Virgilien.

III (3)

In his Memoirs *Berlioz describes his distress at the death of Dido.*

improvisation in the countryside near Rome, when under the stimulus of the landscape's Virgilian associations, guitar in hand, he would hymn the great figures of the later books of the *Aeneid,* and yearn for 'those poetic days when the heroes, sons of the gods, walked the earth'.[7]

In 1848 he began his *Memoirs* and wrote the chapters dealing with childhood and youth, including the famous second chapter which describes his discovery of poetry under the influence of Virgil and his profound distress at the death of Dido. The action of reliving such an experience must have helped to develop and define the still-shadowy, half-formed idea of a great Virgilian work that would bring his career full circle. The year 1848 was a watershed in Berlioz's life – the year of the Revolution (which threatened to make his daily existence even more precarious, and disenchanted him still further with Parisian musical life), the year of his father's death and of

[7] *Ibid.*, p. 155.

his return to the scenes of his adolescent awakening, of the first step in the bizarre pilgrimage that led him back to his boyhood infatuation with Estelle Dubœuf: the year when the nostalgia that is such an important aspect of his nature took decisive hold. But the period that immediately followed, though it produced the Te Deum and *La Fuite en Egypte,* the second part of what was to become *L'Enfance du Christ* – music steeped in a sense of the past – was not propitious for a major dramatic work. The lessons of the calamitous failure of *La Damnation de Faust* were too painfully recent; he was still resolved 'not to stake twenty francs on the popularity of my music with the Parisian public'.[8] It was at about this time that in the same mood of defeatism he deliberately suppressed the inspiration for a new symphony that had come to him. *Les Troyens* continued to grow and take shape in his mind. But it needed help from without.

The impulse to commit himself unreservedly to a project of this kind and on this scale came from the changed circumstances of his external life, combined perhaps with an inward and reckless sense that the moment had come and that, whatever the likely consequences (the taste of Second-Empire Paris being what it was), he must seize it before it was too late. If he finally succumbed to the temptation to write *Les Troyens,* one reason was simply that he could afford to. Since the death of his wife Harriet in 1854, he had no longer had the burden of two separate households to support. By the end of the same year *L'Enfance du Christ* had been completed, and performed with a success that seemed to confound his earlier pessimism. The following year, 1855, apparently confirmed the new trend in his fortunes. His activities during that year kept him busy. Tours of Germany, publication of several major works, the Paris Exhibition and the first performance of the Te Deum, left no time for sustained composition. But the project was certainly discussed at Weimar with Liszt's mistress, Princess Wittgenstein, who urged him to undertake it. By this time he must have known that he would have to: he had no choice. His Virgilian passion must be satisfied; the supreme business of his life was upon him. And in 1856, after further encouragement from the Princess, he began. The first line of the libretto was written on 5 May, the anniversary of Napoleon's death ('an epic date, if there ever was one', he remarks in a letter to his uncle Félix Marmion, a veteran of the Grande Armée).[9] Slightly less than two years later, despite illness and the distractions of journalism, the huge, richly wrought work, words and music, was complete.

Such rapidity of creation was the fruit of a lifelong germination. Berlioz himself acknowledged it in a letter to the Princess which is a prime text for our understanding of the subject:

[8] *Ibid.*, p. 452.

[9] *Correspondance générale*, Vol. V, p. 328.

Study (1873) for a portrait of Princess Carolyne zu Sayn-Wittgenstein by Ernest Héber

As for the principal object of the work, the musical rendering of the characters and the expression of their feelings and passions, it was always the easiest part of my task. I have spent my life with that race of demi-gods; I know them so well that I feel as if they must have known me. And this recalls to me a boyhood experience that will show you how fascinated I was from the first by those splendid creatures of the ancient world. It was during the time in my classical education when I was construing, under my father's direction, the marvellous twelfth book of the *Aeneid*; my imagination was possessed by the glory of its characters – Lavinia, Turnus, Aeneas, Mezentius, Lausus, Pallas, Evander, Amata, Latinus, Camilla and the rest. I became like a sleepwalker 'living within my dream's bright kingdom' (to borrow a line from Victor Hugo).

One Sunday I was taken to Vespers. The sad persistent chant of the psalm *In exitu Israel* produced the magnetic effect on me that it still produces today, and plunged me into the most real and vivid daydreams of the past. I recognised my Virgilian heroes, I heard the clash of their arms, I saw Camilla the beautiful Amazon running, I watched Lavinia, flushed with shame, weeping, and poor Turnus, and his father Daunus and his sister Juturna, I heard the great palaces of Laurentium ring with lamentation – and an immense feeling of grief came over me, my chest tightened, I left the church in floods of tears, and cried the rest of the day, unable to contain my epic affliction. No one could ever get me to confess the reason for it, my parents never knew, had no inkling, what sorrows had seized my childish heart that day.

Is that not a strange and marvellous manifestation of the power of genius? A poet dead thousands of years shakes an artless, ignorant boy to the depths of his soul with a tale handed down across the centuries, and scenes whose radiance devouring time is powerless to dim.[10]

Forty years later, his 'Virgilian passion satisfied',[11] Berlioz dedicated *Les Troyens* 'to the divine Virgil', *Divo Virgilio.* It was a repayment of his debt to 'the poet who first found the way to my heart and opened my budding imagination'.[12] A special sense of affinity bound him to Virgil, an affinity only strengthened by the consuming artistic experience of transmuting his poem into music. Near the end of his life he wrote: 'I must be reconciled [...] to not having known Virgil – I should have loved him'.[13] Much earlier, standing on the site of Maecenas' villa at Tivoli, he could imagine he heard 'Virgil's melancholy voice reciting [...] some splendid fragment of the *Georgics*'.[14] (It was a passage from the *Georgics,* invoked to fill out the bloodless rhymes of the official versifier, that had inspired one of his finest student pieces, the epilogue to the competition cantata *La Mort d'Orphée.*) Only Shakespeare occupied a more personal place in his Pantheon. Shakespeare, to Berlioz, was a kind of humanistic God the Father; artistically, he was the most far-reaching influence of all – an influence vitally felt in *Les Troyens* itself, which, in Berlioz's words, is 'Virgil Shakespeareanised', the libretto articulating the poem by methods learned from the history plays: open form and bold juxtaposition of genres, lofty soliloquy and vernacular conversation, private emotion expressed in a framework of public action. But with Virgil it was something as intimate, a companionship, a sense of identification. While composing *Les Troyens,* he felt that Virgil was alive again in him:

The countryside [at Saint-Germain] seems to make my Virgilian passion more intense than ever. I feel as if I knew Virgil, as if he knew how much I love him. [...] Yesterday I finished an aria for Dido which is simply a paraphrase of

10 *Correspondance générale*, Vol. V, pp. 693–94.

11 *Ibid.*, p. 626.

12 *Memoirs*, pp. 8–9.

13 *Ibid.*, p. 570.

14 *Ibid.*, p. 189.

The title page of the first edition (1861) of the vocal score of Les Troyens, *dedicated 'To the divine Virgil'*

> the famous line: *Haud ignara mali miseris succurrere disco* ['My own troubles teach me to help the unfortunate'].[15] When I had sung it through once, I was naive enough to say, out loud: 'That's it, isn't it, dear Master? *Sunt lacrymae rerum?*', just as though Virgil himself had been there.[16]

He was justified in feeling it. Studying the opera and the poem together, we cannot but become increasingly aware of deep correspondences between the two artists. If this high theme was (in every sense) Berlioz's fated goal, it is equally true that one of the many destinies of the poem, 'across the centuries', was to be its musical incarnation in a work that is among the manifestations of the unique hold of Troy and its legends on the Western imagination.

Les Troyens is Virgilian in countless ways. There is the blend of romantic rhetoric and classical restraint, of monumentality and pictorial vividness; the fondness for mixing genres and in particular for using the lyrical to diversify the tragic and at the same time to bring it into sharper focus; the systematic alternation of scenes or passages of violence and calm as a structural rhythm in the composition of the opera; the combination of an aristocratic aloofness with an awareness of the sufferings of ordinary humanity; the sense of fatality, of obscure inimical powers that lie in wait, and of the madness that can strike a people and drive it blindly to its own destruction. (The two men have also in common their fear of the collapse of civilisation as they knew it, and the doubts that assailed them at the end about the survival of their work.) As with the *Aeneid* in Virgil's life, *Les Troyens* grew from seeds planted in youth. As Virgil went back to Homer in order fully to realise himself, so Berlioz turned to Virgil.

The outward structure of the opera, too, shows Berlioz's fidelity to his model (he has shared the criticism sometimes levelled at Virgil that the character and fate of Dido are treated with such power that they dominate the epic and deflect it from its course). *Les Troyens* follows the *Aeneid* in making the tragic death of an individual the last action that the audience sees enacted on the stage. And just as the *Aeneid* is an epic constructed of two personal tragedies (Dido's and Turnus'), so is *Les Troyens*. Even in consisting of two distinct though interlocking halves the opera reflects the shape of the poem, which is divided into the wanderings of Aeneas, including his narrative of the sack of Troy, and the struggle to found a new Troy in Italy. And though the action of the opera does not take the Trojans as far as Italy, the central idea of the founding of Rome runs through it; Italy is the leitmotiv of the drama.

15 A misquotation for *Non ignara*.

16 *Correspondance générale*, V, p. 502.

A mosaic from the third century AD showing Virgil, holding a copy of the Aeneid, *and flanked by the muses Clio and Melpomene. The oldest-known portrait of Virgil, it was found in Hadremetum, an important town in Roman North Africa, now part of the city of Sousse, and is held in the Bardo National Museum in Tunis.*

A study of the libretto in relation to the poem reveals Virgil as its constant guiding spirit. It is not only that much of it is direct translation or paraphrase of the Latin of the books from which the main action is taken – Books I, II and IV: the whole poem is pressed into use. Even the stage direction at the beginning of the opera, 'three shepherds playing the double flute' – represented in the orchestra by oboes – is derived from the *Aeneid*, echoing a passage in Book IX where the Rutulian warrior Normanus taunts Ascanius with 'Go and dance to the double-mouthed pipe on Mount Dindyma, that's all you're good for'. Where Berlioz adds to the poem for dramatic purposes, he nearly always goes to Virgil for his material or his inspiration, working in ideas taken from anywhere and everywhere in the poem. Thus the scene in Act 1, where Hector's widow Andromache and her son Astyanax, dressed in the ritual white of mourning, lay flowers at the altar and receive Priam's blessing, springs from two sources, one in Book II, where Aeneas, climbing up to the palace roof by a secret postern gate during the sack of the city, remembers that through this gate Andromache used to bring her child to see his grandfather Priam, the other in Book III, where Aeneas meets Andromache in the Epiran city of Buthrotum, performing the rites of the dead at an altar dedicated to the ashes of Hector. Virgil, in fact, has inspired both the visual content and the tragic irony of the scene.

The episode in Book V, where the disgruntled Trojan women gaze out to sea and groan at the thought of the endless voyaging that lies before them, is transmuted into the scene in Act 5 for the two sentries who march up and down by the Trojan ships, grumbling at the prospect of leaving Carthage, where they are comfortably billeted, and entrusting themselves to the tedium of the sea and the rough mercies of the storm (a scene whose Shakespearean ethos was so contrary to orthodox dramatic ideas in France that it was usually cut out when the work was performed there). Cassandra, urging Corebus to fly from the wrath to come, is answered with sentiments similar to those of Aeneas' reply to Anchises in the burning house: *Mene efferre pedem, genitor, te posse relicto/sperasti?*[17] Aeneas' words to his son, spoken before he goes off to fight the Numidians, paraphrase the hero's words in Book XII on the eve of the final battle against Turnus and the Rutulians. The invasion by Iarbas and his Numidian hordes, an interpolation made in order to provide a climax for the third act and give dramatic emphasis to Aeneas' arrival in Carthage, is a development of an idea in the *Aeneid* put forward by Dido's sister Anna when she argues that Dido ought to marry Aeneas and share her kingdom with him: Carthage is surrounded by wild tribesmen, among them the Numidians and their chief Iarbas, who is all the more dangerous since Dido humiliatingly rejected his offer of a dynastic marriage.[18]

The process by which Berlioz fashioned his libretto is most clearly illustrated in Acts 1 and 2. The opera follows the main events of the sack of Troy.[19] But new material is added by the development of hints in the

[17] 'Father, did you really expect me to run away and leave you behind?'

[18] A possible influence here is Piccinni's *Didon* (1783), which Berlioz had got to know during his student days (though written in 1783, it remained in the repertoire at the Opéra until 1826). Much of the action of Jean-François Marmontel's libretto is concerned with Iarbas and his unsuccessful wooing. There are also verbal similarities between the two librettos in the later scenes, where Marmontel stays closer to Virgil.

[19] Originally Act 1 included the episode of the Greek spy Sinon. It was later removed by Berlioz, though not until a few years after the completion of the score. The scene, 235 bars long, has survived (mostly in piano-vocal score) and is published for the first time in the New Berlioz Edition, Vol. 2c, pp. 875–86.

poem, and a good deal else has necessarily been subjected to compression or expansion. Thus the one-and-a-half lines in which Virgil tells of the cold fear that creeps over the Trojans at the news of Laocoön's death are built into a full-scale ensemble which shows the city poised at the fatal moment of decision. In Act 2 Aeneas is made to succeed in his desperate attempt to relieve the citadel (in the poem he merely conceives the wild idea of doing so); and he escapes with the royal insignia of Troy. The motive for this change may partly have been tidiness and coherence: Ascanius later presents a rich selection of Trojan relics to Queen Dido (a scene that is a conflation of two separate passages in Book I). But the main reason, as with the finale of Act 3, is one of dramatic emphasis, to clinch the act with a decisive forward-looking event. In this case the action is not shown. We hear of it, from Cassandra, in the course of a scene which does not figure in the *Aeneid* except by implication, in the cries of the wailing women in Priam's palace (*plangoribus aedes/femineis ululant*), in the glimpse of Helen cowering by the entrance to the temple of Vesta, and in the brief description of Cassandra being dragged from Minerva's sanctuary.

The development of Cassandra into the protagonist of Acts 1 and 2 is the biggest single change that Berlioz made. But here, too, he went to Virgil, deriving the character from a few lines in the *Aeneid* (just as Virgil derived Aeneas from a brief sketch in the *Iliad*). Cassandra fills the role taken in Book II by Aeneas, who in the poem recalls Troy's downfall several years after the event. In the opera the tale comes to us through the eyes of the prophetess cursed with second sight. We see the catastrophe twice over: as it gradually forms in her mind (from the vague fears of 'Malheureux roi' to the fierce clarity of her vision in the following scene), and when it comes. This double process has the dramatic effect of heightening the sense of tragedy and doom. The vehemence and certainty of her unheeded prophecies throws the blindness of her fellow countrymen into more merciless relief – that of Corebus in particular; the young warrior is mentioned briefly by Virgil as being 'on fire with desperate love for Cassandra', to whom he is betrothed, and as refusing to listen to her warnings; in the opera, the lyrical development of these hints sharpens the irony of Cassandra's personal tragedy by holding out the possibility of a happiness that will never be fulfilled. The text of Cassandra's scenes inevitably contains few direct Virgilian echoes; the prophecy, to the Trojan women, of the founding of a new Troy in Italy, based on Anchises' words in Book III, is a rare exception. Yet the whole character and her heroic, despairing utterances are in a sense simply a personification of Aeneas' tragic cry '*0 patria o divum domus Ilium et incluta bello/Moenia*

Dardanidum!'[20] at the moment when he describes the entry of the Wooden Horse into Troy while Cassandra vainly prophesies. Cassandra is the first of the two tragic pillars which support the edifice of *Les Troyens;* across her fate, and Dido's, the epic of Roman destiny marches to its fulfilment. Berlioz had no choice but to kill her off in heroic circumstances at the end of his Act 2. The scene is not in Virgil; but its conception does not dishonour him.

In adapting the *Aeneid* to the totally different medium of opera, Berlioz also made some changes in the order of events as recounted by Virgil. The conversation (already referred to) between Anna and her sister Dido, with its tender urgings on one side and its barely suppressed emotion on the other, prompted the very similar duet in Act 3, 'Reine d'un jeune empire'. But whereas in the *Aeneid* the conversation occurs after the Trojans' arrival in Carthage and is very much concerned with them, Berlioz places it just before, as a means of projecting the state of Dido's heart at the moment of Aeneas' intervention in her life – her restlessness, her half-conscious yearning for love, her ripeness to yield. His dramatic judgement is correct. By doing so he is able partly to compensate for the fact that he has had to unfold the events of the plot in straightforward chronological sequence and therefore to start the Carthaginian part of his story cold. Virgil, on the other hand, by recounting the sack of Troy and its aftermath in flashback, through the mouth of Aeneas, with the fascinated Dido devouring his words, can accumulate tension over two or three thousand lines of verse and so prepare gradually for the explosion of passion which comes at the beginning of Book IV. Yet such is music's power of suggestion, and so vibrant the impression of a woman of peculiar radiance and energy that Dido makes on us in those early scenes of Act 3, that the disadvantage is partly overcome.

The opera also redistributes and telescopes the sequence of events between Aeneas' decision to leave Dido and her death – a sequence that in the poem occupies four or five hundred lines, or well over half of Book IV. A chart of the various sources, line by line, of Dido's soliloquies in Act 5 – 'Dieux immortels, il part', 'Je vais mourir', 'Adieu, fière cité' and the final invocation from the pyre – would show the text as woven of threads freely drawn from many different points in the last 250 lines of the book. The result is clear, logical and compelling, and does no violence to Virgil's psychology.

The third and final category of change concerns the new emphasis that Berlioz gives to certain events or ideas in the poem, his intention normally being to make explicit and theatrically telling what in the poem can afford to take its time and grow by degrees in the reader's mind. To take one of the

[20] 'Oh my country! Oh Ilium, home of gods, fortress of the descendants of Dardanus, renowned in war!'

Philippe Chaperon's set designs for the 1863 production of 'Les Troyens à Carthage' in the Théâtre de la Ville: Dido's throne-room....

most obvious instances: the theme of *fatum,* destiny, which is fundamental to the *Aeneid,* has had necessarily to be much more simply and directly set forth (a process in which the traditional importance of the chorus in French opera plays a vital part). This need applies also to the specifically Italian direction of the destiny of the Trojan survivors; not being native and instantly intelligible to Berlioz's audience as it was to Virgil's, it had to be made plain. In the *Aeneid* there is some doubt about the true identity of the mysterious object of Aeneas' wanderings. The ghost of his wife Creusa tells him, on Troy's last night, that his goal is Hesperia, or Italy. After that, uncertainty descends and it is only subsequently, several false scents later, that Italy is defined as the destined country of Troy reborn. An opera composer cannot afford such inconsistency (if indeed it is not deliberate and subtle poetic realism on Virgil's part) and, as we see, Berlioz is at pains to state the theme clearly and re-emphasise it at regular intervals, so that we shall be in no danger of not recognising it as the majestic impulse of the epic, before which everything must ultimately give way. Contrary to Virgil he makes Hector's ghost specify the object of Aeneas' wanderings. Later, he ends his picture of the sack of Troy with the Trojan women's defiant repeated cry of 'Italie'. Similarly, when the Trojans land in Carthage their spokesman, Panthus, is more emphatic about the god-fated and only temporarily frustrated aim of their voyage than is Ilioneus in the equivalent passage in the *Aeneid*. In the opera, at the peak of the lovers' ecstasy, Mercury appears in the moonlit garden and, striking Aeneas' shield, intones three times 'Italie'. Mercury's larger role in the *Aeneid*, as explicit messenger of the gods, is not sacrificed but is filled, with the directness appropriate to drama, by the spirits of the illustrious Trojan dead, who rise up in turn to whet Aeneas' almost blunted purpose. Again, Berlioz sees to it that Aeneas is fully awake when Hector's ghost delivers his message; in the *Aeneid* the apparition comes to him in a dream, through the veil of sleep. All this makes for a necessary gain in clarity and conciseness, inevitably at a slight cost in poetic suggestiveness and truth to life.

In the same way, Aeneas' heroic role and his consciousness of his destiny as a hero have to be spelled out; the point must be established quickly – it cannot be left to the cumulative effect of epic verse. In *Les Troyens* the last words uttered by Hector's ghost before the vision fades tell of the death Aeneas will meet in Italy; the final line, 'Où la mort des héros t'attend', is not in Virgil. Later, Panthus, in his speech to Dido in Act 3, refers to it as an accepted fact. Aeneas himself, in his monologue in Act 5, says that he could not sway the outraged Dido even by reminding her of 'la triomphale mort par les destins promise' – the end awaiting him on Ausonian fields that is to crown his glory; and almost his last words to her, when she confronts him by the ships, speak of the death to which he is going.

It is sometimes objected that Virgil, concerned with the overriding theme of the epic of Rome, failed to make Aeneas sufficiently sympathetic. This is usually said by people who have fallen in love with his glorious Dido and who consequently regard any man capable of abandoning her as an unspeakable cad. Such indignant charges do more credit to the critics' chivalry than to their careful reading of the poem. Berlioz might appear to belong to their number, from the references in his *Memoirs* to the 'hypocrite', the 'perfidious' Aeneas.[21] But the composer of *Les Troyens* understood the depth of passion hinted at in Virgil's resonant understatements and justly praised silences; and he was quite right, on Virgilian as well as on operatic terms, to make Aeneas' love for Dido wholehearted and avowed and to dramatise the resultant conflict in the hero's mind. The famous duet in Dido's garden is not only obligatory for the composer of grand opera but

21 *Memoirs*, pp. 155 and 9.

Dido's gardens...

also artistically essential to the drama as a whole. The words, adapted from the scene between Lorenzo and Jessica in the moonlit garden at Belmont in the fifth act of *The Merchant of Venice* (whose allusions to Dido and Troilus may have suggested the idea), represent the one major textual innovation that is not Virgilian in origin. Its setting gave Berlioz the opportunity to lavish all his lyrical and orchestral art on a poignant evocation of the warmth and vast splendours of the starlit Mediterranean night. In the *Aeneid* the season of the Trojans' sojourn in Carthage is winter. In *Les Troyens* it is, unequivocally, summertime; the great feasts with their bards and heroic tales and jewel-encrusted goblets take place out of doors under the open sky. Berlioz has also transferred the setting of the hunt and storm from open mountainous country to virgin forest, and has peopled his scene with the woodland satyrs, bathing naiads and glinting streams and waterfalls which help to make it the neoclassical masterpiece it is – a movement that has been compared to some great Claude or Poussin, and that combines attributes of both painters, Poussin's grandeur and universality and dynamic form, Claude's numinous clarity and sense of the golden, fatal moment.

An example of all three types of change – the interpolating of new material derived from Virgil himself, the re-ordering of the sequence of Virgil's narrative, and the making explicit what in the poem is implied – is the Quintet in Act 4, 'Tout conspire à vaincre mes remords'. Here we see Berlioz's dramatic imagination at work on the *Aeneid*, distilling from it a scene that, as such, is not found in the poem but that is necessary to the scheme of a dramatic work based on it – in this case, the moment of Dido's change of heart, from lingering attachment to the memory of her dead husband, Sychaeus, to unreserved commitment to her new love. In the first place, the picture of Dido feasting Aeneas and begging him to repeat the tale of Troy's woes is moved on in time so as to follow the acknowledgement and consummation of their mutual passion; in Virgil it belongs to the preceding stage of their relationship (a part of the poem not included in the opera, except by implication). Then, Virgil's divine intervention (Venus and Juno in league) is discarded. In the *Aeneid* Cupid, in the likeness of Ascanius, fans the flame and 'gradually dispels from Dido's mind all thought of Sychaeus', while she, unaware of his true identity, 'fondles him and holds him close'. Berlioz retains the visual setting but replaces the supernatural with a dramatic idea developed from a reference, in Book III, to Hector's widow Andromache having married Pyrrhus. In the opera it is the discovery that Andromache is now the wife of the man whose father slew Hector that acts as a catalyst on Dido, severing the threads that bound her to her old life (and at the same time setting up in the spectator's mind a sudden resonance with the almost forgotten moment, three acts ago, when the desolate figure in white walked silently through rejoicing crowds by the walls of Troy). Finally, an echo of Cupid substituted for Ascanius survives in the stage direction, which shows the boy 'leaning on his bow, like a statue of Eros', and in the smiling comment of the royal entourage that he resembles Cupid as he slips Sychaeus' ring from the heedless Dido's finger. This last action, taken from Guérin's painting *Enée racontant à Didon les malheurs de Troie*, is one of the very rare non-Virgilian ideas in the libretto.

Most of this examination has shown only the skill with which Berlioz reshaped the *Aeneid* into a fresh mould – a mould for the music that was waiting to pour out of him. It is the music that makes him a true descendant of the poet he loved. 'As for the principal object of the work, the musical rendering of the characters and the expression of their feelings and passions, it was always the easiest part of my task.'[22] But not only the characters' passions, one wants to exclaim, but the Virgilian ambience itself, the whole environment of the epic, has been absorbed by the composer

[22] *Correspondance générale*, Vol. V, p. 693.

...and Dido's apartment

into his inmost being and given back reborn in his own language. A re-reading of the *Aeneid* with the music of *Les Troyens* in one's mind is a startling revelation of artistic correspondence. Feature after feature of the poem reappears in the score. Certain elements may be isolated. On the level of individual images, we find details such as the violin harmonics which in Act 5 suggest the electric effect of the apparitions on Aeneas, matching Virgil's graphic description of the hero rigid with fear, his hair standing on end (*arrectaeque horrore comae*). At the beginning of the opera the combination of shrill, rapidly pulsing woodwind chords, a texture devoid of bass, the absence of strings, and the curiously jaunty melodic material, at once trivial and possessed, conveying a sense of ritual madness, help to establish from the outset the idea of *fatum,* of a people rushing to ruin. An ominous rhythmic figure,[23] first heard as part of the orchestral texture in the opening scenes and stated explicitly in the Octet 'Châtiment effroyable' which follows the death of Laocoön, recurs as a kind of reminder of fatality at moments where the action of destiny is most manifest or the tragic irony most intense: the apparition of Hector's ghost in Act 2 and of the spirits in

[23] Borrowed, perhaps, from Max's *scena* in *Der Freischütz* (itself derived from *Così fan tutte,* Act 1 finale?), via Herod's aria in *L'Enfance du Christ.*

Énée racontant à Didon les malheurs de la ville de Troie,
by Pierre-Narcisse Guérin (1774–1833)

Act 5, the tumultuous exit of Aeneas as king-elect at the head of combined Trojan and Carthaginian forces at the end of Act 3, the climax of the Royal Hunt, Dido's farewell – 'ma carrière est finie' – and the solemnities that precede her immolation. But for the most part the correspondence needs no analysing. It leaps out at us. The Octet, once heard, seems the inevitable setting of the dread words *Tum vero tremefacta novus per pectora cunctis/ Insinuat pavor* – a whole people's blood running cold, panic spreading as an inkling of their doom 'works its way' into the back of their minds. How much of Cassandra's music directly echoes, in its piercing sadness, Aeneas' cry of anguish over the horror, the pity of it – *O patria o divum domus Ilium*!

Or what could be more Virgilian than the scene in Act 2 where Hector 'recalled to life by the will of the gods',[24] appears before Aeneas and lays upon him his sacred mission, then sinks back to nothingness, his task accomplished – the apparition materialising to the sound of stopped horns groping from note to note, accompanied by *pizzicato* strings, then uttering its message on the successive notes of a falling chromatic scale above a dim fabric of divided cellos and basses, with occasional interventions from the

[24] *Correspondance générale*, Vol. V, p. 619.

trombones, at once nightmarish and majestic; Aeneas staring and motionless, except for a sudden lurch in the orchestra, like a missed heartbeat at the words – the most terrible in the *Aeneid* – *hostis habet muros*: 'the enemy's within our walls'. In the orchestral prelude to the same act the very sound and feel of Virgil's lines are reproduced in the rhythm, texture, colour and harmonic movement of the music – *clarescunt sonitus armorumque ingruit horror*:[25] war and rumours of war, the hideous confusion of battle.

Again, how true to Virgil are the music's insights into the effect of war and the great national enterprises born of war on the ordinary human being – poignant in the case of the Palinurus-like figure of the young sailor Hylas, eaten with nostalgia for the homeland he will never see again, humorous in the case of the two grumbling sentries who would like to stay in Carthage and have done with the whole senseless idea of Italy, tragic in the case of Andromache, whose grief, though it pales before the cataclysm to come, remains the ultimate comment on the misery of war. How deeply Berlioz has absorbed the example of the humanity of the *Aeneid* – those little touches that mark Virgil out among ancient writers, like the picture of the women and children waiting in a long line beside the piled-up loot in the courtyard of Priam's blazing palace. Such sudden shifts of viewpoint give a new dimension to the epic, in Berlioz's music as in Virgil's verse.

Dramatic effects of sharply contrasted colours, textures and rhythms are a common feature of the two works. The moment in Book I when the magic cloak shrouding Aeneas is stripped away to reveal him in all his glory is paralleled by the sudden change that occurs in the music when Aeneas throws off his sailor's cloak and steps forward in shining armour. Acts 1 and 2 of *Les Troyens* mirror Book II of the *Aeneid* in their alternation of light and dark, their evocation of flaring light amid surrounding blackness – the doomed splendour of the processional entry of the Horse through the torchlit darkness, the smoky glare in the opening music of the temple scene, shot through with gleams of martial trumpets. The feeling we experience in the opera when the harsh, possessed sound of Berlioz's Troy gives way to the lyrical and sensuous sound of his Carthage (flute and clarinet in octaves, piccolo trills, softer string sonorities), is just such as we experience in Book I of the poem when Virgil cuts from the clangorous description of the frescoes depicting the Trojan War in the temple of Juno to the luminous vision of Dido making her way through the throng, attended by young courtiers.

The criticism sometimes heard of Act 3, that the lengthy ceremonies in which Carthage celebrates its first seven years are a distraction from the

[25] 'The noise grew clearer and the roar of battle swelled.'

main business of the drama and a concession to Meyerbeerian grand opera, is not only misguided but also in effect a criticism of a too close fidelity to Virgil, for the plan of the opening scenes of the act is inspired by the intensely vital and brilliant first impression of Carthage that we receive in Book I. Berlioz's purpose in following Virgil, however, is a dramatic one, being both to provide an interval of repose after the concentrated fury of Act 2 and to emphasise the rising star of the new city so that the tragedy of its fall may be felt to the full. To this end, and perhaps also borrowing an idea from Book VII (the picture of Latium as a kingdom of Saturn, still enjoying the blessings of the golden age), he has made his Carthage something of a matriarchal Garden of Eden, absorbed in the beneficent work of building and cultivation, fearful of the enemies surrounding it, yet defenceless until saved by the hero who is destined to be its destroyer (the limping, melancholy strains of the 'Trojan March' in the minor mode telling not only of Trojan sufferings endured but of Carthaginian disasters to come). But in his development of this gentle pastoral state the composer is, as always, the disciple of the poet – especially the poet of the *Georgics,* who is heard through the mouth of the bard Iopas. In the *Aeneid* Iopas sings of the elements and the movement of the stars, but in *Les Troyens* of the shepherd and the farm-worker and the fruits of the well-tilled earth.

In this fourth act, set in Dido's gardens at night within sound of the sleeping sea, Berlioz matches Virgil's mastery of verbal magic in music beneath whose beauties lies the same sense of the pathos of life and the brevity of human happiness. Yet the fifth and final act is in some ways the most profoundly Virgilian of all, both in its heroic sweep and in its classicism: on the one hand the wide arches of extended melody in Aeneas' *scena* – the huge stride of the vocal line above the surge and stress of the orchestra, the powerful swing of the rhythmic movement between agitation and serene exaltation; on the other hand the simplicity of Dido's grief. In response to the tragic dénouement of Book IV Berlioz strips his art to an extraordinary economy of gesture. One thinks of the gentle swell of the sea cradling Hylas to a death-like sleep; the two-note semitone figure that suggests Aeneas rocking to and fro in the anguish of his indecision; the brief shudder in the strings, like a premonition of a life escaping into air (*in ventos vita recessit*), that abruptly breaks the trancelike calm of Dido's first words from the pyre; the bareness of the vocal line a moment earlier as Dido, speaking as if in a dream, gives the order for the last rites to begin – a passage whose broken phrases and slow chromatic descent through an octave recall the music of Hector's prophecy that was to be the cause of her grief. (Virgil would have recognised here a poetic device of his own, whereby resonances are set up between pairs of similar or ironically contrasted incidents located in different parts of the epic.)

While at work on Dido's recitative 'Je vais mourir', Berlioz wrote of his conviction that the music he was composing had a 'heartrending truthfulness'.[26] What is even more remarkable is the sense of a calm beyond suffering that he achieves in the aria, 'Adieu, fière cite' (*urbem praeclaram statui*), which succeeds the torment of the recitative. Nothing in music is more expressive of utter finality than the concluding bars of the aria – the voice dying away, a last flicker of agony (the flattened sixth on the cor anglais), then a mysterious peace, with a rustle of *pianissimo* strings and, on trombones, the quiet beat of the rhythmic motif of destiny, stilled in a cadence of such purity and simplicity that the silence that follows is almost palpable: there is nothing more to be said. Dido accepts her fate.

In the tragic climate of the ancients, redemption is neither demanded nor expected. Alone among Romantic dramatists, Berlioz was able to re-create it because it was his own imaginative world. It had become his natural element. The memory of the emotional shock that Dido's death had been to him, forty years before, and of all that had followed in his adolescent imaginative life, remained with him, fresh and undiminished. To it was added long experience as a composer of dramatic music and a capacity for feeling, for pain, for regret, that life had sharpened to a fine point. He had been waiting for this. His musical style, with its long flexible melodic line and its use of timbre and rhythm as subtly varied means of poetic expression, was ideally suited to the task. So was his temperament. The call of Virgil's heroic world was irresistible. A concept of human existence as it might once have been in some possible dream of a golden age took root in boyhood and grew till it possessed his mind. The Virgilian vision – a vision of grandeur without illusions, of destruction lying in wait outside and within human beings, and life lived subject to the will of implacable fate but, while it lasts, lived fully and ungrudgingly even in the shadow of doom – answered his deepest longings. It is this heroic temper that is exemplified in the ardent, exalted music to which Aeneas, drunk with his mission, already part of history, apostrophises Dido in sublime farewell, before turning to embrace his fate and the knowledge of his death – the mood expressed in Hecuba's proud prophecy in the final scene of Euripides' *The Trojan Women:*

> We sacrificed in vain. Yet if the god had not seized this city and trampled it beneath the earth, we should have disappeared without trace: we would not have given a theme for music and the songs of men to come.

[26] *Correspondance générale*, Vol. V, p. 539.

Les Troyens, *Act 4: 'the brevity of human happiness' – Berlioz's sketch of the beginning of the love duet, 'Nuit d'ivresse'*

l'im-mortel a — mour
ez à l'a- mour
Par
u-ne telle nuit
Le front ceint de Cy
votre mère Vé-
-nus sui- vit le bel an- chi-se
aux bois-
Celli
C. anglais
R 96-100

As with Aeneas, there could be for Berlioz no turning back once he had begun. But like Aeneas he knew the outcome. 'What agonies I am storing up for myself by becoming so passionate about this work!'[27] Its likely fate had been one of his strongest reasons against being drawn into composing it. The indifference of the French musical establishment was nonetheless a crippling blow. He had schooled himself in a proud stoicism, but his resolve broke down. 'I know I promised you I would resign myself to whatever might happen', he wrote to the Princess, 'and here I am, failing completely to keep my promise. I feel a terrible bitterness of spirit.'[28] The bitterness was not relieved, even by the momentary pleasure of seeing the Carthage acts staged and rewarded with a modest success, despite poor performances and numerous cuts. It is the sense of defeat that *Les Troyens* engendered that, more than anything else, even his son's death and his own painful and incurable disease, accounts for the gloom of Berlioz's last years. At least he was spared the tragi-comedy of the subsequent fortunes of the work in France: non-publication, non-performance, performance in versions mutilated almost beyond recognition, critical dismissal, lawsuits, and the rest of the scene he knew so well. To quote the late Claude Rostand, in an act of public recantation of dramatic completeness:

> Relying purely and simply on received opinion, with a wilful blindness that has persisted, to be precise, for one hundred and seven years, the French have always refused to recognise and accept that *Les Troyens* is a masterpiece, the summit of its author's genius. [...] According to the official view that we were taught, *Les Troyens* was an operatic 'monster', fruit of the old age of an artist in decline, its occasional beauties set in an ocean of feebleness, and in any case humanly impossible to perform and to listen to in one evening. This judgement, this summary condemnation, repeated ad nauseam – till recently even by the most enthusiastic Berliozians – was actually founded not simply on incomprehension but on a large measure of pure ignorance. [...] We have here one of the most astonishing musical scandals of all time.[29]

In the seventh book of the *Aeneid* an indignant Juno looks down on Italy and exclaims in wonder that her hated Trojans have survived so many cruel vicissitudes: half-drowned, blasted with fire, their might scattered, they are still unbowed, and life lies ahead of them. She might have been prophesying the destiny of Berlioz's opera. Despite all that has and has not happened to it, it has survived. Its worth is at last coming to be recognised. In a real sense life lies ahead of it; for, with the publication of the full score (a hundred years after the composer's death), the work may be said for the first time

[27] *Ibid.*, p. 622.

[28] *Ibid.*, p. 706.

[29] *Le Figaro littéraire*, 21–27 September 1970, Rostand's review of the Philips recording of *Les Troyens*.

fully to exist. It can at last be recognised for what it is, the vindication of its creator's faith in his lifelong vision, and proof of the magic power of a great poet working, two thousand years later, on the mind of a kindred genius.

The 1957 *Trojans*

The following note was written to accompany the 2009 Testament recording of the performance of The Trojans *broadcast from the Royal Opera House, Covent Garden, on 20 June 1957.*

From our privileged position, half a century on, there may be a temptation to feel superior and to undervalue the 1957 Covent Garden *Trojans* and what it achieved. We hear these distant sounds with ears familiar with the work from performances – conducted by the likes of Colin Davis, Alexander Gibson, Michael Gielen, Roger Norrington, John Eliot Gardiner, James Levine and others – more assured, more accurate and fuller than was possible for those worthy pioneers, tackling it for the first time.

They had to make do with inaccurate performing material hired from the Paris firm of Choudens, disfigured by mistakes (including a clangorous clarinet wrong note – E natural instead of E flat – in Act 3, just after Aeneas' 'Come, child, embrace thy father'). The New Berlioz Edition full score published in 1969 was still no more than a twinkle in the eye of its future editor, Hugh Macdonald. So, in defiance of dramatic sense, the 'Royal Hunt and Storm' was played after the garden scene instead of before, simply because that was where it figured in the Choudens material, having been omitted from the 1864 vocal score and then, later, put back but in the wrong place.

We may well raise our eyebrows at the cuts that were made in 1957: a sizable chunk of the Act 3 ceremonies and most of the scene in Dido's room in Act 5, as well as six bars removed from the processional entry of the Wooden Horse. And some of Rafael Kubelík's tempos may strike us as strangely excessive, sometimes hectically fast – the chorus' C major *Allegro vivace* in the opening scene, the Wrestlers' Dance – and at other times dragging – Corebus' cavatina, Dido's 'Farewell, Carthage of mine'.

But all that would be to miss the point. What Kubelík and his performers achieved in 1957 and in the revivals of 1958 and 1960 (the latter conducted by John Pritchard and John Matheson) was absolutely crucial. It changed everything. At a stroke the whole picture was transformed. The Covent Garden production vindicated Berlioz's original conception of a five-act opera Shakespeareanly embracing Troy and Carthage in a single span, and

Rafael Kubelík

his belief in the greatness of the work, and it did so in the face of a century of hostile, dismissive opinion.

Until then it had been common to regard *The Trojans* as a deeply flawed, only intermittently inspired work, ripe for dismemberment, and to treat it – when it was performed at all – as an opera consisting of two distinct parts. That was what Berlioz himself had been compelled by *force majeure* to do in 1863, when the Théâtre-Lyrique found the five-act score beyond its resources. It was not how he had planned and composed it; but his original conception had vanished almost without trace. Most subsequent performances presented it in two halves, as *La Prise de Troie* and *Les Troyens à Carthage*. To give the whole five-act opera uncut, everyone agreed, was physically impossible; scholarly works of reference stated authoritatively that it would last anything up to eight hours. The occasional single-evening production (as in Paris in 1921) habitually reduced it by a third or even a half of its proper length.

That is one reason that 1957 was a landmark. Though not complete, it was far fuller than anything heard before. It demonstrated that *The Trojans*, as first conceived by the composer, as a single, integral grand opera, was a viable undertaking, that it worked in the theatre and, by implication, that the music that had been cut – about fifteen minutes – would, when restored, still not make the opera impractically long.

A scene from the Covent Garden production of The Trojans, Act 3: *Dido (Blanche Thebom) addresses her people*

No less vitally, it revealed a different Berlioz, and a composer who, far from being in terminal decline when he wrote it, was at the height of his powers. The impact was summed up by the musicologist Robert Collet, writing in William Glock's journal *The Score* soon after the first night:

> What seems immediately to have struck many people [...] was that this music was utterly different from the idea of Berlioz handed out to us by writers on music, and not only the stupid ones. Until very recently it was customary to hear quite knowledgeable musicians and amateurs talk of Berlioz as a wayward Byronic eccentric, with an interest in the orchestra that was unusual for his day, and an undoubted gift for musical *grotesquerie*, but otherwise a striking figure in musical history rather than a truly great composer. No one who has listened to *The Trojans* with even partial understanding can accept such a superficial and one-sided view any longer.[1]

True, Berlioz had long had devotees in this country, going back to the enthusiasm aroused by his visits to London as composer-conductor in the 1840s and 1850s. After his death his music was championed here by William Ganz, August Manns, Charles Hallé, Felix Mottl, Hans Richter – all of them Germans – and later by Hamilton Harty and Thomas Beecham,

[1] *The Score*, No. 20 (June 1957), p. 66.

among others. But, important though their efforts were in keeping the flame alive, there was something missing. The supreme work, the central key to his artistic being, remained hidden – pontificated about quite freely, but virtually unknown. I remember reading somewhere that Edward Dent (whose English translation of the libretto was used at Covent Garden in 1957 and for the two revivals) had likened it – in the days when the work was still largely unknown – to some buried city of the ancient world, waiting to be discovered.

For some time, almost imperceptibly, the tide had begun to turn. In 1935, in Glasgow, Erik Chisholm conducted a semi-amateur production of the opera, in its two-part form, which moved Donald Tovey – not a writer notably sympathetic to Berlioz – to describe *Les Troyens* as 'one of the most gigantic and convincing masterpieces of music-drama'.[2] It was on Beecham's Covent Garden prospectus for 1939–40, though the season was cancelled because of the outbreak of war. But in 1947 Beecham conducted a concert performance (Troy and Carthage on successive evenings) that, relayed on the Third Programme, caused a stir. Three years later Oxford University Opera Club staged a single-evening production, with cuts, conducted by Jack Westrup.

In other words, the 1957 performances did not come unheralded – they were, rather, the culmination of a gradual process. Yet their effect, experienced in one of the world's leading opera houses, was none the less revelatory. No one was really prepared for it. There was astonishment, exhilaration. People paced the streets afterwards, as had happened years before at the first impact of *Tristan und Isolde*. A typical reaction was that of the musician and critic Tom Heinitz, who had been brought up from childhood in the Austro-German tradition and who had gone to the first night in a spirit of mild curiosity and to hear the new tenor everyone was talking about, Jon Vickers. Five hours later he emerged from the theatre a different being, ready and eager to rethink his whole attitude to the composer.

That was symptomatic. The shock of the revelation created a new awareness of Berlioz's music, setting in motion the modern Berlioz revival, a revival that originated in Britain but had wide repercussions, in America, Germany (where *Les Troyens* is now almost a repertory work), and even among the composer's sceptical French fellow citizens. In this country, in particular, it inspired young musicians, critics and administrators to campaign for full recognition of Berlioz – a movement that resulted in the publication of the full score of the opera in the year of the centenary of his

[2] Donald F. Tovey, *Essays in Musical Analysis*, Oxford University Press, Oxford, Vol. IV, p. 89.

death, 1969, and which continued to gather strength in succeeding years. 1957 was the source, the beginning.

The recording cannot, of course, give any idea of John Gielgud's production. No doubt we would find it very old-fashioned if we could revisit it (we might also be relieved that it foisted no tendentious, self-indulgent concept on the work – that would be for later); but at the time it made its contribution to the excitement generated at Covent Garden on those heady nights in the summer of 1957. The applause at the end of each act is tumultuous. What Gielgud thought of it all is not clear. His celebrated *cri du cœur* – 'Will someone please stop that dreadful music!' – was uttered during a rehearsal of *Don Giovanni*, not (as is sometimes said) of *Les Troyens*. But the story of that other remark of his, made as the ballet boys were struggling to form a pyramid of bodies on the four chords that link the Act 1 March and Hymn to the Wrestlers' Dance, is authentic: 'The poor darlings can't possibly manage it. Mr Kubelík, can't we have another chord?' (Kubelík, in the pit, merely shook his head.) Yet if the genitally well-endowed but otherwise feeble cardboard horse was a disappointment, I can still see in my mind's eye the thrilling climax of Act 3, as the combined Trojan and Carthaginian hordes streamed into the wings in perfect accord with the orchestra and its pulsating *diminuendo*.

Whatever may be their shortcomings, the sounds on these CDs radiate conviction. You feel that everyone involved in it – conductor, soloists, orchestra, chorus, not forgetting the managing director David Webster, whose pet project it was – that everyone believes in the work and is passionate about it. And if we are inclined to criticise this or that detail, we should recall that unlike today's performers, who profit from 50 years of *Trojans* performances, these ones were starting more or less from scratch, getting to know it for the first time. There were practically no models, no tradition, to learn from.

The cast, in the main, give a sterling account of themselves. Amy Shuard's Cassandra is fiery and incisive, delivering Dent's text with exemplary clarity. Perhaps Jess Walters is a rather coarse Corebus (not helped by the slow speed of his 'Beloved heart, cease thy sad repining') and David Kelly an unremarkable Narbal; and perhaps Blanche Thebom sometimes makes heavy weather of Act 3, though in the last two acts her voice gains clearer focus and her singing becomes worthy of Dido's glorious music. Lauris Elms is an outstanding, warmly sympathetic Anna, Richard Verreau's Iopas has rarely if ever been bettered, and the symbolically named Dermot Troy is as good as one remembers in Hylas' haunting song (whose 'Rock me gently, then, on thy bosom leaning, mighty mother sea', for 'Berce mollement sur ton sein sublime, o puissante mer', is one of Dent's happiest

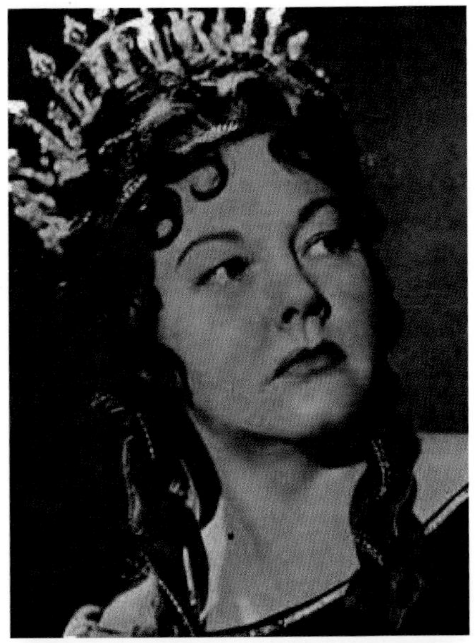

Three of the main singers in the Covent Garden Trojans *in 1957: left, Amy Shuard as Cassandra, Blanche Thebom as Dido and Jon Vickers as Aeneas*

inventions). And Jon Vickers' Aeneas – the voice fresher than when he recorded the role twelve years later, grand though that is – fully lives up to its exalted reputation.

Above all, there is the passion and conviction that Kubelík brings to the score. If, as I say, we may find some of his tempos either too quick or, occasionally, too slow, others seem to me perfectly judged. The whole of

Act 4, whose beauties can tempt a conductor to linger, moves with a lovely natural flow, with no loss of lyrical intensity. So does Andromache's mime scene (the clarinet solo expressively played by Olive Wright, who died last year). All who love *Les Troyens* owe Rafael Kubelík a lasting debt. He laid the foundation and made possible all that has followed.

The Historical Significance of 1957

This piece and the next are taken from the Berlioz Society Bulletin *No. 180 (August 2009).*

The release of the live Testament recording of the Kubelík *Trojans* recalls those heady days in the late 1950s when the revelation of the work changed lives and, even more vitally, transformed the fortunes of Berlioz not only here but worldwide.

Looking back half a century later, one can now concede that those who took up the composer's cause here in the 1960s were – perhaps still are – too insular in their thinking. Charles Munch was performing Berlioz regularly in America some time before those Covent Garden performances and, before him, Pierre Monteux, one of the finest Berlioz conductors, who had learnt the music as principal violist in Colonne's orchestra in Paris, had been active in both Boston and San Francisco.

Even the assumption that Berlioz came into his own in this country only after 1957 has been challenged by the musicologist Leanne Langley, in a brilliantly researched survey, 'Agency and Change: Berlioz in Britain, 1870–1920', published in the *Journal of the Royal Musical Association* in 2007 (I quote from the abstract, but the whole paper should be read):

> Far from being always unjustly neglected until the late twentieth century, as a recent view would have it, Berlioz's music enjoyed dedicated attention and considerable admiration a century earlier. His orchestral works, in particular, were taken up by a range of skilful players and conductors in Britain from the 1870s [...] [a] remarkable reception [...] largely ignored in the historiography of Berlioz's reputation.

She adds that performances of his music 'impressed ordinary listeners much more than many experienced ones'.[1]

That last point seems to me a key one. 'Ordinary listeners' may have responded to the music, and conductors like Hallé and Richter and, later, Harty and Beecham, championed it, and writers like Turner and Wotton and, more equivocally, Tovey and Newman, treated it seriously. But, for 'experienced listeners', and for academics and commentators generally,

[1] 'Agency and Change: Berlioz in Britain, 1870–1920', *Journal of the Royal Musical Association*, Vol. 132, No. 2, 2007, pp. 306–48.

Berlioz remained a figure on the margins of musical history (when he was not actually an embarrassing apology for a composer). That was the official view. Read Wotton's reference to the 'eminent musician' (unfortunately not identified) 'declaring that the opening chords of Faust's Invocation to Nature' – of all pieces! – 'remind him of an adventurous harmony pupil let loose for the first time amongst the joys of diminished triads and augmented sixths'.[2] Read the epigraphs to the chapters of Julian Rushton's *The Musical Language of Berlioz*, of which Arnold Bax's outburst at the *Benvenuto Cellini* Overture is only the most extreme example:

> for a few moments I try to concentrate upon the neuroticism, at once strident and flimsy, of Berlioz's music. [...] Heavens! The bluster of noise the orchestra is making, and all about nothing, with no particular bass to be heard! It is like the gambolling of some monstrous, footloose creature – a drunken walrus, perhaps.[3]

1957 changed that. It was a local, London event but it had international resonance. It completed an unfinished picture by revealing a crucial work, Berlioz's crowning achievement, the key to the whole pattern but largely hidden till then. It started a process of reclamation whereby those who wrote and pontificated about music began to see him differently. From then on he would, increasingly, be treated with respect. Though the old *bêtises* might still be trotted out from time to time, opinion about him was never the same.

[2] Tom S. Wotton, *Hector Berlioz*, Oxford University Press, London, 1935, p. 67.

[3] *Farewell, My Youth*, Longman, Green and Co., London, 1943, p. 84; republished in Lewis Foreman (ed.), *Farewell, My Youth and other Writings by Arnold Bax*, Scolar Press, Aldxershot, 1992, p. 74

Les Troyens: the Philips Recording

As with the previous piece, this one is taken from the Berlioz Society Bulletin *No. 180 (August 2009).*

Listening, the other day, to tapes of the Chelsea Opera Group Berlioz performances from the 1960s I was struck by Josephine Veasey's fiery singing in the finale of Act 2. Has there ever been a finer Cassandra? It reminded me of the discussions that preceded the Philips Covent Garden-based recording of the opera in 1969 – discussions in which the possibility of engaging, for some of the roles, singers different from those in the Covent Garden cast was seriously on the cards. By that time Veasey had, so far as we were concerned, made the role of Dido her own, which ruled her out for Cassandra. I don't remember what made us decide to replace Anja Silja, who was the Covent Garden Cassandra, but I do recall that we barely considered Régine Crespin, who many would say was the obvious choice. In the dark days of the mid-1960s when the record companies wouldn't hear of recording the work – though Colin Davis' concert performances with the LSO and the Philharmonia had been winning golden opinions – the news of Crespin's shredded version of the opera, reduced to two LPs (as reported by Hugh Macdonald, who attended the sessions), filled us with such despair and rage that she became a hate figure. Perhaps we were wrong, and if she had taken part in our recording she would have sung the whole role and would not have insisted on the suppression of the sustained C (flute and oboe) near the end of her Act 1 aria (as Hugh was scandalised to hear her do at the EMI sessions). Before settling on Berit Lindholm, we tried Tatiana Troyanos, whose voice, as well as her name, recommended her. We were too late, of course, for Maria Callas, even if she would ever have agreed to sing it – for her *Les Troyens* was *la barbe* ('a bore'). But what a Cassandra she could have been! As I wrote of her recording of Marguerite's 'D'amour l'ardente flamme':

> The very first phrase establishes an atmosphere of utter forlornness, and she shapes the performance from that point, with supreme intelligence and musicianship and with an understanding of Berliozian phrasing and dramatic style that make it a truly tragic oversight that she never sang Cassandra or

> Dido. There are few Marguerites who would not wither in the flame of her genius.

Roger Soyer and Pierre Thau were brought in (for Narbal, and for the Trojan soldier and the voice of Mercury). We also thought of replacing Peter Glossop, as Corebus, with John Shirley-Quirk (Friar Laurence on the Davis/Philips *Roméo et Juliette*), but had to back down when Glossop said he would not sing the part at Covent Garden if he didn't also do the recording. The other attempt that failed was to have Iopas sung by Léopold Simoneau, by then retired and on the staff of the Montreal Conservatoire but apparently still in excellent voice. In the event we kept with the Covent Garden Iopas, Ian Partridge, whose beautiful singing more than made up for any disappointment.

Les Troyens in Hamburg

The review reproduced here first appeared in The Sunday Times *of 17 October 1982 and then in the* Berlioz Society Bulletin *No. 115 (Autumn/Winter 1982).*

This is being a vintage autumn for Berlioz's music, following a summer when his most exigent admirers could hardly complain that it was being neglected. The publication of Hugh Macdonald's long-awaited 'Master Musicians' study[1] coincides with a profusion of performances. What with the Proms, South Bank Summer Music, and now the activities of the LSO – including their Berlioz/Tippett series in November – it will have been possible to hear most of the major works in London in the course of a few months.

In addition, the Norwich Festival (director Norman del Mar) has been giving its own Berlioz/Tippett concerts this past week, beginning last weekend, in the cathedral, with an account of the Requiem notable for its efficient generalship and for exceptionally fine brass playing, and ending tonight with the Te Deum at precisely the same moment that Abbado and the LSO perform the work in London. No need to go farther afield to satisfy one's appetite.

True: but news that the Hamburg Staatsoper were putting on a production, by Götz Friedrich, of *Les Troyens*, a work not seen on the stage here since the mid-1970s, was too good to resist. And the further information that the young Sylvain Cambreling, a born Berlioz conductor, was in charge of the performance, and that it would begin at 5p.m., augured well for the seriousness of the enterprise.

Alas! *Horrendum dictu!* The inhabitants of Troy were not more deceived. I had forgotten the German-speaking world's passion for cutting – a form of cultural hegemonism, one might think, except that it is inflicted on their own masterpieces (witness the Viennese treatment of *Così fan tutte* and the appalling Paumgartner 'performing edition' of *Idomeneo*[2]). *Les Troyens* began at 5p.m. but it finished at 9p.m., in a lacerated and barely recognisable condition, minus 1,200 bars of music – as though it had not

[1] Hugh Macdonald, *Berlioz*, J. M. Dent, London, 1982; 3rd edn., Oxford University Press, Oxford and London, 2000.

[2] Paumgartner's edition rearranged the score and cut it brutally.

been demonstrated a quarter of a century ago at Covent Garden that the work could be accommodated almost uncut within a single evening, and as though its duration were not literally on record as being no longer than *Siegfried* and shorter than *Götterdämmerung*.

Less than a third of the cuts were of the relatively clean kind, involving the removal of complete numbers or verses. The rest slashed the music anywhere and everywhere, mowing it down regardless of shape, dramatic coherence or, even, syntax. Twenty-two numbers were given in mutilated form. Cambreling can scarcely be blamed for the butchery, having arrived on the scene (as replacement for the indisposed Dohnányi) too late to stop it; he should rather be praised for his courage under fire.

What impression the score made on someone who didn't know it I cannot imagine. To someone who knows it well it was a continual exasperation – you could never tell what was going to happen next. Fifty bars disappeared from the Love Duet, as many from the duet for Dido and Anna, a dozen from the wonderful 'Va, ma soeur, l'implorer', ten from Dido's speech on the pyre – the passage where she prophesies the coming of Hannibal.

I suppose, in retrospect, that it required no second sight to predict that Hannibal would fall victim to Friedrich's deep aversion to the paranormal, of which he has given ample evidence in his Wagner productions. There are also signs of politically motivated manipulation. Dido (who is portrayed as a splendidly democratic monarch in Act 3) is deprived of her imperious 'Je suis reine et j'ordonne'. But, for the most part, the production is Friedrich at his most unthinking, and most crudely illustrative. Cassandra comes into the temple of Vesta carrying the blood-bolter'd corpse of Corebus, thus making an absurdity of the chorus' subsequent question as to what has become of him. In Dido's monologue – one of the most private scenes in all opera – 'ma tendre sœur' is interpreted as a cue for Anna actually to appear on stage. The widowed Andromache flings herself about like a Bacchante, in defiance of the classical restraint of the music.

The staging is constantly creating stumbling-blocks that it then proceeds to fall over. Ekkehard's wooden horse is a Trojan Horse with a vengeance, remaining toweringly on stage during Act 2, to the confusion of the action; Aeneas (Guy Chauvet), so far from being asleep on his couch when Hector's ghost first appears, encounters his dead friend while taking a late-night stroll, during which he entirely fails to notice anything odd about the horse – though its doors are now wide open. 'The Royal Hunt and Storm' is staged, with consummate crassness, as a kind of colonialist war of extermination; of Dido, Aeneas and their coupling to the tumult of the elements, there is no trace. Here, as in all the remaining scenes, the action is crippled by the continued, and inexplicable, presence of the steep wooden amphitheatre used for the popular celebrations in Act 3.

I almost forgot to mention that the opera is generally well sung and in quite passable French, that Karen Armstrong is a vital Cassandra in whose clairvoyance we really believe, Hanna Schwarz a glamorous and touching Dido, Marjana Lipovšek a fine Anna and Robert Gambill an elegant Iopas, that the orchestra and chorus have learnt their parts pretty thoroughly, and that Cambreling conducts lovingly and stylishly, if at times – understandably – with a certain caution. But all this good work is set at naught, for want of a little thought, a little respect. The whole experience took me back to the bad old days – to Paris at its worst, as in the production at the Opéra in the early 1960s, which, awful though it was, did not – if I remember rightly – cut the work more savagely.

Amid the hopeless clutter of the final scene, an unidentified body is removed on a stretcher. Someone suggested that it must be the composer's.

In Defence of the Theatricality of *Les Troyens*

The following article was written as a retort to Hugh Macdonald's 'Les Troyens *Revisited: An Imperfect Masterpiece', a critique prompted by the Covent Garden production of June/July 2012. Both articles appeared in the* Berlioz Society Bulletin *No. 189 (December 2012).*

It's not often I have the temerity to disagree publicly with Hugh Macdonald. But I am emboldened to do so not, I hope, simply because an attack on any aspect of the work we both love is unthinkable but because his arguments seem to me to lack their usual coherence and cogency.

What I am putting forward has nothing to do with the Covent Garden production, about which he is, naturally, entitled to think the worst. But, to my mind, he has allowed his general, all too understandable discontent with all productions of *Les Troyens* to persuade him that the work itself has serious dramaturgical imperfections and, even, might benefit from some judicious cutting. So disillusioned has he become – the latest staging serving as the last straw – that he actually cites with evident approval the *Spectator* review, written by a critic who is at best a very fair-weather Berliozian. 'The work', Hugh Macdonald writes, 'is not sacrosanct, never to be touched or – God forbid – cut. Michael Tanner in *The Spectator* has blamed the "shibboleth" of never cutting a note as "the only reason for the rare performances of this noble work"'; this same Michael Tanner, who, a few sentences earlier, assures us that 'such a mixture of beauty and sublimity and lengthy stretches of intolerable tedium is not to be found anywhere else in opera'. Did Macdonald's eye happen to miss these scathing words about a work which, in the opening sentence of his article, he places 'among the great operas of history'?

To go back to his title, 'an imperfect masterpiece': what great opera – given the strange and unhelpful conditions in which so many of them came to birth – is perfect, or even near-perfect? Very few, I submit: maybe *Dido and Aeneas*, the first version of *Figaro*, *Die Zauberflöte*, the 1814 *Fidelio* (an eccentric view, I agree), *Die Meistersinger*, *Falstaff*, *La bohème*. For that matter (as he says), how many of the greatest operas exist in definitive form? Certainly not *Idomeneo*, nor *Don Giovanni*.

Mentioning *Don Giovanni* reminds me that in more than 50 years of writing about it, I have seen hardly one production that did reasonable justice to what E. T. A. Hoffmann called 'the opera of all operas'. That surely means not that *Don Giovanni* lacks theatricality but that its highly individual character, that unique fusion of dark high drama and comic-strip farce, is extremely difficult to realise on stage. When I asked a friend what he thought of the idea that *Les Troyens* lacks theatricality, he looked at me in blank astonishment. Opera is the art of the possible. Each great opera is theatrical in its own way. I agree with Hugh that concert performances are a boon and not a mere second best. Many of my most completely satisfying experiences of opera, and not only of *Les Troyens*, have been in the concert hall – this not because the opera in question lacks theatricality but because the work was freed from the follies of overweening, concept-obsessed directors and could be itself.

Let me try to examine his detailed charges – charges that lead him to the startling conclusion that 'Berlioz was not truly an opera composer'. '*Les Troyens* was his first serious opera', he says (whereas *Tristan* was Wagner's ninth): 'how could he expect to get it right?' Well, *Das Rheingold* was Wagner's first music-drama; but does anyone suggest he didn't get it right? The *Eroica* was Beethoven's first venture in the vastly expanded scale that inaugurated his so-called second period; yet are there any moments in it where he can be shown to have faltered? Berlioz was highly intelligent; and for more than 30 years he had been attending performances at the Paris Opéra, listening, observing, noting what other composers did. Is it really plausible to represent him, in conceiving and composing *Les Troyens*, as 'forced' against his will to accept the traditional trappings, the ballets, the big choral scenes, with the result that his Virgilian vision necessarily didn't 'fit' the template he was obliged to impose it on?

I don't believe it. To quote Colin Davis, 'this was *his* music, he was making no concessions to anyone'.[1] To me, the exceptionally large role Berlioz gives the chorus shows him embracing the tradition not reluctantly but with enthusiasm, and then bending it to his very different, untraditional purposes. I admit that were I in charge of a production I might omit ballet No. 33b – a splendid piece but arguably too long for the context and too 'Parisian' for a *fête* by the sea shore and under the 'beau ciel d'Afrique'. But none of this music, to my ears, reveals anything but the composer's delight in it.

Nor in the processions of Act 3. Here I must take issue with the claim that 'Berlioz himself permitted a number of cuts in the last three acts' and, a few lines later, that he 'allowed a large cut in the opening scene of Act III', albeit 'in an ironic frame of mind'. You can say that again. Ironic? I would

[1] *Gramophone*, Vol. 79, No. 493, August 2001, p. 9; *cf.* also p. 354, below.

say savagely sarcastic. The three processions (which last all of four minutes) should be cut, Berlioz says, if the stage is too small or the director devoid of ideas. That is pragmatic. But that he sanctioned the cutting of the 'Royal Hunt and Storm' and of the Anna–Narbal duet! Well, read the withering terms in which Berlioz writes of them, cited in the New Berlioz Edition, Vol. 2c, p. 836, the appendix entitled – ironically? – 'Authorised cuts and reductions'. Authorised? I think not.

Berlioz, Hugh Macdonald goes on, 'certainly foresaw conditions in which whole numbers or scenes could be cut'. He did – he knew the theatre world and its laziness, evasions and compromises. But that didn't mean he sanctioned them – or that he had doubts about the theatrical validity and effectiveness of those scenes. Hugh cites many cases of what he calls indecisiveness on Berlioz's part, and attributes them to his lack of experience. But what more natural than that a composer creating a work on this huge scale should have hesitations, second thoughts? That is normal. Mozart, at one moment, was going to interrupt the overture to *Figaro* with a slow middle section (as in the overture to *Die Entführung aus dem Serail*), then thought better of it. We don't blame Verdi (though Ernest Newman did) for thinking of putting in a battle in the middle of *Otello*, because, in the end, he didn't. Nor should we blame Berlioz for thinking of putting a prophecy of the French conquests in North Africa on the lips of the dying Dido. He saw that it was foolish and dropped it. That kind of thing happens during the composition of an opera. The final decision is what counts.

Agreed, the end of Act 4 went through different stages. Why not? That it took him a long time to work out does not have to be seen as a sign of inexperience. Personally, I find the solution that Berlioz finally arrived at wholly convincing. Mercury is not always sprightly or associated with good news (Sappho, in one of the surviving fragments of her poems, describes him as the god who guides the ghosts of the dead to the underworld). The dark conclusion of the act is the logical outcome of those undercurrents of fate and tragedy that run through the Love Duet and the Septet (the rising chromatic figure that echoes the music of Aeneas' words to his son – that duty comes before happiness – and the ominous semitone shift in the Trojan March). The shock of that abrupt descent to E minor is magnificent and right.

Nor, I submit, were the changes to the opening of Act 5 indications of fumbling. What more natural than that he should at first decide to begin the act with Aeneas' monologue, then realise that the sudden shift in perspective from high romance and affairs of state to the experience of ordinary people caught in the tide of epic events would give the drama an extra dimension?

As to the added Dido-Aeneas duet, 'Errante sur tes pas', we will have to agree to disagree. To me Dido's 'Va, ma sœur, l'implorer', following her stinging curse at the end of the duet, is psychologically convincing – the desperately human confusion, the violent mood-swing, of one emotionally on the rack. By now Dido has taken over the opera. Aeneas' 'conviction', his 'sense of epic purpose', is eclipsed by her agony, her nobility, in Berlioz's mind and in the spectator's. That, surely, is why he abandoned the original ending celebrating the triumph of Rome (to quote Colin Davis again, 'we feel Berlioz has seen through all that'[2]) and wrote a new one – an ending that worries some people but that seems to me right.

Yes, as Hugh Macdonald says, Berlioz's imagination 'saw' his concert works as drama. But this was different. This wasn't a dramatic concert work put into the wrong medium. He knew what he was doing when he composed what the American musicologist Donald J. Grout has called 'the unique opera in which the epic has been successfully dramatised'.[3] He knew the medium it was for: a theatre that, like Wagner, he recognised was a mirage. But I shall continue to hope that one day I shall see his vision realised in the opera house.

[2] *Ibid.*, p. 10; *cf.* also p. 357, below.

[3] Donald J. Grout, *A Short History of Opera*, Vol. 1, Columbia University Press, New York, 1947, p. 320.

Les Troyens and Colin Davis

This is a fuller version of an article that appeared in Gramophone, *Vol. 79, No. 493, August 2001.*

The live recording by the LSO of *Les Troyens,* issued this month, marks a new epoch in the fortunes of a great but long-ignored masterpiece of dramatic music, the neglect of which the French critic Claude Rostand called 'one of the most astonishing musical scandals of all time'.[1]

But all that is a long time ago. Berlioz's prediction – that if he could only live to 140, his musical life would 'end by becoming delightful'[2] – has been fulfilled. Various factors coincided to make it so. With the advent of the long-playing record his music began to be widely diffused: he ceased to be more pontificated about than actually heard; his works could at last become familiar. The opening-up of the classical repertoire – for so long dominated by the Austro-German symphonic tradition – has meant that they no longer seem freakish, abnormal. And today more conductors than ever before are interested in performing them.

It's hard now to recall the dismissive comments that used to be routinely made about Berlioz, and the atmosphere of the barricades in which his partisans fought to put things right. We in Britain were conscious that we were embarking on a crusade. We might not be able to do anything about the past – about the wrongs he had suffered in his native France during his lifetime – but we would do our damnedest to make up for it and help spread the word. The watershed was the 1957 Covent Garden production of *The Trojans* under Rafael Kubelík. Everything flowed from that. It set in train a wholesale revaluation of Berlioz and his place in musical history, of which we are still seeing the consequences.

For Colin Davis above all, the new *Trojans* recording – taken from the third of three concert performances given to packed audiences at the Barbican last December – crowns a campaign carried out over nearly half a century. He was one of those for whom discovering Berlioz, in the 1950s, was a defining moment in their lives. Captivated by *The Flight into Egypt*, in which he played under Roger Désormière at the Bryanston Summer School in 1951, he began to explore his music, first with the BBC Scottish,

[1] *Le Figaro littéraire,* 21–27 September 1970.

[2] *Memoirs*, p. 546.

then with Chelsea Opera Group, the orchestra of which he had been one of the founders in 1950, when he was a 22-year-old clarinettist who had been disqualified from taking the conductors' course at the Royal College of Music because he didn't play the piano. Concert performances of *The Trojans* with the LSO and the Philharmonia followed. Then, in 1969, after conducting the work at Covent Garden, he recorded it as part of the Philips Berlioz cycle.

Thirty years later he is still championing him. The Barbican *Trojans* was the culmination of the LSO 'Berlioz Odyssey', the thirteen-month cycle of concerts planned by Davis and the general manager of the orchestra, Clive Gillinson.

When I ask Davis what he feels about completing something he had begun nearly 40 years ago, he pounces on my question:

> I didn't begin it – we all began it. I sound like Stravinsky – 'I was the vessel' – but it was a concerted effort on the part of a great number of people. It fell to me to have a hand in it. That's what really pleases. It's not 'I did this' and 'I did that' but *we* did it. We all needed one another. If it hadn't been for Hugh Macdonald, who edited the first published full score, I wouldn't have had a score of *The Trojans* at all. You meanwhile were writing about Berlioz, and working at Philips, and Richard Macnutt began his great collection of Berlioz manuscripts and letters, and then there was Jacques Barzun across the Atlantic, who'd written that wonderful book. And beyond all that it goes back to Kubelík, and then back further to Beecham, Harty and all the people who championed Berlioz one way or another. This thing found us at the pinnacle of the endeavour and we were able to push it through. I hope they are all as happy as I am that Berlioz is now a composer who's accepted as part of the great tradition.

He agrees, though, that the Barbican performances and the recording taken from them had something special.

> I do believe there's a big advantage in live recording. The tension in the recording studio is not the same. There is tension, but it very seldom approaches the exhilaration of performing before a public in a concert hall where nobody can stop to correct anything and you can't go and listen to what you've just done and come back and try to do better: it's now or never, and you squander all you have on the task before you. I think that must produce better results.

He speaks of the 'amazing freedom' he experienced because of it.

> I felt: I really love this piece, and I'm beginning to know something about it, and I shall never be able to conduct better than I am now, so let's let it all loose

> and see what happens. And what happened was that all the people singing got incredibly excited, the orchestra was, too, and did everything an orchestra can to show off its prowess, and the general excitement of dealing with this masterpiece took over. Those intricate rhythms, those finales that go at such a pace – they're very difficult. To get them right and get them to go like that shows the virtuosity of everyone involved.

I mention the equally extraordinary prowess of the amateur LSO Chorus. 'They got caught up in it, too,' Davis agrees. 'After all, he's a very great composer. It's just like the horse in the Bible that "smelleth the battle afar off and says Ha, ha among the trumpets". As soon as people hear this music their blood begins to circulate – even in England.'

He is particularly pleased with how well Cassandra's prediction of the sack of Troy and Dido's outburst of rage in the fifth act went – both very hard to bring off. With Cassandra, 'it's the joining of text with music: each thing she sings has its own tempo. At the same time you have got to make it a continuous crescendo of intensity'. Of the Cassandra, Petra Lang, Davis adds:

> What a great girl. She learnt it all in a few weeks. She came and sang us an aria from the *Damnation,* and sang it very nicely. And when I asked her whether she'd do Cassandra, her eyes popped out of her head. Her intensity and identification with the character were fantastic. The final scene – Cassandra and the Trojan women – is very difficult to do because it's in the middle of the voice and you can't put much pressure on it in that range. It has mostly to be done through the language. She did an amazingly good job. But it was the same with Michelle DeYoung. She was asked to do Cassandra but she obviously wanted to sing Dido, and she was beside herself with excitement. One has to have people like that for Berlioz. You can't have journeymen.

For Davis, returning to *Les Troyens* after a number of years had been a fresh revelation.

> I think what really struck me was Berlioz's idealism: his music-making was entirely untouched by his dismal experience as a composer in Paris at that time, the prejudice and lack of understanding. It had no effect on him, his integrity was untouched; he was writing his greatest piece and he knew it. This was *his* music and he was making no concessions to anyone. He preserved his inner life in a way that I can only say was equal to Beethoven and Mozart. What a failure Beethoven's life was, outwardly, at the time of the last quartets, yet inwardly…! I think that's why we must continue to admire these people. No pop singer will ever match the suffering they lived through.

We discuss various aspects of the work: for example, the immediacy – today, after the convulsions of the twentieth century – of this ancient tale of the destruction of cities, the migrations of people, the sacrifice of individual lives on the altars of ideology ('it doesn't seem to me at all like something antiquated and remote. The only work I can compare it with is *Idomeneo*, where the people and their emotions are taken seriously, and you feel the power of the composer in making this old tale real: it's the same with Berlioz and *The Trojans*'); the pervasive influence of Shakespeare ('I've been reading nothing but Shakespeare for the last month, I'm besotted'); whether there is one ballet too many in Act 4; and whether – as is sometimes objected – the Carthaginian celebrations in Act 3 go on too long:

> I'm not really by nature a critic – I'm an enthusiast (as you once told me critics ought to be). But, no, I don't think they go on too long at all. Without that sense, after Troy, of expansiveness, of a peaceful future, the disaster that comes wouldn't be half as great. You have to have that, and Berlioz knew it – he was a clever man. And I love Dido's public speeches – the behaviour of the orchestra is so apt, it exactly supports every sentence she says, and does it so beautifully. Only Mozart equals that. Extraordinary how they were both able to enter into psyches so distant from where they were. Mozart and Berlioz are very close – not in orchestral sound or design, but in their depiction of suffering, of tenderness, of all the emotions humans have. When Mozart writes, it's not just notes, he is saying something profound and you have to listen. If you don't understand, it's your fault. I think it's the same with Berlioz. You have to get way down under the skin of the man.

What of other passages, such as the sentries' scene in Act 5?

> We tried to mirror the low-life, Shakespearean character of their duet by putting in portamentos [slides], as people sing or whistle in the streets, in complete contrast to the high-flown aristocratic style of Aeneas and the chiefs – to bring it down to street level. The goings-on of those bigwigs are really of no interest to these poor people who have to obey them.

Then there's Dido's 'Je vais mourir', that 'magnificent piece': the masterly use of the bass clarinet ('it sounds like a serpent – she's turned into Cleopatra'), Berlioz's 'ability to find the crowning cadential phrase for his recitatives, his wonderful sense of arrival'; and the heartbreaking simplicity and finality of her aria of farewell and the way, at the end, 'it's as if her heart has almost stopped, as if the music were bleeding to death.'

He speaks of the important part played by Nature in the work – the juxtaposition of Nature and the doings of human beings.

> It occurred to me the other night, as I watched the sun go down in the countryside, and all the sensational goings-on, especially at this time of year, that the most wonderful thing that we know in this universe is the earth we live on. That's how it used to be. The American Indians lived with the seasons and the creatures, and everything was meaningful. We've completely lost touch with that. And Berlioz reminds us over and over again that this amazing process is going on and it doesn't care about us at all. I love to be reminded of that in *The Trojans*. And let it be in F major, the subdominant of C, because Nature is always connected to the subdominant.
>
> What of the ostensible hero who links the entire opera – Aeneas?
>
> The problem with Aeneas is, who is he? Is it his destiny – is that who he is? Does he find himself, like Shakespeare's tragic heroes – for instance, Leontes at the end of *The Winter's Tale?* Is it his ego that triumphs at the end or his real self? When he sings, in his F major aria, how can I possibly leave her – one of the most beautiful, deeply touching melodies Berlioz ever wrote – is this the real man? Or is he the other, who shouts 'cut the cables, let's be off, to find a glorious death'? If his real self lies with Dido, then he betrays it. Dido is absolutely true to herself. She is a woman and she loves – that's how it has to be. She doesn't lie. But he does.

We agree that the end of the opera answers the question. Aeneas goes off to Italy in the blaze of the Trojan March –

> though, if he'd stayed, it might have spared us the Roman Empire – which might not have been such a bad thing: though they were excellent engineers and plumbers, they were pretty horrible, weren't they? But suddenly the March is sliced in half by that *fortissimo* seventh for the chorus – an amazing effect. Berlioz had his side that responded to *la gloire,* but at the end we feel he's seen through all that. Dido's grief and her death are so overwhelming – they take us apart – that we don't care. For this march, for this trashy empire, we've had to go through Dido's appalling suffering! I think that's what Berlioz is saying. The notion that you're making history is bullshit. You're not, you're just dying for somebody's idea. It casts a deeply ironic light on Aeneas's whole decision. We don't feel it as a triumph.

Does this in any way invalidate the work? 'On the contrary – no: it's enormously effective. For me, it enhances it.'

And what of the future? Has Davis done his work for Berlioz? In 2003, the bicentenary of the composer's birth, will he – as he has threatened – not conduct any Berlioz and 'leave it to the younger men'? Happily he won't. He hopes to perform both *Romeo* and *Faust* in London preparatory to an American tour.

Colin Davis, in a portrait by June Mendoza

> Clive Gillinson plans to take the LSO and me to New York to do the *Fantastique, Harold, Romeo* and *Faust,* and I've also agreed with the New York Phil that we will do *Beatrice and Benedict.* The Met is staging *The Trojans* and *Benvenuto,* so the exposure of Berlioz in New York will be considerable, and Mr Bernard Holland [anti-Berliozian critic on *The New York Times*] will have a ball.

So we haven't heard the last of Davis' Berlioz. But better still would be to reassemble orchestra, chorus and cast – Lang, DeYoung, Ben Heppner ('he has the *perfect* voice for Aeneas') and the rest – for a grand celebratory *Trojans* in 2003. Listening to this electrifying recording, it's simply unthinkable that Colin Davis has conducted it for the last time.

Unthinkable, maybe, but he had. The performance lives on in the LSO Live recording.

Munch or Davis?

This essay first appeared in the Berlioz Society Bulletin *No. 186 (August 2011).*

The old conflict among Berliozians between the Classic and the Romantic lives on, however much one might have supposed that the work of Colin Davis and others had given it its quietus and brought the quondam wild man of music into the fold. I know which side I am on. But Alastair Aberdare reports that recently he met the conductor Paul McCreesh, who informed him that he found Davis' Berlioz 'boring'.[1]

This complaint has been heard before, from Berliozians brought up on the interpretations of Charles Munch. Both in France and in Boston, Munch forged an image of Berlioz, which he established in many music-lovers' minds, as a dazzling and spectacular but flawed genius, guilty (Munch said) of incorrect harmony, as seen in his 'faulty basses' ('fausses basses'), but cherishable for his music's evocative power and brilliance of colour. ('Faulty basses' have long been a cliché of French criticism. I remember Hugues Cuénod complaining of them when he came to London to record the innkeeper in the Philips *Benvenuto Cellini*, though after the Prom performance of the work[2] he admitted that the piece was rather effective in spite of them.)

The Berlioz that Colin Davis has promoted, beginning in the 1960s with his concerts and recordings with the London Symphony Orchestra and his annual concert performances with the Chelsea Opera Group (1961–65), is radically different. The American musicologist Michael Steinberg, in his review of Davis' recording of the overtures with the Dresden Staatskapelle, recalled his

> first experience of hearing Davis conduct Berlioz, more than forty years ago, and thinking, 'this is it'. Here was a musician who taught us two novel ideas:

[1] In an interview with Alastair Aberdare (reproduced in the *Berlioz Society Bulletin* No. 191, September 2013), Paul McCreesh said: 'We come from completely different schools, but I respect profoundly his [Colin Davis'] Berlioz and his legendary recordings, which will always remain absolute benchmark recordings. But as conductors we're not made to emulate each other's work. […] The problem is that everybody likes to create tension between conductors; but what's the point?'

[2] On 24 July 1972; the BBC Symphony Orchestra and Royal Opera Chorus were conducted by Colin Davis; Cellini was sung by Nicolai Gedda.

> that Berlioz's performance directions, almost Mahlerian in quantity and detail, were worth paying attention to, and that Berlioz, even as he was an amazing innovator, was at heart a classicist, the son of Beethoven and the grandson of Gluck. Without resorting to exaggeration and vulgarity, [Davis] has always given us Berlioz's special mix of nobility and fire.[3]

Much earlier, on becoming music critic of *The Boston Globe*, Steinberg caused an uproar by describing a Munch reading of the *Fantastique* as 'abominable'. A similar view was expressed in an article by David St George in the *New Boston Review* (Fall issue, 1976), 'Colin Davis and Berlioz' (reproduced in the *Berlioz Society Bulletin* No. 183). St George said that 'the basic ingredients in the Munch formula' with Berlioz were

> considerable freedom of tempo, with an almost obligatory accelerando toward the end of all fast movements, intense commitment to the purported programmatic content of the orchestral works, accentuation of the fantastic and grotesque elements, and brilliant orchestral sonorities capped by strident, hysterically squawking woodwinds and the blowsiest trumpeting west of the Paris Opéra.

He went on to claim that Munch completely misunderstood Berlioz's radically 'anti-structural' approach to harmony (which looked forward to Debussy and Messiaen, 'with whom harmony is often a specifically colouristic entity, without significance in determining the linear design of the music').

> Munch's great conceptual error in interpreting the works of Berlioz was in not recognising the new principles which underlie Berlioz's basses and thus in conducting the works 'from the ground up', so to speak, and in directing the music vigorously toward apparent points of tonal arrival and quirky harmonic patches which are actually of only local significance, accentuating them both by dynamic and by tempo.

Davis' performances, on the other hand, in emphasising 'the functional role of melody' and in recognising 'the merely local importance of some of Berlioz's more surprising harmonic procedures', were an affirmation that Berlioz's musical qualities have 'no need of either exaggerated emotionalism or of largely *ex post facto* statements of programmatic intent'. 'The genius of Davis's approach to Berlioz is in being able to see him within [the classical] tradition' and, 'while not sacrificing any of its colour or fantasy', in 'finding a way to perform the music "straighter" than before' – the 'very characteristic',

[3] Michael Steinberg, sleeve note for the RCA/Dresden Staatskapelle recording of the overtures (currently released on RCA Red Seal 82876 65839 2).

St George said – classicism – 'which to previous generations would have seemed to disqualify him as an interpreter of Berlioz'.

No doubt some of Berlioz's admirers miss the 'abnormal', outsider figure who dominated the Munch era (until the advent of Davis, Munch's recordings, for many people, *were* Berlioz); but we can live with that. Radical disagreements about the interpretation of a composer's works are a sign that that composer has arrived.

EPILOGUE

Two Hundred Years On

I end with the text of a talk I gave at the Athenaeum in London on the occasion of the dinner held by the Royal Philharmonic Society on 6 November 2003 in celebration of the impending bicentenary of Berlioz's birth.

In November 1847 Berlioz wrote from 76 Harley Street to a friend in Paris, giving an account of his doings in London, where he had just taken up the post of music director of Jullien's Grand English Opera at Drury Lane Theatre. The actor Macready, he said, had held a dinner in his honour. And a French friend had secured him temporary membership of his club – though, Berlioz added, 'God knows what entertainment there is to be had in an English club!'[1]

The club, as it happens, was the Athenaeum. So it is nicely appropriate that the Royal Philharmonic Society should have organised and hosted this splendid dinner here. We may assume, from the minutes, that Berlioz, whatever his misgivings, did attend at least once, because, the following February, he was re-invited, 'for the usual period of two months', by Lord Mahon, his previous proposer being Mr Henry Hallam, father of Tennyson's friend. On that earlier occasion the minutes noted that Monsieur Berlioz was 'a gentleman of high character and an eminent writer on the *Journal des débats*, distinguished also for his musical knowledge'.

In due course London, if not the members of the Athenaeum, discovered that Berlioz was more than an eminent writer on the *Journal des débats*. The five visits he made between 1847 and 1855 established a tradition that has lasted to this day, and which explains why we are here tonight celebrating the bicentenary of his birth. He might well have settled in London, but for the skulduggery of a certain Dr Henry Wylde, a conductor chiefly remarkable for what one observer described as his 'spasmodic gyrations' and 'tremulous stick',[2] but who was a more skilful operator behind the scenes than Berlioz was. As it was, he left behind him a host of admirers and well-wishers – musicians, writers, publishers, administrators – convinced of his genius.

In his last years Berlioz was haunted by the fear that when he was gone there would be nobody who knew how to perform his music – music so

[1] *Correspondance générale*, Vol. III, p. 477.

[2] *Illustrated London News*, 12 June 1852.

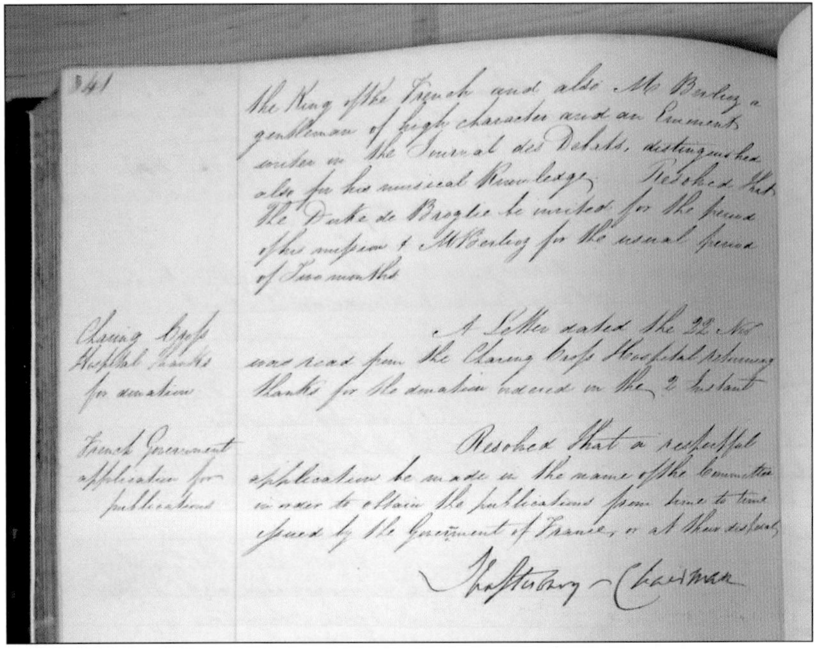

341

the King of the French and also Mr Berlioz a gentleman of high character and an eminent writer in the Journal des Debats, distinguished also for his musical knowledge. Resolved that the Duke de Broglie be invited for the period of his mission & Mr Berlioz for the usual period of Two months

Charing Cross Hospital thanks for donation

A Letter dated the 22 Nov was read from the Charing Cross Hospital returning thanks for the donation ordered on the 2 instant

French Government application for publications

Resolved that a respectful application be made in the name of the Committee in order to obtain the publications from time to time issued by the Government of France, or at their disposal

Shaftesbury — Chairman

Lord Shaftesbury (the sixth earl, father of the social reformer) signs the minutes recording Berlioz's presence in the Athenaeum

difficult to play and to get right. That was never a danger in Germany, where a succession of conductors from Bülow to Mahler and Weingartner understood and championed it. In London, too, for the first few decades after his death, his champions were all Germans (this was the period when English musical life was comprehensively teutonised). There was August Manns, who founded the Crystal Palace concerts; Wilhelm, later William, Ganz, who as a young violinist and percussionist played in Berlioz's London orchestras; Hans Richter, a frequent visitor in the 1880s and '90s, who despised French music – when asked why he never performed any he replied, 'Zer ees no French moosik' – but who made an exception of Berlioz (Berlioz was an honorary German); Felix Mottl, who conducted the first complete performance of *Les Troyens*, in Karlsruhe, and who visited London from time to time; and Berlioz's friend Charles Hallé, from Hagen in Westphalia, the 'pianiste sans peur et sans reproche',[3] who settled in Paris in the late 1830s and then, after the 1848 Revolution, moved to England, where a consortium of Manchester businessmen invited him to form the orchestra that still bears his name.

[3] *Journal des débats,* 31 May 1851; republished in *Critique musicale*, Vol. 7, p. 487.

What were their performances like? How did they interpret Berlioz's music? We can't say, but presumably well enough to keep it afloat. We know about Ganz largely through the writings of Bernard Shaw. Ganz was Adelina Patti's favourite conductor, and there is a famous account by Shaw of a farewell concert given by the diva at the Albert Hall in 1889, with Ganz conducting, just before she left for a tour of South America.[4] Though Ganz played under Berlioz, he may not have learned all that much, if we are to believe Shaw, who found his account of the first movement of the *Symphonie fantastique* too slow: its passions, Shaw said, 'can by no means be represented by an orchestra jogging along under easy sail at the rate of sixteen minims less than Berlioz's explicit tempo'. Shaw also thought that 'the substitution of bass tubas for ophicleides, now nearly always made, produces a more dignified tone in the 'Dies Irae' than Berlioz intended. There is something peculiarly outlandish in the hoot of an ophicleide. No tuba can bellow in quite the same way'.[5] (Shaw was an authenticist *avant la lettre.*) However, he does add that 'the final diabolical orgy came off with great spirit'. It was Ganz who gave the London premiere of the symphony, in 1881, for which he had special bells cast of the right deep funereal tone. Presumably they were melted down in the First World War. A pity – we could do with them today.

Hans Richter seems to have been a better Berlioz conductor than Ganz. Shaw praised his account of *La Damnation de Faust* warmly:

> Call no conductor sensitive in the highest degree to musical impressions until you have heard him in Berlioz and Mozart. I never unreservedly took off my hat to Richter until I saw him conduct Mozart's great symphony in E flat. Now, having heard him conduct Berlioz's Faust, I repeat the salutation. […] The Hungarian March I pass over, though I felt towards the end that if it were to last another minute I must charge out and capture Trafalgar Square singlehanded. But when the scene on the banks of the Elbe began – more slowly than any but a great conductor would have dared to take it – then I knew that I might dream the scene without fear of awakening a disenchanted man. As to the dance of will-o'-the-wisps in the third part, Richter's interpretation of that most supernatural minuet was a masterpiece of conducting.[6]

Best of all, Shaw liked Hallé's conducting of Berlioz. When Hallé brought his orchestra south, they showed London how it should be done. The score, Shaw said (this is again the *Damnation*), 'comes to life in the hands of players

[4] 'Goodbye, Patti', *The Star*, 23 January 1889; republished in *Shaw's Music*, Vol. 1, pp. 545–46.

[5] 'The Fourth Brinsmead Concert', *The Dramatic Review*, 26 December 1885; republished in *ibid.*, p. 430.

[6] 'The Masterly Richter', *The Star*, 9 July 1889, republished in *ibid.*, pp. 692–93.

George Bernard Shaw, an early Berlioz enthusiast in the British press

who understand every bar of it and individualise every phrase'. Hallé, like Richter, seems to have conducted the March at the moderate, steady tempo Berlioz prescribed but that many French conductors have been unable to resist whipping up. 'The Hungarian March', Shaw writes, 'taken at about half the speed at which Lamoureux vainly tries to make it "go", is encored with yells – literally with yells – at St James's Hall'.[7]

With the coming of the twentieth century British conductors appear on the scene: Hamilton Harty and Beecham – Tommy; also Leslie Heward, Constant Lambert and others. The inaugural concert of Beecham's London Philharmonic Orchestra at Queen's Hall in 1932 – a landmark in the history

[7] 'The Absence of Orchestras', *loc. cit.*, p. 519.

of orchestral playing in this country – began with the *Roman Carnival* Overture, which created such a sensation that the applause lasted for five minutes, and – though it sounds improbable, I am assured by a friend who was there that it was so – people stood on their seats to cheer. In 1960, while he was recovering from his first stroke, Beecham made plans to perform all Berlioz's major works in a series of concerts at the Albert Hall; but a second stroke killed him before he could carry them out.

I have now reached, however cursorily, our own time. How, in a brief summary, to do justice to all that has been achieved by the people in this room, not to mention those who went before them?

Looked at from the outside, it might seem to the anti-Berliozians (they still exist, though I'm happy to say they are a diminishing breed) that the whole modern Berlioz movement in this country has been a carefully planned and ruthlessly efficient conspiracy, with cells of dedicated fanatics planted at strategic points throughout the land – 'a tightly knit group of politically motivated men', as Harold Wilson described the left-wing militants at about the same time. Look, for example, at the way certain key professorships in university music departments were occupied by card-carrying Berlioz activists: Hugh Macdonald, having been in the music faculty at Cambridge and then at Oxford, becomes professor of music at Glasgow, Ian Kemp, professor at Leeds then Manchester, succeeded at Leeds by Julian Rushton. Meanwhile John Warrack, after a distinguished career as author and journalist, joins the music faculty at Oxford, where he is influential in spreading the gospel.

Or consider how that knot of conspirators used to gather, in the 1960s, in one of those secluded alcoves that are still a feature of Durrants Hotel in W1, after Colin Davis' concert performances of *Les Troyens* with the LSO or the Philharmonia, and plot to get the full score published and the opera recorded: Macdonald again, Davis himself, Warrack, Nicholas Snowman, Ernest Fleischmann, Richard Macnutt and myself. Or the fact that two of the leading Berlioz conductors of today, Roger Norrington and John Eliot Gardiner, played in the Chelsea Opera Group orchestra in those same 1960s, where they sat at the feet of Colin Davis and imbibed the doctrine – even if their paths have somewhat diverged from his since then.

It is a tempting idea. But the whole thing has been much more haphazard than that – or rather, it was the *Zeitgeist* working, it was many different currents converging, joining their streams to make a river whose course was too strong to be arrested. One of the things that in the past had held Berlioz's music back was that it was simply not heard enough and therefore not known – it was the paucity not merely of faithful performances but of performances at all. When J. H. Elliot wrote the 'Master Musicians' book on

Russell Brown

Hugh Macdonald

Richard Macnutt

Julian Rushton

John Warrack and David Cairns in conversation

Sir Roger Norrington

Sir John Eliot Gardiner

Berlioz, which came out in 1938,[8] he had never – as he later admitted – heard *L'Enfance du Christ;* his not exactly sympathetic and inevitably not very illuminating account of the work was derived from the vocal score. Thanks to Beecham and Harty and others, and to visiting conductors from abroad, Berlioz performances became more frequent, and thanks to the gradual rise in the technical standards of orchestras they generally got better.

But it was above all the advent of gramophone recording, and especially, from about 1950, of the long-playing record, followed by the CD, that was crucial. Crucial in two ways: first because its huge expansion of the repertory helped to relegate to history the notion of a so-called mainstream of music and to abolish the concept of a norm, against which a composer such as Berlioz could be measured and found hopelessly eccentric. It introduced the spirit of pluralism – that pluralism that was the one -ism that Berlioz the independent spirit believed in. Second, recording made his music much more physically accessible. Because of recording, he was ceasing at last to be a composer more talked about than actually known.

Which brings me to *Les Troyens*. The story has often been told, but I hope you will forgive me if I touch on it again, because the Covent Garden production of 1957, conducted by Rafael Kubelík, was in a sense the beginning of the process that has led to Berlioz being accepted as one of the great composers, and that has led to us sitting here (or, in my case,

[8] *Berlioz*, J. M. Dent, London; it was reprinted as late as 1967.

standing) this evening. So much flowed from it. Lives were changed, as was the whole way Berlioz was looked at. *Les Troyens*, his supreme work, had been the repository of more prejudice and ignorance than all the rest of his works put together (which is saying a lot). From now on, everything began to be seen in a new light. In that light the whole of Berlioz's output could be revalued. And, of course, those Covent Garden performances and the revivals of 1958 and 1960 fired numerous individuals to take up the Berlioz cause, to conduct and play and sing and write and plan and promote, in the conviction that here was a great artist and a great human being whose wrongs were terrible but could be redressed.

This time – uncharacteristically for a composer who seemed fated to suffer bad luck – the stars were working for him. By a fortunate accident of dates the momentum gathering during the 1960s found a culminating point to aim at: the centenary of Berlioz's death. The year 1969 was the focus of our united efforts. Here perhaps the word conspiracy, or at any rate premeditation, is apt. In particular, a large debt is owed to Russell Brown, who I am happy to see is here tonight. I think he was bursar of the Royal College of Art at the time. His idea of forming a Berlioz Centenary Committee as early as 1962 or '63 struck the rest of us as slightly odd, even a little premature (as Richard the Lionheart says to Prince John in *The Adventures of Robin Hood*), but he was absolutely right. It needed that amount of time. He got the Earl of Drogheda to preside, and the manager of the Westbury Hotel, Tony de la Rue, another Berlioz enthusiast, to host various functions, and Charles Longman, the press officer of Justerini and Brooks, to lubricate them.

Almost the first action of the committee was to set up a subcommittee charged with launching a new edition of the complete works. (The old one, quite apart from its other deficiencies, had left the operas out altogether.) Hugh Macdonald was made general editor. Through the good offices of Martin Cooper the Gulbenkian Foundation gave a large grant. The first volume, *Symphonie funèbre et triomphale*, was published in 1967, and two years later, coinciding with the centenary and for the first time in its strange but till then largely uneventful history, *Les Troyens*.

It is a pity that Hugh Macdonald, who is now a professor in America, can't be with us this evening. The importance of what he has done for Berlioz cannot be exaggerated. For his Cambridge doctoral thesis, Macdonald had prepared an edition of the full score of *Les Troyens*, and this became the basis of the score that was published under his editorial direction in 1969 and used both for the new production of the work at Covent Garden and for the complete recording made the same year. By the time the recording appeared, in 1970, the Philips Berlioz Cycle was already launched, thanks to the initiative of the Marketing Manager of the Classical Division of Philips London, Jack Boyce. He craftily placed an advertisement for the recently issued *Roméo et Juliette* recording in the programme of a Festival Hall concert that Colin Davis was conducting, describing it as the 'first issue of the Philips Berlioz Cycle', and our Dutch masters woke up to find themselves committed.

To return to the New Berlioz Edition, I want to pay tribute to its work, now nearing completion (it had been hoped to complete it by the end of this bicentenary year; in fact it will run over a little, but as Berlioz will still be alive next year that is maybe no special harm). Gratitude first to the NBE's four chairmen: Wilfrid Mellers, who held the post only briefly, but whose masterly Berlioz chapter in the Harman and Mellers *Man and his Music*[9] was for many years a beacon shining in the musicological darkness; Lionel Robbins, whose wisdom and knowledge and experience of the worlds of scholarship and business were of incalculable value; his equally influential successor Claus Moser (who to his regret could not be here tonight); and finally John Burgh, without whose determination and incisive leadership the edition would certainly not be so near its goal as it is. Then, the general secretaries whose devoted work has kept the whole enterprise going: Richard Macnutt, Ian Kemp, Paul Banks and now, and by no means least, Chris Banks, whose secretaryship has coincided with the tricky problem of funding the final stages of the edition, and who has solved it brilliantly.

I have dwelt on the pioneer days of the 1960s, and they were heady days to live through. But, in this case at least, to arrive is even better than to travel hopefully. Not even the most quirky Berlioz enthusiast, surely, can feel nostalgic for the time when their hero was an outsider, an outcast, a figure on the periphery of musical history, seemingly the eternal maverick (perhaps loved partly for that reason), or can fail to welcome a time when his works are performed regularly and no longer have to be sought out in odd corners of the kingdom; when there are recordings readily available instead of found only on reel-to-reel tapes or on worn-out cassettes passed from hand to hand and at any moment liable to spew out of the machine in Laocoön-like coils. Those were necessary days, but they are over. There has never been a time when so many conductors, worldwide, were interested in Berlioz's music. In the past there were always a few, enough, just, to hold the line. But now we have what St Paul calls a cloud of witnesses, many of them from this country: our guest of honour, Colin Davis; John Eliot Gardiner; Roger Norrington; Simon Rattle; Siân Edwards; Adrian Brown,

[9] 'Berlioz', in Harman and Mellers, *Man and his Music*, pp. 759–81.

to name only some. And reports have recently come from Glasgow, of Ilan Volkov, with the BBC Scottish Symphony Orchestra, performing three Berlioz symphonies – *Harold*, *Roméo* and the *Funèbre et triomphale* – in one day. It is, after all, more satisfactory to celebrate a conquering hero than a defeated one.

We are fortunate to be able to do so. But I should like to recall tonight some of those who did not live to enjoy the bicentenary: the pianist Viola Tunnard, whose long and painful sufferings from motor neurone disease were lightened by her love of Berlioz; Ron Bernheim, founder of the Berlioz Society, which kept the torch alight in those far-off but still remembered days (and whose President, the renowned Jacques Barzun, is still going strong at 95); six other members of the society, who died too soon: Inge Mann, Jim Hacobian, Dick Maidment, Ian Martin, Clifford Smith and Ray Hyatt; Arthur Oldham, the 'Ministre des Chœurs', who was the Orchestre de Paris chorus-master for 27 years until he was forced out, and whose death earlier this year was a shock to many; the conductors John Pritchard and Norman Del Mar; Tom Heinitz, a famous convert of 1957, who came out of the theatre a changed man and thereafter wrote and spoke passionately on behalf of Berlioz; the painter, sculptor and writer Michael Ayrton, a dedicated Berliozian, whom I can still see pacing Bow Street during one of the intervals in the 1969 *Trojans*, murmuring 'I fear the Greeks, especially when bearing sets'. And an American enthusiast, Alan Gore, a Berliozian *hors pairs*, prevented by wretched health from fulfilling his dearest wish, which had been to spend the whole of 2003 in France and England.

Lastly, a dear friend, someone whom a few of us will never cease to cherish, Elizabeth Davison. Elizabeth was head of Arts Council exhibitions in the 1960s, so that when it was decided, by the centenary committee and the Victoria and Albert Museum, that the Arts Council should put on a big exhibition at the V&A, it fell to her to see that it happened. She knew practically nothing of Berlioz, but she set to work to hear and read everything she could, and fell under his spell. The magnificent catalogue that is still one of the prime Berlioz documents was above all her achievement. When shortly afterwards a Byron exhibition was planned, Elizabeth, who had just retired, offered to come back, but John Pope-Hennessy – 'the Pope' – who was chairman of the Byron committee, as he had been of the Berlioz, said no. As a result the Byron catalogue wasn't ready till more than a month after the exhibition opened. That the Berlioz catalogue was finished in time was thanks to Elizabeth and her gentle bullying, and the late-night sessions that she and Richard Macnutt and Jonathan Mayne and I held at her house in Camberwell, sessions that often went on till three or four in the morning.

Nor shall I ever forget the journeys I made with Elizabeth to La Côte-Saint-André to choose objects for the exhibition. Her spoken French was rudimentary but that didn't stop her. I can see her sitting outside the Hôtel de France with a group of inhabitants of the town and saying to the curé, 'Vous connais…' and, despite that, somehow making herself understood. Later, by which time she was a close friend of both me and my wife Rosemary, we went back together more than once to Berlioz's birthplace. On one occasion we took the train from Lyon to the railway station of Le Grand Lemps, a few miles from La Côte, and rang for a taxi to collect us. The hot, dusty station yard had something of the look and atmosphere of those slightly sinister station yards that figure in westerns, which may have influenced what followed. While we waited for the taxi, we found ourselves looking over a wall beyond which a dozen or so men were playing *boules*. Suddenly the men's heads turned as one, like a herd of cattle, or a posse of gunmen, and stared silently and intimidatingly in our direction, whereupon a flustered Elizabeth blurted out: 'C'est permis de regarder le jou?'

But I don't want to end with the past. Berlioz is more important than any of us – Berlioz and his future. I should like to propose a toast to that future. Not long before his death he said that if he could live to be 140 his musical life would become 'decidedly fascinating'.[10] He was a few decades out; but his prophecy has been vindicated. In my family, during the days when he was sometimes felt to be a little over-dominant, there used to be talk of 'life after Berlioz'. That hasn't happened, and perhaps never will. Instead, I would ask you, as this great year nears its end, to drink to 'Berlioz after 2003'. For him this is not the end. It is the beginning of his afterlife. To Berlioz and the next hundred years!

[10] *Memoirs*, p. 546.

Appendix
Three Berlioz People: Appreciations

The appreciation of Catherine Reboul appeared in the Berlioz Society Bulletin *No. 184 (December 2010) and those of Ian Kemp and Pierre Citron in No. 187 (December 2011).*

Catherine Reboul-Berlioz-Vercier

Catherine, great-great-granddaughter of Nancy Pal *née* Berlioz, great-great-great-niece of the composer, and herself a gifted artist, died on 29 August 2010, aged 66.

I had known her since 1969, when she came to London to visit the centenary exhibition at the Victoria and Albert Museum, 'Berlioz and the Romantic Imagination', and with her mother Yvonne was a guest of honour at the gala banquet held there. Later, she stayed with my wife Rosemary and me more than once, captivating our three sons with the charm and vividness of her warm, unconventional personality. Later still, we went to see her on the Île de Ré, staying first with her mother and then with her and her husband Michel Vercier, whom she had known since she was a child and had married in her forties.

She had an intuitive gift for friendship, a generosity of spirit, a sense of fun, a magnetism that drew people to her. At her Paris studio in the rue la Condamine, in the 9th *arrondissement*, you would usually find two or three, often much younger, friends who had dropped in for a cup of coffee (suitably strong) or a drink, and whose admiration and affection for her was palpable, though it never turned her head. She was totally without airs.

I was lucky enough, when working on the first volume of my biography of Berlioz, to have several long and passionate conversations with her about her great forebear. (Once, when dining at the restaurant Le Procope, we became so carried away with enthusiasm that a diner at the next table accused us of being 'mal élevés'.) Of all Berlioz's living descendants there was none so devoted, none who understood him so deeply and perceptively.

The picture overleaf – which shows her at an exhibition of her sculpture and painting in Paris in 1989, with Lucien Chamard-Bois, then an official at the Ministry of Education, and François Lesure, former director of the music department at the Bibliothèque nationale – captures the Catherine that so many of us who knew her loved, and for whom Chamard-Bois spoke truly when he described her as 'une belle âme'.

Catherine Reboul-Berlioz-Vercier, great-great-great-niece of the composer, at an exhibition of her sculpture and painting in Paris in 1989, with (centre) Lucien Chamard-Bois and (right) François Lesure

Ian Kemp

With the death of Ian Kemp in September 2011, at the age of 80, Berlioz has lost one of his most dedicated and knowledgeable advocates. Ian loved Berlioz's music passionately, with a deep, emotional commitment – I remember his exclamation, 'What a composer!', as we left for the interval during a concert performance of *Les Troyens*, after the scene of Cassandra and the Trojan women. But he also had a well-studied, precise and highly articulate understanding of what made Berlioz the composer he was, how the music was constructed, why it was good, and he communicated that understanding to a whole generation of students whom he taught at Aberdeen, Cambridge, Leeds and Manchester.

Ian Kemp defended Berlioz fiercely against his detractors, converting many to the music (including the vice-chancellor of Leeds University, Edward Boyle, who till then had thought it 'grand but amateurish').

Ian Kemp

An article by Rupert Christiansen in *The Spectator* provoked this characteristic rejoinder:

> In his review of David Cairns's biography of Berlioz, Rupert Christiansen reminds us that the earth is flat – that of all great composers Berlioz is still the one about whom a critic can dredge up ancient canards and feel satisfied about it. There is, evidently, a Berlioz 'problem' – lying in his tendency to 'vulgarity', technical 'incompetencies', his failure to 'sustain his noblest ambitions'. Where did Mr Christiansen get this rubbish from? Perhaps he's been reading too many books, especially those upholding the 'drawing-room manners' he sets such store by. As for Berlioz's supposed lapses in this respect, you'd have thought they'd qualify him for applause. And as for his 'shaky technique', if Mr Christiansen would cite chapter and verse I'll prove him wrong.

Perhaps wisely, the critic refrained from doing so, and held his peace.

Had Ian's last years not been blighted by illness (during which he was solaced by the love and unwavering support of his wife, the conductor Siân Edwards), he might have completed the analysis of Berlioz's harmonic procedures that he planned to write. As it is, his published Berlioz legacy consists chiefly of the volume *Songs for Solo Voice and Orchestra* that he edited for the New Berlioz Edition, the Cambridge Opera Handbook on *Les Troyens* and the seminal essay 'Romeo and Juliet and Roméo et Juliette' in Peter Bloom's *Berlioz Studies*.[1]

Pierre Citron

When I was working on my biography of Berlioz, I saw a good deal of Pierre Citron and benefited hugely from my contacts with this friendly and brilliant man, both at the Bibliothèque Nationale and at the apartment of Yvonne Reboul-Berlioz – where I remember her saying admiringly, after a visit from him, 'Que cet homme est épatant!' He *was* – stunning, or however you translate that expressive adjective.

I believe it was only when he became editor of the *Correspondance générale d'Hector Berlioz* that this eminent Balzac and Giono specialist fell fully under Berlioz's spell. Thereafter he worked valiantly and tirelessly for him, and all of us owe him a big debt. For those who knew Citron at all well, he was excellent company. Having spent much of the war in England as a member of de Gaulle's Free French, he leavened his profound and precise scholarship with a remarkable command of English slang and a gratifyingly broad sense of humour. He liked telling the story of a Free-French colleague, exasperated by a telephone conversation with an obstructive bureaucrat, exclaiming as he slammed the phone down, 'Mort aux cons!', to which

[1] Cambridge University Press, Cambridge, 1992, pp. 37–80.

Pierre Citron

de Gaulle, happening to pass the open office-door at that moment, replied, 'Vaste programme'.

Pierre Citron was a wit as well as a polymath. The paper on 'Musical Characters and the Role of Music in Parisian Comic Theatre, 1830–40', which he read at the conference on 'Music in Paris in the Eighteen-Thirties' organised by Peter Bloom at Smith College in 1980,[2] was one of the funniest I have ever heard. At the same conference he set the darkened hall 'on a roar' when, in a moment of silence as Robert Cohen, seated at the lectern, was preparing his talk on Dantan jeune's caricature busts, light from below casting a sinister gleam on his bearded face, Citron called out: '*Robert le Diable*!' John Warrack recalls him coming up during a tea-break and asking, with mock-grave politeness: 'Would you care for a little lemon with your tea?'

[2] Published in Peter Bloom (ed.), *Music in Paris in the Eighteen-Thirties/La Musique à Paris dans les années mil huit cent trente*, Pendragon Press, New York, 1987, pp. 117–32.

Select Bibliography

BANKS, PAUL, 'Byron, Berlioz and *Harold*', *Berlioz Society Bulletin*, No. 205, June 2018

BARZUN, JACQUES, *Berlioz and the Romantic Century*, two vols., Columbia University Press, New York, 3rd edn., 1969

BERLIOZ, HECTOR, *The Memoirs of Hector Berlioz*, transl. and ed. David Cairns, Everyman's Library, London, 2002

—, *Les Soirées de l'orchestre*, ed. Léon Guichard, Gründ, Paris, 1968

—, *Critique musicale, 1823–1863*, Vols. 1–6 ed. H. Robert Cohen, Yves Gérard and others, Buchet/Chastel, Paris, 1996–2008; Vols. 7–8 ed. Anne Bongrain and Marie-Hélène Coudroy-Saghaï, with editorial assistance from Peter Bloom, Pierre Citron, Yves Gérard, Catherine Massip and Jean Mongrédien, Société française de musicologie, Paris, 2013–

—, *Correspondance générale*, Vols. I–VIII, Flammarion, Paris:

I, 1803–1832, ed. Pierre Citron, 1972

II, 1834–1842, ed. Frédéric Robert, 1975

III, 1842–1850, ed. Pierre Citron, 1978

IV, 1851–1855, ed. Pierre Citron, Yves Gérard and Hugh Macdonald, 1983

V, 1855–1859, ed. Hugh Macdonald and François Lesure, 1989

VI, 1859–1863, ed. Hugh Macdonald and François Lesure, 1995

VII, 1864–1869, ed. Hugh Macdonald, 2001

VIII, Supplements, ed. Hugh Macdonald, 2003

IX, *Nouvelles lettres de Berlioz, sa famille, ses contemporains* (suppléments 2), ed. Peter Bloom, Joël-Marie Fauquet, Hugh Macdonald and Cécile Reynaud, Actes Sud and Palazetto Bru Zane, Arles and Venice, 2016

BLOOM, PETER (ed.) *Berlioz Studies*, Cambridge University Press, Cambridge, 1992

—, *The Cambridge Companion to Berlioz*, Cambridge University Press, Cambridge, 2000

—, *Berlioz: Scenes from the Life and Work*, University of Rochester Press, Rochester (NY), 2008

CAIRNS, DAVID *Berlioz*, two vols.: Vol. 1, *The Making of an Artist, 1803–1832*; Vol. 2, *Servitude and Greatness, 1832–1869*, Penguin Books, London, and University of California Press, Berkeley

Chateaubriand, François-René de, *Génie du Christianisme ou beautés de la religion chrétienne*, Migneret, Paris, 1802

Cone, Edward T., *Music: A View from Delft – Selected Essays*, ed. Robert P. Morgan, University of Chicago Press, Chicago, 1989

— (ed.), *Berlioz, Fantastic Symphony*, Norton Critical Scores, New York, 1980

Griepenkerl, Wolfgang Robert, *Ritter Berlioz in Braunschweig: zur Charakteristik dieses Tondichters*, Eduard Leibrock, Brunswick, 1843

Hallé, Sir Charles, *Life and Letters*, Smith, Elder & Co., London, 1896

Harman, Alec, and Mellers, Wilfrid, *Man and his Music*, Barrie and Jenkins, London, 1988

Hiller, Ferdinand, *Künstlerleben*, M. Dumont-Schauberg, Cologne, 1880

Kemp, Ian (ed.), *Hector Berlioz: Les Troyens*, Cambridge University Press, Cambridge, 1988

Legouvé, Ernest, *Soixante ans de souvenirs*, two vols., J. Hetzel, Paris, 1886

Massip, Catherine, and Reynaud, Cécile (eds.), *Berlioz, la Voix du Romantisme*, Bibliothèque nationale de France, Paris, 2003 (catalogue of centenary exhibition, with essays)

Massougnes, Georges de, *Hector Berlioz: son œuvre*, Calmann-Lévy, Paris, 1919

Newman, Ernest, *Berlioz, Romantic and Classic: Writings by Ernest Newman*, ed. Peter Heyworth, Gollancz, London, 1972

Payzant, Geoffrey, *Eduard Hanslick and Ritter Berlioz in Prague*, University of Calgary Press, Calgary, 1991

Rose, Michael, (ed.) *Berlioz Remembered*, Faber and Faber, London, 2001

Rushton, Julian (ed.), *Berlioz Encyclopedia*, Cambridge University Press, Cambridge, 2018

Shaw, George Bernard, *Shaw's Music: The Complete Musical Criticism of Bernard Shaw*, ed. Dan H. Laurence, three vols., The Bodley Head, London, 1981

Spillemaecker, Chantal, and Troncy, Antoine, *Berlioz et l'Italie, voyage musical*, éditions Libel, La Côte-Saint-André, 2012

Stasov, Vladimir, *Selected Essays on Music*, transl. Florence Jonas, Barrie and Rockcliff/The Cresset Press, London, 1968

Tovey, Donald Francis, *Essays in Musical Analysis*, Vol. 4: Illustrative Music, Oxford University Press, London, 1936

Wotton, Tom S., *Hector Berlioz*, Oxford University Press, London, 1935

Index of Berlioz's Works

General Index